ON COMMON GROUND

ON COMMON GROUND

The Ongoing Story of the Commons in Niagara-on-the-Lake

RICHARD D. MERRITT

DUNDURN
TORONTO

Editor: Jennifer McKnight
Cover and text design: Jennifer Scott
Printer: Friesens

Library and Archives Canada Cataloguing in Publication

Merritt, Richard
    On common ground : the ongoing story of the Commons in Niagara-on-the-Lake / Richard D. Merritt.

Includes index.
Also issued in electronic format.
ISBN 978-1-4597-0348-3

1. Commons--Ontario--Niagara-on-the-Lake--History. 2. Niagara-on-the-Lake (Ont.)--History. I. Title.

FC3099.N54M47 2012   971.3'38   C2012-900087-6

1 2 3 4 5   16 15 14 13 12

We acknowledge the support of the **Canada Council for the Arts** and the **Ontario Arts Council** for our publishing program. We also acknowledge the financial support of the **Government of Canada** through the **Canada Book Fund** and **Livres Canada Books**, and the **Government of Ontario** through the **Ontario Book Publishing Tax Credit** and the **Ontario Media Development Corporation**.

Care has been taken to trace the ownership of copyright material used in this book. The author and the publisher welcome any information enabling them to rectify any references or credits in subsequent editions.
                                                                      J. Kirk Howard, President

Printed and bound in Canada.
www.dundurn.com

Dundurn	Gazelle Book Services Limited	Dundurn
3 Church Street, Suite 500	White Cross Mills	2250 Military Road
Toronto, Ontario, Canada	High Town, Lancaster, England	Tonawanda, NY
M5E 1M2	LA1 4XS	U.S.A. 14150

FRONT COVER (TOP): *A View of Niagara Taken from the Heights Near Navy Hall*, artist James Peachey, watercolour, 1783 or 1787. This early painting illustrates a portion of Navy Hall at the water's edge and the British-held Fort Niagara across the river. The open grassy plain on the left, although reserved for military purposes, is being used as common lands.

Library and Archives Canada, James Peachey collection, C-002035.

FRONT COVER (BELOW): *Camp Niagara 1918*, photo, A. Hardwick, 1918. During the Great War, Camp Niagara occupied almost the entire Fort George Military Reserve / Commons.

Courtesy of Jim Smith and Peter Moogk.

BACK COVER: A summer ramble along Sheaffe Road, photo. A side trail of the Bruce Trail on the Commons.

Courtesy Jim Smith.

Table of Contents

Acknowledgements

We are all indebted to teacher, historian, and author, Janet Carnochan. "Miss Janet" considered the Commons as important as the Plains of Abraham and the battlefields of Waterloo and Bannockburn. Without her staunch opposition to any encroachment, the Commons would not have survived. She also preserved many artifacts relating to the Commons and her books and published papers by the Niagara Historical Society are a rich source of information. Her contemporary, military officer and historian General E.A. Cruikshank, edited and published a vast collection of correspondence that has been an invaluable reference source. I am also greatly indebted to life-long resident and historian Joseph Masters (1871–1955) for publishing his voluminous recollections in the local newspaper as "Niagara Reminiscences and Neighbourhood News," which is now available on the internet as *Ars Historica Niagara.*

The much-esteemed current Town Historian, Joy Ormsby, has been my invaluable mentor for the past twenty years.

Special thanks also to the staff and historians of Mayer Heritage Consultants Inc. who conducted and published hundreds of interviews of veterans of the Canadian Army and militia. Without their efforts many stories would have been lost.

The splendid photographs by Cosmo Condina have added another dimension to the story. I was very fortunate to have access to the private photograph and postcard collections of Jim Smith, John Burtniak, Pat Simon, Joe Solomon, Peter Moogk, Chris Allen, Judith Sayers, and others.

Over the years I have enjoyed many interviews with local townsfolk who welcomed me into their homes and their memories. Many have now passed on.

A sincere thanks to each of the following who has assisted me in a variety of ways. Listed in no particular order: Bill Severin, Clark Bernat, Sarah Maloney, Amy Klassen, Neil Rumble, Jarred Picher, Ron Dale, David Webb, Bob Garcia, Daniel Laroche, Peter Martin, Suzanne Plousos, René Chartrand, Gavin A. Watt, Wes Turner, Pat Simon, Erika and Jim Alexander, Jon Jouppien, Noel Haines, Jim Smith, Peter Moogk, Chris Allen, Terry Boulton, Glen Smith, John Harkness, Marie Webber, Kay Toye, Trudi Watson, Richard West, Margo Fyfe, Hope Bradley, John "Ted" Bradley, George Howse, Doug Hunter, Evelyn Campbell, Penny Coles, Anna Tiedtke, Rosi Zirger, Duncan McLaren, Marilyn and Paul Shepherd, Al Derbyshire, John McLeish, Tony Roberts, Bill Lindsay, Donald Combe, Fred Habermehl, Bob Lewis, Tammy Richardson, Susan Merritt, Cameron Williams, Peter Babcock, John Sinclair, Allen S. Merritt, Jere Brubaker, Donald Harrison, Roger Harrison, Harold and Marjorie Clement, Maggie Parnall, Gerda Molson, Sharon Whittaker, Linda Gula and all the current NOTL library staff, Brian Dunnigan, Alun Hughes, Carl Benn, Robert S. Allen, Paul Fortier, Guy St-Denis, Dave Roth, William Smy, Callie Stacey, Tom Braybrook, Mario

Iazzo, Leah Wallace, Cathy MacDonald, Tahir Khan, Nancy Butler, Michael Power, Kathy Powell, Bridget Ker, Debbie Whitehouse, Robert Ritchie, Dennis Schmahl, W. Herbert Crawford, Harry James, Russell Sanderson, Gail and Mike Dietsch, Pat and Ron Balasiuk, Peter Stokes, Gracia Janes, Margherita Howe, Laura Dodson, Judy MacLachlan, Rod and Bev Craig, John Walker, Tony Doyle, David Hemmings, and others whom I have sadly forgotten.

Thanks to my cartographer, Loris Gasparotto, who made it look so easy.

Kirk Howard and Michael Carroll of Dundurn were most patient and helpful as we wended our way through the long publishing process.

Special kudos to my preliminary editor (and dutiful son-in-law) Jonathan Link who gently improved my prose and enlightened me on military culture and terms. The efforts of Dundurn in-house editor Jennifer McKnight are much appreciated.

And finally, a special thank you to my wife Nancy and daughters Tiffany and Susannah who have put up with so many years of repetitive stories, out-of-the-way side trips, library visits, meetings, cluttered dining room and kitchen tables, as well as long walks on the Commons and Paradise Grove in all kinds of weather … and to Tillie the dog, who made it so much fun.

The Parkway, *artist R. Martin, watercolour miniature. On Queen's Parade, under the canopy of Paradise Grove approaching the open Commons.*

Courtesy of R. Martin.

Introduction

Today, the most popular approach to the historic town of Niagara-on-the-Lake is from the south along the Niagara River Parkway. As one emerges from the oak bower of Paradise Grove the wide expansive green on both sides of the road invariably impresses the first time visitor; even lifetime residents marvel at the simple beauty of this verdant tranquil plain edged with mature trees. Visitors to Fort George will learn the role of the fort in the pivotal War of 1812 from the guides and interpretive displays. However, on climbing one of the southwestern bastions of the fort and gazing out over the plains beyond, one would have no inkling just how much this view has changed over the past 250 years.

In the late eighteenth and early nineteenth centuries the Indian Council House stood in the midst of the plain. There thousands of Natives would encamp for their annual presents and for treaty negotiations. For over a century various British and Canadian regiments could be seen marching across those fields along present Otter Trail. Today this "walk into history" is a recreation trail enjoyed by walkers, cyclists, in-line skaters, and dogs alike. Generations of militiamen trained on these fields, including summer encampments "under canvas." During the two world wars, up to twenty thousand men assembled there at any one time for basic training before shipping out overseas. Many never returned. Despite all this military activity, the local citizens always regarded these open spaces and woodlands as common lands — places to graze their livestock, harvest mushrooms, hunt game, gather firewood, play various games, hold country fairs, and enjoy special events.

The British colonial government and the subsequent Dominion of Canada officially referred to these lands as the Fort George Military Reserve. Locally they were called The Common, The Fort George Common, The Garrison Common, The Commons, Niagara Plain, The Green, and others. It was only after the Department of National Defence decided that there was no longer a need for summer camps that the lands were officially turned over to the present Parks Canada. Although declared a "National Historic Park" in 1969, today the Niagara National Historic Sites comprise a complex of National Historic Sites in and near Niagara-on-the-Lake: Fort George, Fort Mississauga, Navy Hall, Butler's Barracks, Queenston Heights, Navy Island, and the Battlefield of Fort George. Although considered "a historic place" as part of the significance of both Fort George and Butler's Barracks, the Commons is *not* designated on its own merits.

This book traces the evolution (some would say degradation) of the original 444 acres of land referred to as the Fort George Military Reserve to the approximately 285 acres protected today. Included are references to the many perimeter properties and structures because they are very much a part of the story. One chapter is devoted to the Fort Mississauga Commons that was a separate military reserve. A final chapter discusses some of the efforts to protect the fragile Commons, preserving it for future generations.

Through my maternal grandfather I am descended from an early Niagara family. As a young boy I was brought to Niagara on several occasions to visit two great-great aunts and one great-great-uncle still living in the then 150 year-old family home. While munching on scrumptious homemade cookies, I was regaled with exciting stories about the old town and "the war" … not the Korean or the Second World War or even the Great War, but the War of 1812. One story particularly intrigued me: an ancestor was out gathering mushrooms on "The Commons" one clear sunny morning when suddenly it became very dark and much cooler as a massive flock of millions of migrating passenger pigeons flew over.

I was fortunate to be able to practise medicine in the Niagara Region, marry, and raise a family in Niagara-on-the-Lake. I became very involved in the heritage community and increasingly aware of ongoing threats to the integrity of the Commons. It seemed the "open spaces" of the Commons were being regarded as a land bank by some politicians and a few bureaucrats with various projects and schemes. For me, the recurring image of the migrating pigeons, now extinct, darkening the skies over the common lands became a metaphor for the ever-present threat of further encroachment of the Commons. The important ongoing story of the Military Reserve/Commons of Niagara deserves to be heard. No doubt I have committed some errors of misinterpretation, omission, and commission in writing this epic; I trust that future researchers will be able to correct some of the deficiencies.

An explanation concerning terminology used in this book is in order. The locals referred to the Fort George Military Reserve as the Common, the Fort George Common, the Niagara Common, the Commons, the Garrison Commons, the common lands, "the Opening," or simply "the plain." The term "the Commons"[1] is used throughout. As Paradise Grove was for most of its history common lands, it too is part of the Commons. Similarly, the cleared grounds around Navy Hall have been for the most part within the public domain and hence part of the story.

The term, "Niagara" refers to the Old Town of Niagara that is now part of the Regional Municipality of Niagara-on-the-Lake. Although "Newark" was Lieutenant-Governor Simcoe's designated name for Niagara when it was the Capital of Upper Canada, it never became popular and reverted back to Niagara shortly after his return to England.[2]

"Camp Niagara" was also called "Niagara Camp" and at least one battalion referred to it as "Paradise Camp."[3] (There was also an American military camp referred to as "New Fort Niagara" across the river at Youngstown, New York, during the Great War.) "Camp Niagara" is used in this book.

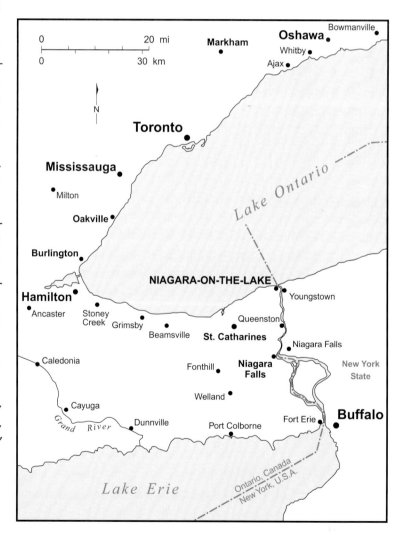

Location of Niagara-on-the-Lake, Ontario, Canada.

Except where specific First Nations or "tribes" or "Indians" are referenced, the term "Natives" is used for North American indigenous peoples. The term "province" refers to the Province of Upper Canada (1791–1841) and the Province of Ontario after 1867. "The Great War" is used for the First World War and "The American Revolutionary War" is used instead of the American War of Independence or the American Revolution. Although there are several variations in spelling, "Mississauga" will be used.

For those of you fortunate enough to have an opportunity to explore some of the Commons, this book may help you to conjure up in your own minds the various natural and historic events that have transpired on these plains over the years. Hopefully generations to come will question future development proposals for this very special place.

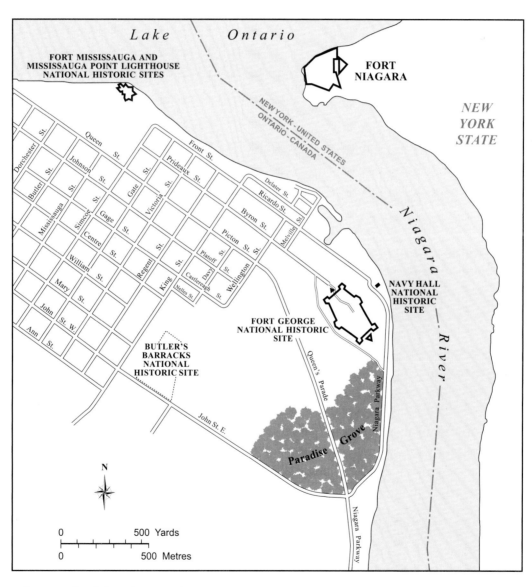

The mouth of the Niagara River, 2011.

CHAPTER 1

Common Lands for Everyone

For most of its history the original 444 acres known today as the Commons in Niagara-on-the-Lake was officially designated the Fort George Military Reserve at Niagara. This implied that the military had exclusive rights on the property. Nevertheless, as early as 1797 a British officer of the Royal Engineers referred to these lands as "commons"[1] and in the same year local civilians petitioned the government to protect their "Common or Lands now used as such."[2]

Ever since early human civilizations began to create villages and eventually city-states, public spaces have played an important role in the social fabric of communities. In the cities, formal plazas, piazzas, squares, forums, agoras, campi, places, quadrangles, and esplanades became the multi-functional public gathering sites for markets, fairs, religious celebrations, political rallies, mustering of troops, public punishments including executions, sports events, or just relaxation. In the smaller communities of Britain "the village green" or "the common" usually referred to an unfenced area of grass for all to use, sometimes for grazing of animals but often serving functions similar to that of the city square. Usually the

Last Day of Carnival on San Marco Square, Venice, artist Gabriel Bella (1730–1799). Public spaces such as historic and popular St. Mark's Square in Venice have always been an important element of urban places.

Courtesy of DeAgostini/Superstock Images.

term "commons" implied a plot of public land either within the town or nearby on the edge of the community that was available to all citizens for communal use such as growing crops, pasturing animals, collecting firewood, etc., as well as all other potential uses for such an urban space. Later, public municipal parks and gardens, which first made their appearance in the early nineteenth century, were created to encompass "retreats, recreation and refreshment."[3] Some social critics decried these urban parks as "the drawing rooms of the poor."[4] Modern urban planners acknowledge the social importance of these public "people spaces."

In North America indigenous peoples did not differentiate between individual property and communal territory.

Swan Green, Hampshire, England, photo. The Open Spaces Society of England and Wales estimates that there are still three thousand village greens/commons in Britain. Quintessential Swan Green with its expansive open spaces and ancient trees is edged by thatched cottages.

Courtesy of Travel Library Limited/SuperStock Images.

However, among Native tribes, spheres of influence were often aggressively maintained.

England and Wales had a long tradition of open common lands under the Saxons. Conquering Norman kings, however, parcelled up much of England to large landowners and set aside large tracts of ancient woodlands such as the "New Forest" for private deer-hunting grounds. Nevertheless, the ordinary people (commoners) retained certain common rights such as to pasture, to fish (piscary), to collect turf and peat (turbury), and to gather wood (estover). During the Tudor period, the process of "enclosure" was introduced whereby common land was taken into fully private ownership and use. This meant that open arable fields and meadows that had been farmed for generations by poor often landless tenants were transferred to the landed gentry or local lord of the manor who then proceeded to fence in the lands and farm the lands for their own profit. In some locales, common lands were retained, but often in the rough less arable regions. With the rise in food prices "enclosure" escalated such that by the early nineteenth century many former common lands in Britain were enclosed by Acts of Parliament, leaving fewer pasturelands and village greens intact.[5] Some argued that the old subsistence type of farming with its perpetual poverty was grossly inefficient while new agricultural techniques of large-scale private farms were far more productive.[6] Nevertheless, thousands who had lost their centuries-old right were reduced to abject poverty while many landowners became very rich. As witness, a period anonymous protest poem:

They hang the man, and flog the woman,
That steals the goose from off the common;
But let the greater villain loose,
That steals the common from the goose.[7]

John Graves Simcoe, the future Lieutenant Governor of Upper Canada, was the owner of Wolford Lodge in Devonshire. Although he considered himself somewhat of a social reformer, he enforced the enclosure act in his own neighbourhood, citing that improved agricultural practices would ultimately benefit the poor.[8] Later he nearly ended up in a duel over a controversy as to who had the right to collect the dung left by a large number of horses kept on nearby Woodbury Common.[9]

Certainly the other British government officials who accompanied Simcoe to Niagara in 1792 would have been aware of the controversial Enclosure Acts in Britain. Perhaps this explains why none of these officials apparently ever referred to the Military Reserve as common land. It was only after they left for York that the term quickly emerged. Interestingly, Mrs. Simcoe does refer to walking on the "garrison common" at Fort Niagara across the river.[10]

Most of the settlers who came to Upper Canada were from the former Thirteen Colonies where nearly every community had the quintessential village green[11] or common: a large central grassy rectangle surrounded by several protestant churches, the meeting house, the court house, and several impressive homes.[12] This tradition had been transplanted from the pre-enclosure seventeenth-century English villages. The Common Lands of New Harlem on Manhattan Island were created by Colonel Nichols, the first British Governor of New York in 1664. Lexington Green, where the first shots of the American Revolutionary War were fired, remains unchanged today and is still enjoyed by its current citizens. Perhaps most famous is the Boston Common, where on the eve of the American Revolutionary War British soldiers trained beside grazing cows. Nearby was "the Public Garden," which was supported and enjoyed by the wealthy citizens and begrudgingly open to the public.[13] The Boston Common was, and is, fearlessly protected by the public. In 1917 when the famous neurosurgeon Harvey Cushing was mobilizing the American Medical Corps he insisted on establishing a temporary military camp on the Boston Common. Despite his reputation and patriotic cause he was advised that such an act was a sacrilege and unthinkable — he eventually backed down.[14]

Given this long colonial tradition of village greens and common lands, it is understandable why the recently arrived settlers in Upper Canada would expect a similar public space. As early as 1783 Governor-General Haldimand had produced the "Cataraqui Plan,"[15] which outlined the recommended configuration of the new townships in the colony. This provided for a "common" of four hundred acres "for the use of the town." However, when the town of Niagara was eventually laid out by surveyor Augustus Jones in 1792, there was still no designation of a commons or true public square. In contrast, in adjacent Township #2 (Stamford), the surveyor Philip Frey had laid out "as much land as a public common to the Township … to amount to 800 acres."[16] Sometimes referred to as "The Town Farm,"[17] the much reduced "Stamford Green" in the present City of Niagara Falls is a much-appreciated remnant of that vision.

Across the lake at the Sixteen Creek, the town of Oakville was surveyed with a large tract along the lake for "common land." At York (Toronto) Lieutenant-Governor Simcoe set aside a Military Reserve of one thousand acres on the eastern edge, of which Fort York was established. The adjacent cleared land became known as the "Garrison Common" which was enjoyed by the townspeople. Eventually a "New Fort York" was built on the Reserve one kilometre to the west (later known as Stanley Barracks), but most of the original Reserve eventually became part of Exhibition Grounds on the south, and the "Provincial Lunatic Asylum"[18] to the north. A portion of the original Garrison Common adjacent to Old Fort York survives today surrounded by expressways and tall buildings of the modern metropolis.

With no designated common lands or village greens in Niagara and a growing population on relatively small

The Village Green Covered with Snow, Woodstock, Vermont, photo, Robert Harding. The concept of village greens and commons was transplanted by English colonists to British North America. The Green in Woodstock is the iconic New England public space.

Courtesy of SuperStock Images.

town lots it was inevitable that the local citizenry would cast an envious eye on that huge expanse of green arable land plus woodlot beyond. Besides, the soldiers were here to protect the town, not antagonize the loyal citizens of Niagara. Prior to the War of 1812 the Commons did in fact resemble a village green, albeit larger than most. The English Church and cemetery were situated on its eastern edge. Overlooking the grassy commons were the court house and jail (gaol), as well as the Freemasons' Hall, which acted as a meeting house. Several handsome homes also faced the Commons. Even two hundred years later,

with the edges of the original Commons nibbled away, the basic village green/common configuration persists: two churches with their ancient cemeteries can be seen from the Commons, the public school and a day care centre face the Commons, the hospital, a seniors' apartment, a nursing home, a renowned repertory theatre, a sports complex, and a veterans' lodge all abut the Commons. Several handsome homes on King and John Streets still overlook the Commons. Most importantly, the remaining 285 acres of grass and trees partially edged by water[19] truly are common lands to be enjoyed by all.[20]

CHAPTER 2

The Early Years

Archaeological digs at the present King's Point site[1] and on the Commons[2] have uncovered artifacts made as early as 7000–6000 BCE. These small points fashioned from chert[3] as well as fragments of ceramic pots probably belonged to small groups of hunters-gatherers living along the Niagara River delta.

The first recorded Aboriginals at the mouth of the Niagara River were the Atiwandaronks — known by the Europeans as the Nation de Petun or the Neutrals who spoke an Iroquoian dialect. Occupying the Niagara peninsula, they were strategically located between arch-enemies: the Hurons to the north-west and the powerful Six Nations Iroquois to the south-east. The Neutrals had several villages on the Niagara peninsula where they grew maize (corn), pumpkins, and beans, as well as tobacco that was traded with the other Natives. The Neutrals referred to the river as Ongiara or Onghiara, from which is derived the modern name, Niagara.[4]

In 1650 the neighbouring Iroquois (Seneca Nation) suddenly turned on the Neutrals, destroying their villages, killing many, but also absorbing some Neutral captives into their own communities. For the next one hundred years the Niagara Peninsula was "empty," with only occasional Mississauga Natives (Chippewa Nation) passing through.

The French explorer Rene Robert Cavelier de La Salle was the first European to actually document stepping ashore on the west bank of the mouth of the Niagara River. Upon reaching the east bank of the river in January 1679 after an exhausting overland trek, La Salle and his Lieutenant Henri de Tonty "were taken across the mouth of the river by friendly Indians, and given a supper of white-fish and corn soup."[5] As such, this simple meal represents the earliest

Projectile Point, early archaic bifurcate (7000–6000 BCE), chert, photo, Sergio Martin. Found at the King's Point Archaeological Site at the bottom of a runoff ravine, this early point probably originated from the uplands (commons) above. King's Point Site, catalogue # 01230.

Courtesy of the Niagara Historical Society and Museum.

Rene-Robert Cavelier de La Salle (1643–1687), purported to be a drawing of the French explorer as a young man. La Salle was the first European to record stepping ashore on the west bank of the mouth of the Niagara River.

Frank Severance, An Old Frontier of France (New York: Dodd, Mead and Company, 1917), 70.

recorded meal consumed in Niagara-on-the-Lake. It is also yet another instance where the indigenous peoples helped "white" strangers to survive.

Successive forts were erected by the French on the site of the present Fort Niagara on the east bank of the Niagara River in present New York State. The French apparently cultivated gardens on the fertile mud flats of the west side of the river to supply produce for the garrison.

During the successful European-style siege of Fort Niagara by British forces in July 1759, the British surreptitiously established a battery on high ground at "Montreal Point"[6] near present Queen's Royal Park. The British invasion flotilla approached Fort Niagara from the east. As the French warship *Iroquoise* controlled the mouth of the river, all the heavy

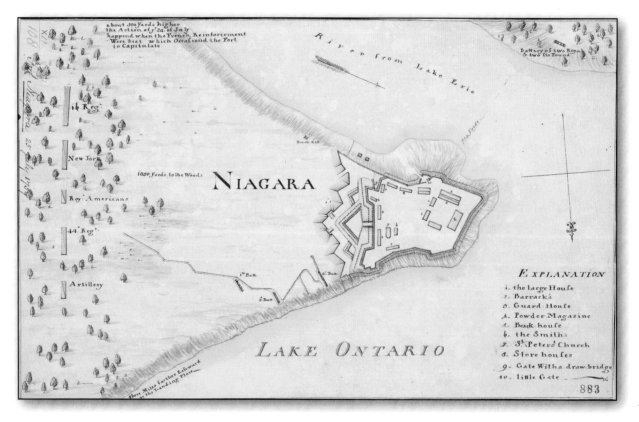

Fort Niagara 25 July 1759, plan on paper. This previously unpublished map shows the battery on the west (Canadian) bank in fine detail, with a "Battery of two Royal and two six pound(ers)" in the upper right-hand corner.

The Royal Collection © 2011, Her Majesty Queen Elizabeth II, RCIN 732108.

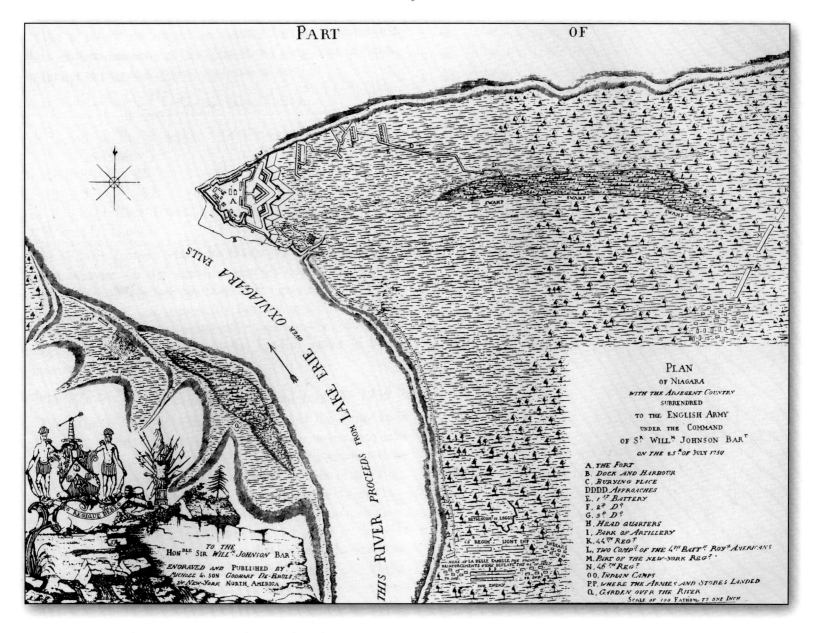

PLAN
OF NIAGARA
WITH THE ADJACENT COUNTRY
SURRENDRED
TO THE ENGLISH ARMY
UNDER THE COMMAND
OF S^R WILL^M JOHNSON BAR^T
ON THE 25TH OF JULY 1759

A. THE FORT
B. DOCK AND HARBOUR
C. BURYING PLACE
DDDD. APPROACHES
E. 1ST BATTERY
F. 2^D D^O
G. 3^D D^O
H. HEAD QUARTERS
I. PARK OF ARTILLERY
K. 44TH REG^T
L. TWO COMP^S OF THE 4TH BATT^N ROY^L AMERICANS
M. PART OF THE NEW-YORK REG^T
N. 46TH REG^T
OO. INDIAN CAMPS
PP. WHERE THE ARMIES AND STORES LANDED
Q. GARDEN OVER THE RIVER
SCALE OF 100 FATHOM^S TO ONE INCH

Plan of Niagara. This map illustrates the mouth of the Niagara River shortly after the British siege of Fort Niagara in July 1759. It shows on the west bank of the Niagara River "ploughed land" on the high land and a "garden over the river" on the marshland. Both had apparently been established by the French before the arrival of the British.

Map published in 1762 and reproduced in the Sir William Johnson Papers, vol. 3 (Albany: University of the State of New York, 1921), photo insert.

artillery, ammunition, and bateaux had to be transported from their landing site at Four Mile Creek (east of the river) overland to the gully of present Bloody Run Creek, two miles upstream from the fort. Transported across the river in the bateaux, the heavy artillery pieces were then dragged laboriously, but apparently without detection, along the crest of the west bank to Montreal Point. Once in place in a new earthen battery, the guns inflicted serious damage on the largely unprotected river side of the fort. Incredibly, the very first cannon ball shot in anger from the Canadian side of the river penetrated the stone chimney of the French commandant's quarters in the "French Castle," crashed down the flue onto the andirons and spun into French Commander François Pouchot's bedroom where he was sleeping.[7] Quite the wake-up call! With the termination of the Seven Years' War in 1763, French Canada, including Niagara, became part of British North America.

In 1764 Sir William Johnson negotiated with the Senecas an oral treaty sealed by a wampum belt whereby a four-mile strip of land along the east side of the Niagara River from its mouth to the escarpment including the strategic portage and a two-mile strip on the corresponding west bank were ceded to the British. The land was to be used for military and trade purposes only. Within a year, the British started construction of the Navy Hall complex at its present site[8] chosen because its wharf provided easier docking for tall-ships[9] and because of its proximity to huge oak trees on the plain above Navy Hall. Oak had long been regarded by the British Navy as the ideal building material for sailing ships.[10]

With the outbreak of the American Revolutionary War, Fort Niagara became headquarters for Colonel John Butler's Rangers, a corps of provincials who waged guerilla-like warfare against the rebels of upstate New York and Pennsylvania. Fort Niagara was overcrowded with Native, white, and black refugees from war and devastation in the Mohawk Valley; hence, Butler received permission in late 1778[11] to start construction of two log barracks and a few small "huts" for his men on the west side (approximately at the site of Chateau Gardens today).[12] The next year more log houses and a hospital were added.[13] With the Rangers now occupying the west bank, they were encouraged, when not out on raiding parties, to till the land — some twenty five acres known as the "King's Field" — now part of the Commons. Such efforts would provide agricultural provisions for the men but even more importantly, for the garrison across the river. Sir Frederick Haldimand, Governor of Quebec (which included present-day Ontario) and an avid gardener himself, had devised an agricultural policy

that provided a system of gardens and farms around each of the British garrisons to produce enough food to enable the garrison to be self-sufficient. However, under the terms of the 1764 treaty, large-scale farming was not permitted by the Senecas on the east side. Moreover, "both from the Soil and Situation, the West side of the river (is) by far preferable to the East."[14]

With the American General Sullivan's destructive swath through the Mohawk Valley in 1779, there was an

Sir Frederick Haldimand (1718–1791), artist Lemuel Francis Abbott, oil on canvas. As governor, Haldimand ordered the land above Navy Hall be reserved for a garrison.

With permission of the Royal Ontario Museum © ROM, #953.215.1.

even greater influx of refugees into Fort Niagara, further taxing the food supply. As a result, Guy Johnson, superintendent general of Indian Affairs, was directed to negotiate a treaty, signed in May 1781, with the Chippewas and Mississaugas who had sovereignty in the Niagara Peninsula. In return for "about the value of three Hundred Suits of Cloathing [*sic*]" a strip of land four miles wide westward from the Niagara River, stretching from Lake Ontario to Lake Erie, was granted to the British.[15] Even before the treaty had been signed, Haldimand granted permission for "amongst the distressed families three or four"[16] to farm full time on the west bank with the understanding that they were tenants only and that they were to sell all their produce to the garrison at prices set by the commanding officer. Within one year the "three or four" farmers had become sixteen households according to Butler's first census of August 1782.[17]

With the Treaty of Paris in 1783, those Loyalists already at Niagara could not return home. Moreover, the influx of new Loyalist families into western Quebec steadily increased. The government would have to establish guidelines for orderly civil settlement in the colony. The result was the "Cataraqui Plan,"[18] a four-point plan to establish townships for the settlement of the Loyalists:

1. Each township was to have a military reserve.
2. Provision was to be made for an Indian settlement "where some of the most noted [Indians] might be allowed to build."
3. A "common" of four hundred acres was to be preserved "for the use of the town" but it could be leased back to settlers "for a term not exceeding 30 years" or until the town needed the land.
4. Each township was to be a six-square mile grid ... similar to what the settlers were used to in their former colonies. There would be approximately seven rows of twenty-five rectangular lots with a road allowance along each row.

The plan also provided for the establishment of churches, grist mills, and saw mills in each township.

The prime prerequisite for such a plan of settlement, of course, would be an accurate official survey. Butler, perhaps to give some legitimacy to the settlers' concerns regarding land tenure of their already settled lands, hired Ranger Allen Macdonell[19] to survey the settlement that was completed before May, 1783.[20] In the Haldimand papers there is an undated and unsigned survey, "The New Settlement Niagara." Although not to scale, it does show the extent of the new settlement, concentrated primarily along the riverbank, and a second block of lots north of the "Due West Line" — now called the East-to-West Line — approximately between the Two and Four Mile Creeks. The large area west of Navy Hall to Two Mile Creek is simply marked "Rangers' Barracks" and probably constituted the tiny settlement of "Butlersburg" and the surrounding military reserve.[21]

Haldimand dismissed the Butler-Macdonell survey and hired a government surveyor, Lieutenant Tinling. One of his prime duties was to set aside "[g]round necessary to be reserved for a Post,"[22] which was to include all the "[h]igh ground above Navy Hall" to the Four Mile Creek north of the Due-West line.[23] Upon Tinling's arrival he was quickly confronted by the reality that several Rangers officers "have cultivated and built good farm houses" on land between Navy Hall and Four Mile Creek and had no intention to leave.[24] Eventually, Tinling produced a survey of Niagara Township that confirmed the general principles of the Cataraqui Plan, including the military reserve as specified by Haldimand.[25] But thanks to heavy Rangers lobbying, several blocks within the reserve were nominated for specific settlers.[26] There was, however, no provision for a commons or Indian reserve.

By 1788 Lord Dorchester, who had succeeded Haldimand as governor, proclaimed that settlers could in fact hold their land as English freehold and also directed officials to begin to lay out a town site within the township. The newly constituted Land Board, comprised of several local prominent citizens, took up the task. Initially they concluded that the most appropriate location for a proper town site

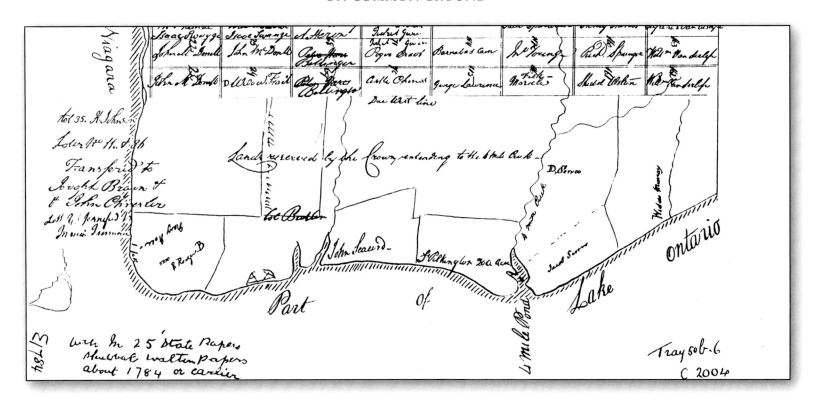

ABOVE: *Plan of Niagara*, circa 1784, paper document hand-copied by J. Simpson, 1909, from the original in the Shubbal-Walton Papers, Library and Archives Canada. This portion of an early official survey of Niagara shows Navy Hall and Rangers Barracks but most of the land from the Niagara River to Four Mile Creek, north of the "Due-West Line" is reserved by the Crown.

Courtesy of the Niagara Historical Society and Museum, #986.003.

RIGHT: *Guy Carleton, 1st Baron Dorchester* (1724–1808), artist unknown, miniature oil on ivory. Carleton introduced a system of land tenure and encouraged the creation of town sites.

Courtesy of the Royal Ontario Museum © ROM, #935.23.1.

would be in the centre of the township, facing the Niagara River halfway between Navy Hall and Queenston. The owners of the lots refused to give up their lands. A year later the colonial government chose the Crown lands on the River just north of the Due-West line, to be named Lenox. The survey was commenced by Augustus Jones,[27] who soon realized that there was insufficient land between the Due-West line and the land already reserved on the high ground above Navy Hall for military purposes. Therefore, the site for the town was shifted to the northwest of Navy Hall — the present King Street, which runs south thirty degrees southwest from the river, would be the boundary between the new town and the military reserve. With the settlement of Butlersburg/Lenox being designated the capital of Upper Canada in 1792 and renamed Newark by Simcoe, a survey of the new capital was produced.[28] This called for lots reserved for churches, schools, and market places, but still no commons or public square. However, provision was made for the speedy erection of a public house (corner of King and Front streets) and a Mason's Lodge next to it[29] — reflecting the social priorities of the male citizens of the town.

During the capital years, with the impending loss of Fort Niagara to the Americans, the strategic importance of the military installations on the Military Reserve increased dramatically. There was great activity in the Navy Hall complex by the river; the Rangers' barracks, vacated by the Rangers who had been disbanded, was used by the militia and the Indian Department and the site was fortified; and the new Fort George garrison site was staked out. Despite this activity there were still some civilian encroachments on the reserve. Widow Murray maintained a farm in the middle of the reserve. Several merchants had shops and wharves along the marshy riverfront.[30] William Dickson, in one of his petitions for land,[31] claimed title for a "small House and Lott" on the reserve (approximate site of present St. Mark's Rectory). He stated that since 1783, the property had been occupied successively by Surgeon Guthrie, silversmith John Bachus,[32] merchant Crooks, and then himself. The claim was disallowed because "it was land reserved for the purpose of fortification."

By 1796 the extent of the Fort George Military Reserve was greatly reduced. The southern and western boundaries of the reserve ran parallel but slightly south of present-day John Street East to the river. Simcoe granted the land now excluded from the reserve south to Due-West Line primarily to "potential Canadian aristocrats."[33] The large acreage between the western border and Four Mile Creek was granted to several Loyalist settlers in addition to those settlers who had been exempted previously.[34] The King Street boundary between the town site and the reserve remained unchanged.

Without any official provision in the town's plan for a commons, green, public square, or park, it is understandable why the local townspeople and visitors alike began to consider the Military Reserves, primarily the large section to the south of King Street and to a lesser extent the smaller Reserve at Mississauga Point, as their commons. Such common lands had been enjoyed and indeed taken for granted back in the former American Thirteen Colonies as well as Great Britain. The commons was a place to graze your cows and sheep, to tether your horses and perhaps till a little garden, to gather firewood or mushrooms, or to provide a venue for various sports and other recreational activities, including a rendezvous for lovers. In the case of Niagara, venturing onto the Commons was always done with a watchful eye on the military installations and personnel, keeping in mind that it was officially a military reserve. It was often an uneasy truce: military officials complained of encroachment on their land and the locals objected to unnecessary high-handed military regulations. But as we will see later, in practice there was also an ongoing symbiotic relationship between the military and the townspeople.

The year 1796 was an important milestone for Newark (Niagara), and the Commons in particular. Construction of Fort George, although laid out as early as 1790, finally began on the high ground above Navy Hall chosen because it was approximately fourteen feet higher than the opposing Fort

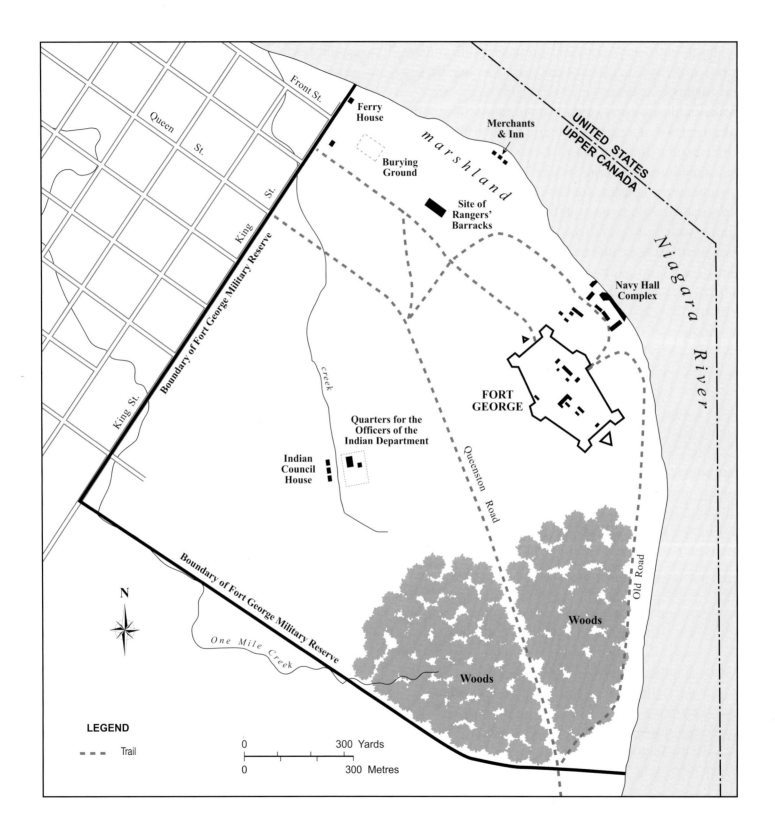

Niagara — an important consideration when lobbing artillery shells onto one's enemy. The mere presence of this military garrison would have a lasting influence on the town's history and that of the Commons.[35]

With the last session of the First Parliament of Upper Canada prorogued in June 1796, the capital of the infant colony officially moved to York (Toronto). Government officials and many military officers reluctantly left Niagara. The mercantile, social, and cultural epicentre of the colony gradually shifted across the lake as well. If the capital had remained at Niagara, the Commons as we know it today would certainly not have survived into the twenty-first century. Moreover, as previously mentioned, with the Crown grants along John Street officially approved in 1796, the boundaries of the Military Reserve were now finalized … or were they? Within one year, two local citizens had requested a grant of a portion of the "Commons or Lands now used as such."[36] This was the first of what was to become a seemingly never-ending succession of proposals (many successful) to nibble away at the edges of the Commons.

If you couldn't purchase a piece of the Commons, at least you could buy a view of the Commons. By 1796 the two most substantial homes in Niagara — D.W. Smith's elegant home and formal gardens on town lots 65, 66, 103, and 104, and William Dickson's Georgian mansion on Lot 64 — both looked out onto the Commons. Moreover, Administrator Russell's home, known as Springfield, was beautifully situated in the midst of the Commons.

The relative tranquility and picturesque green expanse of the Fort George Military Reserve/Commons at the end of the eighteenth century would soon be violently disrupted.

FACING PAGE: Fort George Military Reserve, 1800. This map illustrates the full extent of the Fort George Military Reserve with its Navy Hall Complex, probable site of the Rangers' Barracks, the newly completed Fort George, and the buildings of the British Indian Department. Note the original contour of the Queenston Road is closely followed by today's Queen's Parade and Picton Street. Although this map is based on diligent research, the various trails, creeks, and other landmarks should not be interpreted as their exact original location.

CHAPTER 3

The Captain Cook Connection

With the impending arrival of Lieutenant Governor John Graves Simcoe and his wife at Niagara in the summer of 1792, the original building at Navy Hall was renovated to serve as the residence and offices of the viceregal couple. However, the Simcoes found the accommodation dark and dingy and much preferred to live in "the canvass houses," even through the long, cold Canadian winter. These were not the simple canvas tents that would later be pitched on the Commons by the thousands during the Camp Niagara days. British military officers and government officials during military campaigns or exploratory expeditions throughout the world often lived "under canvas" outfitted with specially designed campaign furniture.[1] The Simcoes' canvas houses, however, were quite unique. Shortly after Simcoe's appointment as Lieutenant Governor, he purchased at a sale of Captain James Cook's effects[2] in England one or two canvas houses. The famous explorer had used these during his three circumnavigating expeditions in the 1760s and 70s. Sketches taken during these voyages illustrate the canvas houses in use.[3] By strange coincidence, at the British conquest of Louisbourg in 1758 John Graves Simcoe's father Captain John Simcoe was commander of HMS *Pembroke*, under whom a young James Cook had served admirably as master.

An itemized account from a Mr. Nathan Smith lists upgrades to the canvas houses commissioned by Simcoe:

Improvements in the Canvas House ... made in frames, 38 feet 4"long by 12 feet wide and 7 feet 2 inches high at the side with 6 glazed windows and a partition to each room, also a cosy iron stove, fender, shovel, poker, and tongs, the inside of the rooms papered complete, the outside painted in oil colour and properly packed, marked and numbered.[4]

A later invoice refers to camp tables and chairs "packed with the canvas houses."[5]

The canvas was apparently applied over a wooden framework and could be boarded up from the outside when necessary for warmth.

Mrs. Simcoe recorded in her diary that upon their arrival in July 1792 they lived in three simple canvas tents, or "marquees," pitched on the hill above Navy Hall that "command a beautiful view of the river and garrison [Fort Niagara] on the opposite side."[6]

Mrs. Simcoe later recorded that the canvas houses finally arrived. After they were reassembled a partition was built so that one part was a bedroom, the other a "sitting-room."[7] The other canvas house was apparently occupied by the "squalling children" and the servants. Such were the domestic arrangements for His Majesty's representative during their first Upper Canadian winter, and quite a

Captain Cook's Canvas Houses, Matavi Bay, Tahiti, April 1769, watercolour. Two of these canvas houses were occupied by the Simcoes at Navy Hall and later on the edge of Garrison Creek at York.

Courtesy of the Toronto Public Library, Toronto Reference Library, John Ross Robertson, JRR #4610.

change from their forty-room mansion in Devonshire with its superb view across the Vale of Honiton.

Surveyor Joseph Bouchette[8] described the canvas house: "Frail as was its substance, it was rendered exceedingly comfortable and soon became as distinguished for the social and urban hospitality of its venerable and gracious host, as for the peculiarity of its structure."[9] Also impressed was an American official, General William Hull, who was attending an Indian Council meeting held in Niagara,

On my account the Governor ordered supper in his canvas-house, which he brought from Europe … It is papered and painted, and you would suppose you were in a common house. The floor is the case for the whole of the room. It is quite a curiosity … Perceiving me so much pleased with the canvas-house, the Governor ordered breakfast in it.[10]

In the summer of 1793 one of the canvas houses was dismantled and transported across Lake Ontario to the site of York (future Toronto). Reassembled on a small knoll above the pristine shore of Lake Ontario, near the mouth of the Garrison Creek across from the chosen site for Fort York, the Simcoe family spent another cozy winter "under canvas." Not all visitors to the canvas house were impressed. Bachelor Peter Russell reported to his half-sister, "you have no conception of the Misery in which they live — The Canvas house being their only residence."[11] Eight months later the canvas house was back in Niagara on the edge of the Military Reserve/Commons and remained the official viceregal's residence until the Simcoes returned to England in 1796. What became of Captain Cook's well-travelled canvas houses is not known.

CHAPTER 4

A "Commodious Dwelling" on the Commons

Standing in the tall, wild grass in the middle of the Commons on the edge of a small creek,[1] it is hard to imagine that a fine Georgian estate stood there as early as 1793. "Springfield" was the home of Peter Russell, a veteran of the Seven Years' and American Revolutionary Wars and an inveterate gambler. As the newly appointed Receiver General for the Province of Upper Canada, Russell arrived at Niagara in 1792 with his half-sister Elizabeth and a young Mary Fleming (possibly Peter's illegitimate daughter).[2] The only accommodation they could find "near the Lieutenant Governor's Residence at Navy Hall"[3] was a two-room "hut"[4] in the middle of the Military Reserve occupied by Widow Murray, for which Russell paid £70.[5] Lieutenant Duncan Murray had been an officer in the 84th Regiment of Foot (Royal Highland Emigrants), garrisoned during the early 1780s across the river at Fort Niagara.[6] While building grist and sawmills on his land grant on the Twelve Mile Creek[7] in 1786, Murray was killed by a falling tree. Perhaps in deference to her late husband, Widow Murray was allowed squatter rights in the middle of the reserve. Russell, realizing that the £70 purchase price was for Mrs. Murray's improvements only, persuaded Simcoe to grant him a twenty-one-year lease for fifty acres, which included the Widow's farm, at a nominal five shillings per year.[8] He also received an outright grant of 160 acres of prime land bordering the southern edge of the military reserve, along what is now John Street, that he would later sell for a very tidy profit.

Peter Russell (1733–1808), artist G.T. Berthon, watercolour. Russell, army officer, office holder, politician, and judge, was also the builder of Springfield on the Fort George Military Reserve/Commons.

Courtesy of the Toronto Public Library, Toronto Reference Library, John Ross Robertson Collection, JRR #T34630.

Before winter set in, the Russells undertook extensive renovations to the hut. Peter complained of the "extravagant wages"[9] of the workmen, with carpenters demanding 7 shillings per day.[10] Within the first year they had already spent £400[11] and by 1796 Russell claimed to have spent £1200[12] on improvements, which included his governmental office on the premises. No exterior views of the house have survived, but a plan of the property drawn in 1797[13] reveals a full two-storey house, along with a coach house, stables, outhouses, root house, and cellars, as well as a formal fruit garden at the rear. Even a spring is shown on the plan. This may explain the name of Springfield, since the fields of the military reserve surrounded the estate. Despite much grumbling about the costs of their "Dear House" the little family seemed to have been very comfortable in their new home. In a letter to a friend in England, Elizabeth wrote:

> We are comfortably settled in our new House and have a nice little farm about us. We eat our own Mutton and Pork and Poultry. Last year we grew our own Buck wheat and Indian corn and had two Oxen, got two Cows with their calves with plenty of pigs and a Mare and Sheep.[14]

Elizabeth's fruit preserves became a much sought-after commodity amongst her fellow colonists. Even Mrs. Simcoe admired Elizabeth's hobby of collecting and preserving botanical specimens gathered in the area.

Not interested in the whirl of social activities at Navy Hall, the Russells were content with small, intimate dinners at Springfield served on the family silver plate, accompanied by fine wines and followed by sonorous renditions given by Peter. This "little threesome" in the commodious house could not possibly have managed without help. The practice of slavery was still alive and well on the Commons in the 1790s. Peter had at least two manservants, Robert Franklin and Pompador. There were also at least two maids/cooks, including Milly and the "troublesome" Peggy. Russell's attitude towards slavery was hypocritical. Although he

supported Simcoe's anti-slavery legislation through parliament,[15] and later as administrator of the province prevented an attempt to reverse the legislation, he owned at least five slaves. He paid for a tutor to teach the son of one of his slaves to read and write, and yet in 1806 he put Peggy and her son Jupiter up for sale.[16]

Well-established in her "commodious dwelling house," Elizabeth Russell commiserated with the Simcoes who had "only a Canvas House"[17] to shelter them from the inclemency of the Canadian weather.

Government officials were well aware of Simcoe's determination to move the temporary capital of Upper Canada across Lake Ontario to York, with the new parliament opening there in 1797. Many government officials were slow to make the move, and quite agreed with Elizabeth who proclaimed, "For my part I am determined to stay here where I am till there is a comfortable Place there to receive me."[18] Eventually, her brother, who had by then been named administrator of the province with Simcoe on sick-leave in England, would find a suitable abode in York. However, the prospect of moving created a major quandary for Peter: how could he possibly recoup his investment in Springfield when he still did not have clear title to the property? One can clearly detect an air of desperation in his correspondence to the new Governor General Robert Prescott, in which Russell suggested that the military reserve need not be so large; if the reserve were to be reduced in size, his property would be outside the reserve and hence his land could be held in freehold.[19] In reply he received a harsh reprimand from Prescott's secretary for even suggesting a change in the military reserve. Moreover, he was advised that the lease was invalid and he had no right to build on the land and would have to remove his house from the reserve.[20] To add to his woes, his new house in York for which he had paid £400, had "just burnt to the ground,"[21] putting his sister "in a low nervous state."[22] In the end, the Governor General relented and permitted the much-chastened Russell to continue to lease

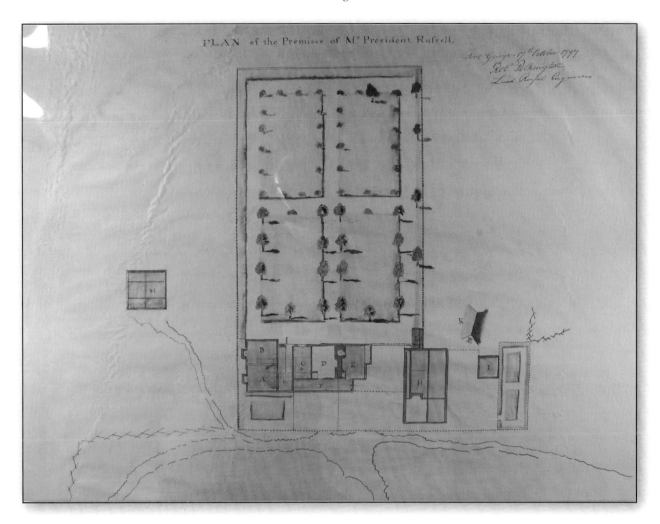

Plan of the Premises of Mr. President Russell, artist Robert Pilkington, 1797, sketch (a 1915 copy of the original in Library and Archives Canada, NMC 0023040). On his fifty-acre leased property in the middle of the Fort George reserve, Russell erected a two-storey "commodious dwelling" with cellars, several out-buildings, plus an extensive garden.

Courtesy of the Niagara Historical Society and Museum, #986.006.

the property on the military reserve. In an effort to sell his leased property in Niagara, Russell placed a large advertisement in the November 1796 edition of the *Upper Canada Gazette* for "A Commodious Dwelling, coach house, stable and other offices all built within three years."[23] He commissioned Lieutenant Robert Pilkington of the Royal Engineers to draw up "a Plan of the Premises of Mr. President Russell,"[24] which apparently was quite widely distributed. After one

year on the market the balance of the lease and the buildings thereon were conveniently taken over by the British Indian Department as a dwelling quarters for its officers at £900.[25]

The British Indian Department was created by the British government in the 1750s as the Crown's military liaison with the Native tribes in North America (see chapter 7). It had initially been concerned with mobilizing His Majesty's Indian Allies against the French during the Seven Years' War. Subsequently during the American Revolutionary War, the Indian Department worked diligently to direct the First Nations against the rebelling colonists, especially along the western frontier. Even after the Revolution, the British maintained this "chain of friendship" with the Natives, keeping them "on side" leading up to the War of 1812 when His Majesty's Indian Allies would play a pivotal role in several battles.[26]

With the Americans' takeover of Forts Niagara, Detroit, and Michilimackinac in 1796 in accordance with Jay's Treaty, the Indian Department was reorganized. It built new Council Houses at Fort George, Fort Malden on the Detroit River, and Fort St. Joseph in the northwest, each with its own officers, including a superintendant of Indian Affairs, a storekeeper/clerk, and interpreters. The timely availability of Russell's house and fifty acres in the midst of the military reserve was a perfect fit for the needs of the Indian Department: the new Council House, storehouses, blacksmith, and other out-buildings on one side of the creek and the officers of the Department ensconced in the "Commodious Dwelling" on the other.

What a sharp contrast between the two households: from the hesitant yet arrogant bachelor-bureaucrat Peter Russell, his gossip-prone, haughty spinster half-sister, and the quiet, young but frail teenage Mary,[27] supported by a household of several slaves, replaced by the boisterous and lusty backwoodsmen employees of the Indian Department. No doubt the house was renovated to meet the needs of the Department. In addition to several bedrooms there would have been an office for the superintendant, a dining/meeting room, a kitchen in a separate building, and a large common room. There, whoever happened to be in town on Department business would probably gather around the fireplace, exchange news and gossip, recall exploits, and perhaps tell some very tall tales, all the while puffing on clay pipes and throwing back swigs of rum or brandy. Raucous games of cards, dice, checkers, or backgammon would have been other popular pastimes. The air would have been heavy with wood and tobacco smoke mixed with the smell of tallow candles and rancid body odours. The common room's walls were probably decorated with maps and proclamations, prints and sketches, portraits of George III and other members of the Royal family, and many colourful and curious Native artifacts.

Effective December 25, 1797,[28] the following Indian Department officers were appointed at Fort George: William Claus, superintendant; Robert Kerr, surgeon; William Johnson Chew, storekeeper and clerk; Barnabas Cain, blacksmith; and George Cowan, David Price, John Norton, and Jean Baptiste Rousseaux as interpreters.[29] Although it is highly unlikely that all these men were assembled together at Niagara at one time, as a group they arguably represent the most colourful and remarkable collection of individuals ever to occupy the Commons or its perimeter.

William Claus

Born into a family of wealth and privilege in the Mohawk Valley, William Claus was a grandson of Sir William Johnson, the powerful Superintendent of Northern Indian Affairs. His father, Christian Daniel Claus, also held important positions in the Indian Department. William's formal education was interrupted by the outbreak of the American Revolutionary War. He enlisted as a volunteer in the King's Royal Regiment of New York under the command of his uncle, Sir John Johnson. After the war, he obtained a lieutenancy in a regular British regiment, the 60th Foot, and made captain by 1795. Meanwhile Uncle John, who was now Superintendant General of Indian Affairs, anxiously sought a position for young William in the Department. With the death of John Butler in 1796, Claus was finally appointed deputy superintendant at Fort George and four years later named Deputy Superintendant General for Upper Canada — a post he held for the next twenty-six years.

Although much of Claus's official time in the service involved "the interminable tedium of Indian councils, gift giving and pledges of British friendship,"[30] Claus was con-

William Claus (1765–1826), artist and medium of portrait, unknown. Claus was a grandson of Sir William Johnson, an army officer, office-holder, deputy superintendant of the British Indian Department for Upper Canada, builder of what became known as the Wilderness, and a horticulturalist.

Courtesy of the Niagara Historical Society and Museum, #984.1.559

fronted by several major challenges. Captain Joseph Brant, civil and war chief of the Six Nations, insisted the Natives of the Haldimand Tract of the Grand River had the right to sell off some of their lands. Claus, acting on behalf of the colonial government, countered that the Six Nations did not have free sovereignty of their land and hence could only sell their land back to the Crown.[31] Although a partial compromise was eventually found, the land ownership issue continues unresolved today.

With the increasing belligerence of the War-Hawks within the United States, Claus was kept busy trying to polish the chain of friendship with the Six Nations and Western Indian Allies in order to keep the Natives "on side." Opposition to his influence within the Six Nations came from an unexpected source. Former employee and sometime fellow occupant in the Commodious House, interpreter John Norton, was persuaded by Joseph Brant to leave the service and move to the Grand Valley where he quickly became Brant's confidant and eventual successor. During the War of 1812, impressed by Norton's outstanding military acumen and leadership skills, the British Army generals deferred to Norton rather than Claus, and by early 1814, commander-in-chief Sir George Prevost proclaimed that Norton was to be the sole spokesman and dispenser of gifts to the Six Nations and Thames Natives until the end of the war.[32] Embarrassed and humiliated, Claus became consumed by jealousy and loathing of Norton's influence, constantly trying to undermine Norton's reputation. The intense rivalry between the two men only diminished after Norton was pensioned off and was succeeded by the young John Brant.

The post-war years were also characterized by a major shift in British colonial policy towards the Natives from one of "allies" to mere wards of the state — a transition supervised by Claus, but a role he played with efficiency and compassion. He was appointed to the prestigious Executive Council of the Province, named a Justice of the Peace, and he served as a school trustee and commissioner of customs.

Although he probably maintained an office in the officers' quarters, it is unlikely that Claus ever intentionally slept over in the officers' quarters; he had inherited his mother's town lots[33] on the edge of the military reserve, where he raised a family. He and his wife, Catherine, kept careful notes of their gardening efforts which provide an interesting glimpse of horticultural practices in early Upper Canada.[34] He died in 1826 after a slow, agonizing battle with disfiguring lip cancer.

Doctor Robert Kerr

Robert Kerr was born circa 1755 in Scotland, and soon after his arrival in North America became a hospital mate in the King's Royal Regiment of New York during the Revolutionary War. In 1788 he was appointed Surgeon to the British Indian Department, no doubt in part due to his fortuitous marriage to Elizabeth, daughter of Sir William Johnson and the indomitable Molly Brant. Settling in Niagara the following year, he attended diligently to his duties with the Indian Department, but also served at times as surgeon to the various regiments garrisoned at Fort George. He also had a large private practice in town. In 1797 he and fellow physician James Muirhead advertised the availability of small pox inoculation for the townspeople, "the poor gratis"[35] — one of the first examples of preventive medicine in Upper Canada.[36]

The doctor had built a substantial house in town for his growing family,[37] so it is unlikely that he actually stayed in the commodious house on the Commons, but he would certainly have attended to ailing Department employees there as well as any visiting Natives. In his war loss claims Kerr lists his medical instruments at the Indian Council House as having been destroyed.[38] Kerr was also a prominent freemason, serving as provincial grandmaster for a remarkable thirteen years. Tall and well proportioned, he enjoyed sports, particularly boxing. Like other early medical men, he supplemented his income with government appointments, serving as a judge of the Surrogate Court, a Land Board member, commissioner of the peace, and trustee for public schools. As one of the earliest physicians of Upper Canada, Kerr was much beloved and respected by the Natives, soldiers, and citizens alike.

Dr. Robert Kerr (1755–1824), attributed to E. Wyly Grier, watercolour over pencil on paper. Kerr served as surgeon to military regiments and the British Indian Department, town physician, judge of the Surrogate Court, and deputy grand master of the Provincial Grand Lodge of Masons. He married Elizabeth, daughter of Molly Brant and Sir William Johnson.

Courtesy of the Toronto Public Library, Toronto Reference Library, John Ross Robertson Collection, JRR #T14843.

William Johnson Chew

William Johnson Chew, born in that fateful year of 1759, was appointed through the influence of his father, Joseph Chew, who had served ably as secretary to the Indian Department. Young William "behaved with attention to his Duties," starting in 1794, although he was "not much conversant with the Indian language."[39] As storekeeper he was responsible for all of the Departmental supplies, as well as the presents and trade goods for the Natives. As clerk he would attend the Indian councils to accurately record the speeches and any resultant agreements. On the morning of May 27, 1813, serving as an officer in the Indian Department with fifty Natives under Captain John Norton, he was killed trying to prevent the American landing at One Mile Creek.[40]

Chew married Margaret Mt. Pleasant, whose mother was a Tuscarora Native.

Barnabas Cain

Barnabas (Barney) Cain is listed as a sergeant in the Indian Department.[41] He was granted town Lot 39 in Niagara, as well as Lots 111 and 114 in Niagara Township (near Virgil). He later served in the Lincoln militia at the Battle of Lundy's Lane and is said to have carried off the battlefield the lifeless body of his friend George Caughill.[42] As the Department's blacksmith he would have been kept busy forging a variety of iron hardware, as well as shoeing horses for the employees and the Natives. In some provincial locales the blacksmith also repaired guns and instruments. The smithy was situated by the Council House. Newly remarried in February 1798 by Reverend Robert Addison,[43] he probably hurried home to his new bride, Cyble Clinton, rather than linger about the commons in the evenings.

INTERPRETERS

Interpreters were chosen for their language skills and trustworthiness. At least one and often two interpreters would be present at the various Indian Council meetings, whether at the Council House at Fort George or at meetings held elsewhere such as Buffaloe Creek,[44] Burlington Heights, or the Grand Valley. On occasion they would be sent out as special emissaries or on secret missions. Given their backwoods origins, most interpreters probably preferred to sleep under the stars by a smoking fire, accepting the housekeeper's invitation to bed down indoors only in inclement weather. Later there may have been separate quarters for the interpreters over by the Council House.

David Price

Born of Welsh parents in the Mohawk Valley in 1750, David Price was captured by the Senecas in 1771 and lived amongst them for seven years. During the American Revolutionary War he served with the much-feared Brant's Volunteers,[45] which consisted of both Natives and whites who fought together under Joseph Brant "in the Indian Fashion." After the war, he became an interpreter first at Oswego and later Fort George. In 1800 he married Margaret Gonder, daughter of loyalist Michael Gonder, who lived on the upper Niagara River. This "old zealous Servant of the King"[46] left the service circa 1812 and took up farming along the Chippawa Creek until his death at ninety-one years.

George Cowan

Probably of Scottish ancestry, Cowan was captured as a young boy by the French at Fort Duquesne (Pitt) in 1758, became fluent in French, and at times assumed a French name, Jean Baptiste Constance or Constant.[47] Although he served on at least one occasion as an interpreter for the Americans in the Ohio Valley,[48] he became a fur trader, guide, and interpreter for the British, establishing a trading post on Matchadesh Bay on Lake Huron. As the guide for Lieutenant Governor Simcoe when he trekked through the region in 1793, Cowan pointed out the ideal site for the future strategic harbour of Penetanguishene.[49] Cowan was considered one of the best Chippewa and Mississauga interpreters in the colony. Whenever these tribes visited the Indian Council House at Fort George he would be summoned. In 1804, a Chippewa chief accused of murder and accompanied by Cowan as an interpreter was being transported aboard the schooner HMS *Speedy* for trial in Newcastle on Lake Ontario. All aboard, including the judge, the Solicitor General for Upper Canada (prosecutor), a member of the Assembly (defence lawyer), the high constable, and several others were lost when the *Speedy* went down in a violent storm.

John Norton (Teyoninhokarawen)

Norton was born in Scotland in 1770, the son of a Scottish mother and a Cherokee father who as a young boy had been rescued by a British officer from a burning village in America. Based on his future writings and great oratory skills, John received a good education before enlisting as a private in the British 65th Regiment of Foot, which arrived in Quebec in 1785. One year later his regiment was posted at Fort Niagara where Norton soon became enamoured with the Native people. Leaving the army shortly thereafter, he served as a schoolmaster for Native children at Deseronto for one year before heading west. Hired by Detroit merchant John Askin, Norton acted as interpreter and fur trader at various trading posts in the Ohio Country and the Old Northwest. With the defeat of the British and their Native allies at Fallen Timbers, he returned to Niagara and was appointed interpreter to the Indian Department. Based on records of Indian councils, Norton appears to have been the most active interpreter and emissary, hence, he probably spent considerable time at the commodious dwelling. Norton soon caught the eye of Captain Joseph Brant, who eventually convinced him to resign from the Indian Department and work with him amongst the First Nations of the Grand Valley. Soon he was adopted as a Mohawk nephew of Brant and given the name Teyoninhokarawen. Brant sent Norton on a secret mission to Britain in 1804 to press the Six Nations' land claims. He was unsuccessful in his prime objective, but the trip was a personal triumph for Norton as he was introduced to reformers and abolitionists as well as the nobility and even the Prince Regent.

Tall, handsome, gregarious, fluent in four European languages and twelve native dialects and blessed with a remarkable memory and oratorical skills, he truly had charisma. He was equally at home in the small intellectual gatherings of the reformers and the grand drawing rooms of the wealthy upper-class of Britain as he was in the frenetic war dances of the First Nations. Before returning home, the newly formed British and Foreign Bible Society convinced him to

John Norton, Teyoninhokarawen, the Mohawk Chief (1770–circa 1830), artist Mary Ann Knight, miniature watercolour on ivory, 1805. He was appointed an interpreter with the British Indian Department at Niagara in 1796 but three years later he was persuaded by Chief Joseph Brant to move to the Six Nations Tract on the Grand River. Note his silver earrings or ear bobs and the many trade silver brooches on his shirt.

Library and Archives Canada, C-123832.

undertake their very first transcription effort: the translation into Mohawk of the Gospel of St. John, a remarkable feat accomplished in less than three months. Shortly after his return to the Grand Valley, Joseph Brant died. Norton assumed Brant's role as a chief of war and diplomacy, introducing reforms in agriculture, industry, education, religion, and social welfare to his adopted people. Although supported by the majority of the chiefs and matrons, the Indian Department and his old protégé William Claus, encouraged by colonial officials at York, constantly tried to undermine his authority. They questioned his parentage, his motives, his chosen way of life — yet the more they attacked his integrity, the stronger his stature became.

In 1809 Norton undertook an odyssey to the land of his Cherokee ancestors in the southern United States where he became acquainted with relatives of this father. He also recorded the legends and lore of the Cherokees as well as their modern adaptation to the incursions of the Europeans.

Back in the Grand Valley, Norton resumed the military leadership[50] of the Six Nations, a position he held throughout the War of 1812; after Tecumseh's death in 1813 he also led His Majesty's Western Native Allies. In addition to Detroit, Norton fought at every major battle but one in the Niagara Peninsula. His military acumen and leadership skills, particularly at Queenston Heights, received glowing praise from British Army generals, and yet the Indian Department, increasingly alarmed at his growing stature, continued their attempt to undermine his integrity and authority among the Natives. By early 1814, however, commander-in-chief Sir George Prevost proclaimed that therein Norton was to be the sole leader and dispenser of gifts among the Six Nations and Thames allies until the end of the war[51] — an unprecedented acknowledgement of Norton's abilities and accomplishments and a total repudiation of William Claus and the Indian Department.

Shortly after the war, Norton with his wife and young son returned to Britain where he was welcomed as a hero — gazetted a brevet major in the British Army, granted a lifetime pension, and awarded personal gifts from the Prince Regent (future George IV) himself. While in Britain he completed his monumental journal dedicated to Northumberland, who was to arrange to have this important work published in Britain. Unfortunately the Duke died shortly thereafter and the manuscript sat on a library shelf nearly forgotten until after the Second World War when it was discovered and eventually published by the Champlain Society.[52] The journal consists of three sections. The first describes his trip to the land of his Cherokee ancestors in which he records details of Cherokee mythology, history, customs, social conditions, and even sports — the accuracy of which has been confirmed by later historians and ethnologists. The second section is devoted to the history of the original five Iroquois nations and contains much heretofore unknown information which had been collected by Brant but subsequently lost and hence is of enormous scholarly importance. The final section is Norton's personal and amazingly accurate narrative recollection of the War of 1812. As such the journal is certainly the most important and by far the most detailed account of the War of 1812 from a Native perspective and is arguably the most comprehensive personal account of the war from the British side as well.

Back on the Grand River again, Norton managed a large farm, constantly extolling to his neighbours the rewards of good agricultural practices and the virtues of good "Christian living." He was also indefatigable in promoting the war claims of his fellow Native war veterans and their families.

In 1823 he became involved in a duel over alleged infidelities by his wife. His protagonist was killed: rather than sully his wife's reputation Norton pleaded guilty to manslaughter and was assessed a fine. Greatly shaken, Norton settled his affairs and headed south again, never to return to British North America which he had so strenuously helped to preserve. In 2011 the Historic Sites and Monuments Board of Canada designated Norton as a National Historic Person.

St. Jean-Baptiste Rousseaux

St. Jean-Baptiste Rousseaux was born in Quebec in 1758. As early as 1770 his father was trading with Natives at the mouth of the St. John's Creek, later known as the Humber River on Lake Ontario. Soon Jean-Baptiste was carrying on this trade and serving as an Indian Department interpreter with the Mohawk and Mississauga tribes. By 1792 he had established a store on the Humber. The following year he welcomed the

Simcoes, who arrived to explore and proclaim the site as the future capital of the province. As such, Rousseaux is considered one of the founders of the city of Toronto.[53] A restless but enterprising soul, he later moved to the Head of the Lake (present day Hamilton Harbour) establishing a general store and later an inn, blacksmith shop, and extensive grist and sawmills at Ancaster. Meanwhile, he continued as an interpreter and respected adviser on Native affairs, hence his appointment at Fort George. Prior to the War of 1812 he was appointed a lieutenant colonel in the militia. Present at the Battle of Queenston Heights, one month later he contracted pleurisy, and despite the efforts of his friend and physician Doctor Kerr, he died at Fort George (possibly in the commodious house) and was buried with full military honours in St. Mark's churchyard.[54]

Many visitors would have been welcomed to the commodious house. The Superintendant General, Sir John Johnson, who occasionally toured the Department's sites, would have expected special attention. Commissioned officers of the Indian Department and veterans of the American Revolutionary War probably dropped in for a little refreshment and camaraderie in the common rooms.

The transfer of Springfield from the Russells to the Indian Department was not quite as smooth as originally planned. Apparently when the Russells departed for York, several army officers took up residence in the vacant premises and were quite incensed when forced to give up their commodious dwelling to officials of the Department.[55] This underscored the ongoing friction between the officers of the British Army, who were primarily from the privileged class in Britain, and the officers and men of the Department, who had spent their entire adult life in North America. Moreover, many of the latter had married into Native families and were much more sympathetic to the First Nations' cultures and perspectives.

Departmental officials also had to deal with other intruders. Townsfolk who regarded the military reserve as their commons were helping themselves to the extensive gardens and orchards on the premises, hence they were told explicitly that "Towns people can have nothing to do with it (any) more than the King can interfere with their property without previous consent."[56]

One gentleman who was welcome was the garrison's commissariat officer. With no space for his offices in the new fort, he was permitted to use one of the outbuildings on the estate.

Although some of the buildings of the Indian Department were destroyed by the bombardment of Fort George in May 1813 and the subsequent occupation by the Americans, a post war map (1817) of the military reserve[57] indicates a building very near the site of the original commodious dwelling's stable, so it may have survived the war, at least in part. It is labeled "Commandant Quarters," which makes sense as it is halfway between the crumbling but still occupied Fort George and Navy Hall to the east and the new Butler's Barracks complex being built to the west. The twenty-one-year lease had expired and the much diminished Indian Department no longer had any need for the building and was gradually transferring its properties back to the British Army.

In 1970 an extensive archaeological excavation of the site was undertaken.[58] It found evidence of a frame building on a stone foundation with cellars dating from the early nineteenth century. The foundations indicated that a number of additions were made to the structure. David McConnell in his exhaustive review of the known references to the Commandant's Quarters[59] confirmed from military reports that indeed repairs and additions had been undertaken in 1817, 1819, and again in 1823. However, E.W. Durnford of the Royal Engineers concluded in his report of 1823 that "[t]his is a very old house to which additions have been made from time to time,"[60] which certainly suggests a much earlier origin.[61]

In 1823 the commandant moved to the more comfortable Commanding Engineer's Quarters near the Niagara River while the more junior Commanding Engineer took up quarters periodically on the Commons. On occasion, the premises were also rented out. The first tenant in the 1830s was "Mr. Powell,"[62] who presumably was John Powell (1809–1881). John was the grandson of two influential personages: William Dummer Powell, the Chief Justice of the province, and Major General Aeneas Shaw, one time Queens Ranger and later Adjuvant General of the Provincial Staff in the War of 1812. John grew up in the home built by his father overlooking the military reserve. The property, later known as Brockamour (see chapter 21) was sold out of the family in 1836. This may have prompted John and his young family to temporarily rent the quarters on the military reserve. In late 1837, however, John was in Toronto where he became embroiled in the rebellion of 1837. He supposedly killed one

Colonel's Residence, 1854, artist uncertain, watercolour. This may be the commandant's quarters on the Commons. Archaeological studies suggest the quarters may have retained elements of Russell's original pre-war commodious dwelling.

Courtesy of the Niagara Historical Society and Museum # 988.273.

of the rebels and sounded the alarm of a threatened rebel attack on the city. For his heroism he was elected Mayor of Toronto at age twenty-eight. John later returned to Niagara, became registrar of the county of Lincoln, and was commanding officer of the Number One Company, a militia unit raised in Niagara during the American Civil War.

A later tenant was Lewis Clement, the son of a famous father, "Ranger John" Clement who had a legendary career as a Butler's Ranger. Carrying on the family tradition, Clement served with distinction in the militia artillery at Vrooman's Battery during the Battle of Queenston Heights. A one-time successful merchant in Niagara, he invested in the financially troubled Niagara Harbour and Dock Company (NHDC), which may explain why he was reduced to renting premises on the Commons for several years.

With the great alarm of Mackenzie's Rebellion in 1837, several regiments were deployed to Niagara. The new commandant appears to have taken up quarters on the Commons once again after they had been extensively renovated. A painting of the quarters in the 1850s has survived, which is the only view we have of any building on this site. While vacant it burned to the ground in 1858.

There is no visible remnant of the "commodious dwelling" on the Commons today. There is still a spring in the area seeping to the grassy surface and occasionally a groundhog digs up a piece of brick or pottery shard at the site. The natural configuration of the nearby creek bed may have been altered over the years. Otherwise, the site today probably looks remarkably as it did that August morning in 1792 when Peter Russell first came out to see Widow Murray on her farm. On an early hot summer's morning with the heavy mist layered across the Commons, it is quite easy to conjure up the restless spirits of some of those characters who had a presence here so many years ago.

CHAPTER 5

Navy Hall

Below the ramparts of Fort George near the edge of the Niagara River, the long, low stone-clad building known as Navy Hall is a popular venue for various social gatherings and educational events. Inside, the exposed hand-hewn beams, interior shutters, and welcoming fire in the huge stone fireplace evoke an ambiance of two centuries ago. Through excellent interpretive displays on the walls, visitors may learn the Navy Hall site is nearly 250 years old. The Navy Hall wharf, now a popular perch for amateur fishermen and the occasional mooring site for commercial marine enterprises, has been a naval and public dock for a similar period. In recognition of its rich and colourful past, Navy Hall was designated a National Historic Site in 1969.

In its formative years, the isolated Fort Niagara was completely dependent on sailing ships bringing in provisions, ammunition, and reinforcements across Lake Ontario from the St. Lawrence River, and later from the more easterly outpost of Oswego. The wharf below the fort was busy and several vessels were built there. However, the site was not ideal, and by late 1765 the British commander of Fort Niagara reported that "they [Naval Department] have been building a Navall Barracks 1200 yards above this Fort upon the opposite side of the river; they have also begun a warfe [*sic*] there."[1] It was easier for tall-ships to get underway from the west side of the river, the site was more protected for ship-building and wintering, plus there was a ready supply of oak beyond the grassy plain above. Initially, the building

consisted of a barracks for seamen and a room for officers and was set at right angles to the shoreline. In order to accommodate increased naval activity during the American Revolutionary War, more barracks, a "house,"[2] and out-buildings including a "rigging and sails loft" were added. The shipyard was busy repairing and building various new vessels for the Provincial Marine and private merchants. The first official use of the name "Navy Hall" appeared in a memorandum in May 1778,[3] but it actually referred to the general area and the complex of buildings on the site.[4] Under the terms of the Treaty of Paris in 1783, the British would eventually have to cede Fort Niagara to the Americans. Almost immediately Governor Haldimand directed his surveyors to reserve the plain above Navy Hall for a protective military post[5] (see chapter 8).

By 1788 the buildings were already "in exceeding bad repair,"[6] so when Lieutenant Governor Simcoe arrived in the summer of 1792, he immediately ordered an extensive renovation of Navy Hall (by then only the original building was still standing) as a residence for his family and for government offices. He complained to a friend back in England that for accommodation he was "fitting up an old hovel that will look exactly like a carrier's ale-house in England when properly decorated and ornamented."[7] While waiting for the renovations to be completed, the Simcoes lived in marquee tents and later the canvas house on the plain just above Navy Hall, which they much preferred. During hot

A View of Niagara Taken from the Heights Near Navy Hall, artist James Peachey, watercolour, 1783 or 1787. This painting clearly shows a portion of Navy Hall at the water's edge and British-held Fort Niagara across the river. The open grassy plain on the left with the Rangers' Barracks in the distance, although already reserved for military purposes, is being used as common lands.

Library and Archives Canada, James Peachey collection, C-002035.

Canadian summer evenings, they would sit outside their canvas tents to catch the breezes. We generally think of the first Lieutenant Governor as one of strict formal military bearing; his wife a young reserved, though proud, wealthy heiress. Yet while writing a letter to Charlotte, one of his daughters who remained back home in England, Simcoe portrays a very relaxed informal domestic scene: sitting in an oak bower on the edge of the Commons (now the site of Fort George), the little family was thoroughly enjoying one another's company as well as the vista to Navy Hall below, the expansive river, and Fort Niagara beyond.[8] Panting at their feet also trying to keep cool would have been their huge "borrowed" Newfoundland dog, Jack Sharp, who was a frequent fixture at Navy Hall during the Simcoe era.[9] When the first member of the Royal Family to visit Upper Canada, Prince Edward, the Duke of Kent,[10] arrived, he chose the canvas accommodation and hence the Simcoes were reluctantly forced back into the "miserable … damp"[11] Navy Hall. Despite the limitations of the old building itself Mrs. Simcoe enjoyed the property with its vistas across the river, the fine turf of the commons, and the woods beyond (known today as Paradise Grove) where she often took walks. She was especially pleased with "thirty large May Duke cherry trees behind the house, and three standard peach trees."[12]

Lt. General Simcoe, artist Jean Laurent Mosnier, oil painting, 1791. John Graves Simcoe (1752–1806) commanded the Queen's Rangers, First American Regiment, during the American Revolutionary War. Upon his appointment as the first Lieutenant Governor of Upper Canada in 1791, Simcoe returned to North America and chose the tiny community opposite Fort Niagara as the first but temporary capital of the province. For the next four years the Navy Hall complex served as his home, administrative offices, and base of operations.

Courtesy of the Toronto Public Library, Toronto Reference Library, #T 30592.

Elizabeth Posthuma Gwillim Simcoe (1762–1850), artist Mary Anne Burges, watercolour. Elizabeth, through her letters, diaries, and sketches portrayed many aspects of life in Niagara and Upper Canada during her husband's tenure as Lieutenant Governor of the province.

Library and Archives Canada, C-095815.

In order to accommodate a growing bureaucracy, several more buildings were erected on site. During the four years Niagara was the temporary capital of Upper Canada, most official government correspondence originated from Navy Hall. Moreover, thousands of hopeful but apprehensive settlers went there with their petitions for land grants. But the old building was much more than a sterile government office; several well-attended "splendid balls" lasting through the night were held there, as well as grand levees. Even visiting American diplomats were impressed.[13]

With the transfer of the government to York in 1796, the bureaucracy reluctantly followed across the lake as well. Simcoe's offices were converted into the officers' mess for Fort George while the other buildings in the complex were used by the Provincial Marine and for commissariat stores. During the tremendous bombardment from the American

Navy Hall from the Fort of Niagara, artist Elizabeth Simcoe, sketch on paper. The verdant plain and woods above the Navy Hall complex are readily visible.

Archives of Ontario, Simcoe family fonds, F 47-11-1-0-13.

guns at Fort Niagara and their river battery in November 1812, the original building at Navy Hall was "entirely consumed."[14] It is believed the rest of the buildings were totally destroyed during the American bombardment just prior to their successful invasion the following May.

Within a year of cessation of hostilities, construction began on a new frame "commissariat store at Navy Hall."[15] Rebuilt on the same location, but slightly smaller at one hundred feet by twenty-five feet, it was complemented by a new "King's Wharf" as well. In 1840, the building was fitted as a barracks to accommodate seventy-two men.[16] Meanwhile, a cross-river ferry was operated from the Navy Hall wharf with a customs house, guard house, and the "Ferry House" tavern nearby. The area was very much in the public domain. By the 1850s the barracks shown on maps as either the Red Barracks or Ferry Barracks had been relegated to storage use again. For a short time during the American Civil War, nine married couples of the Royal Canadian Rifle Regiment occupied the premises.[17]

In 1864, to accommodate a spur line of the Erie and Niagara Railway, the building was ignominiously moved across the road closer to the ruins of Fort George[18] where it was allowed to deteriorate. By the turn of the century the old building was being used as a stable and cow barn and appeared to be about to collapse. Historians, erroneously believing that this building had survived the War of 1812 and had been the actual site of the first parliament of Upper Canada, petitioned the federal government to restore Navy Hall. A small injection of federal funds supplemented by a bequest of the publisher and historian John Ross Robertson stabilized the building, and a marble plaque was erected.

During the Great War the partially restored building was converted into a laboratory for the Canadian Medical Corps to test the Niagara River water supply for Camp Niagara. Other uses included a six-chair clinic for the Dental Corps, stores for medical supplies, and as an inoculation site. Abandoned after the war, the building deteriorated again. In the midst of the Great Depression, local Boy Scouts and Girl Guides occupied the old building until finally in 1934 the Niagara Parks Commission (NPC) reached an agreement with the federal Department of National Defence. As a make-work project, the NPC would restore Navy Hall and Forts George and Mississauga with federal funds, in return for a ninety-nine-year lease "with rental set at an affordable $1.00 per year"[19] (see chapter 8). The rarely used railway spur line had been removed two decades earlier, allowing the old ramshackle building to be moved back to its original site.[20] Actual reconstruction began three years later in 1937. It was set on a new stone foundation with a full basement and encased in stone to protect it from the elements.[21] Many of the original beams had deteriorated, and so a number of beams salvaged from an old barn in Niagara Falls were used in the restoration. All the work was completed by the next summer. To provide vehicle access to Navy Hall, the Niagara Parkway was eventually extended from its intersection with John Street in Paradise Grove along the river to the Navy Hall site. Ricardo Street was extended from the northwest. The small frame one-and-a-half storey Customs

Inoculation in the First Parliament Building in Canada, Niagara Camp 1915, photo postcard, 1915. Soldiers are lined up at the partially restored Navy Hall, patiently waiting for their inoculations prior to being shipped out to Europe.

Courtesy of the author.

House was also restored at this time. Also clad in stone and now situated on the Fort George side of Ricardo Street it is currently used for offices of Parks Canada employees. A new wharf was built to accommodate a proposed shuttle service between Forts George and Niagara, although this never really materialized. Nevertheless, the locals and tourists alike could now enjoy the river site of Navy Hall once again. In 1969, the NPC relinquished its lease to Parks Canada. The wharf was upgraded in 1977[22] and later the building was refurbished and the interpretive displays installed within. Today the restored 1816 commissariat store is a popular site for both indoor and outdoor social gatherings … and on a hot summer's evening, one might see a young family sitting with their dog on the grassy rise above Navy Hall enjoying the view across the river.

Navy Hall today, photo, 2011. The restored 1816 commissariat building clad in stone (1930s). The fortifications of Fort George are barely visible on the rise above.

Courtesy of Cosmo Condina.

CHAPTER 6

The First Butler's Rangers' Barracks

By late summer 1778 Fort Niagara had become dangerously overcrowded. In addition to the regular garrison there were hundreds of Butler's Rangers, some with families, who would need to winter over, as well as desperate loyalist refugees including Six Nations allies streaming in from the Mohawk Valley. Moreover, with Ranger pay slightly higher than that of regular British soldiers, the potential for dissension among the men had to be avoided.[1]

Before winter set in Major John Butler received permission to erect a barracks for his officers and men across the river.[2] It is not clear why the site (now occupied by Chateau Gardens and Queen's Landing) was chosen. Although situated on the edge of the embankment it was not opposite Fort Niagara. In fact, only two years later Fort Niagara's new commandant complained, "[t]here certainly could not be found a more improper spot for the Barracks of the Rangers."[3] He felt from a defensive standpoint, Point Mississauga would have been a far more logical site. Historian E.A. Cruikshank[4] hypothesized the availability of oak logs nearby influenced the decision; in fact at least some of "the timbers" were floated across the river.[5] Perhaps its proximity to the already established Navy Hall, much more protected from the prevailing winds than windswept Point Mississauga, was a deciding factor. Moreover, these log barracks were considered only temporary accommodation.

John Butler, artist Henry Oakley, oil on board, 1834. Butler (1728–1796) raised and commanded the Butler's Rangers Corps until it was disbanded in 1784. At Niagara he served as office holder, judge, Indian Department agent, member of the Land Board, and church warden.

Courtesy of the Niagara Historical Society and Museum, # 988.194.

LEFT: *Private, Butler's Ranger, 1780–82*, artist Don Troiani. Butler's Rangers researcher and re-enactor Calvin Arnt has concluded the military coat worn by the Rangers was forest green with white facing. Headgear may have been cocked "hatts [*sic*]" (turned down in this illustration) or the simpler caps.

Courtesy of *www.historicalartprints.com*.

BELOW: *Plan of Fort Niagara*, artist John Luke, sketch on paper, 1779–1782. This only known surviving plan of the Rangers' Barracks was drawn by an American spy, John Luke. The upper portion shows a primitive rendering of the Rangers' Barracks consisting of two "Rangers Houses" and several small huts.

Courtesy of the American Antiquarian Society, John Bradstreet Papers MSS. B Box 2, Folder 8, BIB 1D Mss 271268.

Butler was ill, so his capable son, Captain Walter Butler,[6] actually supervised intermittently the construction — much of the basic work was performed by the Rangers themselves, supplemented by more experienced artificers and masons.[7] Meanwhile, the Rangers were quartered in tents until they could actually start to move into the new barracks in late January. The barracks were actually part of a complex consisting of two long buildings configured in an *L* shape. The smaller building was at a right angle to the river, with several small log houses, possibly for married rangers, within the hollow of the *L*. The total cost of construction was almost £2,500, half of which was itemized for rum to fortify the Rangers and other workmen during construction.[8]

Later in 1779 another building was erected as a hospital for sick and wounded Rangers.[9] This hospital was the first in the Niagara Peninsula and the earliest purpose-built hospital in what is now Ontario. In the mid-nineteenth century, a buried tombstone was found in present St. Mark's cemetery for "Lenerd Blanck." Ranger Blanck, whose actual name was Planck, had been wounded at Sandusky in the Ohio Valley in June 1782 and was probably brought to the hospital at Niagara where he succumbed to his wounds. He may well have been the first European to be buried in that portion of the military reserve later designated as hallowed land, just north of the Rangers' barracks complex.[10] Interestingly, the house of surgeon Robert Guthrie of the Butler's Rangers was situated just north of the burying ground.[11]

More buildings were added to the complex, including a barracks "for the Savages,"[12] probably the Indian Department's personnel, and for the storage of their trade goods. The Indian Department would maintain a presence at Butler's Barracks[13] until its purchase of Peter Russell's house on the Military Reserve in the late 1790s. With the Butler's Rangers officially disbanded in 1784 and the men and their families eventually dispersed to their new land grants, rental space in the complex became available. In 1790, meetings of the influential Land Board were held in the home of clerk Walter Butler Sheehan "in the Rangers' Barracks."[14] Sometime schoolteacher and land agent Francis Goring also lived in the barracks for a while.[15]

Just as the log buildings had been erected quickly using green wood they also deteriorated rapidly.[16] When Lieutenant-Governor Simcoe arrived in the summer of 1792 he ordered that at least one building in the complex be thoroughly repaired "for the Legislature of the Country"[17] with the addition of two wings.[18] One chamber served as the House of Assembly, and presumably the other wing accommodated the legislative council. Renovations of Butler's Barracks were incomplete when the first session of the first parliament of Upper Canada was opened on September 17, and hence the first session was held in nearby Freemasons' Hall on present King Street, facing the Commons. However, sessions two to five were in fact held at the refurbished Butler's Rangers complex, where many of the formative laws and legislation of Upper Canada were enacted. The legislative chambers were also used by the Church of England for divine services[19] and probably for occasional indoor Indian Council meetings.

With the heightened threat of war with the United States in 1794 and the future Fort George still just a concept outlined by Royal Engineers' stakes in the turf of the Military Reserve, Simcoe ordered at least one of the log buildings in the complex be used as a barracks for the mustered militia[20] and proposed that if the "Heights at Butler's Barracks" were fortified with Carronades, an attack by the Americans and Natives would be "frustrated."[21] In essence, the fortified Butler's Barracks complex was very much the precursor of Fort George.

After the capital of Upper Canada was moved to York, the local militia continued to use the complex as did the Indian Department. The battery became less important with the building of Fort George to the south. In a 1799 list of "Public Property" at Niagara, the reference to Butler's Barracks states simply, "This House was since burnt."[22] However, apparently not all the buildings had been destroyed.

It was already uncomfortably hot and humid at daybreak when a twenty-one-year-old regimental assistant surgeon, Dr. William "Tiger" Dunlop, stepped ashore at the ruinous Navy Hall wharf in July 1814. He and fellow officers of the 89th Regiment of Foot had sailed all night from York

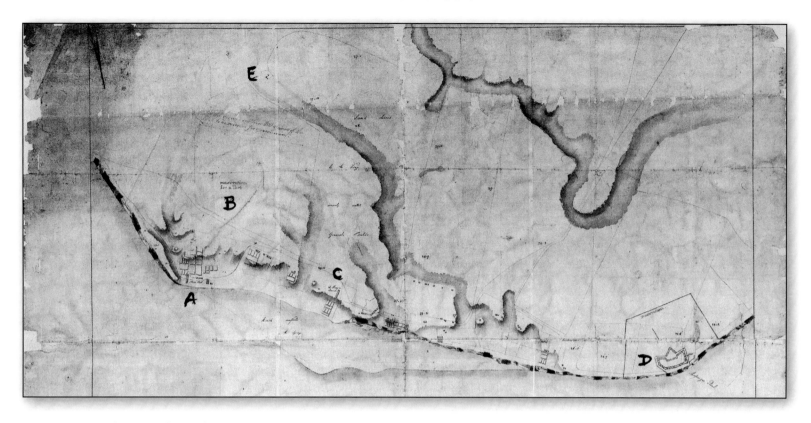

Niagara, 1790. This map shows the waterfront from the Navy Hall Complex (A) on the left with an area behind marked "reservation for a Fort" (B). Part way along a building is identified as the Rangers' Barracks (C). Towards the lake, a fortification is indicated at Mississauga Point (D). The small building (E) is probably the site of Widow Murray's farm.

Library and Archives Canada, NMC 17879.

after a gruelling ride by horseback from Kingston. He was soon informed that a horrific all-night battle near Lundy's Lane had just been fought and that soon wagons carrying the wounded would be arriving. He later recalled:

> Accordingly, upon inquiring where my wounded were to be put, I was shown a ruinous fabric, built of logs, called Butler's Barracks, from having been built during the revolutionary war by Butler's Rangers for their temporary accommodation. Nothing could be worse constructed for an hospital for wounded men — not that it was open to every wind that it blew, for at midsummer in Canada

that is rather an advantage; but there was a great want of room so that many had to be laid on straw on the floor, and they had the best of it, for their comrades were put in berths one above another as in transport or packet, where it was impossible to get round them to dress their wounds, and their removal gave them excruciating pain.[23]

One can barely imagine what horrors were endured by the wounded as they were loaded hastily onto the wagons side by side and transported those fifteen long miles from the battlefield to Niagara under a hot July sun. Many of the men had open abdominal, chest, or head wounds or bloody,

mangled limbs dangling by fragments of skin, muscle, and tendon. As the creaky wagons bounced, lurched, and jolted over the rough, dusty country roads, blood curdling screams, curses, whimpering cries, and agonizing groans were heard from fellow wounded. There was the gut-wrenching stench of acrid gunpowder, vomitus, oozing bowels, bladder wounds, fetid breaths, and sweaty body odours. For many soldiers the last gasps of life transpired before the wagons even pulled up to the old Rangers' Barracks.

Meanwhile, Dunlop was informed the regimental surgeon "had gone to Scotland" and the other assistant surgeon was "of a delicate constitution" and too "exhausted"[24] to assist. Dunlop lamented:

> Waggon after waggon [*sic*] arrived, and before mid-day I found myself in charge of two hundred and twenty wounded, including my own Regiment, prisoners and militia, with no one to assist me but by my hospital serjeant [*sic*], who, luckily for me, was a man of sound sense and great experience, who made a most able second; but with all this the charge was too much for us, and many a poor fellow had to submit to amputation [without anaesthesia] whose limb might have been preserved had there been only time to take reasonable care of it"[25]

In what has become one of the most famous quotes in military medicine, Dunlop recounted the horrors of the week to follow in the old log Rangers' barracks.

> I never underwent such fatigue as I did for the first week at Butler's Barracks. The weather was intensely hot, the flies were in myriads, and lighting on the wounds, deposited their eggs, so that maggots were bred in a few hours, producing dreadful irritation, so that long before I could go round dressing the patients, it was necessary to begin again; and as I had no assistant but my

serjeant [*sic*], our toil was incessant. For two days and two nights, I never sat down; when fatigued I sent my servant down to the river for a change of linen, and having dined and dressed, went back to my work quite refreshed. On the morning of the third day, however, I fell asleep on my feet, with my arm embracing the post of one of the berths. It was found impossible to awaken me, so a truss of clean straw was laid on the floor, on which I was deposited, and an hospital rug thrown over me; and there I slept soundly for five hours without ever turning.[26]

Dunlop related one particularly poignant story that perhaps better than any other sums up the futility of the War of 1812. A stoic American farmer, possibly a militia man or camp follower, was brought in with a smashed thighbone and a severe penetrating injury. His wife arrived from across the river under a flag of truce and while trying to console her husband who was lying on a truss of straw and writhing in great agony, she suddenly exclaimed:

> O that the King and President were both here this moment to see the misery their quarrels led to — they surely would never go to war again without a cause that they could give as a reason to God at the last day, for thus destroying the creatures that He hath made in his own image.[27]

Eventually, all of Dunlop's surviving patients were transferred elsewhere and Dunlop's skills were tested once again at Fort Erie. Presumably, the vestiges of the old building that had served so many purposes were torn down shortly after the war. The land remained part of the Military Reserve but was enjoyed by the townsfolk as their common lands until it was sold off years later. Meanwhile, construction began on a new Butler's Barracks on the Military Reserve, one mile to the west where it would hopefully be out of range of the guns of Fort Niagara.

Some believe there were actually two separate Butler's Barracks built during the American Revolutionary War, one being at the site of the "new" barracks erected after the war. However, to date there is no firm evidence to substantiate such a theory. As we will see in a subsequent chapter, all the surviving buildings at the new site are post-War of 1812.

CHAPTER 7

The British Indian Department and the Covenant Chain of Friendship

Originally, the Board of Trade and Plantations in London was responsible for promoting profitable trade and maintaining the loyalty of the indigenous people of North America to the royal cause. Partly in response to the alarming French incursions into the Ohio Valley on the eve of the Seven Years' War, a more focused and influential British Indian Department received royal approval in 1756. This was a civil agency within the British government representing the Crown in its dealings with the Native peoples of North America. Superintendents of Indian Affairs were appointed for the Northern and Southern areas of the continent east of the Mississippi River.

The first Northern Superintendent of Indian Affairs was the charismatic Sir William Johnson, whose prime responsibility was to maintain the "covenant chain of friendship," which was a symbol of the friendship and mutual understanding that existed between the British government and His Majesty's Indian Allies. The Dutch and Mohawks were the first to refer to this covenant metaphorically as a steel chain of friendship that required constant polishing to keep it shining brightly. After the British replaced the Dutch in the Hudson Valley of New York, they assumed the Covenant but now referred to the silver chain of friendship, as silver was more valuable and could be polished more brightly. Through skillful negotiations and calculated interpersonal relationships with Natives and non-Natives alike, Sir William and his family would have a long-lasting

Sir William Johnson, artist unknown, miniature watercolour on ivory. As northern superintendant of Indian Affairs, Johnson (1715–1774) worked tirelessly to shine brightly the covenant chain of friendship between the British government and His Majesty's Native Allies.

Library and Archives Canada, C-083497.

influence on Native affairs in British North America and, in particular, Upper Canada.

In the summer of 1764, just after Pontiac's nearly successful Indian Uprising, Sir William summoned all the First Nations to a Grand Council at Fort Niagara to burnish once again the chain of friendship. On at least one occasion he symbolically crossed over to the west side of the Niagara River to confer with Natives encamped there on the plain opposite the fort.[1]

During and after the American Revolutionary War, the British Indian Department at Niagara was based in "The Bottoms." This was a collection of ramshackle buildings physically and symbolically outside the bastions of Fort Niagara on the edge of the Niagara River. During the war, the quasi-military Indian Department was permitted by the British Army to grant commissions within the Department.[2] These officers, who often led Native warriors in action, were on the same footing as those fighting in other provincial corps.[3] Most of the men in the Department, known generally as rangers or foresters, eventually became Butler's Rangers after Butler received his "Beating order" in September 1777. With the disbanding of the Rangers in 1784, Lieutenant Colonel John Butler served ably as Deputy Agent for Indian Affairs at Niagara.

In his "Instructions for the good Government of the Branch of the Indian Department,"[4] Sir John Johnson (who inherited his father's baronetcy and eventually assumed the position of superintendant), encouraged the Deputy Agent of Indian Affairs at Detroit, Alexander McKee,

> to employ your utmost endeavours to promote His Majesty's Indian Interest in general, by keeping up a friendly intercourse and Communication between all the Indian Nations assuring them of the King's paternal care and regard as long as they continue to merit them by acting as good and obedient children ought to do … As these people consider themselves free and independent, and are in fact unacquainted with controul

[sic] and subordination, they are alone to be govern by address and persuasion, and they require the utmost attention to ceremonies and external appearances, with an uncommon share of patience, good temper and forbearance.

No doubt a similar document was sent to John Butler at Niagara.

In anticipation that Fort Niagara would eventually be surrendered to the Americans, the British Indian Department maintained its presence at "The Bottoms," but became increasingly more active on the Canadian side of the river. It was imperative that the covenant chain be maintained with the newly arrived peoples of the loyal Six Nations, who would soon take up their tract of land on the Grand River. A traveller to Niagara in 1785 noted that there was a barracks "for the savages" on the west side of the river.[5] Three years later another visitor reported four hundred to five hundred Natives were often encamped near the Rangers' barracks.[6] Soon, the Department received permission to convert one of the old empty Rangers' barracks into a blacksmith shop.[7] Nearby, silversmith John Bachus set up shop.[8] Presumably he was producing Indian trade silver for the Department. With the American occupation of Fort Niagara and the Bottoms in 1796 in compliance with Jay's Treaty, the British Indian Department had to establish quickly a permanent and consolidated presence near but not within the newly built Fort George on the west side of the Niagara River.

The erection of a substantial Council House would signify the British government's firm commitment to maintaining the strong chain of friendship with the Native peoples. In 1797, the Indian Department purchased Administrator Peter Russell's leased property, which included his "Commodious Dwelling" and fifty acres in the midst of the Military Reserve. The comfortable Georgian home was used for offices, meeting rooms, and accommodation for the officials and officers of the Indian Department. Across the creek that ran through the property, the Indian Council House was built at seventy-two feet long, twenty-six feet wide, and twenty feet high. Quarters

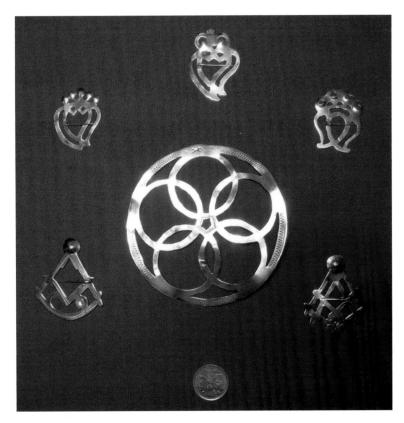

Indian trade silver, photo by Sergio Martin. The indigenous peoples of North America wore shiny shells fashioned into various designs as a form of self-adornment and to reflect away evil spirits. With the arrival of the Europeans brightly polished silver became highly coveted. Pictured in the centre is a large silver brooch or ear wheel, marked by early silversmith John Kinzie. The three "double heart" brooches above, in the Luckenbooth style, were favoured by the Iroquois. The brooches in the Masonic pattern below were also popular among the Iroquois.

Courtesy of the author.

for the store keeper, three interpreters, and a blacksmith were apparently erected nearby.[9] Because of its size, the Council House appears to have been used for other purposes as well. In 1807 Lieutenant Governor Sir Francis Gore held a grand ball and supper in Niagara for which the Indian Council House was fitted up along with a temporary thirty-foot-long shed to accommodate all the guests for supper.[10]

Hundreds, and at times thousands, of Natives encamped on the grounds surrounding the Council House and Officers' Quarters,[11] usually in late summer or fall. Weather permitting, the officials would confer outside in view and within hearing range of all — the principals retreating inside only in inclement weather.

As Sir John intimated, the Natives were sticklers for tradition and deeply resented and resisted any attempt by government officials to speed up the deliberations. Alan Taylor, in his book *The Divided Ground*, describes the strict protocol of Indian councils:

> Upon arriving at the council fire, the visitors entered in ceremonial procession. In welcome, the host conducted the "At the Wood's Edge" ritual, ushering them out of the chaotic world of the forest and into the ordered stability of the council ground. In patient succession, the host cleared eyes, ears, and throats of the dust so that the visitors could watch patiently, listen carefully, and speak freely in the coming days. After at least a night's rest, the formal council began with a condolence ceremony that acknowledged recent losses to death, especially of prominent chiefs or colonial officials. The ceremony metaphorically covered graves, dried tears, and cleansed minds of grief, so that all could think and speak peacefully in the coming days.
>
> Only after these preliminaries could a polite host propose substantial business, with each proposal accompanied by a string or belt of wampum passed across the council fire to an Indian spokesman. Made of many small seashell or glass tubes strung in patterns of alternating dark and light color, wampum represented the interplay of death and life, of war and peace. As a sacred substance, wampum confirmed the earnest importance of a message. Without accompanying wampum, words were frivolous.[12]

Deliberations would last for days. The Natives, being from an oral culture, understandably distrusted the power of the colonials' written documents. As Taylor points out, "[t]o impress memories, Indians preferred the methodical and rhythmic repetition of shared sentiments and histories expressed through prolonged rituals and speeches."[13] Native spokesmen often used many metaphors in their speeches, which lent a simple yet poignant elegance to their messages. The Native spokesmen, chosen for their eloquence, were not necessarily the most powerful of their people. Definitive answers to propositions were never expected to be given until at least the next day. The Natives would return with appropriate wampum strings or belts to be accepted by the colonial host, who was then expected to ponder a reply overnight. For their part, the interpreters with the Indian Department were often young men who had learned Indian dialects from Native childhood friends or had themselves been captives at one time. The Department's agents were encouraged to select "one or two sober and intelligent Chiefs" to act as a prepared "Speaker" who would act as intermediary between the interpreter and the guest Chiefs so that the proper message would be conveyed.[14]

The strict decorum of the daytime public sessions gave way to raucous celebrations on the Council House grounds at day's end. In lingering daylight young Natives engaged in competitive games similar to lacrosse. With nightfall the campfire became the centre of feasting, singing, and dancing to the rhythm of drums and beating sticks. Also at night, colonial hosts often conferred privately with smaller groups of influential chiefs. Known as "speaking in the bushes," these conferences were probably when most deals were really struck.

The council would finally conclude with a sumptuous feast and presentation of gifts and provisions, not only for all those attending, but for the sick and elderly kin at home. British officials would also pledge the king's continued friendship and protection. On occasion the chiefs would be presented with silver peace medals bearing the king's profile.

No first-hand depiction of any councils at Niagara has survived, but it must have been a most impressive vista on the Military Reserve. The British Army officers in regimental dress uniforms and officials of the British Indian Department, also in quasi-British-military coats, would sit on chairs on one side of the secretary's table. Opposite them would be several Indian chiefs in their full regalia, seated in front of a huge semi-circle of Natives, with lesser chiefs at the front and behind. Hundreds or even thousands of warriors and matrons would sit on either benches or colourful blankets on the grass, all watching and listening intently. Around the periphery would be scads of children and camp dogs, beyond which would be hundreds of Native tents, campfires, and tethered horses. The pungent aromas of sweetgrass, tobacco, and wood fires would waft about the assembled. Standing in the grassy midst of the Commons today, one can imagine the drama unfolding with a real life cast of thousands.

One of the most important councils held at Niagara was in November 1796, before the Indian Council House was even built. The council was probably held on the Military Reserve outside the fort that was still under construction or the old Butler's Rangers' Barracks site.[15] With the recent death of John Butler, William Claus,[16] grandson of Sir William Johnson, had just been appointed Deputy Superintendent of the Six Nations at Fort George. At the 1796 Council,[17] Captain Joseph Brant, with power of attorney for all the Six Nations, proclaimed the Six Nations had the sovereign right to sell off some of their Grand River lands to third parties without the consent of the Crown. He argued that although the Iroquois Confederacy had been granted a vast tract of land along the Grand River by Governor Haldimand, only two thousand Natives actually inhabited the land, and hence such a large tract of land exclusively for themselves was not needed since many of the Natives were indifferent to cultivating the land. Moreover, with the surrounding white settlements already encroaching on Indian lands and the game already scarce in the Grand River area, the Native peoples were no longer able to survive on hunting and were already reduced to poverty and, at times, starvation. Brant had devised a plan whereby large sections of the original grant were sold to non-Native investors, with the proceeds of the sales used to set

Thayendanegea (Joseph Brant), artist William Berczy, oil on canvas, circa 1807. As Mohawk chief and principal war leader of the Six Nations on the Grand River tract, Brant (1742–1807) was a frequent spokesman at the Indian Council House on the Commons. His sister, Molly Brant, was the second wife of Sir William Johnson.

Photo © National Gallery of Canada, National Gallery of Canada, Ottawa #5777.

up an annuity fund to provide lasting support for his Native peoples. Claus countered that since the Six Nations' original ancestral lands were in upstate New York, they were not a sovereign nation in Upper Canada since the Grand River lands had been granted to them by the Crown. Moreover, according to the Royal Proclamation of 1763, in the event that the Natives decided to sell some of their reserve lands, only the Crown could purchase such lands. Such arguments would have important constitutional implications for future relations between the Native peoples and the various levels of government in Canada. Brant was furious. With the chain of friendship now grimly tarnished for the next two years, there were very real concerns the Six Nations would "raise the hatchet" in retaliation against the king's subjects.

Eventually a compromise was reached whereby large tracts of land already sold to non-Natives were recognized by the government. When the hesitant Peter Russell, then Upper Canada's administrator, met with Brant in council at Niagara to publicly formalize the agreement the following July, up to three hundred young warriors had unexpectedly accompanied Brant.[18] Since this probably exceeded the entire adult male population of Newark, including the garrison, Russell later admitted to his displeased superiors in London that he had felt "not a little intimidated" to reluctantly sign the agreement without their prior approval.[19] During the ceremony Brant "eagerly" took Russell's hand and declared that, "they would now all fight for the King to the last drop of their Blood."[20] Had Russell delayed signing the agreement, his negotiation stance would have been further compromised with the surprise arrival of Chiefs Red Jacket[21] and Farmers Brother,[22] accompanied by yet another two hundred warriors of the Seneca Nation from the United States[23] the next day.

Until then, the British Indian Department at Niagara served the Six Nations on the Grand River and, theoretically, those still living on reserves on the American side.[24] The Council House was open to the Mississauga Indians and any other Native group that might wander through. In an attempt to thwart Joseph Brant from uniting all the Natives against the interests of the government, the Mississaugas were forced to travel to York, where a new Indian Department was established under Major James Givins.[25]

Meanwhile William Claus carried out his responsibilities at Niagara, dispensing annual presents and provisions to the Natives and calling Indian councils when necessary to address specific domestic and political concerns. In 1799, with the death of Alexander McKee at Amherstburg, William Claus was appointed Deputy Superintendent and Inspector General of Indian Affairs, a post he would hold until 1826. His uncle, Sir John Johnson, pleased with the appointment, commented that Claus was now "set up for life,"[26] although he did worry about his nephew's health given Niagara's reputation as an unhealthy locale.

In August 1808 Claus reported that "a vast number of Indians are at this Post … [and they] complain of the great distress they are in for Bread," but they had also informed him that they would "sit quiet in case of any quarrel between the King and America."[27] The following March he reported on another meeting at the Council House in which the Natives remained aloof to any military alliance but complained of ongoing difficulty with local white settlers "stealing their hogs," working their horses, and settling on their lands, all without redress.[28]

During the War of 1812 the Grand River Six Nations and their allies did eventually side with the British and played an important role in many of the battles.[29] Early in the morning of October 13, 1812, Six Nations warriors were encamped at the Indian Council House; their leader, Chief John Norton, saw General Brock gallop off towards Queenston. Soon the warriors were ordered to follow along the River Road and played a decisive role in the Battle of Queenston Heights. On November 5, 1812, a solemn memorial service was held in the Council House. In the presence of military and British Indian Department officials, Brock was eulogized by Chief Little Cayuga, who presented eight white strings of wampum. A large white belt of wampum was also presented to cover Brock's grave.[30]

Spirits were running high again on the Commons several weeks later. Having successfully repulsed another American

Portrait of Major John Norton (Teyoninhokarawen), artist Solomon Williams, oil, 1804. Adopted as a nephew by Joseph Brant, upon the latter's death Norton eventually became a chief of war and diplomacy among the Mohawks. During the War of 1812 he questioned the authority of the British Indian Department and lead His Majesty's Indian Allies in all the battles on the Niagara Peninsula save one.

© Canadian War Museum #1995009-001.

invading force near Fort Erie, the Natives and some troops returned in triumph to Fort George. As one town person reported they "encamped on the skirts of the woods back of the town [and kept] us alive with their war dances and [made] the dark cedar woods echo with savage yells."[31]

Early in the morning of May 27 the following year, fifty Natives under Chief John Norton, accompanied by several officers of the Indian Department, were lying in wait along the fog-enshrouded shore of Lake Ontario near One Mile Pond. Suddenly a fierce bombardment from American ships offshore cut into the defenders, killing Indian Department clerk and storekeeper Lieutenant William Johnson Chew and several Natives. Despite the valiant but unsuccessful attempt

to defend the town of Niagara and Fort George against the invading Americans, the British forces retreated towards Burlington; the Natives successfully covered their retreat. During the American occupation of the fort and town of Niagara during the summer and fall of 1813, the British Indian Department encouraged up to eight hundred Natives to lurk in the woods nearby and harass the Americans, including their Native allies, whenever they attempted to venture forth outside Fort George.[32] During the occupation, the Americans were especially vengeful towards those families known to be directly connected with the Indian Department.[33]

By the time the war officially ended on Christmas Eve 1814 with the signing of the Treaty of Ghent, perhaps as

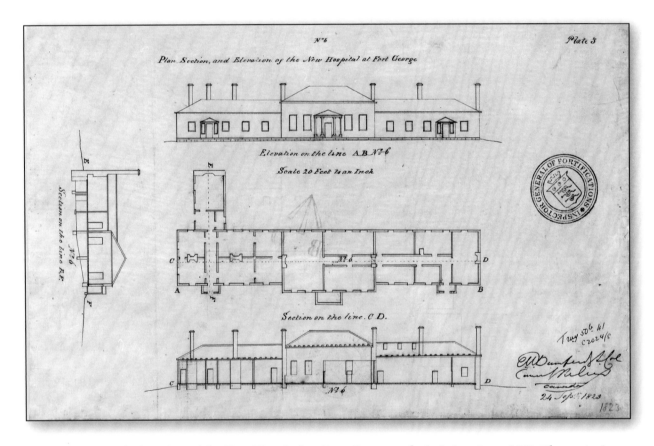

Plan, Section and Elevation of the New Hospital at Fort George, technical drawings, 1823. The central portion of the new hospital was originally the post-war (1816) Indian Council House.

Library and Archives Canada H3/450/Niagara/1823, NMC#5223.

many as half of all the Grand River Six Nations' warriors had been killed or wounded.[34]

In the summer of 1815, an important council of international repercussions was held at Niagara, probably near the site of the old Council House that had been burned during the war. Bitter enemies during the war, the Iroquois of the Grand River and those of New York State met to negotiate peace between them and between the king and the New York Natives. White wampum belts were exchanged to finalize the end of hostilities and the removal of ill will from their hearts.[35]

By August 1815 a contract had been approved to build a new Council House, measuring fifty-five feet by thirty-six feet, along with a "dwelling house" and a store house.[36] However, with the threat of war over, His Majesty's Indian Allies were now less important to the British government, and the British Indian Department's influence at Niagara subsequently dwindled. By 1819 the Six Nations of the Grand River were directed to travel to York or Burlington for their annual bounty. The Indian Council House at Niagara was now empty. The resourceful regimental surgeon at Butler's Barracks, Reid, requested that the empty Council House be used as a temporary hospital.[37] Extensive renovations were carried out, with the building of new foundations and the joining of the three buildings together[38] (see chapter 11). The last physical vestige of the British Indian Department at Niagara was now extinguished.

Nevertheless, there were still occasional Indian Council meetings at Niagara. William Claus, suffering from horribly disfiguring and painful cancer of the lip, presided over his last council meeting at Niagara in August 1826.[39] As late as 1833 the Natives were still coming to Niagara, as an account has survived in which John Claus claimed expenses for "entertaining Indians at Fort George."[40] However, by the 1830s the role of the Indian Department was revised by the colonial government to promote the "civilizing" of the Natives and to establish a system of land reserves.

A hand-written inscription was found on the "south wall of the [powder] magazine on the Garrrison Commons of old Fort George":

A PATRIOT, AUGUST 18, 1890
INDIAN CHIEF, A DESCENDANT OF THE ALLIES OF
GREAT BRITAIN[41]

CHAPTER 8

Fort George on the Commons

British government officials knew they would eventually have to give up Fort Niagara to the Americans, as stipulated in the Treaty of Paris of 1783. Within one year, Governor Haldimand had directed his surveyors to reserve the open ground to the west and south of Navy Hall for a military "post."[1] By 1791 the land had been staked out for a future fortification,[2] but it was another five years before the imminent British evacuation of Fort Niagara forced the start of construction of the new post. This portion of the Military Reserve/ common lands was now officially off limits to the townsfolk.

The detailed story of the evolution, demise, and eventual resurrection of Fort George is better told elsewhere[3]; however, with the encircling grassy open plain of the Commons providing a clear, unobstructed view of an approaching enemy both by land and water, the Commons was always strategically an important component of the fort. Hence, an abbreviated history of the fort and its garrison is warranted.

The British Royal Engineers chose the site above Navy Hall because it was fourteen feet higher in elevation than Fort Niagara, an important consideration when one attempts to lob artillery shells onto an enemy's fortifications. However, this slight advantage was easily overcome by the Americans who established a battery on the river bank directly opposite, which happened to be slightly higher than the west bank. (As a counterpoise, the British later constructed the crescent-shaped Half-Moon Battery on the riverbank, southeast of the fortifications.[4]) More importantly, being situated 1,100 yards upriver, the new fort could not control the mouth of the river. This strategic disadvantage was quickly recognized by the military officers during the War of 1812, and only ameliorated by the construction of Fort Mississauga, which was not completed until the 1820s.

With the improved prospect for peace between Upper Canada and the United States in 1796, all regular British troops were withdrawn from the colony, leaving only the Queen's Rangers, who were mainly assigned elsewhere, and the Royal Canadian Volunteers — all recruits from the province. The second battalion of this provincial regiment was assigned to Niagara for defence and to undertake the construction of the new post. Initially, the new "fort" consisted of a few scattered rudimentary buildings on the heights above Navy Hall. Those included a small blockhouse/barracks for the Volunteers, a stone powder magazine,[5] and two small warehouses,[6] all apparently completed by 1796. However, by 1799, more in response to concerns of a Native uprising than American intentions, the site had undergone a major transformation with construction of six earthen and log bastions linked by a wooden twelve-foot palisade eventually surrounded by a dry ditch.[7] Inside the palisade a guardhouse, five log blockhouses/ barracks, a hospital equipped with sixty beds available for both military and civilian patients, kitchens, workshops, and spacious officers' quarters were constructed. The Volunteers laboriously accomplished all the quarrying of stone, felling of trees, hewing of timber, excavation of the ditches, erection of

Bird's-eye view of Fort George from the east, 1805, artist Tiffany Merritt, graphite on paper, 2011. This is a conjectural drawing showing the six earthen bastions connected by palisades enclosing soldiers' barracks and a large officers' quarters. The stone powder magazine is within the fort. Terrain of the fort's interior is still somewhat uneven.

Drawing based on conjectural drawings in an unpublished report. Gouhar Shemdin, David Bouse, "A Report on Fort George" (Ottawa: Department of Indian and Northern Affairs, 1975). With permission of Parks Canada.

FACING PAGE: *The Esplanade, Fort George, Upper Canada*, artist Edward Walsh, watercolour, circa 1805. Note the somewhat uneven terrain of the parade ground. In the centre, the artist has incorporated himself holding a fox on a leash and possibly feeding one of the bear mascots of the 49th Regiment.

William L. Clements Library, University of Michigan.

the palisades, plus the construction of all the buildings. With the work completed, the regiment was disbanded in 1802, their garrison duties taken over by the 41st British Regiment of Foot.

In the year 1800 a traveller reported, "The situation is pretty … the fort new and remarkably neat, built on the edge of a handsome green or common."[8]

During the first decade of the nineteenth century, tensions between Great Britain and the United States escalated. Just before the outbreak of hostilities in June 1812, Major General Brock and his staff apparently concluded that Fort George, headquarters of the Central Division of the British Army in Upper Canada, was too large to defend. Plans were drawn up to reduce the fort's size by one third, abandoning

the two southern bastions, the octagonal blockhouse, and the stone powder magazine, and building a palisade "curtain" across the southern exposure of the fort.[9] It is not clear how much of this work was completed by the British before the American invasion in May 1813.[10]

We do know that in early October 1812 Brock had supervised the strengthening of the strategic northeast "York" bastion, apparently so named by Brock in recognition of the York militiamen who had laboured strenuously towards its completion.[11] Within a fortnight both he and Macdonell would be buried in this same bastion, known as the Brock bastion ever since.

Early in the morning of the ill-fated American invasion at Queenston in October 1812, Fort Niagara's artillery

shelled Fort George using red hot shot as a diversionary tactic. These superheated cannon balls ignited several wooden buildings within the fort. One month later more buildings were set on fire by a similar bombardment. But it was not until May 1813, as a prelude to the successful American invasion, that virtually every wooden building within the fort was destroyed by horrendous and incessant artillery fire from both land and shipboard batteries (see chapter 10).

The Battle of Fort George concluded with the abandonment of the fort and the retreat of the combined British forces towards Burlington. The occupying Americans immediately strengthened the fort's southern flank by constructing a new major bastion of earthworks and palisades. They eventually threw up extensive earthworks extending from the northwest bastion as far as St. Mark's cemetery (where remnants can still be traced today) and then eastward towards the river's edge.[12] No new buildings were erected by the Americans inside the fort during their occupation. The Americans established several small outlying posts, or "piquets," within a mile or two of the fort. Similar British piquets lay beyond. There were multiple skirmishes across this no man's land throughout the summer and early fall. Taking part in these skirmishes on the side of the Americans were two new groups of combatants.

Bird's-eye view of Fort George, 1812 from the east, artist Tiffany Merritt, graphite on paper, 2011. By the fall of 1812 or early the following spring, the Royal Engineers were directed to truncate the fort, abandoning the two southern bastions and stone powder magazine with wooden palisades across the southern exposure. The soldiers' barracks were also to be reduced in height. It is not clear how much of this work was actually accomplished.

Drawing based on conjectural drawings in an unpublished report. Gouhar Shemdin, David Bouse, "A Report on Fort George" (Ottawa: Department of Indian and Northern Affairs, 1975). With permission of Parks Canada.

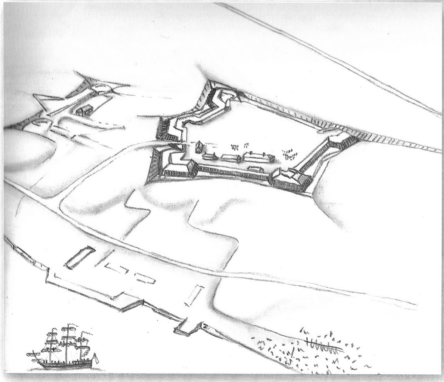

Bird's-eye view of Fort George, 1814 from the east, artist Tiffany Merritt, graphite on paper, 2011. During their occupation the Americans greatly fortified Fort George with stronger earthen bastions, including earthworks extending across the southern half of the truncated fort as well as earthworks extending from the northwest bastion towards St. Mark's burying ground. They apparently did not erect any significant buildings within. Upon recapture by the British in late 1813, new log barracks and possibly a brick/stone inner powder magazine were erected.

Drawing based on conjectural drawings in an unpublished report. Gouhar Shemdin, David Bouse, "A Report on Fort George" (Ottawa: Department of Indian and Northern Affairs, 1975). With permission of Parks Canada.

For the first time in the war "volunteer"[13] Native Americans were fighting on the Canadian side of the river, often in direct confrontation with their cousins, the Grand River Six Nations, a pivotal event in Iroquoian history.

Also fighting with the Americans were the "Canadian Volunteers." One-time member of the House of Assembly, newspaper publisher and citizen of Niagara Joseph Willcocks[14] convinced American General Dearborn at Fort George in July 1813 to allow him to establish a corps of disaffected Canadian volunteers to fight alongside the American army in Upper Canada. As such, the Canadian Volunteers are the only military corps to be actually raised at Fort George.

Six thousand American soldiers, their Native allies, and the Canadian Volunteers were encamped in tents on the plains outside the fort behind the new trenches. They were much decimated by disease,[15] desertion, and eventual redeployment elsewhere. One disgusted American General reported:

> We have an army at Fort George which for two months past has lain panic-struck, shut up and whipped in by a few hundred miserable savages leaving the whole of the frontier, except the mile in extent which they occupy, exposed to the inroads and depredations of the enemy.[16]

By December there were only sixty remaining occupying troops that happily returned to American soil, but not before they torched the town of Niagara. Surprisingly, the fortifications and the Americans' pitched tents were left intact although, according to one observer, no barracks were left standing.[17] When the British reoccupied the fort the rebuilding process began once again: two log barracks for three hundred men, a small frame quarters for officers, and possibly a new stone/brick powder magazine[18] within the fortifications.

During the summer of 1814, after the American success at the Battle of Chippawa, the American army laid siege to Fort George and dug trenches on the Commons. Years later, a young U.S. drummer recalled an incident on the Commons during this abbreviated siege. Their commander, Colonel Winfield Scott,[19] was sitting on his horse a few yards in front of the American line, when suddenly a whistling sound was heard coming from the fort's artillery (probably a howitzer). Scott calmly held up his sword to sight the incoming shell, concluded that he was vulnerable, and immediately wheeled his charger to the side just before the shell landed on the very site he had been occupying seconds before.[20] Despite this one inspiring moment, the Americans, having waited in vain for promised naval support, withdrew after only a few days.

After the war, realizing the shortcomings of the Fort George site, all efforts were directed to building Fort Mississauga (see chapter 23) at the entrance to the Niagara River and the new Butler's Barracks (see chapter 11) at the westerly end of the Military Reserve, out of clear range of American artillery. Initially, some troops were still quartered in the old log barracks within the fort. Both surviving powder magazines served as supply depots for the Royal Artillery stationed at Fort Mississauga.

In 1817, while on a good-will tour, the President of the United States, James Monroe was entertained with great civility by British officers somewhere in the historic Fort.[21]

By 1825, however, Fort George was reported to be "in ruins."[22] The bodies of Brock and Macdonell, buried in 1812 with great ceremony in the Northeast Bastion (now known as the Brock bastion), were disinterred and reburied in the base of the first Brock's Monument at Queenston Heights. British military headquarters were moved to York, much to the annoyance of the locals. By 1839, the remaining soldiers were using the rebuilt Navy Hall complex as their barracks while the old barracks within the fort were downgraded to stables. Some of the adjacent Military Reserve was granted to merchant James Crooks in exchange for his strategic lands at Mississauga Point (see chapter 12).

In November 1844, Lieutenant Colonel R.H. Bonnycastle of the Royal Engineers received an unusual request from Mr. Edward Campbell of Niagara to purchase a ten-foot square of land on the southwest bastion of Fort George. Campbell claimed that he was the eldest son of Donald Campbell who had served honorably as Fort Major of Fort George until his untimely death in December 1812. Apparently he had been buried near the southwest bastion and his son wanted to erect a memorial on the site. Although the Board of Ordnance approved the request it is not known whether the son ever erected a cairn.[23] He may have changed his mind, as a large memorial plaque for the Fort Major is situated inside St. Mark's Church "Erected By His Eldest Son 1848."

With the Fort no longer a military installation, the eight-acre parcel of land was leased intermittently to private citizens, including John Meneilly in the 1840s and '50s and later the Wright family from 1882 until the eve of the Great War. Rent was sixteen dollars per annum. The small officers' quarters (circa 1814) was incorporated into a larger farmhouse, while the esplanade was cultivated as a garden and used for grazing animals. The original stone powder magazine was intermittently occupied by squatters or used for the storing of hay. The

townsfolk's livestock grazed on the grassy bastions and youngsters played "fort" or dug for artifacts on the slowly eroding earthworks. One former student of schoolmistress Miss Janet Carnochan recalled being excused for "habitual tardiness or failure in [his] studies" by bringing in regimental buttons he had found while "ransacking the dust heaps of Fort George." A found military cross-belt plate atoned for major truancies.[24]

In 1897 a Toronto newspaper reporter described the pastoral vista.

A visitor naturally asks on approaching the Commons from the town, where is Fort George? He is pointed to a grassy hillock surmounted by a grand old tree [the Lonely Sycamore]. A nearer approach shows the grassy depression compassing the old earth works that did service in the moat. Here, where once the murky cloud from cannon dulled the sunlight, a little streak of

Bird's-eye view of Fort George, 1880s, artist Tiffany Merritt, drawing, graphite on paper, 2011. By the 1880s the bastions were deteriorating as well as both powder magazines. The 1816 officers' barracks was occupied by a custodian and some of the land both inside the fort and on the outer earthworks was being cultivated.

Drawing based on conjectural drawings in an unpublished report. Gouhar Shemdin, David Bouse, "A Report on Fort George" (Ottawa: Department of Indian and Northern Affairs, 1975). With permission of Parks Canada.

The Wright Cottage, photo, circa 1910. For over one hundred years the interior of Fort George was intermittently leased to custodian-tenants, the Wright family being the longest occupants. The cottage incorporated the small 1814 officers' barracks and was eventually restored as such in the 1930s.

Private collection.

blue smoke rises from a small frame homestead nested in the heart of the old fortifications. The ruins of the magazine are there. Strong and massive in those days long ago; if the cow is out you can enter and look around....[25]

However, such a peaceful scene belied a major controversy. In the 1880s a golf club had laid out a nine-hole course on a portion of the ruins and adjacent Commons. By 1895 it had expanded to eighteen holes and a total distance of over five thousand yards. Janet Carnochan, herself a daughter of Scotland, described the unique course so eloquently:

> … surely never had the players of the game such historic surroundings. The very names of these holes are suggestive of those days when, instead of a white sphere, the leaden bullet sped on its way of death or the deadly shell burst in fragments to kill and destroy. The terms used in describing the course — Rifle Pit, Magazine, Half-Moon Battery, Fort George, Barracks — tell the tale.[26]

The club, whose membership was predominately American summer residents, proposed cleaning up the old fort site and erecting a clubhouse within. Increasingly impassioned letters to the editor and editorials in the local and Toronto newspapers referred to the desecration of sacred heroic sites as a sellout to "Sabbath-breaking Americans," while others countered "predatory bovines now wander at their sweet will through the bastions, the inner court is used as an oat field … A five minute ramble serves to cover one to the elbows with burs, and this is the place that patriotic 'Canadian' wishes to save from desecration!"[27] Surprised and bewildered by the opposition of the townsfolk, the golf club quietly abandoned its plans (see chapter 20).

In 1912 Robert Reid, a former local chief of police, was hired as caretaker of Fort George by the Department of National Defence. He undertook an aggressive cleanup of the site, and by the following spring the local newspaper exclaimed, "a wondrous change has taken place."[28] The locals once again were enjoying the "ruins" on the Commons, but soon all would change. With the outbreak of war in 1914, Camp Niagara on the Commons was thrown into high gear (see chapter 14). The Wright's lease was not renewed and the Fort George golf links were closed. The southern portion of the fort's former esplanade was soon the site of a fifty-bed military hospital complete with one fully equipped operating room. It was officially opened by Lady Borden, wife of the Canadian Prime Minister. Several other auxiliary buildings were erected, including a mess, kitchens, guardhouse, and toilets.

With the end of the Great War the buildings within the ruins sat unused, but the site was finally beginning to attract some recognition from historians and politicians. The newly formed Historic Sites and Monuments Board of Canada dedicated a stone cairn on the site to recognize the importance of Fort George. To provide better public access to the site a road was built in 1931 from the Niagara Parkway's intersection with John Street northwards along the river and then skirting the western edge of the ruins to connect with the end of Byron Street. (The portion skirting the fort was removed in 1990 and replaced by the Recreation Trail.) Seven years later the Parkway was also extended down to Navy Hall to connect with Ricardo Street.

In the mid 1930s, with Canada in the depths of the Depression, the federal and provincial governments were looking for make-work projects. The Niagara Parks Commission (NPC) proposed to the Department of National Defence that they would undertake the restoration/reconstruction of Forts George and Mississauga, as well as Navy Hall, if they were granted a ninety-nine-year lease for a nominal one dollar per annum. The offer was quickly accepted, but with some stipulations. To be eligible for federal funding preference would have to be given to workmen who were presently unemployed and married with dependants, they should be from the area, and the work should include as many workmen as possible. The Department of National Defence, mindful of past experience, also reserved the right to reclaim the lands with six months notice.

The two men who were instrumental in the eventual success of this ambitious undertaking were the Honourable Thomas McQuesten and Ronald Wray. McQuesten was chairman of the NPC as well as Minister of Public Works and Minister of Highways. An overachiever, this tireless visionary proposed and supervised many similar restoration projects and was the driving force behind the Queen Elizabeth

Way superhighway and the Niagara River Parkway. Wray was the project historian and director of all the Niagara projects. Considered one of the historical restoration experts of the time, he was also in charge of the Fort Henry restoration in Kingston at the same time. Despite frequent commutes between Niagara and Kingston, Wray found the time to court and marry a local Niagara girl.[29]

After considerable archival research but no archaeological survey,[30] the decision was made to reconstruct the fort to its original 1799 layout. A careful survey of the site was not easy:

> A century of erosion had reduced the earthworks to little more than five or six feet above the overall level of the site. In some places they were barely discernible at all … The survey … went slowly due to the almost impenetrable growth of brush and thorns which again covered the earthworks.[31]

Work began on Navy Hall in August 1937. A few weeks later a Michigan Central freight train came puffing and hissing down the King Street tracks carrying heavy excavating equipment. Such was the announcement to the sleepy little town that work was soon to start on Fort George as well. The initial restoration and reshaping of the earthworks using bulldozers took several months.[32] Only the two northern bastions had retained any semblance of their original configuration. The military hospital, mess hall, kitchens, and one caretaker's cottage were relocated to the edge of Paradise Grove. The original 1796 stone powder magazine, particularly its interior brick lining, was in very poor shape but was eventually completely restored. The small officers' quarters (1814) was moved to a new location[33] and restored to its presumed original appearance. All the timber for the fortifications was pressure creosoted for longevity. They lasted until 2010.

As previously described, much of the long-neglected site had become overgrown with trees of various sizes, all of which were cut down with one exception: a giant sycamore (buttonwood) tree some eighty feet tall standing as if on guard on the edge of the northeast (Brock) bastion. There

was great public concern for this beautiful and impressive "Lonely Sycamore" that had become part of local lore, a favorite venue for family picnics, and praised both in prose and poetry.[34] An heroic and monumental effort[35] was made to move this landmark, which weighed an estimated one hundred tons, under the supervision of students at the Niagara Parks Commission's School of Horticulture. In May 1939 the tree was replanted in a new location just outside the northwest bastion. The tree seemed to be viable at first, but with each succeeding spring it sprouted fewer and fewer leaves, and finally the Lonely Sycamore succumbed. A small rise in the turf near the bastion marks it final spot.

In the spring of 1939 the second phase of Fort George's phoenix-like rise began. After the stone foundations had been completed, the fort's lost buildings were reconstructed based on the research available at that time. All the timber used came from a first-growth white pine forest in northern Ontario.[36] Many of the logs were so immense that they had to be hand-cut by whipsaw on the site. The pit used for this laborious work remains evident inside the fort today. All exposed wood surfaces were fashioned using early hand tools. Soon, all the present buildings on the site were erected. The massive front gates were the last to be completed. A log "Trading Post" was built as a reception centre well outside the fort's reconstructed perimeter.

The first official visitors to the fort never stepped inside. In June 1939, Niagara-on-the-Lake was included in the Royal Visit by King George VI[37] and his consort Queen Elizabeth.[38] As the Royal cavalcade proceeded along the road skirting the western flank of the fort, three thousand excited school children cheered and waved their flags. Even the recently transplanted Lonely Sycamore bravely showed its leaves.

With the work finally completed, plans were underway for a gala opening party. The restored Fort Niagara across the river had enjoyed a grand celebration in 1934, as had Fort Erie in 1939. But Canada was now in the midst of another world war and the NPC decided that such a party was not appropriate. The gates quietly opened to the public on July 1, 1940. There was even concern that the Department of National Defence might exercise its right to reclaim the fort site for military purposes. Much to the relief of local officials, the fort itself was not needed as part of the war effort. In fact, for the tens of thousands of service men and women training on the Commons at Camp Niagara, the fort became a gentle reminder of their rich military heritage.

Finally, in June 1950 the official opening and dedication of Fort George was held in the presence of ten thousand spectators with marching bands and a cross-border exchange of cannon salutes. Festivities were capped off with a very twentieth-century phenomenon — a stirring fly-past by American and Canadian Air Forces. Initially Fort George was operated as a passive museum with displays of military

St. George's Lonely Sycamore at Fort George Heights, Niagara, photo, circa 1890. The eighty-foot tall Lonely Sycamore stood proudly near Brock's Bastion. A favourite picnic spot, it inspired patriotic prose and poetry.

Courtesy of the Toronto Public Library, Toronto Reference Library, T 13478.

Moving the Lonely Sycamore, photo, 1938. This was the largest known tree removal of such a mature tree attempted at that time. The huge root was balled and burlapped. Under the careful supervision of students from the newly inaugurated Niagara Parks School of Horticulture, the tree was pulled through a timber-lined trench to its new site outside the fort.

Courtesy of the Niagara Parks Commission Archives.

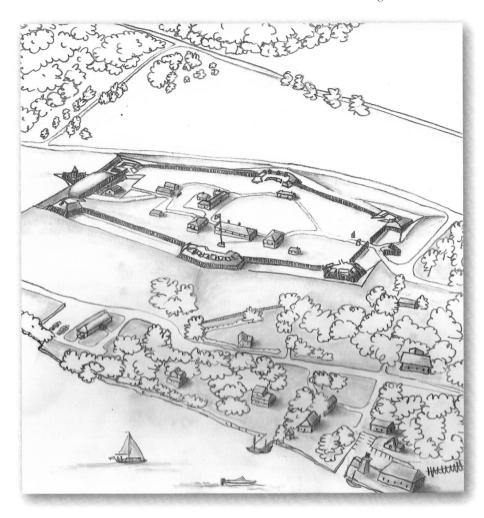

Bird's-eye view of Fort George, 1950, artist Tiffany Merritt, graphite on paper, 2011. Although not exactly as it was originally built, the restored Fort George captures the essence of the original fort as a living museum.

Drawing based on conjectural drawings in an unpublished report. Gouhar Shemdin, David Bouse, "A Report on Fort George" (Ottawa: Department of Indian and Northern Affairs, 1975). With permission of Parks Canada.

artifacts in the blockhouses. A custodian lived on the premises (the site of the garrison hospital in the original 1799 fort). In 1969 the ninety-nine-year lease was broken and the NPC officially transferred ownership of the site to the federal Parks Canada. Navy Hall and Fort George were named a "National Historic Park." Reflecting changing attitudes about museums, Fort George became a "living history" site with emphasis on interpreting the garrison on the eve of the War of 1812 with live demonstrations of various aspects of garrison life, including the soldiers and camp-followers.

To accommodate increased visitation, a larger parking lot was carved out of the Commons to the west and north of the fort site, partially camouflaged with berms and a newly planted small forest of native trees. Part of the American earthworks and campsite (1813) and possibly an American soldiers' burial site may lie under the northeast edge of the parking lot, the bush, and the grassy fields beyond, along Byron Street.

One question often posed by visitors to Fort George today concerns the accuracy of the restoration. If Brock were to march into the fort today he would probably be very surprised by the expansive flat esplanade in the middle of the fort. Early maps and an 1805 interior drawing of the fort[39] as well as later sketches of the fort "in ruins" indicate a somewhat uneven terrain of the interior grounds, possibly due to old dried up creek beds that are still evident in other parts of the Commons. The 1930s bulldozers reforming the

Fort George, photo, 1970s. In the silent early morning mists of autumn, restored Fort George stands guard on the Commons with Paradise Grove beyond. The fog-bound Niagara River has been a peaceful international border for two hundred years.

Sam Abell, National Geographic Stock, #623359.

earthworks simply flattened out the fort's interior space. Brock would note that the reconstructed guardhouse is not on its precise original site; the three blockhouses are not quite accurate as the new blockhouses were based on surviving contemporary blockhouses at Fort York in Toronto. He would be pleasantly surprised that there is now a tunnel to the octagonal blockhouse. Some of these discrepancies can be blamed on the lack of any archaeological assessment and the limited research resources available to the restoration historians. Nevertheless, on spending a couple of hours inside Fort George today, one is faithfully transported back in time to a period when Upper Canada's military survival was very much in doubt.

With paid admission to the site, this portion of the Military Reserve/Commons became no longer readily accessible to the townspeople as "common lands." After the restoration, it was as if there were two unwritten solitudes: the restored museum-fort — run by the NPC with its own live-in custodian and a few locals who worked in the Trading Post — and the townspeople who were for the most part indifferent to Fort George. On occasion locals were invited to special events within the fort. This attitude changed with the formation in 1987 of the Friends of Fort George, an association of interested and concerned local citizens. The Friends is dedicated to encouraging awareness and appreciation of Fort George and its artifacts and to support Parks Canada's mandate to protect, preserve, and interpret the military significance and historical resources of Fort George and its surroundings (including the Commons). Primarily as a result of the Friends' efforts many local citizens have become involved in the activities of the fort as volunteers and re-enactors. Funds raised by the Friends through their gift shops and other activities have been used by the permanent staff to hire more well-trained interpreters for the fort and to develop new programs such as the excellent period military fife and drum corps.

For over twenty years the Canada Day Committee, of which the Friends is an important partner, has celebrated Canada's birthday with a list of fun events, including breakfast and lunch in Simcoe Park, entertainment in the bandshell, and the grand parade of the birthday cake. In the evening the gates to Fort George are thrown wide open to welcome one and all. Citizens and visitors of all ages and backgrounds stream in, open up their lawn chairs, and spread out their blankets on the grass of the esplanade and sit back and enjoy the camaraderie of the long summer evening, the period music, the short historical vignettes, and then the fireworks (a faint echo of the cannon rumblings and Congreve rockets of so long ago). For a few precious hours the locals and their guests have reclaimed this special place as their "common lands," their land to enjoy in common.

A re-enactors' encampment inside Fort George, photo, 2010. Where cows once grazed, today the reconstructed Fort George is a living museum.

Courtesy Cosmo Condina.

CHAPTER 9

The Stone Powder Magazine

Fort George's stone powder magazine survived three years of warfare, during which it sustained one near disastrous direct hit, occupation by animals, and disrespectful human squatters, as well as over a century of neglect.

During the War of 1812 most contemporary powder magazines had short life expectancies. The Grand Magazine at Fort York was intentionally lit by slow fuse as American invaders approached the abandoned fort. The explosion resulted in hundreds of casualties including the American commander, Zebulon Pike. The blast was heard forty miles away. Similarly, during the siege of Fort Erie in 1814 an unexplained explosion of the bastion magazine resulted in over one thousand British casualties. Today, Fort George's restored stone powder magazine is the oldest surviving military building in Canada west of Montreal.

The evacuation of Fort Niagara by the British in 1796 necessitated the careful transfer of barrels of gunpowder (much of it left over from the American Revolutionary War) to Navy Hall — hardly a secure or defensible location, hence construction began immediately on a new powder magazine. The high ground above Navy Hall was cut by several deep ravines that provided a natural depression in which to build a powder magazine. The open side of the ravine facing the river was then filled in so that only the magazine's roof ridge could be sighted from Fort Niagara. Later, a defensive earthwork was fashioned just to the northeast

of the magazine to provide even more protection. There were two grassy ramps down to the level of the magazine. Following strict European military engineering principles, construction began on the building, which measured thirty-five by twenty-one feet with the walls eight to nine feet thick. The frame consisted of limestone (probably brought down by barge from an early quarry at Queenston) on the outside, while the roof and inner layer were constructed with thousands of bricks, including a three-foot thick arched inner ceiling for greater strength. Shuttered small windows and doors were sheathed in copper that would not strike a spark that could ignite the gunpowder. The roof was covered with sheet iron. To reduce the chances of sabotage, narrow ventilation slits penetrated the stone walls in a zig-zag fashion with a copper screen on the inside. Double wooden floors were pegged rather than nailed.[1] Once completed, the magazine could store up to three hundred barrels of coarse black gunpowder, and it continued this function even after it was no longer within the modified fortifications in 1813. A slightly smaller stone and brick magazine built by the British within the truncated fort in 1814 eventually was allowed to deteriorate, although the ruins of this "inner magazine" were still evident until the 1930s.

On the morning of the Battle of Queenston Heights the Americans fired "hot shot" (cannon balls heated red-hot in a special furnace to start fires on their intended targets). Suddenly the magazine's roof was ablaze and the structural

Inner powder magazine, photo, circa 1903. This deteriorating brick and stone magazine was built inside the truncated fort by the British in 1814. Note the cultivated land and French Thorns nearby. Remnants of the magazine survived until the 1930s.

Courtesy of Pat Simon and Joe Solomon.

wooden beams ignited. A quick-thinking and very brave Captain Henry Vigoreux of the Royal Engineers, along with several "volunteers," immediately climbed onto the roof, tore off the metal covering, and extinguished the blazing wooden beams, avoiding catastrophe.[2]

Water was the other potentially destructive element. Sitting enclosed in the deep ravine with resultant poor drainage, the magazine's floors tended to rot, and the damp atmosphere presented a constant challenge to keeping the powder dry. Drains were installed but moisture was an ongoing problem.

With the war over and Fort George eventually abandoned as a military post, the old stone powder magazine was still used by the Royal Artillery garrison at Fort Mississauga to store its gunpowder. After two decades, however, its primary military function had ended. The old building was occupied intermittently by squatters and used for the storage of hay. When American historian B. Lossing toured the site in 1860 he found the old powder magazine "occupied as a dwelling by the family of an English soldier named Lee." He then commended Niagara's hospitality:

> Mrs. Lee was an intelligent woman, very communicative and free in the dispensation of hospitalities. We were refreshed with cakes, harvest apples and cold spring-water. She filled a small basket with copper coins and other relics, and as I parted with her she wished me good luck....[3]

Lossing noted that the smaller inner magazine was being used as a pigsty by an Irish family.[4] Gradually deteriorating, but easily accessible to the public, the original stone magazine became the last visible reminder of the war for both locals and tourists alike. In response to local historians' concerns, in 1893 the Federal government commenced some remedial work on the old building. Most of the badly

French Powder Magazine at Fort George, artist Benson Lossing, pen and ink sketch. This sketch illustrates the 1796 powder magazine as occupied by the Lee family when Lossing visited the site in 1860.

Benson Lossing, *The Pictorial Field Book of the War of 1812* (New York: Harper & Brothers,1868), 418.

The Fort George Powder Magazine, photo, circa 1895. The 1796 stone powder magazine, nearly forgotten and slowly deteriorating.

Courtesy of Pat Simon and Joe Solomon.

The 1796 stone powder magazine, photo, Cosmo Condina, 2011. The 1796 stone powder magazine is once again within the fortifications of restored Fort George.

Courtesy of Cosmo Condina.

deteriorated interior brickwork was replaced, three stone buttresses were added to the north and south walls, the foundations were reinforced with cement, the tin roof was repaired, and the old clogged drains were replaced.

When the Niagara Parks Commission decided to restore the magazine in the 1930s, a replica of the 1799 plan of the fort was chosen; hence, the old powder magazine is now back inside the fortifications. Again extensive repairs to the roof and buttresses were carried out.[5] Further renovations were carried out in the 1970s. Remarkably, most of the original building is still intact and appears today much as it did upon its completion in late 1796.[6] As such, the stone powder magazine represents the only building in the Old Town of Niagara-on-the-Lake to have survived the War of 1812.

CHAPTER 10

The Battle of Fort George[1]

It must have been a very long night for hundreds of British soldiers and Canadian militiamen lying on their arms in the tall grass out on the Commons. For days everyone knew the Americans were massing a huge invasionary force,[2] and false alarms had already made for many restless nights. Two days earlier Fort George had been subjected to a horrific bombardment from American batteries. By 2:00 p.m. virtually every wooden building and gun deck within the fort had been destroyed.

The town had also sustained collateral damage from the bombardment. Anticipating a major battle most of the townspeople had already packed up their treasured belongings and sought shelter in the township. Four year-old John Carrol later recalled the great excitement within his own household during this period. With "bullets" and cannon balls raining down on their little house, John's mother hurriedly gathered up the children and some household effects, seeking refuge on an open wheat field where they rested on a blanket. When a cannonball ploughed into the ground nearby they escaped to Four Mile Creek, leaving behind their horses on the "common." Meanwhile, "the militia men [went] pouring into the house to receive a badge of white cotton or linen on the arm to let the Indians know that [they] were British."[3]

With only a small detachment retained inside the smoldering defenceless fort, the entire garrison had been forced to sleep on the Commons under the stars. Covered in heavy dew, the men were chilled lying in their soaked, heavy wool uniforms. Shortly after a rousing reveille had been sounded by a British bugler, a single rocket was fired above Fort Niagara, followed by a thirty-minute unanswered American cannonade from the fort. Was this the signal that the Americans were finally coming? A thick layer of fog hung over the lake and river obscuring any activity. Occasionally sounds could be heard: the splash of oars, the creaking of ropes, the flap of sails. Finally, several hours past daybreak, the fog banks rolled away revealing a huge armada across the mouth of the river two miles out on the lake — sixteen ships and over one hundred boats and scows each conveying thirty to fifty men.[4] The much-anticipated American invasion had indeed begun on the morning of May 27, 1813.

Three armed American schooners quickly took out the one gun at the lighthouse battery. The other one-gun battery along the lakeshore near Two Mile Creek was also disabled. A small piquet of Glengarry Light Infantry Fencibles, fifty Natives under Chief John Norton, and officers of the Indian Department, stationed at one anticipated landing site near One Mile Creek were subjected to withering offshore cannon fire and were soon forced to withdraw with heavy casualties.[5] At 9:00 a.m., with the firepower of over fifty naval guns firing broadside over their heads, the invaders, under the command of the young aggressive Colonel Winfield Scott, began the assault on the beach near Mr. James Crooks's house at One Mile Creek.[6] As the Americans ascended the

Capture of Fort George, artist unknown, coloured, engraved aquatint, Philadelphia *Port Folio*, July 1817, p. 175. This is a naïve view of the American amphibious invasion, May 27, 1813.

Courtesy of the Niagara Historical Society and Museum, #988.259.

low sandbanks along the shore, they were twice forced back by a small but determined combined force of Glengarries, men of the Royal Newfoundland Regiment, Lincoln militia including Runchey's black corps, and soldiers of the 8th Regiment. Eventually, however, 2,300 Americans gained the plains and were faced down by approximately 560 combined British forces. In what is considered one of the fiercest battles of the entire war, "for fifteen minutes the two lines in front, at a distance of from six to ten yards, exchanged a destructive and rapid fire."[7] With every field officer killed or wounded, the British withdrew, leaving nearly three hundred dead and wounded on the field. Although reinforced by fresh troops and field artillery, the British could only delay the relentless southward advance of the Americans, who had gained another two thousand landed reinforcements and extensive field artillery. The Americans advanced in three columns: their left flank proceeding past the lighthouse and along the river, their right flank proceeding through the woods west of the Two Mile Creek, and the main force cautiously marching through the western section of town[8] with their band playing "Yankee Doodle."[9] Their advance was temporarily halted at the Presbyterian Meeting House by British field artillery covering the British withdrawal. By 11:00 a.m. the British had re-assembled on the Commons near the Indian Council House, preparing to make a stand. British artillery firing for half an hour from one surviving manned battery near the fort effectively stopped the American advance. However, it became apparent that the American flank companies were moving to cut off any possible British withdrawal. Just before noon, British commander Brigadier General John Vincent reluctantly ordered Colonel William Claus to evacuate Fort George, but not before spiking the guns and exploding the small powder magazines within the fort.[10] Quietly, the British infantry forces retreated through the woods towards St. Davids. Meanwhile the field artillery and some baggage carts withdrew along the River Road towards Queenston and then on to St. Davids, the DeCew House, and eventually Burlington Heights. John Norton and a small band of Natives covered the escape. Surprisingly, the Americans made no serious attempt to follow until June 1. When later chastised for missing this opportunity to capture the British Army, the commanding officer, Major General Henry Dearborn,[11] explained that his men were just too exhausted, having been up since one o'clock in the morning when they had boarded the assault boats. Moreover, not wanting a repeat of the disaster at Fort York one month earlier,[12] the Americans very cautiously approached the "abandoned" fort; inside they found a few soldiers of the 49th trying desperately to cut down the flagstaff in a failed effort to prevent the enemy's capture of the garrison flag. They also

found 124 sick and wounded in the garrison "hospital,"[13] as well as several military wives cowering inside a storage compartment within one of the bastions. Commodore Isaac Chauncey, whose navy had made the amphibious capture of the British Army's Central Division Headquarters possible, proudly reported, "I am happy to have it in my power to say, that the American flag is flying upon Fort George."[14]

Undoubtedly there were many acts of heroism performed that day. One enduring story relates to Dominick Henry, the keeper of the lighthouse at Mississauga Point. Amidst the carnage of all the bombardments from the ships and Fort Niagara, Henry (a retired Royal Artillery officer) bravely assisted the wounded while his wife provided refreshments to the troops.[15]

Besides losing the fort with most of its ordnance, supplies, and soldiers' baggage,[16] Brigadier General Vincent reported over 350 regulars killed, wounded, or missing. Five officers and eighty men were killed or missing in the Lincoln Militia. At least two Natives had been killed, as well as officers of the Indian Department. The Glengarries lost seventy-seven men of 108 deployed. Many of the British killed were buried in unmarked graves on site. The official total loss for the Americans was 150 killed or wounded.[17] The only American officer to perish was Henry Dearborn's grandson, Lieutenant Henry Hobart.[18]

The American flag would cast its long shadow of occupation over Fort George, the town and the Commons for the next seven months.

One hundred and seventy years later, seven teenagers were "hanging out" on the Commons having a beer or two. As they relaxed in the tall grass, suddenly "a blue-coated soldier ran by them his back on fire."[19] After a long pause, one of the boys questioned whether anyone else had just witnessed something strange; each of the seven had seen the same thing. A search of the area failed to find any trace of the poor fellow. Some believe this was the spirit of a British artillery officer who had stayed in the fort as it was consumed by fire from American bombardment; others surmise the apparition may have been an American infantryman who had torched the town.

***8th Regiment of Foot**, colour illustration of the 1813–1815 uniforms of a private and an officer. At least five companies of the 8th King's Regiment were present at the Battle of Fort George.*

Courtesy of René Chartrand, from *Historical Record of the King's Liverpool Regiment of Foot* (London: 1883).

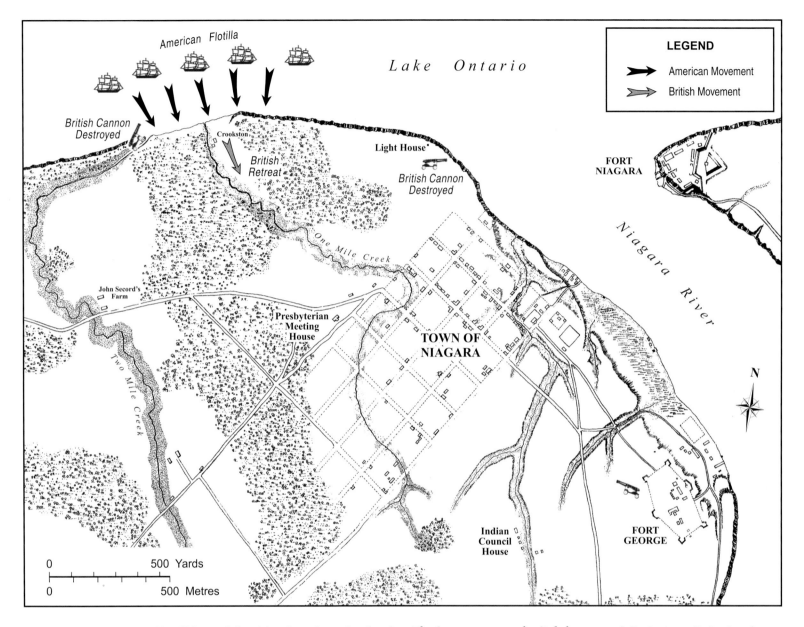

May 27, 1813, 8:45 a.m. Fog lifts and the American invasion begins. The lone gun near the lighthouse on Mississauga Point is taken out as well as the gun at Two Mile Creek. A small piquet of Natives under John Norton and Glengarry Light Infantry men near One Mile Creek retreat under withering fire from the American ships.

Although based on diligent research, the exact timelines and geographic locations of the order of the battle are still somewhat conjectural. The original topographical map used for this and the subsequent timelines for the Battle of Fort George is "The Upper Canada Plan of Niagara," A.Gray, 1810, Library and Archives Canada, NMC 001955.

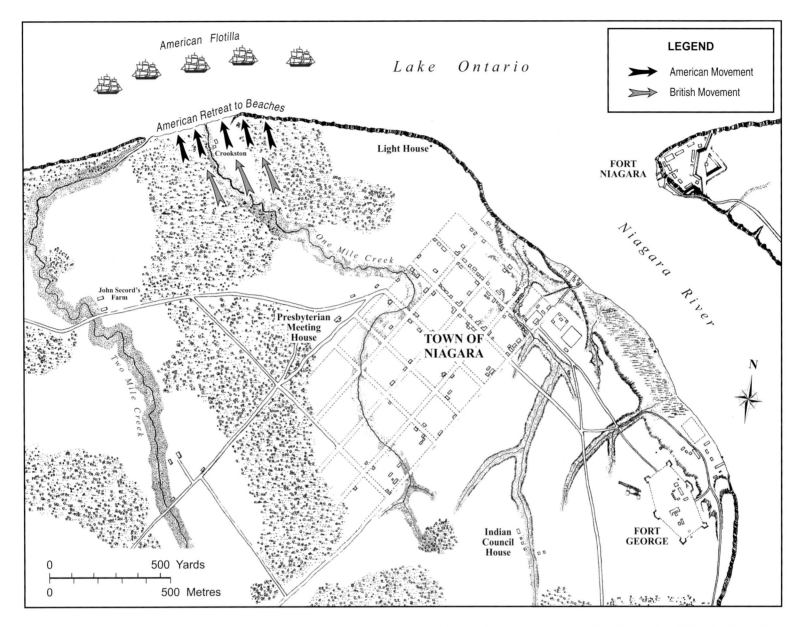

May 27, 1813, 9:15 a.m. American landing and subsequent temporary withdrawls. American forces land near One Mile Creek under cover of their ships' artillery and climb up onto the banks. Twice they are forced back to the beach by British combined forces.

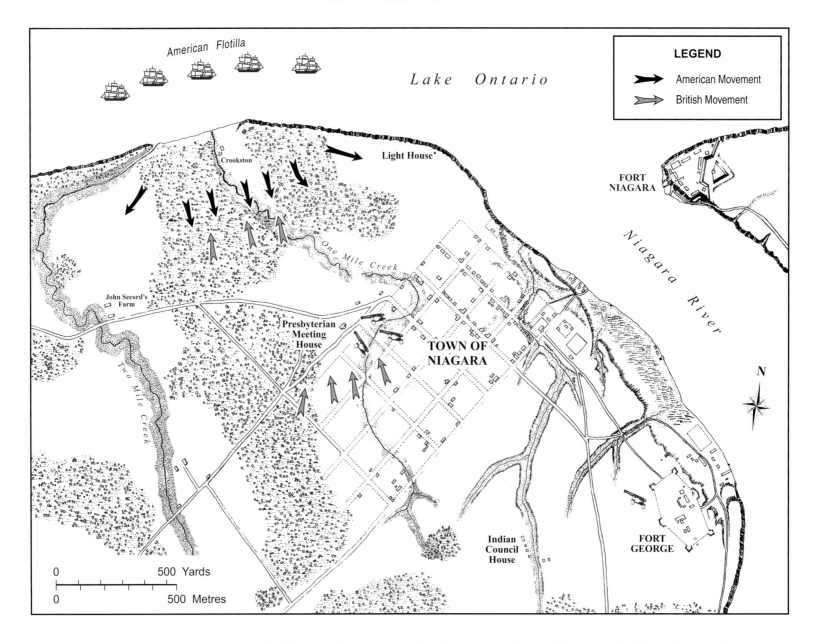

May 27, 1813, 9:30–9:45 a.m. Intense combat. Intense close contact, only six to ten yards apart between 2,300 Americans and 560 combined British forces lasts fifteen minutes and is arguably the fiercest single encounter during the entire war. Taking heavy casualties, the British forces withdraw southeast. Meanwhile, Lieutenant Colonel Harvey brings up companies of the British 49th Regiment held in reserve as well as field artillery to the area of the Presbyterian Meeting House.

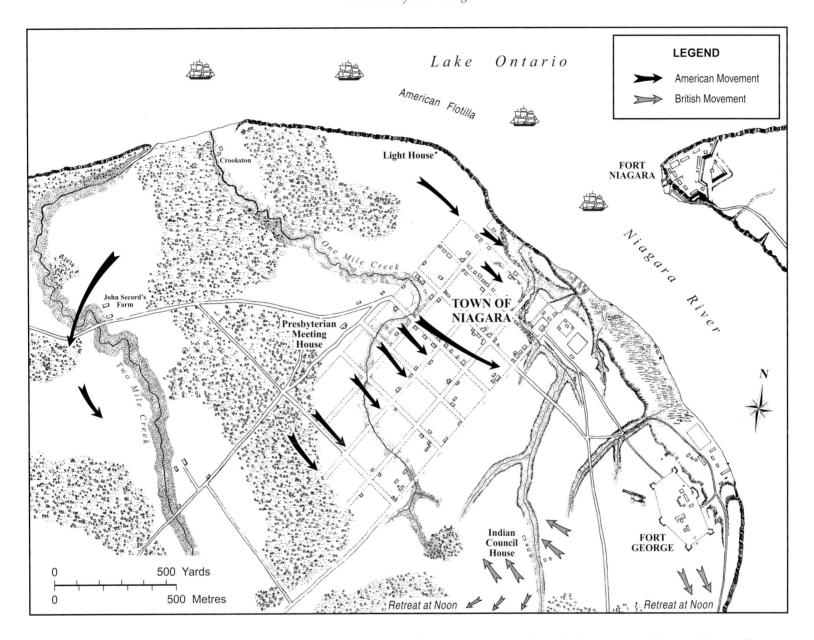

May 27, 1813, 10:30–11:15 a.m.–noon Standoffs and retreat. After a thirty-minute standoff at the Presbyterian Meeting House, the British withdraw to the Commons where they hold steady near the Indian Council House for half an hour supported by effective artillery firing from their one remaining manned battery just outside Fort George. Meanwhile the Americans are advancing cautiously in three columns: their right column is gradually making its way through the woods in the west; their left column under hesitant General Lewis is proceeding along the lakeshore, river, and edge of town; the main central American thrust also moves very cautiously through town. The American flagship enters the mouth of the river and American soldiers at Youngstown can be seen boarding bateaux on the river. By noon, the British forces, fearing entrapment by these American flanking manoeuvres begin a quiet retreat: the infantry through the woods towards St. Davids and the British field artillery and baggage wagons along the River Road to Queenston. The Americans do not pursue.

Re-enactors marching across the Commons with the King's and Regimental (41st) Colours, 2011.

Courtesy of Cosmo Condina.

CHAPTER 11

The New Butler's Barracks Complex

There has long been confusion among historians and locals about the Butler's Rangers' Barracks built in the winter of 1778 overlooking the Niagara River and the preserved Butler's Barracks buildings situated on the western edge of the Commons today. At least one historian claims that a small Butler's Rangers' Barracks was indeed present at the modern site in the late eighteenth century, but thus far there is no credible documented evidence. According to Mrs. Simcoe's diary, upon arrival in 1792 the Queen's Rangers encamped "within half a mile"[1] behind Navy Hall, but no permanent building would have been erected as they soon were dispatched to Queenston where they established a more permanent encampment. Quite clearly the surviving buildings of the Butler's Barracks complex do not predate 1814. With the final destruction/decay of the original Rangers' Barracks during the War of 1812, the name was probably given to the new military complex in recognition of the noteworthy military leadership of John Butler during the American Revolutionary War.

Early in the War of 1812 it became painfully obvious that Fort George and Navy Hall could not withstand the horrific bombardments from the American batteries both at Fort Niagara and directly across the river. By early 1814 the Royal Engineers were ordered to relocate many of the storage facilities to the western edge of the Military Reserve, which, although possibly still within range of American guns, would at least be out of sight of American artillery officers. It

appears the new Butler's Barracks complex grew initially in an unplanned and haphazard manner as a cluster of buildings on the open plain. By 1817 there were already a dozen buildings onsite, including log barracks, dwellings, storehouses, a hospital, and outbuildings. Only the Commissariat Officer's dwelling house has survived from this early period.

The Butler's Barracks complex had two primary functions. The first was to provide storage, or "stores," for all the military installations in the Niagara Peninsula. The second purpose was to provide the living quarters for most of the British garrison at Niagara. (Fort Mississauga, which was not completed until 1826, housed the Royal Artillery defending the mouth of the Niagara River; the decaying barracks of Fort George were no longer fit for British regiments; Navy Hall, although primarily a storage depot, at times was converted into temporary barracks.) The types of buildings at Butler's Barracks reflect the multiple functions of the site: the commissariat officers' quarters, the commissariat stores and offices and for the regular army, officers' quarters and mess, barrack master's house, single and two-storey barracks, gun sheds, and Dragoons' stables.

On reading the many reports for the various buildings at Butler's Barracks, one quickly concludes that most of the buildings were built in haste with inadequate foundations, using unseasoned timber and wood. Most of the buildings underwent many repairs and revisions, and the function of individual buildings was frequently altered.

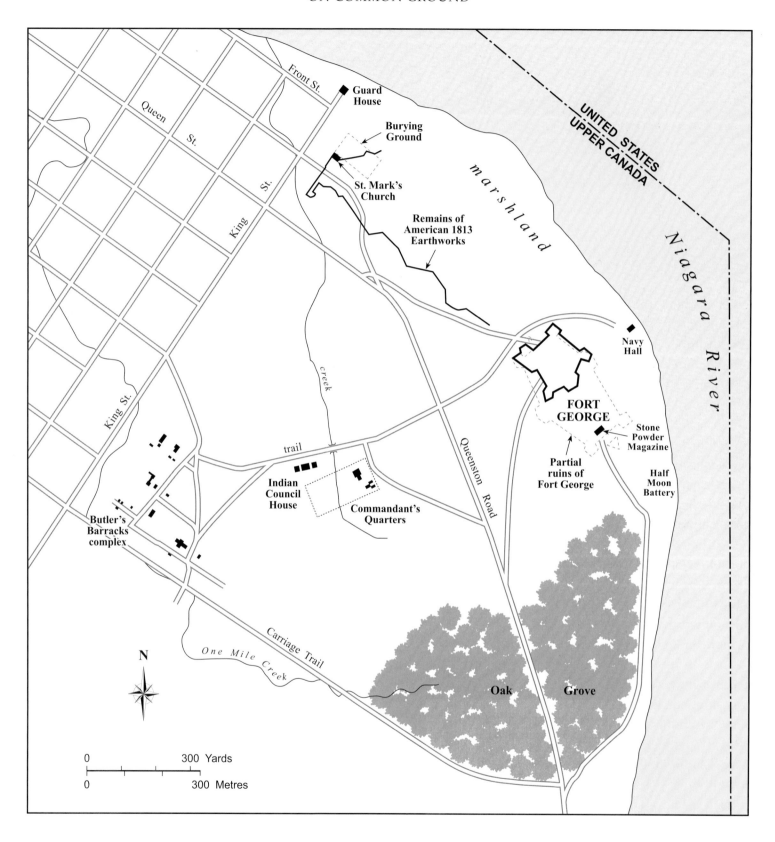

Butlers Barracks, built about 1783,
Niagara-On-The-Lake, Canada.

ABOVE: *Butler's Barracks*, postcard, circa 1910. In the foreground is the officers' quarters and mess with the two-storey barracks behind. Note the grazing animal and the two sets of tracks of the railroad spur line along John Street East.

Courtesy of the author.

FACING PAGE: Fort George Military Reserve/Commons, 1817. By 1817 Fort George was already deteriorating. A new Indian Council House and a commandant's quarters were built in the middle of the Commons. Several new buildings were established in the Butler's Barracks Complex.

One historian noted that the organization of the British Army in the eighteenth [and nineteenth] century was "weird and wonderful."[2] The British military establishment consisted of many departments with varying and often overlapping functions and responsibilities. As another historian points out:

In order to support a fighting soldier in the field, the army required a broad range of services including food supplies, adequate living quarters, camp equipment clothing and the armaments of war.[3]

Vegetable dish, photo, George Vandervlugt. Obverse decorated in "Chinese Garden" pattern by Wedgwood. This dish was found during the 1978 archaeological excavations at the 1816 officers' quarters and mess.

Courtesy of Parks Canada, #RAO2P.

Vegetable dish, photo, George Vandervlugt. Reverse, insignia of the 70th Regiment, which was stationed at Fort George April–June 1817.

Courtesy of Parks Canada, #RAO1P.

Board of Ordnance stone marker, 2012. The Board of Ordnance was responsible for all military lands and buildings in Upper Canada. Such markers inscribed with BO and the broad arrow were used to identify military buildings and the boundaries of the Military Reserve. This marker has probably stood sentinel in front of the Junior Commissariat Officer's Quarters since circa 1816.

Courtesy of the author.

To meet these requirements the military bureaucracy was often stifling and contentious. For example, the Board of Ordnance, responsible for all military lands and buildings in Canada, supervised the actual construction of the barracks through the Royal Engineers on site. The quartermaster assigned the barracks space within the fort, but the barrack master outfitted the barracks according to strict regulations. The commissariat officer had to tender and purchase the supplies for the barracks, but the storage of those supplies was the responsibility of the storekeeper.

Weapons and ammunition were the purview of the Ordnance Board; it was the responsibility of the Commissariat Department to tender and purchase all other supplies for the army, including the inspection and procurement of all food supplies, fodder for the animals, and fuel. The commissariat officers were administrative rather than military personnel and answered to the Lord Commissioners of the Treasury. Although these civilian officers did not hold the king's commissions, they were issued quasi-military uniforms.[4] To ensure security and efficiency, their offices and residences were usually on the edge of the military complex, but they were readily accessible to the local suppliers as well.

Most military garrisons enjoyed expansive boom years, alternating with stagnant periods of benign neglect with the ever present fear of closure of the site altogether. In the decades after the War of 1812, the Niagara installations were subject to these same fluctuations. On several occasions the threat of closure nearly proved disastrous to the integrity of the Commons as we know it today. In the early 1830s, burdened by the high costs of maintaining their world-wide empire, the British government decided to withdraw its regular troops from Upper Canada's frontier posts. The buildings and adjoining lands at the Niagara sites were divided into lots and advertised for rent,[5] but subject to cancellation should a military crisis arise. The surprising outbreak of the rebellion of 1837 and the establishment of William Lyon Mackenzie's provisional republican government on Navy Island in the upper Niagara River quickly brought such plans to a halt, with the government rushing fresh troops

1ˢᵗ (King's) Dragoon Guards Marching Order, artist M.A. Hayes, lithograph by Spooner, 1840.

Courtesy Anne S.K. Brown Military Collection, Brown University Library.

and arms to the much agitated Niagara frontier. One British regiment assigned to Niagara was a detachment of the 1st King's Dragoon Guards, arguably the most handsome regiment ever to march or ride across the Military Reserve. One local resident recalled:

perhaps the finest military body that ever came to the district, the King's Dragoon Guards' officered by men of wealth and title. The men were all six feet in height with fine well trained horses. Butler's Barracks was put in order for them, many of the officers were in private houses. Some of the young officers when on a lark often carried off the big gilded boot of P. Flinn, shoemaker, and sometimes paid a fine of $25 for this, so that it proved very profitable to the owner.[6]

The troop arrived in Niagara in mid-1838, creating quite a sensation among the women of the town and also reluctant admiration from the men. During their stay, the officers of the regiment were active members of various social clubs in town, including the prestigious Niagara Sleigh Club. No doubt there were amorous liaisons with local belles. In August 1842 Sergeant John Morgan of the King's, by then stationed in Chambly, Lower Canada (now Quebec), was granted a one month furlough (which was later extended) to return to Niagara.[7] We may never know why this furlough was granted, but we can surmise that he had left a loved one behind, perhaps a love child, or perhaps he simply had an old score to settle.

To meet the needs of the elite dragoons the barracks were refurbished and the officers' quarters renovated; special stables were erected for the cavalry horses, as were veterinary stables, a forge, and a saddler store. Responding to the heightened military activity at Niagara and need for increased stores, construction began on the two-and-a-half-storey commissariat store and office in 1839. In the same year the Royal Engineers constructed a rectangular defensible picket stockade with mock bastion corners and two gates around the twenty-acre complex. Interestingly, the officers' quarters and mess, the barracks officer's quarters, the barrack master's quarters, the Junior Commissariat Officer's Quarters, and the military hospital were all left outside the fortifications. At its peak there were over thirty buildings or structures in the complex. Later, responding to complaints that during certain seasons access to the hospital was almost impassable due to mud and water, a plank walkway 1,218 feet in length was laid down between the front door of the military hospital in the middle of the Commons to the two-storey soldiers' barracks inside the stockade.

Dress Helmet, Non-commissioned Officer, 1st King's Dragoon Guards, ornate beaten brass, circa 1838. Large plume illustrated in previous print is missing.

Courtesy of the Niagara Historical Society and Museum #972.917.1.

Much to the locals' disappointment, the 1st King's Dragoon Guards were withdrawn to Lower Canada in July 1841, and for two years all was depressingly quiet at Butler's Barracks. However, in March 1843, a company of the newly formed Royal Canadian Rifle Regiment (RCRR) established its headquarters at Niagara (a second company settled there later). This regiment was raised to guard border posts and consisted of long service volunteers of good conduct raised from other line regiments serving in Canada. Upon arrival the new commanding officer insisted that the Commandant's Quarters out on the Commons be completely refurbished.[8] For the next thirteen years the RCRR became an integral part of the community. Many of the officers and some of the enlisted men lived in town with their families. Military tattoos, band concerts, and picnics encouraged the military and civilians to mingle. Many of the men later returned to Niagara to retire.

However, by the late 1840s the colonial office was once again trying to reduce the costs of defending its far-flung colonies. The colonial secretary, Earl Grey, devised a plan whereby the regulars would be withdrawn but retired soldiers and pensioners would perform garrison duty in return, for which they would be granted small two- to three-acre plots of "surplus lands" on the Military Reserve. Here they could erect a dwelling and cultivate their holdings. In the event of a crisis they could quickly respond until regular troops could be rushed in. Although this "Enrolled Pensioner Scheme"[9] was actually attempted elsewhere, it fortunately never gained traction in Niagara, partly due to resistance from local inhabitants who did not want to lose their "common."[10] Moreover, by 1858 the British government transferred jurisdiction of the military lands to the Crown Lands department of the provincial government, but still with the stipulation of military readiness. A preliminary report to the province by Ordnance Lands Agent William Coffin recommended the buildings of the Butler's Barracks complex be converted into "a Deaf and Dumb and Blind Asylum for Upper Canada"[11] while the nearby Commons be divided into "convenient farming lots and let on lease for

five or seven years."[12] But Coffin seems to have had second thoughts, for in a later report he appeals for restraint[13]: "The government does not possess in Canada a more beautiful piece of land than the Ordnance Reserve at Niagara or one better suited to purposes of drill and militia instruction." He also railed against the Erie and Niagara Railway Company for cutting a disfiguring slice across the oak forest (later known as Paradise Grove) on the edge of the Commons.[14]

When the remaining detachment of the RCRR was withdrawn from Butlers' Barracks in 1858, the provincial government attempted to rent out the buildings once again, always with the proviso that the properties could be taken back for military emergencies. Various uses for the buildings and adjacent lands were proposed. Plans were drawn up to convert "No 6 Cavalry Stables as a school room for 84 scholars,"[15] apparently to accommodate the growing population of children in Niagara. This plan never materialized. William Kirby,[16] who was paid a salary of $1 per day as live-in caretaker[17] of the Reserve, suggested the Commons be converted into a "pleasure ground to attract tourists and encourage games and other sporting events."[18]

Unease along the Canadian-American border during the American Civil War and the subsequent Fenian Raids in the 1860s once again brought the RCRR back to the Military Reserve, but because of rental agreements some of the buildings were not available for the troops when needed. This seems to have been the last straw and further attempts at renting with "the proviso" for the military ended. Moreover, with Confederation achieved, the new government of Canada decided to retain the Military

FACING PAGE: Fort George Military Reserve/Commons, 1850. By 1850 the Niagara Harbour and Dock Company was working at full capacity on its waterfront properties on Ricardo Street. James Crooks was slowly developing his properties southeast of King Street that he had acquired in the great swap. The hospital on the Commons was serving both the military and civilian population. Part of Butler's Barracks was enclosed within a palisade.

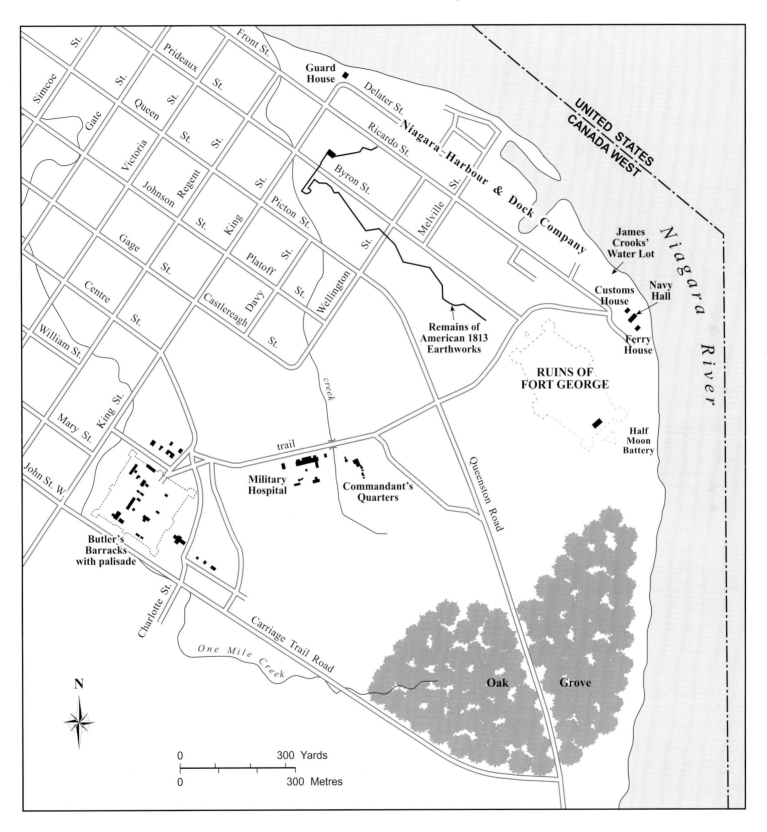

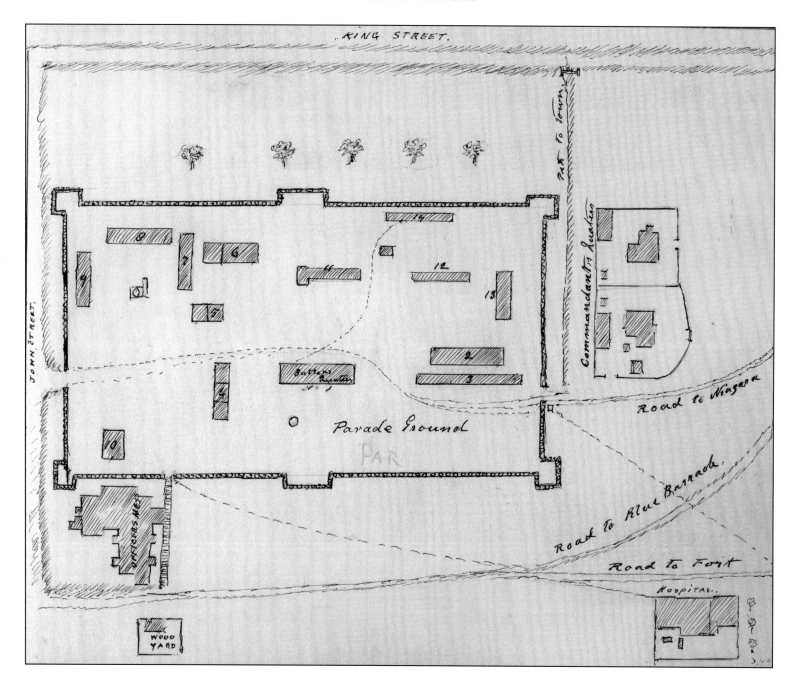

Plan of Butler's Barracks, pen and ink on linen, circa 1855. Many of the buildings of Butler's Barracks were enclosed within a palisade.

Courtesy of the Toronto Public Library, Toronto Reference Library, T13470.

Illustrations for Plan of Butler's Barracks, pen and ink, circa 1855. Buildings 1, 2, and 3 are still standing today.

Courtesy of the Toronto Public Library, Toronto Reference Library, T 13468.

Reserve at Niagara for defensive military purposes, and no consideration would be given to selling off this "most beautiful piece of land"[19] (at least for another forty years). The buildings of the Butler's Barracks complex would form the nucleus for the summer militia training at Camp Niagara for the next ninety-nine years.

SURVIVORS

Only four of the original buildings of the Butler's Barracks complex have survived into the twenty-first century.

JUNIOR COMMISSARIAT OFFICERS' QUARTERS

The Junior Commissariat Officer's Quarters is the oldest surviving building of the Butler's Barracks complex, having been built as early as 1814, possibly using materials salvaged from earlier buildings. It apparently began life as a stable, but on the commissariat's insistence, plans were altered to transform it into a residence.[20] The building was of frame construction with brick infill between the timbers. It was a simple one-and-a-half-storey cottage on a stone foundation with four rooms on the ground floor and a dividing hallway down the middle. There were two sets of back-to-back interior fireplaces. The upper space was unfinished. A separate cookhouse and servants' quarters were built to the rear of the residence. A well and root house were probably constructed at the same time. A second residence to accommodate another commissariat officer was erected to the north. It soon became the barrack master's house, but never received the same attention as its neighbour though both shared the same enclosure. Within five years the Commissariat officer in residence requested approval to add a porch at the front as well as a porch at the rear to connect the main house with the cookhouse, various "sundry repairs,"[21] and a fence around the perimeter. When the British troops were withdrawn from Niagara in 1836 the quarters were abandoned, but underwent extensive repairs after the British Army returned in response to Mackenzie's Rebellion. An enclosed stairway to the attic was completed with several rooms upstairs partitioned and plastered. The stable and coach house were also refurbished. Within ten years it was recommended that the ceiling of the first floor be raised to add height to the ground floors apparently to overcome dampness attributed to the main floor being so close to the outside ground level.[22]

Over the next twenty years, occupancy of the quarters alternated between military personnel during periods of heightened military readiness and civilian tenants. Not only did the latter provide a little revenue for the government but it was generally felt that occupied buildings would be better maintained and less likely to be vandalized. In May 1867 the aforementioned William Kirby moved into the recently repaired quarters as resident caretaker of the Military Reserve. Three years later Kirby had to vacate the quarters, which was turned into the commandant's quarters for the summer militia camps (see chapter 13). Over the next forty years the two buildings were used during summer camps as the commandant's quarters, headquarters, or officers' mess. Here the military elite and politicians of the day were entertained in high style. During the late nineteenth century the building also served as the clubhouse for the Fort George eighteen-hole golf course (see chapter 20) before reverting back to the military just prior to the Great War. The two old buildings were appropriated by the military for the headquarters' staff and renovations carried out. Together, these were now officially known as "the compound" until the end of the Second World War.

After the Second World War the surplus buildings at Camp Niagara were turned over to the War Assets Corporation for disposal. The Niagara Town and Township Recreational Council purchased from the Federal government fourteen acres of the Reserve, which included the two buildings of the compound. The old barrack master's house unfortunately was quickly demolished. The former Junior Commissariat Officer's Quarters, however, was used by various young peoples groups. Boys' Town, with its motto "Busy as a Bee," sponsored regular activities for teens, including boxing, crafts, and floor hockey. Teen Town held Saturday night dances in the old quarters in the 1940s and '50s.[23] The Girl Guides and Brownies also used the building. The Council also signed a lease for the nominal sum of one dollar per year on a twenty-year term, for the other three surviving buildings of the Butlers' Barracks complex. In 1952 with resumption of the summer camps primarily because of the Korean War, the government cancelled the sale and leases. Finally, in 1966, with the summer camps at Camp Niagara declared surplus to the needs of the armed forces, the Department of National Defence transferred the property to the National Park Branch (Parks Canada). The latter stabilized the building in the 1980s.

Today, within earshot of a children's playground, modern baseball diamonds, soccer fields, tennis courts, and the public swimming pool, the old quarters sits quietly nestled amongst mature trees partially hidden behind its tall fence. Many of those passing by on "Brock Road," walking their dogs, jogging or cycling, are unaware of this little building's extraordinarily rich history. Yet for all its varied uses the interior retains much of its original fabric and layout. In 2011 Parks Canada in consultation with local heritage groups sponsored another in-depth study of the property. Given its unique cultural heritage and key landscape features it is hoped that a sympathetic adaptive reuse of the property can be found soon. Time is running out for the Junior Commissariat Officer's Quarters — possibly the oldest surviving military dwelling in Ontario.

Headquarters, Niagara Camp, postcard, circa 1910. Together the former Junior Commissariat Officer's Quarters and the barrack master's house were known variously as the commandant's quarters, headquarters, and officers' mess, and later the compound.

Courtesy of the author.

SOLDIERS' BARRACKS

The two-storey hip-roofed soldiers' barracks was constructed in 1817 or 1818. The lower wall is composed of horizontal logs while the upper walls were originally frame but later filled with bricks to make the building more splinter proof against rifle fire. The exterior walls are now sheathed in clapboard. The interior of the two floors is identical: two large rooms flanking a central hall. The second floor is accessible only by an enclosed exterior stairs. The barracks could accommodate one hundred men, but for most of its life it was used simply for storage. For nearly two hundred years this building has dominated the Butler's Barracks complex by its sheer size. Being of log construction it has often been confused with the original 1778 Butler's Rangers' Barracks that were built near the

The two-storey soldiers' barracks (1817), photo, Cosmo Condina, 2011. Today the two-storey soldiers' barracks is the home of the Lincoln and Welland Regimental Museum.

Courtesy of Cosmo Condina.

Niagara River. The ground floor of the soldiers' barracks today is the museum of the Lincoln and Welland Regiment which traces its origins to Butler's Rangers. The second floor holds the regiment's archives.

ORDNANCE GUN SHED

The ordnance gun shed was constructed circa 1821. An early description portrays a clapboarded, wooden frame building, one storey high, built on a stone foundation, with a ramp extending along the entire thirty-three yard front of the building, which is divided into seven bays. Built to store heavy ordnance it was later used as a barracks and storage facility. The building has been restored and is now used for storage by Parks Canada and the Lincoln & Welland Regiment.

THE COMMISSARIAT STORE AND OFFICE

The commissariat store and office was constructed during the frantic military build-up of the complex in the late 1830s. This impressive two-and-a-half-storey frame structure also had a full basement. In order to hoist up the heavy crates and containers of stores, a windlass or crane consisting of a huge wheel, eight feet in diameter, with ropes and hooks was installed on the top floor. Several years after the building was completed a huge brick money vault with eighteen-inch thick walls was installed on the first floor. Large sums of money passed through the commissariat department. Today this interesting building has retained much of its original fabric and continues its original use as yet another storage facility.

Today, facing the old parade ground, the soldiers' barracks, gun shed, and commissariat store sit silently in their government-issue grey paint as mute testimony to the hundreds of thousands of soldiers who have passed this way.

A NOTABLE NON-SURVIVOR

In 1815 the Canadian Fencibles[24] garrisoning Niagara were still using the Count de Puisaye's house[25] on the River Road as their hospital. Being three miles out of town it was inconvenient for the surgeon's daily visits.[26] The Fencibles requested a new hospital in the Butler's Barracks complex, but only a recently built stable was available. With great reluctance and a promise that a new purpose-built hospital would be forthcoming, the modified stable was accepted as a temporary hospital. In addition to a leaking roof it soon became apparent that it was situated in a very unsuitable location in the southwest corner of the Military Reserve. One officer noted:

> The Hospital is also situated near to an extensive Swamp, and the Miasmata arising in the summer months from the decay of a luxuriant profusion of vegetable matter (combined with other causes) is sufficient in my opinion to warrant the conclusion that these are the causes of the varieties of remittent and Intermittent Fevers, which I am informed are occasionally prevalent.[27]

It is a swampy portion of One Mile Creek to this day.

Surgeon James Reid of the 68th Regiment was apparently the first to suggest that the soon-to-be-empty Indian Council House buildings could be converted into a hospital.[28] Responding to his request, extensive renovations were carried out with the laying of new foundations and joining the three original buildings together, which resulted in quite a handsome building looking out over the Commons. A plan of the building[29] illustrates "the left wing of the structure was self-contained, and included the surgeon's quarters, his kitchen and medical storeroom." The centre and right sections were the hospital proper, including the wards, surgery, kitchen, and the hospital sergeant's room. "The interior included a long room with a large fireplace, with fine woodwork and carving."[30] Apparently the building was well maintained, for in 1836 it was described as "[o]ne of the best hospitals in the command."[31]

Again with the excitement of Mackenzie's rebellion and the resultant return of troops to Butler's Barracks the hospital was upgraded. A frame one-storey building measuring twenty-four feet by fourteen feet was erected just to the west of the hospital. One half served as a guardroom complete with bed and an arms' rack for four muskets. On the other side of a thin partition was the "deadhouse" (morgue). Many a sentry probably had stories to tell about guard duty at the hospital. New stables and a new privy at the rear to replace the former privy situated near the hospital's front entrance were also completed. The entire hospital complex was surrounded by a close-pale fence. By 1864 the hospital was also being primarily used as a civilian hospital for the townspeople, and hence the recommendation for "one ward at least for women."[32]

With the British Army relinquishing control of the Fort George complex upon Confederation, the building continued to serve both as civilian hospital for the town and military hospital during the summer militia encampments. However, in February 1882 this old building burned to the ground. According to local historian Janet Carnochan, the foundation stones were "harvested by an enterprising local resident."[33] In the early twentieth century the Niagara Historical Society erected a commemorative stone cairn.[34] After years of standing forlornly and almost forgotten in the tall prairie grasses it has only recently been recognized as one of the commemorative sites on Parks Canada's "Spirit, Combat, and Lore: A Walk to Remember" trail. If one stands nearby with the wind blowing you may be able to conjure up blood-curdling Native war-whoops, the screams of terrified patients subjected to surgery without anaesthetic, or the frightened wails of poor souls dying from various afflictions that are readily preventable today.

Queen's Own Rifles, photo, circa 1865. This is the earliest known photo of the military hospital, readily discernible in the background. The central portion of the building was originally the post-war Indian Council House. Note the deteriorating palisade of Butler's Barracks Complex and the dog, mascot or stray, in front of the formation.

Courtesy of the Niagara Historical Society #984.201.

CHAPTER 12

The Great Swap

In order to defend the mouth of the Niagara River and the Town of Niagara, plans were drawn up in early 1814 for a new fortification on Mississauga Point. A portion of the land had been set aside in 1796[1] as a military reserve (approximately one half the size of the present Mississauga Common/Golf Course). A stone lighthouse (1804) and small earthen battery were established on this reserve. However, it is curious why the government did not reserve the entire strategic Mississauga Point property from the very beginning. Instead, the acting surveyor general of the province, David William Smith (see chapter 21), convinced the Crown to grant him the remaining half of the Point extending all the way to the One Mile Creek in 1796.[2] This was not the only important property that Smith secured for himself. As the contemporary Lord Selkirk complained, "The lots marked DWS are sure to be choice spots."[3] When Smith, suffering from the "ague," departed the province for England in 1802, he listed his properties in Niagara for sale.

The plans for the new Fort Mississauga on the reserve were for "a temporary field work," consisting of irregular star-shaped earthworks with picketed ramparts enclosing several log barracks and a unique central masonry tower. Construction began in March 1814, and most of the work was completed by July, with the exception of the tower.[4] The Royal Engineers, however, were concerned that the reserve did not provide a clear perimeter zone of at least eight hundred yards.[5] Moreover, the grandiose plans[6] for a mammoth garrison on the site, ten times larger than the current Fort Mississauga, had been drawn up. Such a fortress would have necessitated a much larger reserve. The rest of the land, bordered by Queen Street, Lake Ontario, the Niagara River, and Simcoe Street, would have to be expropriated for military use.

The current owner of the property was not to be trifled with. The Honourable James Crooks (1778–1860) arrived from his native Scotland when he was thirteen years old to join his half-brother Francis, a merchant at Fort Niagara. Eventually he and another brother went into the mercantile business in the Town of Niagara. They were the first to ship wheat and flour from Upper Canada to lucrative markets in Montreal. To facilitate this trade, Crooks had commissioned the shipwright Asa Stanard to build the schooner *Lord Nelson* at Niagara (probably Navy Hall). This ship was later commandeered and renamed *The Scourge*[7] by the Americans on the eve of the War of 1812. At the age of twenty-four, James Crooks purchased Smith's property at Mississauga Point, which included land at the mouth of the One Mile Creek. There he built a comfortable brick home on an estate he called Crookston.[8] As captain of the First Lincoln Regiment he was honorably mentioned for his leadership role in the Battle of Queenston Heights. Although Crooks suffered huge war losses, he proceeded with the industrial development of his significant properties elsewhere in the province, including several mill-sites, one being the first paper-making mill[9] in the province. Other interests included the Bank of Upper Canada, the promotion of several canals, and politics. He served as a member of the House of Assembly for several terms and eventually was appointed to the prestigious Legislative Council of the province. Although his Niagara properties were only a small portion of his fortune, Crooks nevertheless was determined to drive a hard bargain with the British government.

In the early 1820s negotiations commenced between Crooks and H. Vavasour of the Royal Engineers.[10] The

Niagara's first public school, artist Captain John D. Shawe, oil painting, 1946. The first purpose-built public school was erected in 1859 on land obtained by James Crooks as part of the great swap. This wonderful painting captures the excitement of a winter recess on the playground in the rear of this handsome building that was soon to be replaced by the new Parliament Oak School.

Courtesy of Parliament Oak School, photo by Jim Smith.

government proposed an exchange of land — upon surrendering his 21.25 acres at Mississauga Point, Crooks would receive four blocks of vacant property on the Military Reserve/Commons suitable for development bounded by present King, Picton, Wellington, and Castlereagh Streets (sixteen acres). He would also receive another four-acre block of the Reserve on present Ricardo Street plus a small adjacent "water lot," which would allow Crooks to maintain a wharf on the river next to Navy Hall. The deal was complicated by the fact that a one-acre plot at the corner of Queen and Simcoe had already been severed.[11] Moreover, Crooks had granted leases to two small houses on his property,[12] which were quickly removed from the newly enlarged Military Reserve.

The agreement was formally approved at a meeting of the province's Executive Council on April 16, 1823.[13]

The Crooks swap was the first and largest surrender of a portion of the Military Reserve since its original boundaries were set in 1796. Fortunately Fort Mississauga was never subsequently called upon to fire a shot in anger and the enlarged clear defensive perimeter was not necessary. The expansive site was eventually used to good purpose as a military encampment during some of the Camp Niagara years, and was also leased as a golf course (see chapter 20). Had it not been designated as a military reserve the Crooks portion of the Point would probably have been developed and the unique and arguably most historic golf course in Canada would not exist today.

Crooks's newly acquired properties were called the "New Survey," and new names, many with military connections,[14] were assigned to all the new streets southeast of King Street. The lots were slowly developed and are now an integral part of the town. World-class hotels and restaurants now occupy the Picton Street properties while most of the rest of the four blocks is residential. One exception is part of Lot 39. In 1854, for £200 Crooks sold the partial lot to the Town Council for "uses of Common Schools and Grammar Schools in the Town of Niagara forever."[15] As part of the deal, scholarships called the

"Crooks Endowment" were established for two scholars from each of the two schools "each and every year ... in perpetuity."[16] The funds were to be provided by the town or any subsequent owner of the land. In 1859 Niagara's first permanent common or public school was erected at the corner of Platoff and Davy Streets. A handsome two-storey brick building, it continued as a school until it was replaced by Parliament Oak School. Recently restored, it is now a private residence. One wonders about the legal stipulation that scholarships were to be provided "in perpetuity" by the town or subsequent owners of the property. The commodious brick outhouse behind the school has also been renovated. Although Niagara boasted one of the first grammar (high) schools in the province, it never had a permanent home until the erection of a purpose-built brick structure complete with bell tower on the portion of the Crooks school lot at the corner of Davy and Castlereagh Streets in 1875. In 1909 a separate gymnasium was erected behind the High School on Davy Street in honour of former teacher Janet Carnochan. Too small to meet the requirements of a growing enrollment, the school was closed in the 1940s and the students were bused to Niagara Falls.

Arguably the most important institution on this section of Crooks's New Survey is the Niagara Historical Society's Museum. Under the guidance of its founding president Janet Carnochan, the Niagara Historical Society had accumulated a vast collection of early Niagara artifacts. To house this collection the decision was made to erect a purpose-built museum — the first in Ontario. The site selected was Simcoe Park, but this met strong opposition in town. The final choice was a portion of Lot 39 on Castlereagh Street, donated by Miss Janet. Thanks to her indomitable spirit, sufficient funds were raised. Finally on June 4, 1907, the two-and-one-half storey red brick museum, Memorial Hall, facing southwest across the Commons, was officially opened. After opening speeches, guests repaired to a marquee on the Commons for afternoon tea. Years later the Society acquired the old high

Portico window, Memorial Hall, photo, Cosmo Condina, 2011. The decorative window provided natural light to the third floor of Memorial Hall (1906), the first purpose-built museum in Ontario.

Courtesy of Cosmo Condina.

school next door and a bridge building was completed in 1973.[17] The school's old gymnasium in the rear, facing Davy Street, remains in private hands.

The James Crooks block on Ricardo Street remained residential despite the heavy industrialization of the adjoining Harbour and Dock Company's premises. It is now part of a handsome condominium development. The water lot across the street with its wharf out into the river complemented Crooks's extensive mercantile business. A portion of the lot was used by the town and later the region for a water treatment plant. This has since been converted into an artists' centre and gallery known as The Pump House Visual Arts Centre. The rest of the original lot is now occupied by expensive waterfront residential properties.

The Niagara Historical Society's museum, photo, Cosmo Condina, 2011. The brick central portion and the wing to the right of today's museum comprised the original Niagara High (Grammar) School.

Courtesy of Cosmo Condina.

CHAPTER 13

Militiamen and Camp Niagara

The story of the local militia very much reflects the evolution of the Commons. After the American Revolutionary War, many of the new settlers at Niagara already had some military experience, having served in Butler's Rangers, the British Indian Department, or other Provincial Corps. A few were veterans of regular British regiments.[1] In 1788 these former soldiers formed the nucleus of the newly created Militia of the District of Nassau (still part of Quebec) that included the little settlement at Niagara.[2]

By 1792, despite the ongoing threat of renewed hostilities with the new Republic to the south, even fewer British regiments were posted to the newly created Province of Upper Canada. Recognizing that a ready civilian military force would have to assume some responsibility for the defence of the province, the first Militia Act was passed at the second session of the First Parliament of Upper Canada, held in the refurbished Rangers' Barracks on the Commons. This Act required all adult males between sixteen and fifty years of age to perform military service in both war and peace. At their own expense they were required to supply themselves with clothing, arms, ammunition, and accoutrements. Subsequent amendments increased the age to sixty years and stipulated that a muster be held at least once a year. Failure to attend the annual muster resulted in a stiff fine.[3]

The amended Act also allowed for the marching of the militia outside the province. Regiments were to be established in each of the province's counties. In the County of Lincoln five regiments were established on the basis of the political electoral boundaries.[4] The First Lincoln Regiment included the town and township of Niagara and was the most numerous in the province. The annual musters of the militia were held on June 4, the king's birthday. In most parts of the province these were often just an excuse for a boisterous festive party. A keg of whiskey or beer was usually drawn up, the men half-heartedly practised their drills marching about with various improvised weapons, but resting of course every few minutes for yet another draught and toast to the king.[5] The 1st Lincoln Militia held its musters on the Commons and no doubt ended in similar debauchery. However, the fact that they were able to provide a 1,600-man colour party for a dinner given by the Lieutenant Governor on the grounds of the Indian Council House in 1807[6] indicates a well organized unit.

With the threat of war with the United States building, Isaac Brock as administrator and commander of British Forces in Upper Canada was confronted with several sobering facts: he had only 1,100 regular British troops in the entire province, the loyalty of recent immigrants from the United States was questionable, the Six Nations on the Grand River were refusing to take up the hatchet, and the militia were clearly poorly trained and ill-equipped. Moreover, most militiamen were farmers with many responsibilities at home. Brock devised a plan whereby each militia regiment of one thousand men in the province was ordered to set aside two flank companies of not more than one hundred men each. These volunteers, who were equipped with arms, would train intensively six times per month. Once deemed proficient, their training was reduced to monthly sessions. If necessary they could be placed on full-time duty for up to six months.[7] The officers of the flank companies were for the most part experienced veterans from the American Revolutionary War. The rest of the men in the regiment (the sedentary militia) could be called out (embodied) should an emergency arise.

In Niagara several special units were created. With only one Royal Artillery company in the whole province, Brock established two companies of volunteer Lincoln Militia artillery trained by the Royal Artillery. In the spring of 1812 the volunteer Car Brigade (later the Provincial Artillery Drivers) was established to haul and mount field artillery. The citizens of Niagara donated one hundred horses to this brigade.[8] As the 19th Light Dragoons were the only British cavalry regiment in the entire province, Sheriff Thomas Merritt[9] was commissioned as major commandant of a newly raised troop of Niagara Light Dragoons. The troopers supplied their own horses and equipment and the government provided their weapons. The troop was disbanded during the short-lived ceasefire late in 1812. The following year, however, Merritt's nineteen-year-old son[10] was authorized to raise the Niagara Frontier Guides that were part of the Provincial Dragoons. These spirited volunteer cavalry units of the militia provided invaluable service throughout the war. A group of free blacks volunteered to form the Coloured Corps[11] (later called the Corps of Provincial Artificers), which fought in several engagements including the Battle of Queenston Heights and the Battle of Fort George.

Training of all the militia groups intensified during the spring and summer of 1812. One muster on the Commons was described:

> Yesterday we had a grand display on the plains. Col. Procter with the 41st in the centre, Major Merritt with his light horse on the right and Captain Powell with his company of artillery on the left and to do them no more justice they fired remarkably well.[12]

During the early part of the war, the flank companies of the militia performed well in battle. Later, as more regular British regiments arrived, the flank companies saw less battlefield action. In 1813 a new Volunteer Incorporated Militia was established in which volunteers recruited from the regular militia agreed to serve full-time until the end of the war. They were fully uniformed, equipped, and well trained.[13] This further relegated the flank companies to more supportive roles. They were assigned to dangerous picquet duty as well as guarding and transporting prisoners and deserters. Also, with their knowledge of the local countryside, they were often sent out to seek out food supplies for the military.

Intense patriotism followed the war and the local militia became the recipient of grossly exaggerated accolades from an adoring public. Later the pendulum swung the other way, dismissing the role of the militia in the war. Today, most historians agree that the flank and various volunteer units raised in Lincoln County and elsewhere did play an important role in the defence of Upper Canada, especially in the early phase of the war when the province was perhaps most vulnerable.

There were many casualties among the militiamen, with resultant widows and orphans. In the midst of the war, the Loyal and Patriotic Society of Upper Canada was created to raise funds to assist Upper Canadians deprived of their homes, health, or livelihood as a result of American depredations and to assist the families of militiamen killed or incapacitated by their wounds. Significant funds were raised both in the colonies and Great Britain. Cash grants were then disbursed to over eight hundred militiamen and their families, including many in Niagara.[14] The Society also struck a medal to reward militiamen for heroism. However, the medal was never officially awarded because of disagreement over the design and eligible recipients. Most of the medals were melted down and the proceeds along with the considerable excess funds raised by the Society were used to establish the York General Hospital, now Toronto General Hospital.

ABOVE: *Private, Niagara Light Dragoons or Frontier Guides*, artist Derek FitzJames, drawing, 1973.

Courtesy of Anne S.K. Brown Military Collection, Brown University Library

RIGHT: *Illustration of Officer of the Upper Canada Militia 1814*, drawing, artist G.A.Embleton. Although this may have been the official uniform of an officer of the militia, due to chronic shortages during the war, officers and men were often forced to wear makeshift uniforms.

Reproduced with the permission of the Minister of Public Works and Government Services, 2011, photo by René Chartrand.

On enlisting, each new recruit received a cash bounty as well as a daily stipend for their duty days served. If they completed their term most veteran militiamen were eligible for a grant of Crown land known as "the Prince Regent's Bounty." These land grants were usually located in distant parts of the province and later quietly sold by the men or their heirs.

After the war the special units were disbanded, but the routine annual musters of the regular (sedentary) militia continued on the Commons. In response to Mackenzie's rebellion in December 1837, nineteen hundred militiamen were assembled "on the common"[15] within twenty-four hours of the "alarm." Militiamen performed sentry duty along the Niagara River and later the Welland Canal. Incorporated Militia regiments were reactivated and regular British regiments were rushed in from England to man the military posts. Two new Coloured Corps were also formed at Niagara.[16] Within a few years tensions eased again along the Niagara frontier, but all males aged eighteen to sixty years were still required to attend the annual musters.

In 1855 with most of the regular British regiments withdrawn from Canada for service in the Crimean War, a new Militia Act was passed to provide for more active local militia units. Volunteers were to be trained weekly in local drill halls or drill sheds. With the rise of Irish Fenian sympathies in the United States and the American Civil War, relations between the two neighbours were strained again. There was a very real fear of invasion from the south. The British increased their garrison in the Canadas to a level unseen since the War of 1812, and a general call to arms was issued to the active militia to guard the Niagara frontier. (Interestingly, during the American Civil War many Niagara men found employment across the river building the new extensive ramparts and casemates of Fort Niagara.[17])

Although tensions eventually subsided, the newly formed Dominion of Canada, emboldened with a sense of national pride, recognized the need for a stronger, more effective military presence. New military orders set aside sufficient funds to establish brigade summer camps to include infantry, cavalry, and artillery. After two small summer camps at Thorold and Grimsby, the first Camp Niagara (the largest summer camp in the country by far) was held in 1871 — the same year that the last British regiment officially left Canada. Camp Niagara, sometimes called Niagara Camp, was the summer camp for Military District No. 2 with headquarters in Toronto. Eleven battalions of infantry, seven troops of cavalry with 511 horses, and three batteries of field artillery with cannons — over 4,600 men — attended that first year from June 5 to 19. Most came by steamer or train, "fully equipped," including their Snider-Enfield muskets. The Commons was home base for one unit, "Number One Company, Niagara Volunteers." Formed in the old town by Captain John Powell[18] ten years earlier, it had answered the call to arms along the Niagara River, Quebec, and Fort Erie during the various border threats of the 1860s.[19] It would later be absorbed into the St. Catharines 19th Battalion.[20]

Each trainee had a strict daily ration of food and was paid at a daily rate ranging from fifty cents for privates to $4.87 for a lieutenant colonel per day. The troops were instructed in drill, musketry, signaling, cavalry, and artillery. The camp was "under canvas" for the men and officers. The remaining buildings of the Butler's Barracks complex were used for storage. Although the old Junior Commissariat Officer's Quarters was the Headquarters even the camp's commandant slept in a tent. As with all future camps at Niagara, the soldiers' day followed a certain rhythm as laid down by militia orders:[21] the firing of a gun at daybreak followed by reveille played by a band or bugle corps; special bugle calls throughout the day; another gun at sunset followed by the playing of retreat; lights out a 10:00 p.m. with a final bugle call. On June 9 a "grand field day" was held, which included a march past of all the regiments, accompanied by six brass bands and two fife and drum bands.[22] On the last full day of activity a grand inspection was held by Sir George-Etienne Cartier who congratulated the men on their newly acquired skills and good behavior.

The Toronto *Globe* had sent a correspondent to cover that first camp. His observations of the old Town are noteworthy:

The Camp at Niagara, woodcut, *Canadian Illustrated News*, July 15, 1871. Local citizens and visitors turned out to watch a grand march past at the first Camp Niagara.

Courtesy of the author.

The large influx of strangers appears to have reanimated the old capital, usually so very dull, and trade has all at once received great stimulus. Last night the scarlet tunics of the infantry or the dark green of the rifles was to be seen in almost every store, and the streets resounded with their martial tread. There is ample opportunity too for amusement in the evening…. female minstrel performances, the inevitable collection of monstrosities, the entertainment of the Gaiety Vaudeville Company … concert and dancing hall, etc.[23]

Written narratives by the rank and file in the nineteenth century are rare, but an insightful journal by Private Andrew Greenhill of the Hamilton 13th Battalion who attended that first camp has survived. For the most part he is very upbeat about his camp experience.

Greenhill's battalion arrived by train from Hamilton via Niagara Falls. He gives a vivid and perhaps unique description of the arriving soldiers' first glimpse of Camp Niagara:

> We now busied ourselves getting buckled up and sat anxiously waiting for the first view of the "tented field." It came at last. We rounded a curve [John onto King Streets] and the first thing that met our gaze by the track was a row of the largest willows I ever saw [some still there] with a long line of artillery horses picketed below them. Beyond that a lot of old solid built military looking buildings, [Butler's Barracks] then numerous tents thinly scattered over a wide expanse of green common and beyond all a background of beautiful green woods [Paradise Grove].[24]

Once they disembarked from the train, the order to march was given and:

> … we began to trudge across the common which seemed as if it was never to end…. at last hot & thirsty we halted a short distance from the beautiful woods before alluded to.[25]

Although Greenhill understandably disliked some aspects of camp life, such as standing at attention and inspection, he showed no concern for the perceived deficiencies and lack of preparation decried in officers' accounts of the camp.[26] He was critical of "officers who are so emphatic in their order to be in time are generally the last on the ground themselves."[27] For this young city man, his two-week stint at camp was a welcome escape, a time of fun and memorable hijinks. One unique observation of life in camp was the seemingly ever-present background martial music drifting across the Commons. This perhaps is understandable given so many military bands attending camp but at times he "got tired and sick of it."[28] He does, however, describe what would today be called a "jam session" one evening.

> Music music all over tonight every band banging away at its best & not to be behind we got up a nice little concert in our tent which was crammed full with guests from our own and other Coys [Companies].[29]

The young soldier describes one experience when he and his friend Jim were put on guard duty at Fort Mississauga:

> It was pitch dark and the time dragged wearily along. The only sound that broke the deathlike stillness was the waves washing against the lake front of the fort. The only thing we saw in that long two hours were a dog & a tall figure in a black robe. It glided along the top of the wall swiftly & and was seen by Jim as well as myself…. I fixed my bayonet gave chase & challenged but it glided out of sight.[30]

The YMCA tent on the Commons received much praise from Greenhill, as it served as a refuge from one's "noisy comrades." Books and periodicals were always available, as was a quiet spot to write letters home. Evening prayer meetings were also well attended.

Greenhill, as with generations of trainees after him, regarded "tricks and jokes … an essential feature of life under canvas. Any opportunity is eagerly taken hold of to create fun & jollity. Blanket tossing became a great sport."[31]

Greenhill's journal unfortunately ends abruptly half way through that first camp. Nevertheless, his surviving narrative describes the unique Camp Niagara experience that would be relived by tens of thousands of the rank and file on the Commons over the next ninety-four years.

Indian Band 37th Regiment, postcard, circa 1900. The Six Nations were known for their military bands at Camp Niagara.

Courtesy of the author.

The Blanket Throw.

Photo published in E. Cruikshank, *Camp Niagara* (Niagara Falls: Frank H. Leslie, 1906).

The second camp at Niagara the following year was even larger: over 5,800 officers and men, including a cavalry regiment, three field batteries of artillery, and fifteen infantry battalions. Rather than use the old officers' mess of Butler's Barracks, canvas marquee tents were provided for the officers' use. The unfortunate drowning of a trainee in the treacherous Niagara River resulted in a directive that future swimming was restricted to the lake.

Due to budget restraint, the militia camp was cancelled the following year but Camp Niagara continued intermittently for the next thirty years depending on funding available and perceived military threats. Although there were the usual drills, instruction in musketry, and cavalry exercises, there was more emphasis placed on tactical exercises including "sham battles." Evening tattoos and sham battles on the Commons were always popular, attracting up to ten thousand spectators.

Complaints were raised occasionally over the quality of the food and refreshments provided to the men in camp. On one occasion two companies claimed that they were quite familiar with "coffee, café au lait, café noir, demi tasse and all that." Hence they refused to "respond to the notes of the bugle" until they were served coffee, which was better

Niagara Commons Christmas 1899, artist E. Wyly Grier, watercolour, 1899. This delightful bird's-eye view of an evening tattoo on the Commons was used as a Christmas card. Note the compound on the right, flanked by several officers' tents.

Courtesy of the Niagara Historical Society and Museum, # 1998.087.

than that being served in their mess that "was not fit for a hog to drink."[32]

A Camp Niagara *Daily Duty Order Book* for the 12th Battalion (York Rangers) for the years 1888–1900 has survived.[33] Lieutenant Colonel William Otter[34] was the camp commandant for most of this period. Otter had no time for "Sunday soldiers" and was anxious to erase the view that summer militia camp was merely a glorified holiday for the men. His intense training program would result in a well-trained militia and ultimately a professional regular

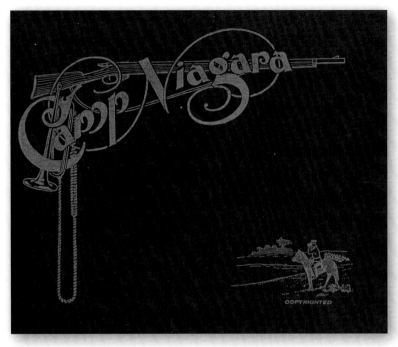

Camp Niagara, graphic, 1906. Art nouveau cover of the souvenir booklet by E.A. Cruikshank, *Camp Niagara* (Niagara Falls: Frank H. Leslie, 1906).

Visiting day at Camp Niagara, photo, circa 1893. Lieutenant Colonel Orlando Dunn was then-acting commanding officer of the Governor General's Body Guards at Camp Niagara. Among his lady visitors were his wife on far left, Mary Magdalen Secord, a grand-niece of Laura Secord, and, sitting on the right, Laura Secord Clarke, a grand-daughter of the heroine.

Courtesy of the author.

Camp Niagara, Butler's Barracks, photo, circa 1910. Photo shows the ordnance gun shed and two-storey soldiers' barracks on the right and the officers' quarters and mess on the left.

Private collection.

Cavalry Manoeuvres, Niagara Camp, postcard, circa 1910. Governor General's Body Guards are practising manoeuvres on the Commons.

Courtesy of the author.

A March Past — 1911 Niagara Camp, photo, 1911. Thousands of trainees on the Fort George Military Reserve/Commons are being reviewed by dignitaries.

Courtesy of the author.

Canadian army that would be recognized during the Great War to follow. The first Canadian-born senior officer of the Canadian army, Major General Otter, was eventually knighted and is commemorated today by the Otter Trail, the main east-west pathway cutting across the Commons. The order book contains the daily duty roster and assignments for the camp each day. Ominously, both a medical officer and assistant surgeon would be assigned to the ranges each day. Accidents did happen: the local newspaper reported in 1896 that a twenty-two-year-old trainee was fatally wounded at the rifle range on the Mississauga Reserve.[35] In addition to the usual manoeuvres and musket and firing practices for the men, there were "sword exercises" and lectures in the YMCA tent for the officers. Some entries would include lists of the promotions for NCOs and leaves of absence. Occasionally the men had to be reminded that they were "not to pass through the lines of Officers' Tents," but they were to go around. "Profane language, swearing and obscenity is strictly prohibited." Loitering around the camp kitchens before the sounding of appropriate bugle call was also strictly forbidden. The men and NCOs were warned not to steal fruit from the orchards of adjacent farms or they would be turned over to the "Civil Power."

Occasionally the trainees were invited to provide a military presence at special events. On June 21, 1888, Queen Victoria Park along the edge of the Niagara River overlooking Niagara Falls was to be officially opened. Some seven hundred infantry and cavalry officers and men along with their bands boarded the train "at the Grove siding" for the trip to Niagara Falls. Later the camp commandant praised the participants "for their uniform good conduct and steadiness from first to last: it reflects great credit upon the militia."[36]

The summer militia camps continued at Niagara into the twentieth century. Veterans of the Camp served in the North-West Rebellion in 1885 and the Boer War. As early as 1903 the men were beginning to practise trench warfare on the grassy Commons. To augment the rifle ranges in Paradise Grove and the "Rifle Butts" just to the west of Fort Mississauga, the government purchased a large tract of land on Lakeshore Road in 1908 beside Camp Chautauqua. This was turned into a large rifle range with a barn erected on the property. To the west, vacant farmland, originally part of the John Secord family Crown grant, was now used for practice skirmishes and manoeuvres. Thus began another defining aspect of life in the town of Niagara: the daily parades of soldiers escorted by their rousing regimental bands, marching from the encampments on the Commons on various routes to the Ranges on Lakeshore Road. After the routine summer camp of 1914, the old Military Reserve/Commons became the site for the training of Overseas Battalions for the Canadian Expeditionary Forces. However, summer militia camps continued even through the war years into the 1960s.

CHAPTER 14

The Great War and Camp Niagara

The summer of 1914 started out like so many previous Niagara-on-the-Lake summers: the militia brigades were back at Camp Niagara; the wealthy Americans had returned to their expansive summer homes; the Queen's Royal Hotel was full; the steamships and railway were busy bringing in more tourists; tennis, golf, lawn bowling, and yachting were in full swing; the fruit was ripening in the township's orchards; and the old town's year-round citizens were enjoying long, languid evenings on their verandas. Canada had just completed a century of relative peace, but on August 5 the daily newspapers reported that Great Britain had declared war on Germany and the Austro-Hungarian Empire. With Canada following suit within twenty-four hours, Camp Niagara and the sleepy little town of Niagara-on-the-Lake suddenly became an integral part of Canada's war effort. Of the 619,000 Canadian troops who fought in Europe, one in ten did not return home. Of the sixty thousand who made the supreme sacrifice during the Great War, a significant proportion trained at Camp Niagara.[1]

Five years earlier at the Imperial Defence Conference in London an agreement had been reached whereby in the event of war, all military forces within the British Empire would be harmonized into a single fighting force under British command. As a result, Canada's military lost much of its independence and regimental uniqueness. Moreover, the British military hierarchy, which clearly differentiated between officers and the "other ranks," was further reinforced. Hence while the officers would continue to wear the comfortable open-necked tunics with ties, the "other ranks" were required to wear the uncomfortable uniforms introduced a decade earlier: the tight tunics of drab rough khaki serge with rigid, high collars that buttoned up to the neck causing chafing and even open ulcers[2]; collarless grey shirts; trousers also of the khaki serge that irritated the skin, especially when perspiring; and woolen undergarments. The men's legs were wrapped from ankles to the knees in a bandage-like material called "putties." Although difficult to apply properly and hot during the summer, the water-resistant putties did offer some protection in the wet muddy trenches of France. Brown leather boots and peaked caps decorated with a bronze maple leaf completed the uniform. While in training the men often wore casual civilian clothes topped up by the same straw hats, cocked on one side, which had been issued to the militia ten years earlier and which the men referred to as "cow's breakfast." The men were often issued their official uniforms at Camp Niagara just before embarking.

The energetic and opinionated Minister of the Militia and Defence Colonel Sam Hughes directed much of the Canadian war effort. He insisted that the troops use the Canadian designed and manufactured Ross rifle. Although effective if kept clean and not fired too rapidly, in the trenches of France the Ross would easily jam. Occasionally the bayonet would drop off while firing. Frustrated, the men at the Front were always on the lookout for abandoned, more

Soldier "Frank," photo postcard (damaged), circa 1915. Trainees could have their photograph taken in their new uniform before being shipped out. Note the "Camp Niagara" backdrop.

Courtesy of the author.

Within a few days of its declaration of war, the Canadian government raised the First Division of the Canadian Expeditionary Force. This consisted primarily of trained volunteers from various militia and permanent regiments. They quickly assembled at the yet uncompleted Valcartier Camp, were formed into battalions, and along with a cavalry brigade were shipped out to England shortly thereafter. Camp Niagara became the training camp for the Second Division, receiving recruits from mostly southern and central Ontario battalions for eventual service in Europe.[5]

The recruiting offices were initially inundated with volunteers anxious to be part of the war effort; after all, almost everyone predicted that the war would be over by Christmas. And who were these recruits? Many were young men looking for adventure, some were anxious to escape the boredom of the family farm, some enlisted with boyhood chums or felt compelled to volunteer when a friend or family member had been killed. Many were underage.

Most of the battalions arrived at Camp Niagara by steamship from Toronto. Upon arrival the men would regroup on the dock and then march up to camp, usually led by their regimental band. Many were encouraged by the sight of so many young local girls lining the streets welcoming them to town. Unfortunately, with the exception of carefully chaperoned dances, these young ladies seemed to just disappear until they once more lined the parade route as the men marched back down to the docks to embark for Europe several weeks later.[6] Many of the men arrived in civvies; some had inadequate if any boots or shoes. It could take some time before they were fitted for their khaki uniforms and boots and issued kit.

reliable, and slightly shorter Lee-Enfields. Early in the war, Hughes dismissed Camp Niagara as just too small for an effective training camp[3] and directed resources towards the creation of a huge new camp at Valcartier, Quebec. Despite these early threats of closure, tens of thousands of soldiers received their basic training at Camp Niagara.

Another Hughes initiative was a government call to arms in which all the original named and numbered militia infantry regiments with their strong traditions and esprit de corps were forced to reassign their men to new numbered "Overseas Battalions" of the Canadian Expeditionary Forces (CEF).[4] Hence, the locally raised 19th Lincoln Regiment and the 44th Lincoln and Welland Regiments did not fight as separate units but instead contributed men to the various numbered battalions of the CEF. Over the course of the war several other numbered battalions were raised in the Niagara Peninsula. (Three outstanding battalions with a local connection were 81st, 98th, and 176th.)

With the exception of the Polish army, Camp Niagara during the Great War operated from spring through fall; hence, the camp was "under canvas." Long rows of canvas tents were pitched on most of the Commons west of present Queen's Parade. For the "other ranks," under canvas meant up to nine men with their guns and other equipment sleeping in a small bell tent, feet towards the centre pole with a ground sheet, straw palisses,[7] and, if lucky, three blankets. In

The Girls at
NIAGARA CAMP
Will greet you
with smiles.

The Girls at Niagara Camp, postcard, circa 1915. Not the postcard a soldier would likely send home to Mother.

Judith Sayers Collection.

the morning "each man's kit was piled neatly, in geometrically precise lines in front of his own tent. The side walls of the tent were rolled up to provide ventilation."[8] With the men away on duty, a sentry was assigned to patrol the lines. There were occasional stray animals in camp; sometimes dogs or even goats were adopted as mascots. The 76th Battalion had a black bear as a mascot[9] — an interesting throw-back to a century earlier when the 49th apparently had bears as mascots in Fort George just prior to the War of 1812. The higher the rank, the fewer men per tent, and there would probably be a wooden floor with mattress. Even the camp commandant slept in a tent in the compound of camp headquarters, the former Junior Commissariat Officer's Quarters. However, some of the officers of battalions encamped on the Mississauga Commons stayed at the nearby Oban Inn.[10]

A daily rhythm soon emerged for the infantry battalions. Reveille was sounded by the camp bugler at 5:30 a.m., followed shortly thereafter by the regimental bugler sounding a few bars of the battalion's song, followed by more reveille. For Scottish regiments, a piper sounded the calls. After roll call at 6:00 a.m. it was time to wash and shave outdoors with cold water, dress, put the tent in order, and exercise, all before breakfast at seven. One hour later everyone fell in for duties. After dinner at twelve it was time for parade and more drills until just before supper at 6:00 p.m. Evenings were usually free until roll call at 9:30 p.m., in bed by ten, and lights out fifteen minutes later. Each of these milestones in the daily schedule was announced by a different bugle call[11] — no need for timepieces.

For the infantry, most of their days were occupied by physical training, endless foot drills, lectures, and hands-on instruction with various armaments. Although they were introduced to the newly developed hand grenade, they still spent considerable time on the intricacies of bayoneting straw dummies with "blood curdling yells."[12] In anticipation of the type of warfare the men would be subjected to in France, great attention was made to trenches. Situated near the river on the edge of Paradise Grove were "first line trenches with barbed wire entanglements and steps and pegs for assisting in charges, trenches with dugouts and look outs, connecting by underground passages with other trenches built with ramparts of sand bags and zigzag to prevent damage from enfilading fire."[13] Although some live ammunition was used,[14] these simulated trenches on the idyllic Commons could never prepare the men for the horrific mayhem into which they would be immersed on the Front, where if not soon killed or maimed, were often subjected to debilitating shell-shock long afterwards.[15] After the war the trenches on the Fort George Commons were bulldozed over, leaving no evidence of them today. However, there were also trenches dug on the Mississauga Commons, and although they were to be all filled in[16] there is evidence of a least one trench on the golf course near the sixth green.

Parades were an important element of life in Camp Niagara and the town. There were the marching parades on Mary Street to the firing range on the Lakeshore Road, usually accompanied by a band. It was common for the locals to come out and watch the young soldiers march by, with young boys and dogs often running excitedly alongside. There were the "bathing parades"; since there was no running hot water in camp the men were marched to the lake at the end of Queen Street from May to October. Lake Ontario is cold even in August, so swimming in the nude must have been a very chilling experience. On Sundays there were "church parades" to the various established churches in town or on occasion to a large open-air service on the Commons. At these drumhead services the men formed a hollow square (U shaped fashion) with regimental drums stacked at the open end to form an altar. Several chaplains would conduct the service and regimental bands would provide the music. "Onward Christian Soldiers" was a favourite.[17] Any trainee feeling really unwell would be marched over on "sick parade" to the hospital where the genuinely sick would be sorted out from the slackers.[18] Every Friday there was a "route march" to Queenston Heights, a distance of approximately ten miles with a two-hour rest on the Heights before marching home.

The full-scale march could involve as many as ten thousand men each carrying their weapons and sixty- to seventy-pound packs. Individual battalions would march with a proper distance in between with "scouts on the side and in vanguard ahead, climbing fences and crawling under brush to ferret out any 'enemy' that might be near, and which could threaten the mass of troops."[19] Signallers maintained constant communication. The march usually proceeded up Pancake Lane, later known as Progressive Avenue,[20] and returned down the River Road. Marching bands and various ditties maintained morale and the marching rhythm. Sore, blistered feet were the usual complaint afterwards, but on at least two occasions tragedy occurred. During a severe electrical storm, lightning struck the coffee tent on the Heights. One man was killed, two were blinded, and forty-eight injured, many having been burned when their straw "cow's breakfast" hats burst into flames.[21] On another occasion when a summer storm became violent, nine soldiers were killed when lightning struck a willow tree, under which they had sought refuge.[22]

The supreme route march was the Great Trek of 1915 from Camp Niagara to the Exhibition Grounds in Toronto. On October 25 the first battalion left for Toronto, and for each of the next eleven days another battalion broke camp. Every night on the Commons before their departure the battalion would have a huge gala bonfire, around which they marched "shouting and singing and having an hilarious time."[23] One Scottish battalion, perhaps "excited by the pipes" (this was officially a dry camp), burned down the judges' stand on the racecourse.[24] The eighty-seven mile trek was conducted at a relatively leisurely pace; six days of marching on dirt roads with a rifle and a sixty- to seventy-pound backpack. The worst part was the dust. "You couldn't tell your own pal's face because of the sweat and the dust caked on his face."[25] Some were fortunate to finally have a bath on the fifth day in large vats of the St. Lawrence Starch Company in Port Credit.[26] Another special treat was at Fruitland, where all the men were presented with slices of pie served by "lovely girls."[27] Within a few weeks of reaching Toronto they were on their way to Europe.

CEF Bathing Parade Niagara-on-the-Lake Canada, postcard, circa 1916. Heading for the icy-cold waters of Lake Ontario.

Courtesy of the author.

The cavalry brigades were encamped between the Fort George ruins and Paradise Grove. They followed a similar routine, although much of their time was spent with the horses: grooming, drills, and so forth (see chapter 15). As one cavalry officer recalled, the general order of responsibility was always "Guns first, horses second, men last!"[28]

Many other units also trained at Camp Niagara, including artillery batteries, machine gun batteries, armoured car and motorcycle detachments, field engineers, and various detachments of the Canadian Permanent Army Service Corps. University students were trained through the recently formed Canadian Officers Training Corps. Although most of the men were encamped on the Fort George Commons, hundreds of infantry tents were also pitched on the Mississauga or "Lake" Commons, formerly the Niagara Golf Course. At the far end of the latter was a small firing range.

There were always several brass bands training in camp, as well as buglers and trumpeters. In addition to accompanying the battalions in various endeavours they would occasionally engage in competitions and tattoos, to which the townspeople were invited.

Machine Gun Instruction Class Niagara Camp 1918, photo postcard, 1918. This photograph was taken at the edge of Paradise Grove. Note the puttees on the trainees' legs.

Courtesy of the author.

The health of the recruits was of prime importance. The soldiers' feet were a special concern, and regular "foot parades" were conducted by the medical staff. Another monthly medical ritual was known colloquially as the "short arm inspection" in which the men were lined up and checked for any signs of venereal disease.[29] (A graphic film on the dangers of venereal disease was also shown to the men.) The men's lines were inspected every day, and any concerns were reported to the camp commandant. Rules for camp cleanliness were strictly adhered to. The town's water supply was the source of the camp's drinking and washing water. This was tested several times a day in a laboratory unit in the old Navy Hall building that was also the site of a six-chair clinic operated by the Dental Corps. Mass inoculations and vaccinations were also conducted periodically in this historic building. The camp's stationary hospital consisted of rows of tents for the patients within the bastions of the ruins of Fort George. The operating tent was replaced in 1915 by a more permanent operating room officially opened by Lady Borden, wife of the prime minister. At the far end of the enclosure were the tents of the Army Medical Corps. At the end of the season any remaining in-patients were transported by a special Red Cross hospital train to Toronto.[30]

Although the men were kept busy with their training, recreational activities were also promoted to discourage "idle" activities. Besides swimming, there were pick-up games and more structured inter-battalion competitions in lacrosse, baseball, football, and track and field. Battalion canteens were a popular refuge for refreshments and camaraderie. Thanks to Sam Hughes, Camp Niagara was declared "dry." This may explain why the graduates were noted to be the thirstiest beer drinkers of all the overseas battalions once they reached Europe.

All trainees were encouraged to send letters or postcards to their families and friends back home. This was the golden age for postcards, and, as any card collector will attest, many have survived from the Great War. They were readily affordable for both officers and the ranks. For two cents postage a soldier could send a postcard with a message showing various activities or buildings at Camp Niagara, or he could send more expensive photo cards of his battalion or even of himself standing in front of his tent. The postal station in

Panoramic View of a March Past on the Commons, photo, 1915. This march past of CEF troops, 2nd Divisional Area, was reviewed by HRH Duke of Connaught on October 7, 1915, just prior to the start of the Great Trek.

Courtesy of the Niagara Historical Society and Museum, #972.741.2.

Military Hospital Building Built 1915, Niagara Camp, postcard, 1915. This hospital complex was built inside the remaining earthworks of Fort George. The horse-drawn ambulance on the left is marked with the Red Cross.

Courtesy of the author.

TOP: *Camp Niagara 1918*, photo by A. Hardwick, 1918. On the right is the administrative building and in the centre is the camp's field post office marked with a two-colour flag in front.

Courtesy of Peter Moogk.

BOTTOM: **Field post office cancellation, Niagara Camp**, postcard. This is the most common stamp cancellation used in Camp Niagara's busy post office.

Courtesy of Peter Moogk.

The St. Andrew's Brotherhood of the Anglican Church just outside the camp provided similar services and was known for serving especially good food.[33]

There were many other diversions outside the camp, including a vaudeville theatre and a movie hall, built on Queen Street by a Mrs. Norris.[34] There were several shooting galleries and "refreshment stands" in town. Many shops popped up along Picton Street selling souvenirs to the soldiers and their families who arrived by steamship to visit the camp on Sundays. In the warmer summer months concerts and dances were offered in Simcoe Park.

As with any military encampment there were the usual camp-followers: the sutlers, the boot-leggers, the card sharps, and "the ladies." Harry James recalled as a boy being told that a long wagon-caravan of "Gypsies" rumbling by along Queenston Street in St. Catharines towards Niagara was on its way to Camp Niagara.[35]

The training of overseas battalions and other groups continued at Camp Niagara for five years. It was not until 1917, however, that a standardized fourteen-week training course was introduced. (During the winter the training

camp used the cancellation "Field Post Office Niagara Camp Ont" plus date.

The YMCA operated large tents on both Commons. There souvenirs, various amusements, sports, games, reading room, and even movies were available.[31] Volunteers in the tents encouraged and even assisted the soldiers in writing their letters and postcards home. Sing-songs and concerts were occasionally offered.[32] The popular entertainment group The Dumbells performed at Camp Niagara.

TOP: *YMCA, Niagara Camp*, postcard, circa 1915. There were three large YMCA tents: one on the Mississauga Commons, another serving the Fort George encampment, and later a third tent for the Polish trainees.

Courtesy of the author.

BOTTOM: *St. Andrew's Brotherhood*, photo postcard, circa 1915. Just at the edge of camp the Brotherhood of the Anglican Church served especially good food.

Courtesy of the John Burtniak Collection.

continued at the Exhibition Grounds in Toronto.) At times there were as many as eighteen thousand personnel in camp either in various stages of training or as support staff. For many, these weeks spent at Camp Niagara would be their last on Canadian soil.

The initial patriotic and optimistic enthusiasm of 1914 waned as the growing lists of casualties in Europe appeared in the daily newspapers and local families received word that loved ones were not coming home. Recruitment posters became more forceful, some even directed to young women to encourage their "best boy" to enlist. Because so many men were in training or overseas, women were assuming much more responsibility. Although they continued their important roles as nursing sisters and ambulance drivers both at home and abroad, they were now working at occupations once restricted to men in the munitions factories and at clerical jobs in banks and insurance offices. Locally more women were working the farms, canning factories, and operating the canteens.

With the grim reality of horrific battles still raging in Europe and the prospect of voluntary enlistments dropping off, the Canadian government introduced conscription under the Military Service Act of 1917. Although divisive for the country, it did continue the stream of recruits to Camp Niagara.

What a relief when the Armistice was finally signed on November 11, 1918, ending the most destructive global war ever — the war to end all wars. However, the overwhelming joy was somewhat tempered by the Spanish Influenza, which was spreading around the world. Camp Niagara would not be spared, although the overseas battalions still in training were not as severely afflicted as the Polish army in training five hundred yards away.

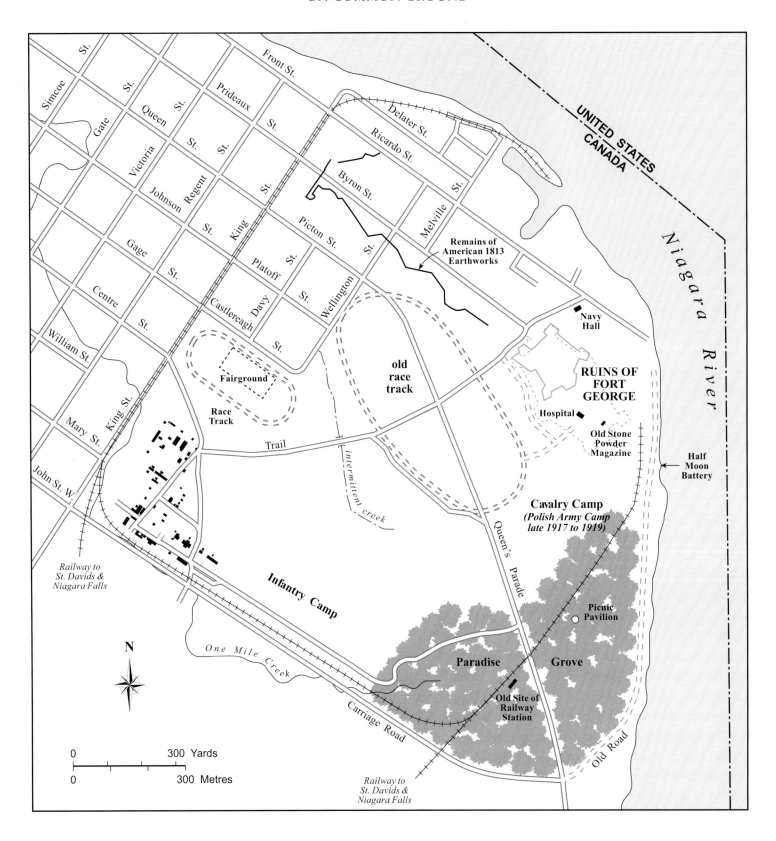

During the Great War's years, over a hundred thousand young men spent several weeks on the grassy plains of the Commons. Each one of them had hopes and fears, dreams and demons, friends and loved ones. For many these would all be snuffed out within months. Others would endure years of physical disabling pain and/or mental anguish. Some would faithfully attend cold rainy Remembrance Day ceremonies with aging comrades for the next eighty years as their numbers relentlessly dwindled away.

The preservation of the Commons is a testament to their sacrifice.

THE POLISH ARMY

The training of the Polish army at Camp Niagara is surely unique in the annals of Canadian military history. The story is even more remarkable because it has inspired an annual commemorative pilgrimage to Niagara-on-the-Lake ever since.

For over 125 years the homeland of Poland had been partitioned by Austria, Germany, and Russia. The military and social upheavals created by the Great War encouraged ex-patriot Poles to form a Polish military force to fight alongside the western allies in France with the ultimate goal of repatriating their country. By 1917 thousands of young Americans of Polish descent had volunteered, but with the United States still at peace with Germany, Congress refused to allow their training on American soil. While touring the United States, renowned Polish pianist Ignacy Jan Paderewski persuaded President Woodrow Wilson to support a scheme whereby Polish Americans would be trained by Canadian officers in Canadian camps, all paid for by the French government.

In early 1917 the first of 295 young Polish American "probationers" began intensive training as officers in the School of Infantry at Camp Borden, north of Toronto.[36] In June the president of France officially authorized the formation within the French army of an autonomous Polish army. Early in the morning of September 28, the Canadian staff and new Polish officers arrived at Camp Niagara to establish their campsite on the eastern half of the Commons. Shortly thereafter, over three thousand raw recruits arrived by train from Buffalo. As this was to be the first winter Camp Niagara, the recruits began construction on four tarpaper-covered barracks

FACING PAGE: Fort George Military Reserve/Commons 1917. In 1917 Camp Niagara was probably near its peak capacity. In the fall of 1917 the cavalry camp was moved towards the western end of the camp and the new year-round Polish army camp was established.

RIGHT: Polish army camp, photo postcard, 1918. Four barracks were quickly erected in the fall of 1917 on the former cavalry campsite between the ruins of Fort George and Paradise Grove.

Courtesy of the John Burtniak Collection.

NIAGARA-ON-THE-LAKE, CANADA

situated between the ruins of Fort George and Paradise Grove. Deep trenches for water and sewage lines below the frost line had to be dug quickly as well. Completion of the barracks by early December only provided accommodation for 1,200 men. With an unusually early and severe winter, some two thousand men had to be billeted throughout the town, all provided free by the citizens of the town: at the town hall, the bath house, unoccupied hotels, empty stores, canning factory, the Sherlock house and garage, and several buildings down by the waterfront.[37] The band was lodged on the main floor of the Masonic Hall. Many officers enjoyed the comforts of the Plumb House on King Street[38] and the old Western Home.[39]

Bayonet Practice Niagara Camp, artist C.W. Jefferys, sketch, ink on paper, 1919. Jefferys was commissioned by the federal government to paint various scenes of life in the Polish army camp both in summer and winter.

Beaverbrook Collection of War Art © Canadian War Museum, 1 9710261-0213.

Polish Soldiers Crossing the Commons, artist C.W. Jefferys, sketch drawing, carbon pencil on paper, 1918.

Beaverbrook Collection of War Art © Canadian War Museum 19710261-0241.

The actual headquarters was in the American (later King George III) Hotel on Delater Street. Visiting family members usually stayed at Doyle's Hotel on Picton Street, which was owned by a Polish family.

Over the next eighteen months a constant turnover of volunteer recruits arrived and left by train throughout the day and night. At any one time there were approximately four thousand eager recruits in camp undergoing a month of rigorous basic training. Instructions were given in British and French drill, and in English or Polish languages by acting Polish officers and NCOs under the supervision of Canadian officers. No musketry training or rifle drill was given. Two brass and one bugle band were trained in camp. The volunteer recruits were paid the princely sum of five cents per day; acting officers received $1.12 per day. In addition, each man was entitled to a premium of $150 per year.[40] Initially the recruits were outfitted with surplus discontinued nineteenth-century Canadian militia uniforms. Instead of the drab khaki uniforms of the regular expeditionary overseas forces still training at Camp Niagara, Polish recruits marched in the more colourful scarlets, dark blues, and rifle greens of the old militia.[41] Eventually they were outfitted with the "horizon blue" uniforms of the French army, and so became known as the "Blue Army."[42]

After their month of training, the recruits decamped by train back to Buffalo for eventual embarkation to Europe via New York or Halifax. Even after the Americans declared war on Germany, Congress refused to allow the training of a foreign army on American soil. Nevertheless, for a short time overflow recruits were allowed to camp at a "Depot" at Fort Niagara. Another depot at St. Johns, Quebec, now Saint-Jean-sur-Richelieu, also accepted an overflow of recruits for a short period of time.[43]

ABOVE: *Soldiers of the Polish Army in the YMCA Tent at the Camp Niagara, Niagara-on-the-Lake*, artist C.W. Jefferys, gouache, watercolour, graphite pencil on board, 1918. Note that the Polish trainees are wearing old Canada militia uniforms and the signs are in both Polish and English.

Beaverbrook Collection of War Art © Canadian War Museum 19710261-0207.

FACING PAGE: *Polish Soldiers Bathing at Niagara*, artist C.W.Jefferys, watercolour on paper, 1918. As with all the other trainees at Camp Niagara, the Polish volunteers took part in their own bathing parades. Note on the right is Fort Mississauga and Fort Niagara beyond, across the river. Guards served as lifeguards and kept away the curious.

© Canadian War Museum, 20070151-001.

In the spring, the camp returned under canvas. The following winter most of the recruits had to be billeted once again, but on this occasion, there was a nominal fee.

The supervising Canadian officers, including the medical staff, were headed by Camp Commandant Lieutenant Colonel Arthur D'Orr LePan, who at age thirty-two already had a distinguished career, both in the military and education. Many of the officers had served overseas in the Boer War or the Great War. One officer of note, Captain Alexander G. Smith, a Native of the Six Nations Reserve, had served with distinction in France and been awarded the Military Cross.[44]

The Polish camp on the Commons was officially named Tadeusz Kosciuszko Camp after the American Revolutionary War hero Kosciuszko who fought bravely with George Washington — a strange irony as the camp was only a stone's throw from the site of Loyalist John Butler's Rangers' Barracks.

Poland's national emblem, the white eagle, watched over the campsite. On a summer's evening haunting and melancholic Polish folk music could often be heard drifting across the Commons. During their hard-earned rest periods, the recruits, wearing the *czapka*, the traditional square-topped headdress of the Polish military, were often seen "dancing the mazur [*sic*] and the polka on the green."[45]

Although the local citizenry were initially concerned when these young "aliens"[46] first arrived, these dedicated young men, so passionate about their homeland, soon were accepted with open arms. It was not unusual for crowds of townspeople to turn out for their emotional departures; many homes were opened for billets; new books on Polish history and culture appeared in the library. And there was other support for the men. The Canadian YMCA furnished a large tent on the Commons as well as a recreation hall and reading room in town. Facilities included halls for three "movie picture machines," a branch post office, and bank. Assistance was freely offered to the recruits to write letters home and even write wills. Recreation halls were converted into chapels on Sundays. Arrangements were made for sports and entertainment. Profits from the canteen were donated to the soldiers.[47] The American Red Cross sisters travelled regularly to Niagara with their motor ambulances to distribute "comfort kits" to each of the men.[48] They also established a "service station" for relatives visiting the camp.

The soldiers responded in kind. One event long-remembered by the locals was a special parade on Armistice Day.[49] The recruits and their Canadian officers mounted a huge parade, including ordnance, bands, flags, banners, and a float with the "Kaiser" in a cage which marched from Camp Kosciuszko, across the Commons, through town, and out to Fort Mississauga. Some of the recruits enjoyed carving ice sculptures in Simcoe Park and down by the waterfront, much to the delight of local children.[50] The supervising Canadian officers and the locals all agreed that the Polish recruits were "the best behaved soldiers who served [at

Armistice parade, photo, 1918. The Polish volunteers organized a huge special parade on Armistice Day (somewhat prematurely). A "Kaiser" in a large cage was paraded across the Commons and through town.

Courtesy of the John Burtniak Collection.

Niagara] at any time."[51] On one occasion Father Rydlewski, who had left a large comfortable church in Pittsburgh to serve as chaplain to the recruits, appeared at a meeting of town council. After receiving a warm commendation for his men's exemplary behaviour he explained, "But I'm afraid gentlemen, they wouldn't have been so good if they could have got the viskey."[52] A few of the boys did apparently succumb to another vice: an upstairs apartment on Queen Street was staffed by "ladies from Buffalo."[53]

In recognition of the historic significance of the training of the Polish army on Canadian soil, several distinguished personages visited Camp Kosciuoszko. These included HRH Prince Arthur, Duke of Connaught,[54] the Duke of Devonshire, the then-Governor General of Canada, and Polish Prince Poniowtoski.[55] But the most revered visitor was Paderewski himself who had worked so hard to establish a Polish army in exile. He was honored with a march past on the Commons. He later became prime minister of the newly independent Republic of Poland.

During the eighteen months of its existence 22,395 men were trained on the Commons for the Polish army, with 20,720 actually sent to France. Less than 1 percent were enlistments from Canada, the balance coming from the United States.[56] These statistics, however, belie an underlying tragedy that struck the young "rugged strong" Polish soldiers.[57] In early September 1918 the first cases of Spanish Flu in Canada appeared among recently arrived recruits from the United States. Part of a worldwide pandemic of viral influenza originating from the American Midwest, the virus spread quickly through young soldiers in over-crowded barracks all over North America and then the rest of the world. The deadliest disease in human history, it was eventually responsible for more deaths than the Great War.[58] At the Polish camp on the Commons the medical personnel were soon overwhelmed with hundreds of cases resulting in twenty-four deaths during the initial wave that lasted six weeks. A second outbreak in 1919 was mercifully not quite as severe. Interestingly, it was several weeks after the Polish outbreak before the first case of

Ignacy Jan Paderewski, photo, 1918. In July 1918 the world-renowned pianist Ignacy Jan Paderewski (1860–1941) was honoured with a march past on the Commons. He would later become prime minister of the free Republic of Poland.

Courtesy of the Niagara Historical Society and Museum, #97911.2

Volunteers from the Red Cross, photo, 1918. Many local women, some of whom were former nurses, volunteered to work with the Red Cross during the influenza outbreak at the Polish army camp. They encamped on the Commons near the Polish barracks.

Courtesy of Pat Simon.

Sovereign Poland in Niagara-on-the-Lake, photo, 2011. This hallowed piece of land in St. Vincent de Paul cemetery was given to the Government of Poland by the Government of Canada to commemorate the Polish trainees who died at Camp Niagara and in recognition of the Polish people as valued allies.

Courtesy of the author.

influenza presented among the Canadian soldiers encamped near Butler's Barracks at the far end of the Commons. Of the forty-three deaths at Camp Kosciuoszko, at least twenty-five (including a Canadian officer in the Polish camp) were directly attributed to the Spanish Flu.[59] Many of the stricken Poles were buried in the parish cemetery of St. Vincent de Paul Roman Catholic Church.

In recognition of the sacrifices of these young men for their beloved homeland and for the support given by the citizens of Niagara, members of the Polish community in North America make an annual pilgrimage to St. Vincent de Paul cemetery on "Polish Sunday," usually the second Sunday in June. A special service is held in the "Polish Enclosure," which is the location of the burials of twenty-five young men and one of their chaplains, Father Jan Jozef Dekowski, who asked to be buried here. This hallowed place has been designated

as sovereign Polish soil. In September 1969, Karol Cardinal Wojtyla, the future Pope John Paul II, visited the site.[60]

One of the last surviving veterans of the Blue Army recalled:

> … in Canada, it was just like having good parents, you know. The Canadian people were wonderful and they are wonderful now. The Canadians welcomed us like brothers.[61]

There was one local citizen who became especially connected with the Polish army camp. Elizabeth (Lizzie) Masters Ascher (1869–1941) was born in Niagara[62] and became a journalist, writing articles for newspapers in St. Catharines, Buffalo, and Toronto. During the Great War she became particularly interested in the Polish army

Lt. Col. A.D. LePan Commandant and Staff Polish Army Camp. Photo by Ficar, January 15, 1919. The Polish army camp at Niagara was demobilized in early 1919. By this time most of the Polish trainees were fighting in Europe against Russian Bolsheviks for the independence of their homeland.

Courtesy of the Niagara Historical Society and Museum, # 991.737.

camp, and during the Spanish Flu epidemic she fearlessly cared for stricken young recruits. Even after the last volunteer had left Camp Kosciuszko she tirelessly spearheaded local relief efforts to collect clothing, medical supplies, and money for villages in newly independent Poland.[63] She even tended the graves of the fallen. For her dedication she was awarded Poland's highest civilian honour, the Order of Polonia Restituta. As part of the annual Polish Sunday commemorations a wreath is placed on her gravesite in St. Mark's Cemetery.

CHAPTER 15

Between the Wars

Now that the war to end all wars was finally over, there was less interest in summer camps for the militia. Moreover, a much greater proportion of defence spending was directed towards the fledgling Canadian air force and navy. Camp Niagara, even with the lakeshore properties, could not provide the space or resources of the much larger camps in Quebec and Manitoba. Nevertheless, and much to the relief of the local population, Camp Niagara resumed in the summer of 1921. The extensive wartime practice trenches on the Fort George Commons were gradually filled in[1] as were some of the trench works on the Mississauga Commons.[2] The Niagara Golf Club eventually reclaimed the latter for their golf links.

Two regular army units were assigned to Camp Niagara for the duration of the summer: the infantry Royal Canadian Regiment (RCR) and the Royal Canadian Dragoons (RCD).[3] The Dragoons wintered in Stanley Barracks in Toronto, but there was always great excitement in town when they arrived in the spring. Having ridden for three days from Toronto on their own steeds, the Dragoons usually assembled near the corner of Mary and King Streets. There the cavalrymen and their horses would be "spiffied up" before making their grand parade march into camp at the Centre Street entrance.[4] The officers and NCOs often brought along their wives and families, who would find accommodation in town and return year after year. There was much socializing with the town folk, including town socials, dinners, and dances in

RCR's garden party, photo, circa 1936. Garden parties in the compound for the military personnel, their families, and invited townsfolk were popular events during the Depression. Behind is the former Junior Commissariat Officer's Quarters, still standing today awaiting restoration.

Courtesy of Peter Moogk.

The Compound, photo by Willis Moogk, 1936. Within the picket fence under stately trees on the left is the former Junior Commissariat Officer's Quarters with newer additions. On the right is the former barrack master's house. Visible behind is the two-storey soldiers' barracks.

Courtesy of Peter Moogk.

the officers' and sergeant's messes, garden parties, and even "Christmas in July" celebrations on the campgrounds.[5]

In addition to improving their own skills, the prime function of the regular regiments was to train the summer militia attendees. After the war the overseas battalions of the Canadian Expeditionary Forces were disbanded and the old named militia units were reactivated. Eventually men from the original 81st, 98th, and 176th CEF battalions during the Great War became the Lincoln and Welland Regiment,[6] the non-permanent active militia in the Niagara Peninsula.

The militia units from the Toronto area still arrived by steamship, while those from southwestern Ontario generally came by train. With reduced resources for the militia, most regiments expected their men to supply their own uniform and boots and received no pay. Many of the trainees arrived only in threadbare civvies and often sub-standard shoes or boots, if any. This became even more desperate in the depths of the Depression. An officer of the prestigious Governor General's Body Guard, which did supply boots, claimed that "many men signed up to get 'issue' boots and the streetcar tickets to attend parade."[7] The infantry camp provided instruction in the basic skills: the various marching drills, musketry, target practice and general military etiquette. Because so many of the men lacked suitable footwear the route marches were limited to five or six miles.[8] The camp was still under canvas. For the men this entailed sleeping up to nine in a bell tent with only a ground sheet and three blankets. The official uniform for the men, if you could afford it, was still the khaki outfit with stiff collars and putties wrapped around the legs.

The role of horses in the military was soon to be relegated to strictly occasional formal affairs; however, until the start of the Second World War there was still great emphasis on training men to be "one with their horse." This not only

Camp Life, A Work Out, photo postcard. During and after the Great War, the cavalry was still an important element of Camp Niagara.

Courtesy of Peter Moogk.

included troopers in the cavalry regiments, but all infantry field officers and military medical officers. Most of the horses used for training the militia cavalry at Camp Niagara were rented from the Six Nations Reserve near Brantford, Ontario. The Ferrier sergeant had to inspect the horses, most of which were farm horses; not all were halter broken. The chosen horses were then transported by cattle cars to camp. One subaltern in the Governor General's Body Guard at Camp

Niagara in 1933 recalled being assigned to "rough riding detail," which meant attempting to saddle, bridle, and even ride the unbroken horses so that the horses would be ready for the camp's rookie incoming troopers. Of the two hundred horses that arrived from the reserve, fifty refused to be ridden and were "hidden" in Paradise Grove to forage for themselves.[9] The cavalry lines were usually set up between the ruins of Fort George and Paradise Grove because of the

Aerial view of the Military Reserve, photo, 1934. Aerial mapping of the country was an important project during the 1920s and 30s. In this view, the restoration of Fort George and Navy Hall has not yet begun. Two race tracks are readily visible, as are several trails. One of the fields northeast of Queen's Parade was a polo field while the town's baseball diamond can be seen within the larger track near the present site of the Shaw Festival Theatre.

Canada Department of Energy, Mines & Resources. Niagara air photo, 1934. Ca. 1:6000. Brock University Map Library.

ready access to water in the river. Much time was spent washing and grooming their mounts but for the most part they practised their riding skills or "equitation."

When not instructing, the officers of the Royal Canadian Dragoons practised their "Musical Ride" for which they would return to Toronto in mid-August to perform at the CNE.[10]

To hone their riding skills the Dragoons set up a polo field next to the fort. They also practised the ancient game of tent peg spearing.[11] Arguably, the ultimate goal of the cavalry was to execute an effective "charge" upon the enemy with drawn swords or sabres. The last recorded charge at Camp Niagara was filmed for posterity, but unfortunately the reel has since gone missing:

> ... one of the most outstanding pieces of filmwork I've seen ... was a charge we made in line down this big field and there was a post in the middle of the field where the fellow was standing with his camera. And I don't know if you've ever seen a couple of hundred horses with lances coming at you, but the guy's movie camera just disappears into the sky as he faints dead away.[12]

As with previous camps, the brass and bugle bands, as well as occasional Scottish pipers, were an important part of camp life. Many of the bandsmen were also taught as ambulance stretcher bearers. There were several highly regarded marching bands from the Six Nations Reserve that made the annual trek to Camp Niagara.

Aviation was not an important aspect of Camp Niagara. However, in 1936 the Governor General's Horse Guards[13] performed exercises during which low flying planes practised dropping "bombs" (bags of flour) on moving targets below (cavalrymen on horses.)[14] Between the wars, Barn Stormers occasionally came to town. These civilian-operated biplanes could land and take off from the grassy Commons. Rides were offered for a stiff fee; acrobatics and parachute demonstrations also were performed. On one occasion, to the horror of all the spectators assembled on the Commons,

the performer's parachute failed to open; on impact, the lifeless body sunk a foot into the turf.[15]

High school "cadets" also trained at Camp Niagara. For these teenagers the two-week camps under canvas were often their first trip away from home. The boys studied the military chain of command, practised drills, enjoyed the swimming parades, and might even venture into a tattoo parlour on Picton Street. There was a cadet corps at the local Niagara High School on Castlereagh Street. They often practised their marching drills after class on the Commons across the street from their school.[16]

University students attended Camp Niagara with the Canadian Officer Training Corps (COTC). These "gentlemen cadets," many of whom would eventually become officers in the armed forces, received military instruction during the school year and were expected to attend summer camp for practical training. Many had very fond memories of their summer sojourn on the Commons.[17]

Niagara River Parkway, photo, 1934. The old River Road northward from the John Street East intersection along the Niagara River was greatly improved in 1931 by the Niagara Parks Commission prior to the restoration of Fort George and Navy Hall.

Courtesy of Pat Simon and Joe Solomon.

During its long history Camp Niagara was fortunate to have several outstanding camp commandants and brigade commanders. Brigadier Oliver M. Martin, commander of the 13th Brigade, was particularly revered by both the campers and the townspeople.[18] An early riser, this impressive figure would often be seen touring the camp astride his white horse. Born a Mohawk on the Six Nations reserve, he joined the army at age seventeen as a bugler and worked his way up the ranks. After the Second World War he was appointed a magistrate. Firm but always courteous, he was much admired by both his officers and other ranks.

The annual rhythm of the summer camps on the Commons rolled along through the 1930s but the rumblings of yet another world conflict were getting louder. Meanwhile, to the northeast of Queen's Parade there was much activity with the restoration of Fort George and Navy Hall.

CHAPTER 16

Global War Again, 1939–1945

In the late summer of 1939, with summer militia camp just completed and the threat of war in Europe imminent, B Company of the Royal Canadian Regiment was ordered to remain in Camp Niagara. Within days, its commander, Colonel Willis Moogk, received orders to erect nine miles of barbed wire fencing on the Commons for an internment camp to house enemy aliens gathered up by the RCMP. After five frantic and strenuous days the job was completed and celebrated with a huge bonfire on the Commons. When Moogk called his superiors the next morning to announce completion of the job, there was a long pause followed by "Haven't you heard? It's all been changed!"[1]

Needless to say the locals would not have been pleased with the presence of a POW camp and the constant prospect of desperate escapees within town limits.[2]

Instead, Camp Niagara once again became the military training ground for tens of thousands of Canadian men and women. Most small communities in Ontario experienced a great exodus of their young people to the war effort overseas or to urban factories; however, Niagara-on-the-Lake became the temporary home to thousands of anxious soldiers about to leave for Europe, many of whom would never return home. For the sleepy little town of Niagara just emerging from the Great Depression, Camp Niagara provided once again a tremendous stimulant to the town's economy and psyche.

In many respects the Camp Niagara experience in the 1940s was similar to that of the Great War. However, with increased mechanization and more sophisticated weaponry, training became more specialized. Cavalry and horse-drawn wagons, although still present early on, were soon gone — the stables were converted into garages and workshops.

But this time, in addition to its traditional role as a training facility, Camp Niagara was to be the home base for regiments guarding the Niagara Peninsula's "Vulnerable Points." Throughout the Second World War there was genuine concern by the Canadian military that enemy terrorists would attempt to sabotage the major hydroelectric plants at Queenston and Niagara Falls or the international bridges, or that they would try to disrupt the flow of military supplies through the Welland Canal. Moreover, guard duty was required along the border to capture and intern "enemy nationals" attempting to escape into the United States prior to its entry into the war in late 1941. Many regiments stationed at Camp Niagara spent a third of their time training at Niagara and two thirds rotating through "Guard Posts" at sites such as Queenston Heights, Niagara Falls, Chippawa, and Allanburg.

Another innovation for Camp Niagara during the Second World War was the "electrification" of the camp. Candlelight was replaced by electric wiring and lamps in the officers' tents, messes, canteens, and quartermasters' stores.[3] With the canvas tents so inflammable there was always the risk of fire as the insulation on the wiring would wear off due to constant chaffing from the shifting tents. Fire alarms were frequent. With the cold fall weather of 1939 setting in,

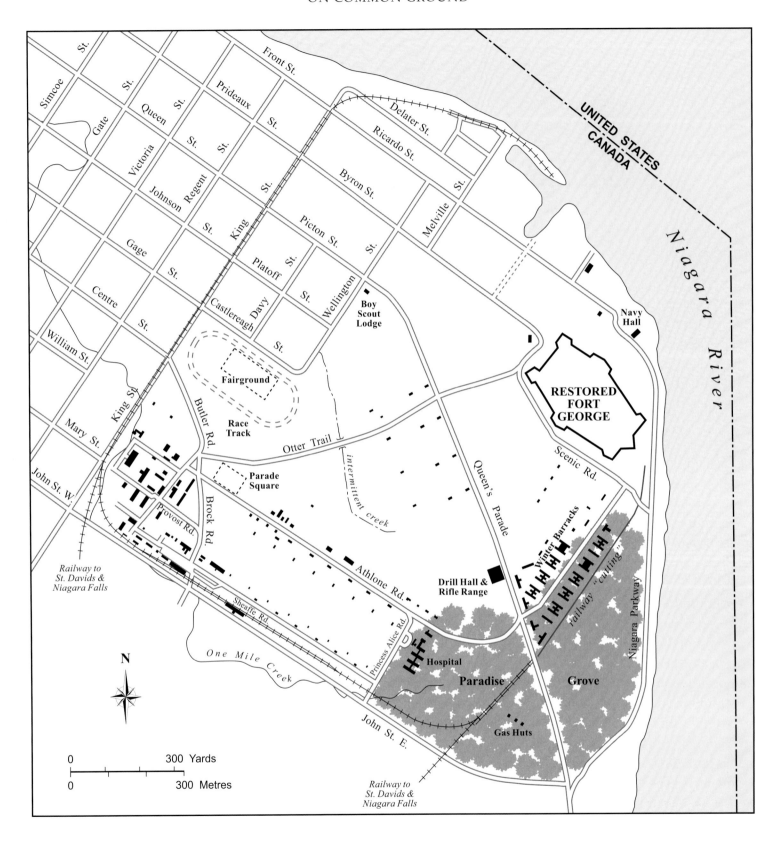

FACING PAGE: Military Reserve, 1941. With the exception of the restored Fort George and Navy Hall sites, Camp Niagara occupied the entire Military Reserve. As it was now a year-round camp, and many new permanent buildings were erected, including the avenue of H-huts between Paradise Grove and Fort George and the new hospital on the western edge of the Paradise Grove. Provost Road was eventually extended to meet King Street at the end of Mary Street.

ABOVE: The SS *Cayuga*, photo, circa 1939. During the Second World War, the SS *Cayuga* was the only trans-lake passenger boat still in operation. Thousands of soldiers and their visiting friends and family came to Camp Niagara aboard "the graceful lady."

Courtesy Pat Simon and Joe Solomon.

the ever-resourceful troops took advantage of the recently installed hydro lines by hooking up electric heaters, electric razors, and electric toasters to the outdoor wires, which overloaded the transformers. It wasn't long before the order came down from brigade headquarters that "All ranks are warned that, on no account will they interfere with electric wiring or appliances, either inside or outside of buildings in camps or barracks,"[4] and so it was back to basics. The use of candlelight and tobacco smoking under canvas would continue to be very risky practices.

As with the previous war, most of the soldiers arrived at Camp Niagara by steam railway or passenger boat. Only a few were brought in by bus or truck convoy due to the severe limitations on gasoline during the war years. The only railway into town was still the Michigan Central owned by New York Central, which cut across the township along

Concession 1, now called Railroad Street (see chapter 18). With connections at St. Davids and Niagara Falls, soldiers could be brought in from all over southern Ontario.

The only passenger boat still in operation during the Second World War was the steamship *Cayuga*, which made the two-hour trip across Lake Ontario from Toronto several times a day. It could carry 2,500 passengers and ran eight months of the year (see chapter 18).

Once the soldiers had disembarked from their train or boat they would fall into formation and march to the camp-site, led by their regimental band or, in the case of the Scottish regiments, their pipers, thus proudly announcing their arrival to their brothers in arms and welcoming townspeople.

There were some motorized vehicles in camp. The Royal Canadian Army Service Corps erected a fifteen-car garage and a gasoline filling station along John Street East. The Camp's fire truck had its own station. Jeeps and buses were used sparingly, the latter to transport troops up to the vulnerable points, although the men would frequently march to these sites. In July 1940, twenty-one new trucks arrived from the Windsor truck factory, and these were used primarily by military truck trainees.[5] Bren Gun universal carriers and even a Sherman tank arrived later in the war and were kept at the rifle range on the lakeshore properties.

As with previous generations of soldiers, the enlisted men were housed in canvas bell tents. For this camp the men usually slept six to a tent, feet towards the central pole on straw paliasses laid on floorboards. NCOs slept two to a tent while the regimental sergeant major and the officers had a tent to themselves. Some officers even had some camp furniture under canvas. The summer militia trainees continued to sleep under canvas throughout the war years. As the war effort dragged on and Camp Niagara became a year-round destination for the overseas battalions in training, more substantial buildings were erected. Eventually, ten large H-hut barracks along with outbuildings were erected on the Commons northeast of Queen's Parade, just north of Paradise Grove. A drill hall with a small indoor firing range was built on the opposite side of Queen's Parade. A new

military hospital was built on the edge of Paradise Grove. However, many of the century-old buildings of Butler's Barracks were also used: the officers' mess and quarters became the administration building. The nearby barrack officer's quarters became the Nursing Sisters' quarters. The two-storey barracks, gun shed, and commissariat stores were used for storage. The compound consisting of the old Junior Commissariat Officer's Quarters and barrack master's quarters continued to be the headquarters. The previously abandoned flower gardens were rejuvenated, trees were planted along the parade roads, and even ornamental shrubs were added to help beautify some of the buildings' entrances.[6]

The Canadian Women Army Corps (CWAC) stationed at Camp Niagara was housed off-site in a large clapboard house on Regent Street, now the Morgan Funeral Home. A large coach house at the rear, a smaller residence on William Street, and the large house at the corner of King and Mary (now known as Brockamour) provided extra accommodation. The sleeping arrangements consisted of bunk beds with two or more women sharing a room; kitchen facilities were available for snacks.[7] Many of the CWACS (affectionately known as the Quacks) performed secretarial and stenographic duties in various camp offices; they were also assigned to operate the camp switchboard 24/7. Delivering the official mail around the camp was another responsibility.

Some women were trained in various trades with the Ordnance Corps, including motor mechanics and welding and would be paid accordingly. Although the CWACs had received basic training before being assigned to Camp Niagara, on occasion they were expected to take part in route marches and parades. Marching with the men could prove very frustrating: generally the stride of the women was significantly shorter than their male counterparts; hence, they were often out of step.[8]

The CWACs' barracks were strictly off limits to the men. A man courting a CWAC would have to present himself at the front desk, whereupon his date would be summoned. With so many men in camp, the women could be very choosy. Although the more highly paid officers were

Winter Quarters, Niagara Camp, souvenir card, circa 1942. To accommodate the trainees through the winter months, ten large H-hut buildings were quickly erected. This photo is taken from near the river bank looking westward towards Paradise Grove.

Courtesy of the author.

considered prime candidates, it was forbidden for officers to date "other ranks" … but then rules were bound to be broken, especially with affairs of the heart!

Married officers' wives and children were housed in private homes in town.[9]

Once the newly arrived active servicemen were unpacked and received orientation, training at Camp Niagara commenced with basic section drill, squad drill, platoon drill, rifle, machine gun, and hand grenades training. On the 30th of each month a new detail was added.[10] Some of the training was carried out at the rifle range on Lakeshore Road. As with previous generations of trainees these daily parade marches out to the Lakeshore Road properties were led by rousing regimental bands, much to the excitement of the locals, especially the youngsters who were often seen excitedly beating their homemade toy drums by the roadside.[11] If they were lucky the trainees would get back to camp in time for dinner in the mess hall. Newly acquired skills in defensive manoeuvres and tactics were put to the test in mock battles conducted on the vacant land to the

west of the rifle range. (This land has remained contaminated and posted "off limits" for over half a century for fear of unexploded ammunition from the Camp Niagara years. Now transferred from the Department of National Defence to Parks Canada, the future of these lands is uncertain.)

All units had to report to the dreaded "Gas Hut." This actually consisted of three buildings: a gas chamber and two gas stores and/or quarters, all of which was surrounded with barbed wire, in Paradise Grove at the south end of the camp. Here recruits were taught to don protective clothing and respirators in a fog of gas, but as part of the training they would also be submitted to the horrors of an unprotected gassing so that they would know what to expect. It was suspected, however, that the authorities were experimenting with various new gasses and antidotes that were tried on the men.[12]

One of the many strengthening and conditioning exercises the men were subjected to at camp was the occasional twelve kilometre parade march up to Queenston Heights and then back, sometimes in full battle dress.

Taking a break, circa 1942. Men taking a break during intensive training exercises on the Commons. The drill hall can be seen in the background.

Courtesy Niagara Historical Society and Museum, #2011.020.001E.

Gas huts, photo, 1939. The dreaded gas huts were three small buildings situated in an area surrounded by barbed wire, deep in Paradise Grove.

Courtesy St. Catharines Museum, The St. Catharines Standard Collection, S1939.44.10.1.

Although the militia would continue to attend the summer camps "the mood was more serious and the training more focused and intense."[13] In fact, during the Second World War the militia often formed a 2nd battalion of a regiment, many of whom would eventually be transferred to full active service in the regiment's 1st Battalion.

As previously mentioned, two-thirds of the regiment's time at Camp Niagara was spent rotating through the vulnerable points where they were billeted. Generally the men found the shifts in the guard huts very boring and lonely. They much preferred the intense training and camaraderie at the camp. As the war dragged on and the training of the active regiments accelerated, their guard duties were taken up by the Veteran Guards of Canada, considered too old for battlefront duty. Perhaps out of boredom, some of these "old guards" became heavy drinkers, which alarmed the townsfolk.[14]

A successful military encampment depends on three key components: discipline, dependable communications, and the good health and well-being of the soldiers. The Canadian army adopted the strict traditional no-nonsense top-down chain of command so characteristic of the British Army. The *esprit de corps* of a regiment required all components to act quickly and appropriately in concert with one another, regardless of adversity. Unity of appearance and the soldiers' standard of dress (for example, the "spit and polish" tradition that all boots, buttons, and badges be kept highly polished) all contributed to a soldier's personal pride in one's regiment. Soldiers, identified by special armbands, were also assigned on a rotation basis to serve as camp and regimental military police (provosts).[15] There was also tight perimeter security to attempt to prevent unauthorized persons from entering or leaving the camp. Although there was no actual barrier fence, the few roads into camp were controlled by guards manning special gates. It was always tempting for locals to take shortcuts across the camp.

When a new regiment arrived, one of the very first duties was for the regimental signallers to establish and operate their own field switchboard for communications with all units within the regiment, but also with the main central camp switchboard and with the vulnerable points installations throughout the Niagara Peninsula. From the 6:00 a.m. wake-up call of reveille to the lights out reminder at night, the regimental buglers continued to play an important role in the daily routine of the soldiers.[16] Buglers called the men to meals, marches, and even announced the arrival of the mail. Lyrics were often matched to the distinctive calls that became such a part of their everyday existence: one ditty for the mail call ran, "a letter for me, a letter for you, a letter from Lousy Lizzie." The Scottish regiments had their pipes and drums to play their distinctive calls.[17] Traditional "dinner sets" were also played in the officers' mess. Depending on the wind direction, the frequent bugle and pipe calls could be heard throughout much of the town. In fact, citizens of Youngstown, New York, across the river, bemoaned the loud early-morning skirling bagpipe calls emanating from Camp Niagara.[18] Of course similar wake-up calls would also be heard coming from the American training camp at Fort Niagara after 1941.

Song at Twilight, Niagara, souvenir card, circa 1940. The Scottish regiments always had their pipers who could be heard throughout town and across the river.

Courtesy of the author.

The health of the men and women was of prime concern. The regimental medical officer was responsible for the welfare of his servicemen, and any concerns were to be reported to the camp's commanding officer, stat. Vaccinations and inoculations were kept up to date. All men's hair was to be kept short. In good weather barbers would be seen cutting hair outside under a shady tree. An enterprising barber could perform seventy haircuts per day.[19] The new arrivals were subjected to lectures and graphic movies on the spectre of venereal diseases.

Understandably, special attention was paid to the men's feet, with special instructions issued that feet were to be bathed daily and clean socks worn. Daily showers were supplemented with the mandatory use of footbaths containing antiseptics, which were changed daily. However, many soldiers complained that such communal immersions only increased the risk of athletes' foot.[20] Special care was also given to the proper fitting of soldiers' boots.

A new hospital building (the eighth hospital to be built on the Commons) was erected on the edge of Paradise

Camp Life, "NEXT," photo postcard, circa 1915. Throughout its ninety-five-year history, outdoor haircuts were a tradition at Camp Niagara. In this scene the impromptu barbershop has been set up on the edge of Paradise Grove. Here the men appear to be in civvies and the barber and two of the customers are wearing the straw "cow's breakfast" hats.

Courtesy of the author.

Grove, and included a thirty-six-bed open ward and a twenty-eight-bed isolation ward for those with communicable diseases. Even a fully equipped operating room was available. Regimental physicians and Nursing Sisters of the Royal Canadian Army Medical Corps staffed the hospital. The Sisters' residence near the administrative headquarters was strictly out of bounds to all others.[21]

The Royal Canadian Army Medical Corps with the Ambulance Corps and Casualty Clearing Stations also trained at Camp Niagara. Unlike the horse-drawn ambulance wagons of the Great War, ambulances now were usually jeeps or small trucks often identified by a large red cross. Mock battles offered a great opportunity for field ambulance trainees to practise their newly acquired skills on mock or "notional" injuries. The commonest real wounds were embedded thorns acquired from the many native French hawthorn trees on the various camp sites.

Feeling ill, one would have the option to go on "sick parade." After waiting for breakfast to be finished, you would report to a superior that you were not feeling well and then be escorted to the military hospital. Usually after a cursory exam by a camp doctor one would be instructed to go home and take an aspirin. Consequently, unless desperately ill, most trainees would simply avoid sick parade.[22] Moreover, too many days on sick parade would draw suspicions of malingering from one's comrades.

The food at camp was generally wholesome and plentiful — all prepared on the premises. Soups and stews were popular fare in order to use up leftovers, even incorporating the skins of vegetables normally discarded.[23] Recycling was a necessity during the war years so even the cooking fats were either reused or sold for the manufacture of soaps and glycerine-based products including explosives. With all their rigorous activities, the campers would always have good appetites; the trainees could have as much food as they wanted as long as they ate everything they took. The method of cleansing their eating utensils also followed strict regulations. After scrapping off their mess tin plate and cutlery, the utensils were dipped into a bucket of hot soapy water, then a

bucket of chlorine water solution followed by a third bucket of clean water and dried by simply waving them in the air as they walked back to their tent or barracks.[24] In the officers' mess, the meal was served and entirely different protocol observed, befitting an "officer and a gentleman."

Without indoor plumbing, outhouses were still much in use — the "honey pots" emptied daily by a contactor from town.

The mental health of the recruits was always a concern. For many, Camp Niagara was their first experience away from home and their loved ones. The ever-present spectre of impending warfare, the strict discipline, and the lack of privacy all weighed heavily on the minds of many. The YMCA set up a special area for the writing of letters and even supplied the stationery. The Salvation Army was always there for support. In an effort to meet the spiritual needs of the men and women, church parades were held with separate services for Protestants (St. Andrews, St. Mark's and Grace United), Roman Catholics (St. Vincent), and Jewish personnel. After their respective services, the troops would reassemble at the old Fair Ground's Race Track (now the site of the Veterans' Carnochan sub-division) and march through downtown Niagara-on-the-Lake for a "march past" before dismissal. In the warmer weather, ecumenical Drumhead services were sometimes conducted by regimental padres on the Commons for soldiers and townspeople.

In camp, amateur theatricals and professional concerts[25] were staged and movies were shown weekly in the recreation centre. In 1941 the Brock Movie Theatre (now the Royal George) opened, providing welcome entertainment for soldiers and locals alike. Many local organizations invited off-duty men and women to social activities in town including card games, dances, and theatrical productions; during the summer, strawberry socials, garden parties, and Friday and Saturday night dances in Simcoe Park welcomed the soldiers. The General Nelles branch of the local Legion opened its doors to the enlisted men as well. Starting in 1940, the Legion sponsored the Sunday Evening Song Service (SESS) in Simcoe Park during the warm summer months. Sacred and patriotic music with words projected onto a screen were performed by military bands or local musicians. These rousing sing-alongs, usually led by Archie and Charles Haines,[26] were enjoyed by all. At the season's finale in September over two thousand people would be in attendance.[27] In the winter the locals and soldiers could skate to music on the ice rinks on the Commons or in Simcoe Park.

Many of the off-duty trainees would relieve some of their stress with a pint or two. The wet canteens and messes in camp had strictly controlled hours of operation. Some of the local hotels, restaurants, and beer parlours welcomed soldiers, but many were "Out of Bounds."[28]

If a soldier were lucky enough to obtain a temporary pass out of camp, he could hitchhike in his uniform to St. Catharines, Niagara Falls, or even Buffalo for a few hours of shopping and recreation.

Sports also played an important role in relieving stress for the soldiers. League softball games with the other regiments, as well as civic teams, track and field events, hockey, soccer, boxing, and judo were all available.

Occasionally there were visitor days. Friends and loved ones would usually arrive by the *Cayuga* and be met at the dock by taxis owned by Tom May and Steve Sherlock for transport to the camp.[29] Inspection of their living quarters and a tour of camp would be de rigeur; sometimes a demonstration practice, tattoo, or a march past would be performed for visitors and townspeople alike. Many souvenir shops in town catered to the servicemen and their families. The day would end with fond farewells. Some would never see their loved ones again, as many regiments were mobilized to Europe directly from Camp Niagara.

Another diversion for the servicemen was the War Savings Certificate campaign to help finance the war effort. In an effort to remind and encourage civilians to participate, the soldiers would march through the neighbouring cities of St. Catharines and Niagara Falls followed by a few army vehicles and an ambulance. Of course the officers and enlisted men would also be encouraged to buy the Victory Bonds, thus setting an example to the civilian population.[30]

Despite all these activities and support for the troops, tragedies still occurred. Kaye Toye, who has lived most of her life in the Dickson-Potter Cottage on John Street across from the Commons, recalls one peaceful summer afternoon suddenly being shattered by a single gunshot from the

Hockey players in camp for training, photo by Jack Williams, 1940. Toronto Maple Leaf hockey players including Red Horner, Syl Apps, Turk Broda, and Art Jackson get some rugby tips while in camp for military training.

Courtesy St. Catharines Museum, The St. Catharines Standard Collection, S1940. 30.4.3.

Special guests, photo, 1940. The monotony of camp routine was sometimes relieved by visits of VIPs. In August 1940, Governor General the Earl of Athlone and his wife visited Camp Niagara. This photo was taken at the corner of King and Queen Streets looking across towards Simcoe Park. Note the railway tracks through the intersection.

Courtesy of the Judith Sayers Collection.

direction of the enlisted men's tents. There was great commotion and she soon learned that a young soldier had taken his own life in his tent; his companions took many months to recover from the shock.[31]

During the summer fruit season, with so many young people away for the war effort, the local farmers were always short of help. At 7:30 a.m. farmers' truck would be waiting at the camp gates to whisk off-duty servicemen to the orchards for the day. The military pickers were well paid compared to army standards,[32] and they could eat as much fresh fruit as they wanted. Many of these same farms also hired young women, known as Farmerettes,[33] an added attraction for the young men to work the orchards. As the war dragged on the Veteran Guards were also called upon to help harvest the crop. Colonel Willis Moogk, perhaps in cahoots with his subordinates, reported another good use for Niagara's fruit:

Military training is notoriously dry work, however, and liquor was becoming both scarce and expensive. Someone secured a local genius, who, with unwritten approval, set up a still in the camp. It

yielded an alcoholic "screech" which [was] mixed with Niagara fruit juices to produce a very inexpensive and authoritative drink. Distribution to the various messes was arranged, and life was good once more — until some wretch tipped off the R.C.M.P. News of the departure of two of their operatives on the "Cayuga" somehow reached camp before the steamer cleared Toronto harbour. On their arrival nothing could be found but an alcoholic odour.[34]

With the much-anticipated announcement of VE Day on May 8 marking the end of hostilities in Europe, exuberant celebrations broke out spontaneously throughout much of the world — Camp Niagara and the town included. The CWAC on duty when the news arrived reminisced that "the colonel came tearing over and was phoning for the Provosts to go and board up downtown, the liquor store and all that."[35] "There were men all over the [women's] barracks."[36] Two thousand citizens and soldiers attended a thanksgiving service in the park followed by a mile-long parade through town.

The 1,200-strong 1st Canadian Parachute Battalion returned to Canada after VE Day, and after a thirty-day leave of absence they reassembled at Camp Niagara in late July 1945 to prepare for duty in the Pacific. The men became very bored because "they had no weapons, no aircraft available for flying and no parachute equipment! They would roll call in bathing suits or whatever, then be dismissed for the day."[37] For many of the men who had just returned from the horrors of European warfare, "the sunny and warm summer [of] '45 made Niagara-on-the-Lake look like Paradise."[38]

With the announcement of VJ Day on August 9, similar celebrations erupted again in Niagara. Some of the soldiers headed to Buffalo and got themselves into trouble, and two sergeants were arrested by the Buffalo police. The commanding officer had to personally rescue them, thus defusing an international incident.[39] Eventually, the Parachute Battalion officially de-mobilized Camp Niagara.[40]

Generally, the men and women who trained at Camp Niagara and survived the war retained very fond memories of Niagara. Many often brought their families back to Niagara-on-the-Lake to look around town but especially to revisit the site of Camp Niagara — the Commons — and remember.

CHAPTER 17

The Final Years of Camp Niagara and the Military Reserve

With the Second World War finally over, the need for a year-round Camp Niagara with all its facilities quickly evaporated. The locals, at least for most of the year, could reclaim their Commons. Within two years of cessation of hostilities, the Department of National Defence (DND) hired contractors to demolish many of the camp's buildings, including the historic former officers' mess and quarters of Butler's Barracks. Shocked by such wanton destruction of the town's military heritage, the Niagara Town and Township Recreational Council purchased approximately fourteen acres of the Commons, which included the two historic buildings in the compound, and negotiated a lease for three other surviving historic buildings.[1] Meanwhile, the War Assets Board sold some of the buildings for removal offsite. Some were sold to veterans and converted into homes; one wing of an H-hut was moved to the corner of Simcoe and Gate Streets in town and renovated as the new Kirk Hall for St. Andrews Church. The camp's gymnasium was moved to Davy Street for St. Vincent de Paul's parish hall. Some buildings were moved to area farms to serve as barns or packing sheds. The large drill hall was dismantled and reassembled in Welland as the Welland Curling Club. Another dismantled H-hut was transported to Port Hope, Ontario, and used as an annex for the Dr. Powers's School.[2]

For years, the raised grass-covered foundations of several of the early administrative buildings along John Street West served as silent reminders of the extensive collection of buildings of Camp Niagara and its predecessor, Butler's Barracks. However, in the 1990s the foundations were leveled (to facilitate grass-cutting maintenance) with the promise from Parks Canada that the foundations would be outlined with flat stones — a commitment which so far has not been kept. The only temporary building on the Commons today, the small Company B barrack, was one of several constructed in the late 1950s or early '60s. All the others were eventually moved off-site.

Trees planted at Camp Niagara during the Second World War still stand as living silent sentinels along the interior roads and walkways on which tens of thousands of Canadian soldiers have proudly marched. The old parade ground is now barely visible and the small oval running track nearby has disappeared. Meanwhile, Paradise Grove has gradually reclaimed the lands once occupied by the military hospital and the gas huts.

The present-day Genaire building just off King and Mary Street was originally a canning factory on lands purchased from the town. Established just after the war, Genaire continues to produce aeronautical equipment. A veterans' housing site on the Commons, known as the Carnochan Subdivision or "The Project," bounded by King, Nelles, Davy, and Castlereagh Streets, was designated for returning soldiers and their families (see chapter 22). An adjacent piece of the Commons was set aside in 1949 by the town as a sports

Coming down, photo, 1947. One of the buildings of Camp Niagara is being dismantled after the Second World War.

Courtesy of the St. Catharines Museum, the St .Catharines Standard Collection, S1947.53.16.2.

On the move, photo, 1947. One of the buildings of Camp Niagara is being moved off site.

Courtesy of the St. Catharines Museum, the St. Catharines Standard Collection, S1947.53.16.1.

park and eventually designated "Veterans Memorial Park."[3] In 1965 the General Nelles branch of the Royal Canadian Legion obtained a grant of town land adjacent to Memorial Park for the site of their new legion hall.[4]

After a short hiatus, summer militia camps resumed in 1952 on the Commons under canvas. Camps usually lasted one week only. Many soldiers happily returned year after year. Although some militiamen and women still arrived at Niagara on the SS *Cayuga*, by train, or even chartered bus, most now came to camp in truck convoys, often towing artillery hardware behind. "Despatch riders" or DRs, who usually were veteran sergeants, often led such convoys on Harley Davidson motorcycles.[5] Arriving at the main gate, the campers were "told off" into platoons and then quick marched proudly into camp, led by a bugle, trumpet, or pipe band.[6]

One officer recalled:

In camps of those days, with Queen's Parade running almost north and south of you, envisage … On the east side of the road would be the main Orderly Room which was a large marquee and on the west side of the road you'd start with the officers' tents, then there were some QM tents if I recall correctly, then the bell tents for the enlisted men, and down at the other end were the Sergeants' tents and various messes in each unit, so there was a whole series of unit lines running at right angles to the Queen's Parade. And there were common showers, I just forget exactly where they were but I can recall them being set up in big marquee tents. And the latrines were old wooden types which were dragged there, brought there by truck and then dragged into position…. the female camp in those days was up against Butler's Barracks, just to the rear of the barracks. The Canadian Women's Army Corps usually occupied that, and that was their tented area.[7]

All training exercises during these summer camps were held at the Lakeshore Road site. Once again, every morning during summer camp, townsfolk would hear the soldiers with their marching bands parade out John or Mary Streets to Lakeshore Road. Just west of Shakespeare Street on the lake side were the rifle ranges, and further west (what is now the sewage lagoon area) was a rocket launcher range to practise lobbing blank shells out over the lake; the "stay away flag" was raised and sentries had to be placed on the lakeshore to watch for unsuspecting boats or stragglers out wandering along the beaches. Also on site was a steel Quonset hut covered with sod, towards which artillery would be fired. Officers inside would soon learn to detect the type and direction of incoming fire.[8] An old barn from the Great War period served as daytime mess hall and for storage. (Having survived decades of army use, it suspiciously burned down early in the twenty-first century.)

Challenging training courses in the driving of military trucks, Bren gun carriers, and tracked personnel carriers, including four Sherman tanks, were all carried out on military property south of the Lakeshore Road. Today this land is a peaceful parkette and cemetery. Although the Lakeshore Road training area was considered very tight, the site provided a good opportunity for the trainees to gain some experience with various weaponry and armoured vehicles.[9]

Competitions within the regiment and against other regiments were always popular events, as were the "end of camp" parties … one of which ended abruptly when a Sherman tank was driven over the embankment into the lake twenty-five feet below! Another camp tradition involved someone on a white horse, requisitioned from the local bakery or dairy, riding through camp as King William of Orange on the "Glorious 12th" of July[10] — an anachronism of old protestant Ontario.

Niagara has always been known for its voracious mosquito population. In the 1950s DDT spraying in camp was carried out by an outside contractor using fogging trucks, which would drive up and down the lines spraying the pesticides, usually when the troops were away. However, on at least one memorable occasion when a certain officer was still in the latrine, the sprayer's nozzle "sort of" hit the bottom of the latrine's door and "the door exploded open and out he came clutching his trousers and shaking his fist."[11] On other occasions the fogging truck would stall just outside the officers' mess. Herbicides were also sprayed particularly near Paradise Grove.

Other groups also used Camp Niagara during the summer — instructors and teachers of Army Cadet Programs attended camp. Wolf Cubs and Boy Scouts held nature treks on the Commons. In 1955 the 8th World Boy Scout Jamboree was held there (see chapter 19).

The last public function at Camp Niagara was the wedding reception for Warrant Officer Bill Bowman's daughter Gail and the young groundskeeper/fogger Mike Dietsch.[12] The Lincoln and Welland's sergeant's mess, on the upper floor of the two-storey Butler's Barracks,[13] was the venue for the festivities.

With the advent of the Cold War and proliferation of nuclear weapons, militia training in Canada radically changed direction. In the event of a nuclear war there would be limited need for conventional weaponry, hence, a new emphasis on "National Survival" and civil defence. Men and women of the militia now received specialized training in first aid, search, and rescue, particularly with regards to controlled entry into "bombed out" urban areas. A "survival village" was constructed at the rifle range to simulate a series of partially destroyed buildings so that the militiamen could practise their skills.

In 1964 the Minister of Defence released a White Paper calling for the militia to be the "back up" for the regular army and align their training with that of the regular forces. Regiments were disbanded or amalgamated with nearby regiments. A total of seventy-two militia units were disbanded across the country.[14]

The 1964 Camp Niagara consisted of officers only with specialized training in tactical manoeuvres. Finally,

Canadian Army Training Camp, postcard, 1950s. In the 1950s Camp Niagara was still a popular venue for summer militia camps and other groups.

Peterborough Post Card © H.R. Oakman, author's collection.

in 1966 Camp Niagara was officially closed after ninety-five years of military training. However, in April 1968 the Lincoln and Welland Regiment held a three-day "Exercise Lincoln Green" inside Fort George — the first time that the fort had been officially occupied by a military unit in more than 150 years.[15] Small weekend camps were held at the Lakeshore Road site well into the 1970s. Finally in 1969 the jurisdiction of the site was officially transferred from DND to Parks Canada. The Fort George Military Reserve was now truly a commons.

Camp Niagara was never a large, important military base like Valcartier, Petawawa, or Borden. However, because of its compact size, picturesque location, and the strong military heritage of the site, Camp Niagara was always the favourite destination of the men and women trainees. As

one commanding officer noted, "You could go down there for a week and do your training and you'd come back feeling that you belonged to something important. And that's the essence of a militia camp."[16]

Many years later a memorial cairn was erected on the Commons with the inscription:

THEY WILL NEVER KNOW THE BEAUTY OF THIS PLACE, SEE THE SEASONS CHANGE, ENJOY NATURE'S CHORUS. ALL WE ENJOY WE OWE TO THEM, MEN AND WOMEN WHO LIE BURIED IN THE EARTH OF FOREIGN LAND AND IN THE SEVEN SEAS. DEDICATED TO THE MEMORY OF CANADIANS WHO DIED OVERSEAS IN THE SERVICE OF THEIR COUNTRY AND SO PRESERVED OUR HERITAGE.

CHAPTER 18

By Water and By Rail

Camp Niagara was a successful military camp in part because of its ready railway access and the introduction of large trans-lake passenger steamships.

BY WATER

Indigenous peoples plied the waters of Lake Ontario in their bark canoes long before the French introduced sailing vessels as they expanded west of the St. Lawrence Valley. In the early 1700s the isolated and struggling Fort Niagara at the mouth of the Niagara River was completely dependent on sailing ships supplying provisions, ammunition, and military reinforcements, as well as shipping out valuable beaver pelts harvested in North America's hinterland. With the defeat of the French in the Seven Years' War and a verbal treaty with the Seneca nation, the British established Navy Hall on the west bank of the Niagara River. Thanks to a ready supply of oak trees, a hastily constructed shipyard was soon busy repairing and building new vessels for the Provincial Marine.[1] By the time Niagara was the capital of Upper Canada, most of the ships on Lake Ontario were operated by the Provincial Marine, transporting military and civilian personnel as well as various trade goods; a few cargo ships were owned by enterprising merchants.[2] During the War of 1812 the American capture of York and Niagara was accomplished by amphibious invasions from the lake; although, for most of the war the British and American navies chased one another about the lake without any actual naval engagement.[3]

After the war the Rush-Bagot Agreement of 1817 severely curtailed naval activity on Lake Ontario. However, commercial traffic on the lake quickly revived. Sailing vessels, mostly schooners, continued to ply the waters of Lake Ontario, but the 1816 launch of the *Frontenac*, the first steamship on the lake, signalled a new era in passenger transportation. Queenston-born John Hamilton[4] and several competitors built and operated increasingly larger and more efficient steamships, which offered regular comfortable passenger service between the growing communities of Niagara, York, Kingston, and Prescott.[5]

In addition to their regular runs, steamships would occasionally be called upon for special duty. On a cold December day in 1837 locals were surprised to see the steamship *Transit*, which they knew had already been laid up for winter in Toronto, approaching Niagara. With news that Mackenzie's rebellion had broken out in Toronto, 250 men of the local militia were called out and left immediately aboard the *Transit*.[6] Another steamer, the *Britannica*, also set out with great fanfare with one hundred volunteers of militia troopers plus twenty horses aboard, only to be turned back by a violent storm.[7]

Five years earlier the Niagara Harbour and Dock Company (NHDC) had been formed at Niagara. It drained and reclaimed forty acres of marshland and became a major

Fort Niagara, photo, Cosmo Condina, 2011. For nearly three hundred years the "French Castle" has stood guard at the mouth of the Niagara River.

Courtesy of Cosmo Condina.

ship building concern on the waterfront (see chapter 21). By the 1850s, however, the steamship companies were confronted by growing competition for passengers and freight from the emerging railways. Local businessman Samuel Zimmerman purchased the assets of the bankrupt NHDC and extended the railway to Niagara in an effort to coordinate the schedules of the two modes of transportation and attract more customers. After Zimmerman's untimely death, Captain Duncan Milloy[8] gained control of the Niagara dock from which he operated his *City of Toronto*.[9] The mercantile business in Niagara was in serious decline due to the Welland Canal and loss of the county seat. Nevertheless, the Town of Niagara continued to be a regular stopover point for the popular pilgrimage-like excursions from Toronto to Queenston and the battlefield of Queenston Heights. One commentator described the excitement and anticipation of the visit of HRH Edward, the Prince of Wales to the new Brock's Monument in September 1860:

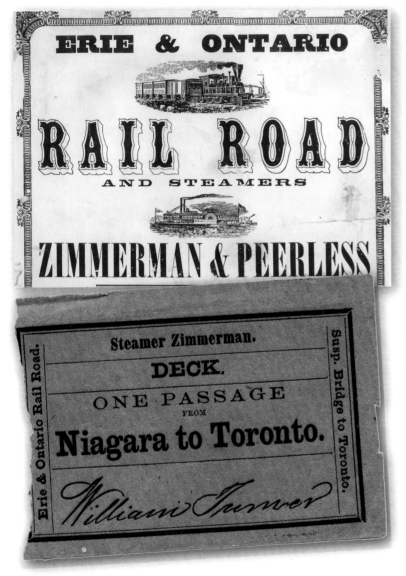

TOP: Rail Road and Steamers, advertisement, circa 1854. Entrepreneur Samuel Zimmerman coordinated the schedule of his Erie and Ontario Railroad with trans-lake steamers, thus making Niagara an important transportation hub.

Courtesy of the Niagara Historical Society and Museum, #988.5.208.

BOTTOM: Rail Road and Steamship ticket, paper, circa 1860. This is part of a ticket for one passage from the Suspension Bridge station at Niagara Falls to the Town of Niagara via the Erie & Ontario Rail Road and then by the Steamship *Zimmerman* to Toronto.

Courtesy of Roger Harrison.

… the steamer *Peerless* left Toronto at the early hour of five o'clock, yet with 500 passengers, a motley gathering of civil and military, volunteer rifles, a Highland company, Yorkville cavalry and many veterans of 1812, dressed many of them in the uniforms of their times. Rival pipers appeared and in the language of the newspaper account of the day the air seemed alive with the shrillest and most maddening music that ever was invented. At Port Dalhousie a company of St. Catharines Rifles joined them with a band, and at Niagara another addition was made and on nearing Queenston it was seen that the heights were dark with people.[10]

And after the speeches and unveilings the Prince embarked on the *Zimmerman* under Captain Milloy for Niagara, where:

… a handsome arch had been erected and also a pavilion on the wharf. A band of pretty little girls strewed flowers before the Prince and school children sang God Save the Queen … and the Mayor read the address …[11]

One of the prime reasons for choosing the old Military Reserve at Niagara as a site for annual summer camps for militia was its ready access to water transportation. Thousands of soldiers with all their equipment would have to be transported back and forth from Toronto. The Milloy family's lone passenger ship could not meet the need, and so the Niagara Navigation Company (NNC) emerged.

The first boat in its fleet was the *Chicora*, the "Land of Flowers." Built in England, she initially served as a successful Confederate blockade runner into Charleston, South Carolina. With the American Civil War over, she was cut in half to pass through the canals into the Great Lakes. Reassembled, this 210-foot side-wheeler transported troops for the Red River Expedition during the first Riel Rebellion in Manitoba, 1869–1870. Purchased by the NNC in 1878, the *Chicora* spent its last forty years on the more peaceful Lake Ontario run.[12] Initially the NNC was refused landing rights at the Niagara Dock and ran from Toronto to Lewiston/Queenston. Responding to demand, a second boat, the *Cibola*, was added to the fleet, followed by her sister ship, the *Chippewa*,[13] described as a floating palace with a 192-foot salon. By then the ships were allowed to dock at Niagara. When the *Cibola* burned at her berth in Lewiston in 1895 she was replaced by the *Corona* the following year. At the turn of the century, all three ships of the NNC's fleet — all their ships' names began with *C* and ended in an *A* — operated on the Toronto-Niagara run and offered six round-trips a day with a full load of passengers and freight.[14]

The Pan American Exposition in Buffalo in 1901 popularized the water and rail route between Toronto and Buffalo. In response, the *Cayuga* was launched in Toronto in 1906. At 317-feet long and capable of carrying 2,500 passengers, she was the largest passenger ship on the lake. A few automobiles could also be transported on the lower deck. Over the next half-century she would carry over 15 million passengers.

For the young soldiers travelling from the Toronto area to Camp Niagara, the boat ride aboard one of these steamships was a much-anticipated bonus. The various regiments would either march or travel by train or streetcar to the docks at the foot of Yonge Street. There would be much commotion — up to two thousand men with their officers barking out commands, as well as their baggage, supplies, cavalry horses, and even ordnance, would have to be loaded aboard before embarking. Once underway a military band or lone piper would often entertain the soldiers and any civilian passengers during the two-hour trip.[15]

It was not always a warm, sunny day with clear sailing on a placid lake. One young cadet on his first trip away from home recalled spending the night before sailing with some pals indulging in numerous banana splits. Aboard one of the side wheelers the next day, "the heaviest storm in many years" struck. "[We] arrived at Niagara a very, very sick bunch of boys. Boy, it was really something."[16] An easterly wind caused many a soldier to lose his breakfast sailing across Lake Ontario.

As the *Cayuga* approached the mouth of the Niagara River, a loud blast of her steam whistle would

SS *Chippewa*, photo, circa 1910. The steamer *Chippewa* was described as a "floating palace."

Courtesy of Pat Simon and Joe Solomon.

TOP LEFT: *Troops Disembarking for Niagara Camp*, postcard, circa 1910.

Courtesy of the author.

TOP RIGHT: *Troops Landing for Camp, Niagara-on-the-Lake, Canada*, postcard, circa 1912.

Courtesy of the John Burtniak Collection.

CENTRE: *Troops Leaving Niagara-on-the-Lake for the Front*, postcard, 1915. A time of emotional farewells as many of the boys would never return home.

Courtesy of the John Burtniak Collection.

BOTTOM RIGHT: *Are We Down-Hearted? No!*, photo postcard, 1915. Soldiers leaving Camp Niagara aboard steamer with contented mascot.

Courtesy of the John Burtniak Collection.

announce her imminent arrival. In summer months during the slow disembarkation process on the docks, young boys would dive for silver coins thrown by soldiers or tourists who lined the boat's rail.[17]

Once back on terra firma, the regiments would form up. Then, with flags and banners flying, they marched up King Street, often taking a circuitous route towards Camp Niagara led by bands playing rousing regimental music. It often seemed as if the whole town had turned out to welcome them, enthusiastically crowding the dock and lining the streets. Meanwhile, with another blast of the horn, the ship would gradually pull away from the dock[18] and head up to Queenston and then over to Lewiston, often to take on fuel before turning down river and making another stop at the town dock.

During the war years when departing soldiers were re-embarking ships for Toronto and deployment overseas, there were many emotional and heart-rending sendoffs as the steamer gradually pulled away from the dock. For many of these boys Camp Niagara would be their last meaningful life experience in Canada.

Quite aside from Camp Niagara's dependence on water transportation, the steamships, and in particular the *Cayuga*, held a special place in the social fabric of the town. The *Cayuga* always made her first trip of the season around May 24 with a boatload of people from Toronto. All the local school children and a few parents would then be treated to a free boat ride aboard the *Cayuga* up the Niagara River and back. Kaye Toye recalled the excitement of the day:

> This was the day long anticipated by every child.... Long before it was time to see the boat rounding Fort Niagara, we were all at the dock, standing tiptoe, breathless with expectancy. Finally the shout went up, "We see her, we see her! Look at the Union Jack flying atop the centre spar!"[19]

As another citizen remarked years later, "It was just the greatest thing."[20]

Throughout the summer season, the boats were so regular that golfers on the Mississauga links knew the time simply by the steam whistles of arriving or departing ships. With up to three round trips a day, thousands of tourists arrived daily to visit the town or proceed up to Queenston Heights for group picnics or connect by train to Niagara Falls and Buffalo. Some of these were family and friends visiting the soldiers on Sundays. During the summer local fruit growers shipped fresh tender fruit to ready markets in Toronto. For two special weeks in August 1955, international campers and visitors crowded the *Cayuga* during the 8th World Boy Scout Jamboree (see chapter 19). For the local citizens and servicemen on leave, the ships offered an easy and cheap opportunity to "escape" to Toronto.[21] For several generations of young people and the young at heart, the midnight cruises with live bands and lots of refreshments were indeed memorable. Some of these cruises crossed the lake to Toronto, returning in the wee hours of the morning.

The *Cayuga* was the last of the great steamships on Lake Ontario.[22] With the popularity of the automobile, and in particular the easy access of the Queen Elizabeth Way, the passenger lists dwindled, and after a few half-hearted attempts to revive the service, the *Cayuga* made its final crossing in 1957. There have been several varied attempts to revive regular cross-lake passenger service, but so far none has survived.

BY RAIL

The first railway in the province had been established tantalizingly near Niagara. The Erie and Ontario Railroad was chartered in 1835, running between Queenston and the Welland River; shortly thereafter it was extended to Chippawa on the Niagara River. It ran on wooden rails covered with iron, and the cars were pulled by up to three horses in tandem, so it was really a horse-operated tramway. Although it coordinated its schedule with a steamship at Queenston, it could not compete with the Welland Canal and soon fell into disuse.

Queen Street Station, M.C.R.R., Niagara-on-the-Lake, postcard, published by F.H. Leslie, circa 1912. The Michigan Central train chugs northward across the intersection of King and Queen Streets. Note on the left the Hotel Niagara, now The Prince of Wales Hotel, situated on land that was originally part of the Military Reserve/Commons and the great swap.

Courtesy of the Niagara Historical Society and Museum, #2009.030.001.

The entrepreneurs of the province were slow to catch the "railway fever" that was gripping the United States. However, in 1853 the enterprising Samuel Zimmerman[23] purchased the assets of Niagara's bankrupt Niagara Harbour and Dock Company, and with the thought of producing locomotives and railway cars at the Company's foundry, he revised the Erie and Ontario's charter. The track was upgraded to carry steam engines and it followed a new easier grade down the escarpment near St. Davids and travelled beside Concession 1 (later called Railroad Street) to East-to-West Line. Here it split with the main line cutting across country to the corner of John and King Streets. It then followed along the east side of King Street down to Ricardo Street where it then turned down towards the dock area after crossing over Delater

Street on a high trestle. A stone turn table[24] allowed for the engine to turn 180 degrees for the trip back up. At King and John Streets a collateral branch followed along John Street East. This line met the spur line that traversed John Street East and passed through Paradise Grove along a trench, "the cutting" twenty feet deep and eighty feet wide ending near present Navy Hall.[25]

Although the new railway did not save the Niagara Harbour and Dock Company it was a financial godsend for the town and ultimately made Camp Niagara possible. The local newspaper, *The Niagara Mail*, writing in the midst of the Crimean War, heralded the dawn of the railway era in town and compared the train's raucous steam whistle to "a scream like a Russian's, in the hands of a Connaught Ranger."[26] Eventually the railway was extended to Fort Erie and by railway bridge across the Niagara River to Buffalo. Passengers from Toronto could travel by steamship to Niagara and then take the train all the way to Niagara Falls or Buffalo. With connections at St. Davids and the Suspension Bridge station in the Falls, one could connect with railways all over southern Ontario, as well as Michigan and New York States. Conversely, soldiers from all over southern Ontario (and later

Soldiers boarding a train, circa 1917. Soldiers are boarding a train on railroad spur-line along John Street East at Charlotte Street. Note the cement bridge over One Mile Creek at the left.

Courtesy of Jim Smith.

Niagara Central Ry. Cars leaving Simcoe Park
Niagara-on-the-Lake, Canada.

Niagara Central Ry. Cars Leaving Simcoe Park, photo, circa 1920. A crowded electric streetcar is about to cross the King and Queen intersection.

Courtesy of the Niagara Historical Society and Museum, #2000.012.

Buffalo) could be transported into and out of camp in long trains along with their baggage, supplies, horses, and ordnance. There was even a Red Cross train set up as a hospital to transport seriously ill or wounded men out of camp to military hospitals. In the balmy days of this railway there were six passenger trains using the line daily,[27] and extra trains were added to meet the needs of the army. The men usually detrained along John Street East where there was a siding spur, thus accommodating two trains at the same time. On occasion the men detrained along King Street. The officers had their own train stop. Many friends and family members would also come by train, usually on Sundays, to visit their loved ones in camp. Military tattoos performing with precision on the Military Reserve also attracted paying customers. The same railway was used during the annual migration of wealthy Americans to their summer homes in Niagara as well as affluent visitors to the Queen's Royal Hotel. The many visitors to Chautauqua Park often arrived by train.

The railway line went through several name changes and ownership.[28] In an effort to keep the line viable, the town and township were on occasion called upon to purchase shares or advance funds to the railway to ensure its continued operation.[29] Nevertheless, as with the steamships, the railway eventually fell victim to asphalt highways. The last train chugged out of Niagara in 1959.[30]

For a period there was also an electric railway line coming into Niagara from St. Catharines. With both freight and passenger service, "the car" was used primarily by the locals on shopping expeditions and by some students attending schools in St. Catharines. Soldiers on leave could hop on the trolley to "escape" to the city. The line entered town near Mississauga and John Streets, travelled along John Street and then ran down King Street. The original station on King Street at Market Street still stands today. The electric power was turned off in 1931.

CHAPTER 19

Special Events on the Commons

THE FUNERAL OF SIR ISAAC BROCK AND THE CONDOLENCE CEREMONY

Perhaps the most sombre events ever recorded on the Commons were the funeral of Major General Sir Isaac Brock and his provincial aide-de-camp, Lieutenant Colonel John Macdonell, on October 16, 1812, and the Natives' Condolence Ceremony one month later.

It fell upon Captain John Glegg to make the funeral arrangements. Brock's body was laid in state on October 14 in Government House, the former home of D.W. Smith (see chapter 21) facing the Commons. Soon he was joined by young Macdonell, who had suffered a slow and agonizing death. On October 16 the funeral procession got underway, with detachments from the regular army, militia, and Indian

Major General Sir Isaac Brock, K.B. (1769–1812), miniature pastel attributed to Gerrit Schipper (as part of research by Guy St.Denis), circa 1809–10. Brock's energetic efforts to organize the militia prior to the war and his audacious capture of Fort Detroit emboldened the combined British forces as well as the population of the Province. His death at Queenston Heights created an enduring symbol of patriotism in Upper Canada. This is the only authenticated portrait of Brock as an adult approaching middle age. At the time of his sitting Brock was a brigadier general on the staff of Sir James H. Craig.

Courtesy of the Guernsey Museums and Galleries, GMAG 2009.52.

Department lining each side of the route from Government House across the Commons to Fort George. All officers were required to wear black armbands and black crepe on their sword knots during the funeral and for one month afterwards. During the procession, the Royal Artillery fired minute guns with two nine-pounders. Fort Major Campbell led the procession, followed by a company of the 41st Regiment and a company of militiamen. Next came the band of the 41st playing a dirge, its drums muffled and draped in black cloth. Four grooms led Brock's horse draped in ornamental coverings, after which came three groups: the general's personal servants, four surgeons, and Fort George's chaplain, the Reverend Robert Addison.

A team of horses drew the first caisson bearing the casket containing the body of Macdonell, attended by six pallbearers and three mourners, foremost of whom was his brother Alexander Macdonell. Brock's caisson followed, accompanied by nine pallbearers and several chief mourners, including Major General Sheaffe. Staff from the provincial government, civilian friends, and the general public followed behind.

After Reverend Addison read the service the two caskets were lowered into a single grave dug in the cavalier York bastion (known thereafter as the Brock bastion). At that point a twenty-one-gun salute was fired in three salvoes of seven guns each. (This was echoed by a similar salute from Fort Niagara whose flag was at half-mast.[1]) A twenty-four-pound cannon captured at Detroit was placed at Brock's head.[2] "A more solemn and affecting spectacle"[3] had never before been witnessed by the thousands of spectators present that day.

Three weeks later a Native Council of Condolence ceremony was performed at the Indian Council House on the Commons. Present were members of the Six Nations, Hurons, Chippewas, and Potawatomies, among others. Representatives of the Indian Department included William Claus, Captain John Norton, and Captain John Baptiste Rousseaux. Chief Little Cayuga was the chief speaker who presented eight strings of wampum and declared:

… now seeing you darkened with grief, your eyes dim with tears and your throat stopped with the force of your affliction, with these strings of wampum we wipe away your tears, that you may view clearly the surrounding objects. We clear the passage in your throats that you may have free utterance for your thoughts.…[4]

He then explained that he was presenting a large white belt of wampum to be placed over Brock's body to protect his remains from injury[5] and grant him a happy afterlife. Finally, on addressing Brock's successor, Major General Sheaffe, he pledged the Natives' confidence and continued support for his leadership.

SECOND FUNERAL FOR BROCK AND MACDONELL

Twelve years later thousands more gathered on the Commons on a "remarkably fine"[6] October morning to witness a similar ceremony. A Tuscan-style column had been erected at Queenston Heights as a permanent memorial and final resting place for Brock and Macdonell. In a solemn ceremony, the remains of the two were removed from the Brock bastion of Fort George (which was already in a state of ruin) and transferred to a black hearse drawn by four black horses, each with its own leader. To the sound of sombre band music and a nineteen-gun salute, the cortege slowly made its way across the Commons, followed by a procession of military officials, chiefs of the Six Nations, and civilian dignitaries, with common folk falling in behind. The procession to Queenston Heights took three hours and ended with the remains being deposited in a crypt in the base of the column. Poor Brock and Macdonell would be reburied twice again.[7]

PROVINCIAL AGRICULTURAL FAIR

When the first Agricultural Society in Upper Canada was formed in Niagara in 1792, one of their first acts was to encourage an annual fall fair as a celebration of the bountiful harvest. The Niagara Fair continued annually for at least 150 years and was held in various locations. However, in September 1850, with financial assistance from the town, the Provincial Agricultural Exhibition was held on fourteen acres of the Commons demarcated with a "substantial octagonal fence. The Floral Hall was 140' X 42', Agriculturists' Hall and Mechanics' Hall, each 100 X 24'."[8] A grandstand and half-mile racetrack were other features. Events included a ploughing match, presumably on the turf of the Commons. Some indoor exhibits and lectures were also held in the court house. In a predominantly rural province, this was a very important event at the time, even attended by the Governor General. The exhibition buildings apparently were soon taken down and the grandstand was accidentally burned by Camp Niagara trainees during the Great War. Nevertheless, fall fairs including horse racing continued at this site until the building of the senior citizens' apartments and the Carnochan subdivision in the mid-twentieth century.

THE DAY OF THE TORNADO

One of the greatest recorded natural events to hit the area was a tornado that swept in from the northeast off of Lake Ontario early in the morning of April 18, 1855. First to be hit were several buildings of the recently built Niagara Car Works at the waterfront. The twister then bounced over to the park where a large "Daguerrean Saloon"[9] was flipped over two or three times, scattering its contents on the Commons. The tornado then took off the roof of St. Andrew's church as well as the Angel Gabriel weathervane on the steeple.[10]

LOYALIST CENTENNIAL CELEBRATIONS IN 1884

A large proportion of the Ontario population still claimed Loyalist ancestors in the 1880s. Hence there was much interest in commemorating the centennial of the arrival of the United Empire Loyalists in 1884. Three specific events were planned. In June a three day celebration was held in Adolphustown, Prince Edward County to mark the actual arrival of the loyalists in the Bay of Quinte area. The festivities then moved on to Toronto for a day of rousing speeches and special exhibitions. On a sunny day in August, two thousand spectators gathered in a "glade in the Oak Grove" on the Commons. At one o'clock the invited dignitaries took their places on a specially built platform. Measuring thirty-six by twenty-four feet, the stage was dominated by

> a large flagstaff with the Union Jack in the centre and British ensigns at each of the corners. In front was a large painting of the Royal Arms, and around the platform were festoons of oak and maple leaves. Tablets on the sides and front of the structure bore the names of the men of the Lincoln militia who fell during the War of 1812.[11]

With this patriotic backdrop various dignitaries spoke, including Lieutenant Governor John Beverley Robinson, Senator J.B Plumb, local politicians, and two chiefs of the Six Nations who led a delegation of forty-eight chiefs from the Grand River Reserve (two of whom were in their nineties and had fought in the War of 1812). Chief A.G. Smith concluded his remarks with, "I firmly believe that the day is not far distant when the Indians will be able to take their stand among the whites on equal footing."[12] The program finished with five aged chiefs of the Cayuga and Onondaga nations, in their traditional dress, performing a traditional war dance followed by three rousing cheers for the queen.

CENTENNIAL OF THE FIRST PARLIAMENT OF UPPER CANADA

To celebrate the Province of Ontario's one hundredth birthday in 1892, the government of Ontario provided $2,000 towards the cost of two successive celebrations held in Niagara and Toronto. Recognizing that Niagara was the first capital of Upper Canada, the celebration on July 16 would commemorate the date on which the proclamation was issued, summoning elected members to the first parliament. Most of the dignitaries arrived by steamer and were escorted by marching bands through the gaily decorated town[13] to the Commons near the ruins of Fort George, where they were joined by a large crowd of locals. After the Lieutenant Governor read the original Proclamation there followed a royal salute of twenty-one guns by the Welland Field Battery. After a long rambling speech by the vice-regal representative, Canon Bull read prayers from Captain Joseph Brant's prayer book. Dignitaries and guests then "partook of luncheon at the Queen's Royal Hotel."[14] The party reconvened in what is now Simcoe Park at four o'clock when the premier of the province, Sir Oliver Mowat,[15] reviewed the history of Canada and spoke glowingly of the bright future for Canada as an independent country. The program concluded with short addresses by other politicians and the singing of patriotic songs. Although there is no reference in the official program, it appears that an exhibition game of lacrosse was held probably on the Commons sometime during the day, as there is an item in the statement of expenses for Niagara of $41 for "Lacrosse Match." A memorial water-drinking foundation was commissioned and this still stands on Queen Street today. A medal to commemorate the centennial celebrations was struck and widely distributed.

On September 17, 1892, the actual anniversary of the opening of the first parliament, an extensive program was held in front of the new provincial parliament buildings at Queen's Park in Toronto.

These various centennial celebrations were much appreciated at the time and their memories lingered. They fostered

Ribbon for the centennial of the landing of the Loyalists, textile, 1884. Each Loyalist attendee of the centennial celebrations on the Commons was issued a Red Ribbon to wear proudly.

Courtesy of Gail Woodruff.

an enthusiastic interest in local history that culminated in the formation of several historical societies which have survived to this day.

On September 17, 1992, a re-enactment of the first parliament was held in a sunny Simcoe Park, Niagara-on-the-Lake, with Premier Bob Rae and most of the members of the provincial parliament in attendance. A reception followed in restored Navy Hall.

BONFIRES ON THE COMMONS

Periodically, bonfires on the Commons have signalled to the townspeople something of great import. The progress of the Crimean War, 1853–1856, had been followed with great interest in Canada. When news arrived that the British had taken Sebastopol, "[a]n immense bonfire was made on the common,

a whole ox was roasted, and with bread and ale *ad libitum* a memorable feast was held in honour of the victory."[16] There was singing, dancing, and firing of cannon till morning.[17]

THE WORLD BOY SCOUT JAMBOREE

It was an inauspicious start. Hurricane Connie swept in off Lake Ontario with high winds and driving rain flattening the large canteen tent that measured one hundred feet by four hundred feet as well as several smaller marquees and bell tents. They had already been set up in anticipation of the Jamboree set to start five days later, but with the help of hundreds of volunteers the damage was rectified. The next day dawned bright and clear.

The 8th World Boy Scout Jamboree was the first to be held outside Europe.[18] The title "Jamboree" is derived from

Air photo of the Jamboree, photo, 1955. Looking northward across the Commons. A small portion of John Street East can be seen in the lower left-hand corner.

Courtesy of the Niagara Historical Society and Museum, #2000.007.

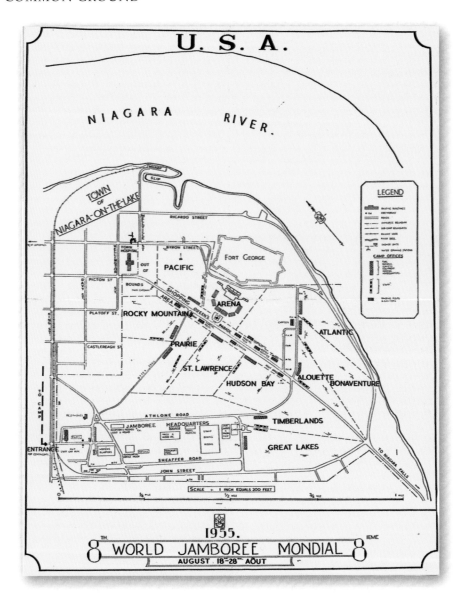

Plan of the Jamboree, paper, 1955. This plan shows the locations of the various sub-camps and the administrative buildings.

Courtesy of the author.

an American Native word meaning "a joyful meeting of the tribes" — certainly appropriate for this huge international gathering of scouts on the Commons during a hot August 1955. In the decades following the Second World War, Scouting was immensely popular. By the mid-1950s Lord Baden-Powell's troop of young men was six million strong and it was estimated that at least thirty million young men around the world had spent at least part of their youth in scouts. In 1955 Niagara-on-the-Lake was a very quiet, sleepy town. The mayor of Niagara-on-the-Lake, William Greaves, in his welcoming address admitted that he doubted if the town had ever been as excited since the War of 1812 as it was about the Jamboree. For ten days the Commons would be alive with 11,000 campers and 250,000 spectators who paid 25 cents to enter the campsite.[19]

The happy campers from sixty different "free nations"[20] started arriving by boat, train, bus, and bicycle[21] on Thursday, August 18. Probably the scout with the shortest distance to travel was Steven Scott, who lived on King Street.[22] Much of the Commons to the south and west of Queen's Parade was divided up into various sub-camps with distinctly North

184

American names such as Alouette, Timberlands, Hudson Bay, Great Lakes, Rocky Mountain, and Pacific. Two of the sub-camps were actually in part of Paradise Grove, which had been chemically cleared of poison ivy. Each country's delegation was assigned to one of these sub-camps. Most of the countries then created their own unique "gateways" to their campsite. In the section between Queen's Parade and Fort George a huge arena was built on the grassy turf.

A tiered three-sided grandstand seating 10,000 was built facing a 3,250-square-foot canopied stage, with a large deep-blue backdrop and Fort George's palisades beyond. A mammoth floral replica of the First Class Scout Badge using 5,500 plants[23] and the Flag Plaza were in front of the arena. Scattered throughout were canteens, showers, and toilets; along Queen's Parade were more canteens, a camp post office, bank, and trading posts.

Aerial view of the grandstand, photo, 1955. The tiered grandstand could seat 10,000 spectators with space for a similar number within the inner circle. The temporary facility was located between Queen's Parade and the restored Fort George.

Courtesy of the St. Catharines Musem, the St. Catharines Standard Collection, S1955.12.6.1.

In the rectangle between Sheaffe and Athlone Roads were the Jamboree headquarters, which included facilities for all the support staff. There a media tent serviced three hundred reporters, photographers, and technicians. The CBC transmitted live coverage of the Jamboree to its listeners and viewers by means of a ninety-foot tower erected for the purpose. The American CBS television network also covered the event.

The Jamboree hospital was set up by the Tri-Services Staff of the Department of National Defence in Parliament Oak School opposite the Commons. A ward of 102 beds was created in the school while tents were pitched on the school grounds for the staff. Before the end of the Jamboree, there were nearly six hundred visits and over two hundred admissions to the hospital. At least two patients were referred for appendectomies, and one photo-journalist died when he fell off one of the camp's media towers.[24]

The Niagara Parks Commission planted extensive floral gardens at the entrances to the camp as well as the previously described huge raised bed at the Flag Plaza.

The opening ceremonies for the 8th World Jamboree — with the slogan "New Horizons" — were held in the arena in blistering heat on the afternoon of Saturday, August 20. The chief scout and Governor General for Canada, the Right Honourable Vincent Massey, was escorted into the camp by motorcycle cavalcade, where he was welcomed by fellow Canadian Mr. Jackson Dodds, Jamboree camp chief. Also present was Olave, Lady Baden-Powell, widow of the founder of Scouting. After a short speech, the chief scout declared the Jamboree open, followed by a five gun salute from Fort George. He then reviewed the mile-long parade of countries in alphabetical order, each preceded by their flag and a plaque bearing the country's name carried by two Canadian scouts … much like other stirring march pasts seen at international sports meets. Within the large French delegation of marchers was a group of twelve blind campers.

The international importance of the day was recognized by the issuing of a commemorative stamp by the Canadian Post Office with first-day covers originating at the camp's own post office — 150,000 stamps were sold the first day.

TOP: First day cover, August 20, 1955.

Courtesy of the author.

BOTTOM: Badge, textile, 1955. This badge was presented to each attendee of the 8th World Boy Scout Jamboree.

Courtesy of the Niagara Historical Society and Museum, #2005.002.001.

On Sunday morning the campers dispersed to various places of worship. The Roman Catholic Church had erected an impressive chapel on the Commons to the east of the arena where two cardinals[25] celebrated Holy Mass. Three thousands scouts lined up outside St. Mark's Church while large numbers attended other church services in town. Non-denominational services were also held in the open arena. In the afternoon the town was open to the scouts: no admission fees at the museum, no golf fees, exhibition baseball games, water skiing, and boat races at the docks. Some lucky campers were invited into private homes for refreshments.

Over the next week the scouts were kept busy learning new skills and maintaining their own campsites, but also visiting other campers, swapping various articles, and trying to keep cool with scheduled swims on Niagara's beaches. Pick-up games of baseball, lacrosse, and cricket were common, as well as music jam sessions. One surprised American camper found a five-pound cannon ball when placing a dining table in the turf. There was a schedule of concerts performed in the arena, and each evening several countries would perform pageants portraying their history and culture. Understandably, the largest pageant was performed by the large Canadian contingent[26] portraying the rich history of Canada. On three occasions the scout troops from Toronto performed a pageant inside Fort George portraying the King's Colours being presented to the Guards regiment by "Brock." Most of these events were open to the general public.

All interested campers were driven by chartered buses to experience the various tourist sites in the Niagara Peninsula. On the Friday, using five trains and the steamer, *Cayuga*, nine thousand scouts were transported to the CNE where they performed a march past for an enthusiastic Toronto audience.

An emotional closing service was held in the arena on Saturday afternoon with a final concert in the evening.

On Sunday, August 28, it was time to make those final strategic swaps, exchange addresses, pack up, and start for home. Soon all 7,500 tents and other temporary buildings would be gone — only the packed down turf would bear witness to the fact that something glorious had just happened on this common land.

Fifty years later, a two-day reunion was held of former campers of the 8th World Boy Scout Jamboree on September 16–17, 2005. A reception and meet-and-greet was held at Navy Hall on the Friday evening. The following morning a plaque was unveiled near Butler's Barracks[27] commemorating the Jamboree, and in the afternoon a memorial oak tree was planted by the Niagara Parks Commission on the edge of Paradise Grove. A celebration banquet followed in the evening. This reunion was held on the same weekend as the annual Scout's Brigade. This encampment on the Commons has been held now for over ten years and usually attracts two- to three-thousand scouts from Ontario and New York State. A march through town in period costume and a re-enactment of a War of 1812 battle provide a valuable experience in living history for these young people. It also adds a little extra colour to the Commons in September.[28]

OUTDOOR CONCERTS

The Fort George Military Reserve/Commons has witnessed many military tattoos, concerts, and outdoor (drumhead) church services, often attracting thousands of participants and spectators. Moreover, concerts and pageants were performed in the ten-thousand-seat temporary grandstand during the Jamboree in 1955, and Tchaikovsky's 1812 Overture has been performed in Fort George.

As this book was going to press, it was announced by the AEG Live production company that on June 30, 2012, the iconic Canadian band the Tragically Hip would be headlining a massive outdoor concert on the grassy rectangle portion of the Commons along John Street. Parks Canada has reassured concerned citizens that the natural and cultural integrity of the historic site will be carefully protected. If well received, similar concerts may be entertained.

ROYAL VISITS

The lands that were once part of the original Military Reserve have been honoured with several Royal Visits. His Royal Highness Prince Edward, Duke of Kent, visited Niagara and stayed in Lieutenant Governor Simcoe's canvas tents at Navy Hall in 1792. His grandson, His Royal Highness Edward, Prince of Wales, future King Edward VII, stopped at Niagara's waterfront for a formal presentation from the town in 1860. His Royal Highness Prince George, Duke of Cornwall, and later King George V, and his wife visited Niagara in 1901. Their son His Royal Highness King George VI and his wife Queen Elizabeth drove around the fortifications of the partially restored Fort George in 1939. Elizabeth returned as Her Majesty Queen Elizabeth the Queen Mother for a ceremony at Fort George to commemorate the town's bicentennial in 1981. Her Majesty Queen Elizabeth II and His Royal Highness The Duke of Edinburgh were honored at a Civic Ceremony at Fort

ABOVE: *H.R.H. Edward Duke of Kent and Strathearn* (1767–1820), artist William Bate, enamel on copper, 1810. The Simcoes reluctantly gave up their comfortable canvas habitation at Navy Hall for the prince's accommodation during his visit to Niagara in August 1792. Edward was the father of the future Queen Victoria.

Courtesy of the Royal Ontario Museum © ROM, #962.32.

LEFT: Royal visit of the Duke and Duchess of Cornwall 1901, photo. This photo, taken at the foot of King Street opposite the Old Bank House, shows the future King George V and his wife Mary about to board the train.

Courtesy of the Niagara Historical Society and Museum, #993.067.60.

Her Majesty Queen Elizabeth II and HRH The Duke of Edinburgh inspecting War of 1812 re-enactors at Fort George, photo, 1973.

Courtesy of Pat Simon.

George in 1973. His Royal Highness Prince Edward visited the Lincoln and Welland Regimental Museum in Butler's Barracks as well as Fort George in 2003.

CHAPTER 20

Sports on the Commons

EQUESTRIAN SPORTS

Garrison towns have long been associated with horse racing, and certainly Niagara was no exception. Within one year of the commencement of construction of Fort George, there appeared in the *The Upper Canada Gazette* for June 27, 1797, the following announcement signed by three prominent local citizens: "Races will be run for over the new Course on the plains of Niagara. A purse of 20 guineas, 10 guineas etc."[1] The races were run over three days in July. Shortly thereafter the Turf Club was established "to promote an intercourse of commerce, friendship and sociability between the people of this province and those of the neighboring parts of the United States."[2]

In a letter to the editor of a local Niagara newspaper in 1801, a "Sportsman's Friend" warns all unwary local "sons of the turf" not to be taken in by a scheming "famous jockey … capt. Skanundaigua alias Black Legs," who was known to frequent the local "bar-room"[3]

Following the War of 1812, "matches and sweepstakes" were reintroduced over the course near Fort George. A description of one such event during the race season in 1817 confirmed that horse racing had become one of the social highlights of the year for both the military and civilian elite of the town:

The charming music of the band of the 70th Regiment was heard. The officers of the 70th gave a dinner, ball and supper to a large party in their messroom [at Butler's Barracks]. Dancing was kept up till five in the morning.

Over the next several decades the Turf Club continued to sponsor races on the Commons. An announcement for the Niagara Race Meeting in 1840 records a list of stewards including officers of the King's Dragoon Guards, all excellent horsemen themselves. The races would be run over three days, starting at twelve o'clock. Various categories were listed for "one or two mile heets [sic]" for a host of purses and plates.[4] Spectators had the advantage of simply climbing the ramparts of old Fort George to gain a good view of the races. Someone recalled that the races could be viewed from the belvedere of the rectory of St. Mark's. Nevertheless, the spectacle of horses and their riders charging towards the finish line could be a dangerous one. An entry in St. Mark's Record of Burials noted, "1850 Aug. 8, Frederick Tench, died 5th Aug., in consequence of being dashed against a tree on the common near the race-course, in running a horse of Capt. Jones, aged 38."[5] An obituary in the *St. Catharines Journal* in 1858 noted the death of long-time resident, Adam Crysler: "for many years a tavern keeper in Niagara, was killed on Thursday last by the falling of the grandstand at the race course. Several other persons were injured."[6] Apparently, he was operating a refreshment stand under the spectators' stand when it collapsed.

Turf, with Jockey Up, at Newmarket, artist George Stubbs, circa 1765. Although this remarkable image was painted in England, the broad turf and trees beyond evoke the old racecourse on the Commons.

Yale Center for British Art, Paul Mellon Collection, B1981.25.621.

It appears that horse racing on the old racecourse on the Commons became less frequent as the British garrison at Niagara dwindled in size. The annual agricultural fair with its grandstand and racetrack on the edge of the Commons continued to offer horse racing well into the twentieth century.[7] The larger original racetrack in the centre of the Commons was incorporated into the golf links in 1895. A generation later, racing on the old course took on a modern twist when American summer residents would organize clandestine races of their fancy automobiles around the old track.[8]

Interestingly, even today aerial views of the commons reveal the outline of the old racetracks.

Polo is another sport brought to Niagara by various British regiments. Although not recorded, the elite King's Dragoon Guards probably played polo on the commons turf during their stay at Niagara, 1838–1842. Long time Niagara resident Kaye Toye recalled that "summer evenings rang with the sound of the polo mallets as the Royal Canadian Dragoons galloped across the polo field by Fort George"[9] in the 1930s.

But it was not until the 1980s when a real resurgence of interest in polo on the Commons was developed as a fundraiser. First, the field between the Sheaffe and Athlone Roads had to be converted into a regulation field at considerable expense. For several years the Chamber of Commerce ran

the annual event, and in 1993 it became the annual Heart Niagara Tournament.

Recently dressage and steeplechase have returned to the Commons. Although well attended such activity has reportedly damaged the polo fields.

The fourth equestrian sport associated with the military is "tent pegging." This is an ancient East-Indian sport apparently developed to improve an equestrian's battle skills. It involves a trooper riding at full gallop across a timed course on the flat and over jumps. Armed with sword, sabre, and/or

LEFT: *Niagara Race Meeting 1840*, paper, 1840. An announcement for a busy racing session on the Commons. Note the race session concludes on the final day with "gymnastics games" including "quoits," a blind wheelbarrow race, and a "jingling match" with prizes.

Courtesy of the Niagara Historical Society and Museum, #972.701.

ABOVE: *Goals on the Common, one Common Gaol*, paper, 1998. This was an invitation to the Annual Polo for Heart Niagara Tournament held on the Commons for several years in the 1990s. Walker Industries Holdings Limited was one of the prime sponsors of this "spectacular" fundraising event.

Courtesy of Walker Industries.

lance, the rider attempts to smite a succession of ground and elevated targets. Canadian dragoon regiments training on the Commons used elements of tent pegging to improve their riding skills.[10]

CRICKET

Another popular sport in British garrison towns was the game of cricket. Newspaper advertisements indicate that there were several cricket clubs in town: in 1837 one club met in Graham's Hotel, Dr. Lundy's Classical School had a club, and so did the Grammar School, which was close to the Commons. The Niagara Cricket Club was meeting in the local lawyer's office in the 1860s. Interestingly, all the clubs' executives seem to have been civilians with no military officers listed. One local boy, T. D. Phillips, apparently became best all-round player in the Dominion.[11] Although none of the announcements indicate where the actual cricket pitches were located, an 1843 map of the Reserve[12] indicates a "Proposed Cricket Ground" at the site eventually occupied by the provincial agricultural fair. With the British regiments leaving in the 1860s and the emergent popularity of field lacrosse, interest in cricket seems to have waned. In more recent years, however, a friendly match of cricket is played annually between staff of the Shaw Festival and the Stratford Fesitval, alternating between a pitch on the Commons and Stratford.

Baseball became more popular in the twentieth century. One of the first baseball diamonds in the area was on the Commons just behind the Boy Scout lodge at the present-day site of the Shaw Festival Theatre. As many as one thousand spectators would turn out for a game.[13] In the 1960s the new diamond was established as part of the Recreational Sports Park at Veterans Memorial Park (see chapter 22).

Cricket on the Commons, photo, Cosmo Condina, circa 2010. As a British garrison town, cricket was a popular sport on the Military Reserve. This tradition continues every other year on the Commons, the locale of a friendly match of cricket between the Shaw and Stratford Festivals.

Courtesy of Cosmo Condina.

GOLF

Many local golf enthusiasts are aware the Niagara-on-the-Lake golf course on the Mississauga Commons is one of North America's oldest. Yet for a generation, a unique eighteen-hole golf course, the site of many international tournaments,[14] was situated on the Fort George Commons.

J. Geale Dickson grew up in what is now Brunswick House overlooking the Commons. His grandfather, William Dickson, had been a prominent lawyer and merchant who owned much of the land along John Street East (see chapter 22). Geale had served as an officer in a British regiment in England where he had been smitten by the game of golf. He returned home in 1877, and along with friend Ingersoll Merritt,[15] laid out a few practice holes on the Commons across from his ancestral home.[16] A year later, the two enthusiasts with Charles Hunter, a Scot by birth, laid out a nine-hole golf course on the Mississauga common. We have a description of one of the first rounds of golf played by Dickson, Hunter, and four friends:

… a pony cart followed them from hole to hole, laden with every possible beverage which the human tongue could desire.[After the morning round, they lunched all afternoon, dallied over cigars,] by which time it was too late to renew the contest of the morning.[17]

Several years later Geale's twin brother Robert Dickson also returned home, and when the Niagara Golf Club was organized in 1881 he became first captain. It is important to note that at this time there were only five golf clubs in all of North America and all were in Canada: Royal Montreal, Quebec, Toronto, Brantford, and Niagara. Although the other four clubs were established earlier, the Niagara club is the only

The Hunter Family on the Fort George Links, "The Thorn" hole, photo, 1887. The members of the Charles Hunter family whose large home overlooked the Mississauga Links were avid golfers. Note the three caddies.

Courtesy of the Niagara Historical Society and Museum, #982.384.b.11.

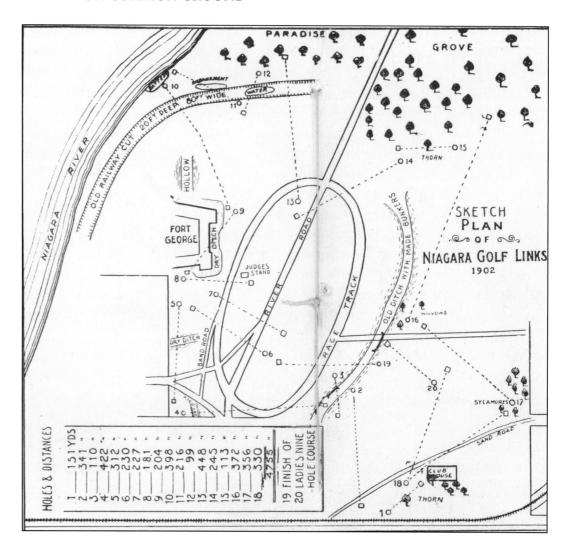

Sketch Plan of Niagara Golf Links 1902, 1902. This plan illustrates the layout for eighteen holes on the Fort George Commons. Note the club house is in the compound.

Courtesy of the Niagara Historical Society and Museum, #994.208-2-large.

one that still retains the original site; hence its claim as the oldest surviving links[18] in North America. In 1882 the Toronto *Globe* enthused that the Niagara club "bids fair to become the St. Andrews of Canada."[19] The following year the club played host to the first interprovincial golf match held in Canada. Nevertheless over the next ten years the club struggled to survive. For the wealthy Americans who summered in Niagara, as well as a few well-connected locals, yachting, tennis, and lawn bowling were the popular forms of recreation.

In the 1890s the sport of golf became fashionable in North America. Niagara, with its luxury hotel, the Queen's Royal, became a golfing destination.

Sometime in the early 1890s Geale Dickson laid out another nine-hole course on the Fort George commons opposite his family home. In 1895 the first International Golf Tournament was held at Niagara. The first nine holes were played on the Mississauga Course and then the competitors were transported by horse-drawn conveyance to the Fort George links on the other side of town. This was not too satisfactory so in 1896 the nine-hole Fort George course was converted to eighteen while the original Mississauga Links were designated for ladies only. Both courses apparently flourished, and in 1901 the visiting Prince of Wales (future King George V) was made an honorary member of the club but regretfully didn't have time to play a round.

Historian and golfer Janet Carnochan waxed eloquently on the uniqueness of the Fort George Links:

> Surely never had the players of a game such historic surroundings. The very names of the holes are suggestive of those days when, instead of the white sphere, the leaden bullet sped on its way of death or the deadly shell burst in fragments to kill and destroy. The terms used in describing the course — Rifle Pit, Magazine, Half-Moon Battery, Fort George, Hawthorns, Oaks, Officers' Quarters, Barracks — tell the tale.[20]

The clubhouse for the Fort George links was in the compound that included the former Junior Commissariat Officer's Quarters, still standing today. During the summer militia camps the building was also used as headquarters.

The men's trophy winner for the International Tournament in 1895 was American, Charles B. McDonald, whose grandfather had been a British Army surgeon at Fort George in 1812. In a strange twist of fate, two of his chief competitors, the Dickson twins, were grandsons of William Dickson who had been imprisoned by the Americans in the War of 1812. The female champion was Miss Madeleine Geale, described as "having the prettiest golf stroke among women players."[21]

In 1895 McDonald had won the prize for longest drive at 179 yards. With improvements in golf club design and construction, and in particular introduction of the new rubber-cored golf ball,[22] longer drives were inevitable and the length of the fairways had to be increased several times.

In the languid years leading up to the Great War, the golf course at Niagara was a very pleasant place to spend a summer's day.

> … the black man with roller, shears and cart, the caddies lazily or eagerly searching for a lost ball,

Golf Club House, Niagara-on-the-Lake, postcard, circa 1902. The eighteenth green was in front of the golf clubhouse, shared with the Camp Niagara commandant in the compound.

Courtesy of the John Burtniak Collection.

the scarlet coats, white shirt waists, the graceful swinging movement in a long drive, and the intent gaze forward as the ball rises, and falls true to aim to the destined spot.[23]

There was apparently room on the Mississauga Common for two courses, as in 1905 the Queen's Royal Hotel formed a second golf club. All this came to an abrupt end on the eve of the Great War as both commons were eventually converted into military training camps. Soon the links were covered in canvas tents. The commandant's headquarters occupied the compound full time.

The eighteen-hole Fort George links were never reopened although the club retained the lease on the property until the 1960s. Play resumed on the Mississauga Commons, initially operated by the Queen's Royal Hotel. However, when the latter was closed the 1920s, a group of enthusiastic golfers formed the Niagara-on-the-Lake Golf Club. Originally the course used only the perimeter of the Mississauga common with one green within the ramparts of the fort. Reconfiguration of the course allowed for longer fairways; the green for the second hole was still within the ramparts and there were at least two tees built on the ramparts. During the Great Depression many a local lad worked as caddies for thirty five cents an eighteen-hole round, but if the ball were lost, the caddy was held responsible and there would be no pay![24]

In the 1960s the federal government decided to renovate Fort Mississauga and convert the Mississauga common into a National Historic Park. Initially it was proposed that the golf club could reactivate its lease on the Fort George common and construct a new eighteen-hole course there. After much correspondence it was eventually decided that the golf club and the fort could continue to co-exist on the Mississauga common, provided that the second hole be relocated outside the ramparts and the tees on the ramparts be eliminated. In 2002 a new walkway was created from the corner of Front and Simcoe Streets out to the fort's entrance providing greater public access to the historic site.

Miss Madelaine Geale, photo, circa 1895. A local girl, Miss Geale, won the Women's International Tournament held at Niagara in 1895.

Courtesy of the Niagara Historical Society and Museum, #982.384.b-18.

Today the Niagara-on-the-Lake Golf Club continues as a privately owned club with a long-term lease from Parks Canada. The recently rebuilt clubhouse and pro shop sits on private property. There are few golf courses in North America with such a vista across an international river to

Fort Niagara and along leafy fairways towards an original two-hundred-year-old Fort Mississauga. Many club trophies have been awarded since the 1800s.

Any discussion of golfing on the two commons would be remiss without reference to one of Niagara's native sons, Lancelot Cressy Servos. As a young man he travelled to the United States, which was just starting to embrace the game of golf. A tournament champion and golf pro himself, he also wrote one of the first instruction manuals for golf.[25] He laid out and constructed some of the earliest golf courses in the southern states and also designed innovative golf equipment. For anyone who has ever picked up a golf club, the introduction to his book says it all:

> Time marches on. Man conspires, respires, aspires, and expires. During which sojourn, if he is fortunate he plays a little golf and perspires. He may get so he plays it well, or he may not get to play it as well as he would like. It is for those who would like to improve their golf that this book is published. For what gaineth a man if he acquire the whole world and yet is unable to play golf.[26]

LACROSSE AND BANDY

The Indian Council House in the middle of the Commons symbolized the covenant chain of friendship between His Majesty's Indian Allies and the British government. Every year thousands of Natives from much of what is now southern Ontario, and to a lesser extent western New York, would come here for their annual presents, to air their grievances, and to negotiate treaties. With so many young Natives assembled in one place, the wide-open grassy plains of the Commons were a natural playing field for stick-and-ball games such as lacrosse and bandy. After a long day of council meetings, lacrosse and bandy were often played in the lingering summer daylight.

Stick-and-ball games were played among First Nations long before Europeans arrived in North America. Lacrosse

Drinks the Juice of the Stone, in ball-player's dress (Choctaw, 1834), artist George Catlin, hand-coloured print. Various forms of stick-and-ball games were played among the indigenous peoples of North America. The Military Reserve / Commons with its Indian Council House was a popular venue.

Originally published in George Catlin, *Letters and Notes on the Manners, Customs, and Condition of the North American Indians* (London: Tosswill and Myers, 1841), 223.

may have originated among the Algonquins, but arguably the Iroquois became the masters. The Ojibwa called the game "baggataway," but soon after contact the French called the game lacrosse because the playing stick resembled a bishop's crosier.

In its early Native version, the playing field could be several miles long and hundreds of feet wide. The object of the game was to hit a single pole by the ball or to get the ball between two posts that could be tens of feet apart. The sticks, made of various types of wood, were strung with strands of spruce roots or deer hide. They were often decorated and were the owner's prize possession. The "ball" could be simply a knot of wood or more commonly a ball made of hide stuffed with hair.[27]

The game was considered a gift of the gods and had a strong spiritual component. Natives might travel hundreds of miles to participate in the larger contests. The men would prepare themselves physically, emotionally, and spiritually, encouraged by their shaman who acted very much like a coach. At the start of the contest they would strip down to their breech-cloth, decorate themselves in war paint, and take to the field. It's a small wonder the Cherokee called this sport, which stimulated such intense exhilaration, "the little brother of war." The only two rules of the game were there had to be an equal number of players on both teams (which could be hundreds of players) and it was forbidden to touch the ball on the ground with your hand. Otherwise, the sky was the limit. The famous American artist George Catlin, who recorded the demise of the Native way of life in nineteenth-century America, described a typical match:

> ...hundreds are running together and leaping, actually over each other's heads, and darting between their adversaries' legs, tripping and throwing and foiling each other in every possible manner, and every voice raised to the highest key, in shrill yelps and barks.[28]

The games could go on for three days. There were often thousands of spectators to watch such contests. Besides the pride and sheer exhilaration of it all, the winners were often rewarded with strings of wampum, bracelets, necklaces, etc. Sometimes Natives and non-Natives would place wagers on the outcome.

It was a non-Native Montreal dentist George Beers who felt compelled to modify and codify the game of lacrosse, specifying the size of the field, rules of the game, equipment, and so on. At the time of Confederation, lacrosse was so popular that it was unofficially the national game of Canada.[29] Ivy League American colleges adopted the game and exhibition teams travelled to England where it became very popular, especially among women.[30] Sadly, many of the best players who were Native were unable to play in the big "amateur" tournaments because they couldn't afford the travel costs yet couldn't accept travel subsidies.

By the turn of the century baseball was becoming more popular than lacrosse during the summer months. With growing enthusiasm for ice hockey, arenas were being built. This resulted in the introduction of "box lacrosse," which could be played in the empty hockey arenas during the summer. Today, field and box lacrosse are flourishing once again at both the amateur and professional levels.

It is not known how many spirited matches of lacrosse were played on the Commons by visiting Native tribes in the shadow of the Indian Council House. We do know that in 1804, poet Thomas Moore, the bard of Ireland, visited Niagara and was entertained by then Colonel Isaac Brock for ten days. Years later, he recorded that he accompanied Brock "on his going to distribute among [the Natives] the customary presents and prizes ... the young men exhibited for our amusement in the race, the bat-game, [sic] and other sports."[31] This may have transpired at the Fort George Indian Council House or farther afield.

The last recorded international lacrosse tournament on the Commons was held in 1860 between the old rivals, the Mohawk Nation of the Grand River and the Seneca Nation of western New York. There was "an immense" number of

Natives in attendance and "thousands of spectators" watching the contest. After many hours the Senecas won the day.[32]

The game of bandy is also mentioned in early references to the Natives at Niagara. In the Memoirs of John Clark,[33] whose father was barrack master at Fort George until his death in 1808, he refers to the visit of HRH Prince Edward to Niagara in September 1792. According to Clark, "The most youthful Indians entertained His Royal Highness and suite with a game of bandy ball and foot races, on the common of Niagara." Later Clark refers to this game of bandy where "there is a deal of animation and dexterity" as "resembling cricket." There were likely many variations of the Natives' stick and ball games: some perhaps similar to cricket, but others were probably more like field hockey or the more popular lacrosse.

HOCKEY

Informal games of "shinny" or "shinty," described as hockey without skates, were played on frozen ponds on the Commons long before the advent of organized ice hockey.[34] During the first half of the twentieth century there was an ice rink within the racetrack of the agricultural grounds on Castlereagh Street. Niagara produced several very competitive hockey teams.

FOOT RACES, WALKING, HIKING, AND JOGGING

Anyone familiar with the Commons today knows that walking or walking the dog are probably the most common recreational pursuits on the Commons today. Whether following the various established trails, many of which are now paved, or blazing your own path across the greens or through Paradise Grove, the vista is forever changing and the air fresh. Recalling the wonderful[35] Indian foot-races of days gone by, joggers may want to quicken their pace as they pass the Indian Council House site on the Commons.

CYCLING

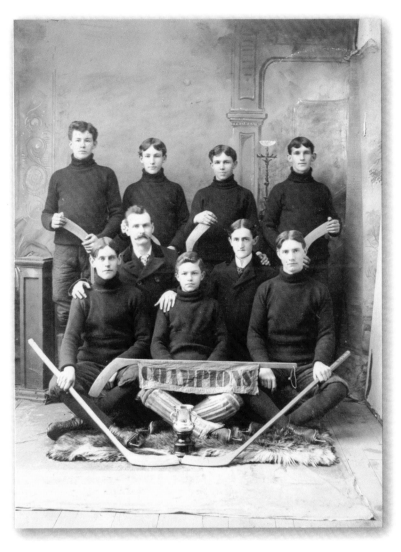

Champions, photo, circa 1900. Niagara produced several ice hockey championship teams who practised on the ice rink within the half-mile racetrack at Castlereagh and King Streets.

Courtesy of the Niagara Historical Society and Museum, #989.5.407.3.

Since some of the trails of the Commons are now part of the Bruce Trail, the Waterfront Trail, the Greater Niagara Circle Route, and the Upper Canada Recreation Trail systems, cycling on the Commons can be a leisurely pastime or

Early morning walk, Cosmo Condina, 2011.

Courtesy of Cosmo Condina.

part of a real physical workout. Since its invention, the bicycle has been a popular mode of transport in town used by locals travelling about, often cutting through the Commons to get from point A to point B. Because of the large size of Camp Niagara, bicycles were often used by military couriers within the camp.

TENNIS

The first recorded tennis courts were situated on the King Street edge of the Commons near the grandstand. Later they were moved to their present site in Veterans Memorial Park, where they are maintained by an active tennis club.

The Otter Trail, photo Cosmo Condina, 2010. The historic Otter Trail in autumn. Note the modern soccer pitches on the left. The grassy field on the right was the site of the Indian Council Houses and later the military and civilian hospital.

Courtesy of Cosmo Condina.

RECREATIONAL FISHING AND HUNTING

We know that for thousands of years Native peoples have had campsites at the mouth of the Niagara River primarily because of abundant fish: whitefish, bass, and in particular sturgeon. Off-duty soldiers would often be seen at the Navy Hall wharf trying their luck. A very significant commercial fishery also thrived in Niagara for over one hundred years (see chapter 21). Surprisingly, there was a spring-fed fishpond on the Commons just below the northeast bastion of the fort. Built of stone, the pond was stocked with fish and was the exclusive preserve of the officers of the garrison.[36] Years later an archaeological dig confirmed its existence. The spring is still there, but the pond disappeared long ago.

In earlier times boys would often be seen on the Commons hunting birds and various small animals. One such expedition ended in tragedy when twelve-year-old Master Stocking, while in the company of several boys on the Commons, accidentally shot himself in both thighs.[37] Joseph Masters recalled that boys often trapped birds such as pigeons, sparrow, and snowbirds in nets strung out on the Commons. The captured birds would later be used for shooting matches. "Not much sport for the birds."[38]

SOCCER

An early version of this now very popular team sport was known as "Association Football"[39] and was played on the Commons. Two regulation fields with night lighting now grace the Commons. So as not to disturb the possibly rich archaeologically original sub-soil of the Commons, much topsoil was brought in to top up the fields.

KITE FLYING

Wide open green spaces and a brisk wind will always make for an exhilarating day of flying one's kite, especially if it's homemade.

CHAPTER 21

On the Edge:
Overlooking the Commons

Although the Military Reserve/Commons at Niagara in 1800 was considerably larger than most contemporary commons or greens, it still retained elements of the quintessential village green because its large, open green space was bordered by public and private buildings. This attribute was recognized by citizens and visitors alike. A walk around the edge of the official boundaries of the Military Reserve on the eve of the War of 1812 would mean strolling from the river's edge at the foot of present King Street southwest to John Street, turning south, and then eastward along what is now John Street East to the banks of the Niagara River. With the exception of the stone powder magazine in Fort George, all the original buildings in the town were destroyed during or shortly after the War of 1812. Most streets in town were not assigned their present names until the 1820s.[1]

It is important to remember in the original survey, King Street was laid out with a generous ninety-nine-foot-wide street allowance (one and a half chains),[2] and was aligned due south-southwest. It appears that until the 1870s there was a guardhouse in the middle of the road allowance at the river's edge and at times a "Ferry house."

All the land bounded by King and Front Streets and the Niagara River was also designated a Military Reserve but from the earliest years most of the site[3] was occupied by the Royal Engineers' Yard. This "complex," rebuilt after the War of 1812, consisted of a number of buildings including the commanding officer's quarters[4] with various outbuildings, offices, a carpenter's shop, and quarters. As with the rest of the garrison at Niagara, activity here varied according to the perceived military threats of the day. With the final redeployment of British forces to other parts of the empire, the land with its fabulous view of the mouth of the Niagara River was acquired by the town in the late 1860s for the luxurious Queen's Royal Hotel.[5] Tennis courts and a lawn bowling green were laid out at this end of the property and became the venue for important international tournaments well into the twentieth century. The area fell silent with the final dismantling of the hotel and its sports facilities in the 1930s. The town acquired the property in a tax arrears sale and set aside this usually quiet idyllic spot as Queen's Royal Park, enlivened by annual Lions Club's carnivals, a community skating rink, and the popular "Niagara Lions Beach" for public swimming. These facilities are now long forgotten by most or moved to other venues; the park still comes alive with an annual art show on Canada Day. The gazebo was built as a prop for a motion picture shoot in 1983[6] but has become a popular fixture of the waterfront. The site has also been the starting point for many famous cross-lake swimming marathons.

Lot 1 at the corner of King and Front was granted to merchant Francis Crooks. Facing the Commons, an early inn, The Yellow House, also known as the King's Arms Hotel, was operated by Thomas Hind who welcomed many guests,

The Foot of King Street, artist Francis H. Granger, watercolour, circa 1856. Looking up from the river's edge, the Guardhouse stands in the midst of the wide expanse of King Street. On the left is the Elliot House or Whale Inn built on land leased and later purchased from the Niagara Harbour and Dock Company. This Niagara icon still stands today at the water's edge. On the right are the Gleaner printing office and adjoining Oates tavern. The green space beyond to Front Street is reserved for the Royal Engineers. Soon all the buildings on the right would be demolished to make way for the Queen's Royal Hotel.

Courtesy of the Niagara Historical Society and Museum, #988.189.

including the celebrated transcontinental explorer Alexander Mackenzie.[7] After the war the present building was erected and for many years served as offices of the Bank of Upper Canada. Somewhat altered, including the addition of a veranda, the home is now the Old Bank House Bed and Breakfast.

On the adjacent lot stood the town's original jail and temporary court house. Private residences now occupy the site.

At the northwest corner of King and Prideaux stood the Freemasons' Hall, described as "a neat compact building of wood and plaster."[8] When Lieutenant Governor Simcoe arrived in 1792 he opened the first session of the first parliament of Upper Canada in this multi-purpose hall with great pomp and ceremony. (The newly renovated Rangers' Barracks on the Reserve would host the remaining sessions.)

In addition to its prime function as a Masonic lodge, it served on occasion as a court house, ballroom, meeting place for the British Indian Department, and for divine services. In 1818 John Eaglesum erected the present substantial building of stone (later plastered and grooved to resemble blocks), apparently much of it gathered from the rubble of the burned town. It too served many functions in town including a store, a tavern, a private school, a public school, a grammar school, a dancing academy, and, during the Rebellion and Fenian alarms, as a barracks, hence its common name, "the Stone Barracks." In 1877 it was purchased by Niagara Lodge No. 2, A.F. & A.M., and has served as their lodge ever since. Today the Masons meet in the upper rooms, where they maintain a significant archives of early artifacts. The downstairs is currently leased as a gallery. Before 1812, inkeeper John Emery owned a portion of this lot on which he built a substantial house and/or inn facing the Commons.

Prior to the war, the intersection of King and Queen Streets was the most prestigious residential address in town,

flanked by William Dickson's Georgian brick mansion on the northeast corner and David William Smith's equally impressive home on the opposite block. Both residences enjoyed views of the Commons.

William Dickson obtained the half-acre Lot 64 from Crown grantee David Secord.[9] There, as early as 1793, Dickson erected his impressive two-and-a-half-storey brick

Niagara Masonic Lodge No. 2., postcard, circa 1920. Standing on the site of the original Freemasons' Hall, the present building, known on occasion as the Stone Barracks, has served many functions. The Masons currently occupy the upstairs.

Published by F.H. Leslie, Ltd. Author's collection.

William Dickson's house, 1815. In his extensive war loss claims, Dickson declared his town house was the first brick house in the province. The fine architectural embellishments of his home's front façade were remarkable in eighteenth-century Upper Canada.

Library and Archives Canada, NMC C-126553.

mansion facing King Street and the Commons. Interestingly, according to his war loss claims, Dickson and his family had taken up residence in his "new" home on his John Street property on the eve of the war. Dickson had acceded to Brock's personal request that his King Street residence be used as a barracks. Ten months later, just before the American invasion, he had signed a formal lease of £75 Halifax currency

The Niagara Apothecary, photo Cosmo Condina, 2010. Light and shadows on Italianate glory.

Courtesy of Cosmo Condina.

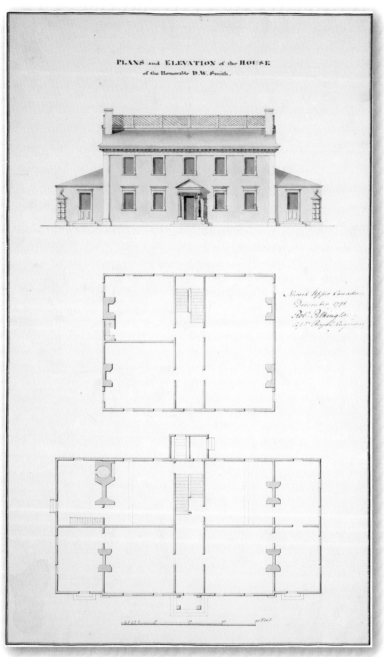

Plans and Elevations of the House of the Honourable D.W. Smith, artist Robert Pilkington R.E., drawings on paper, 1797. Georgian elegance overlooking the Commons.

Courtesy of the Toronto Public Library, Toronto Reference Library, Baldwin Room, D.W. Smith Papers, B 15-39.

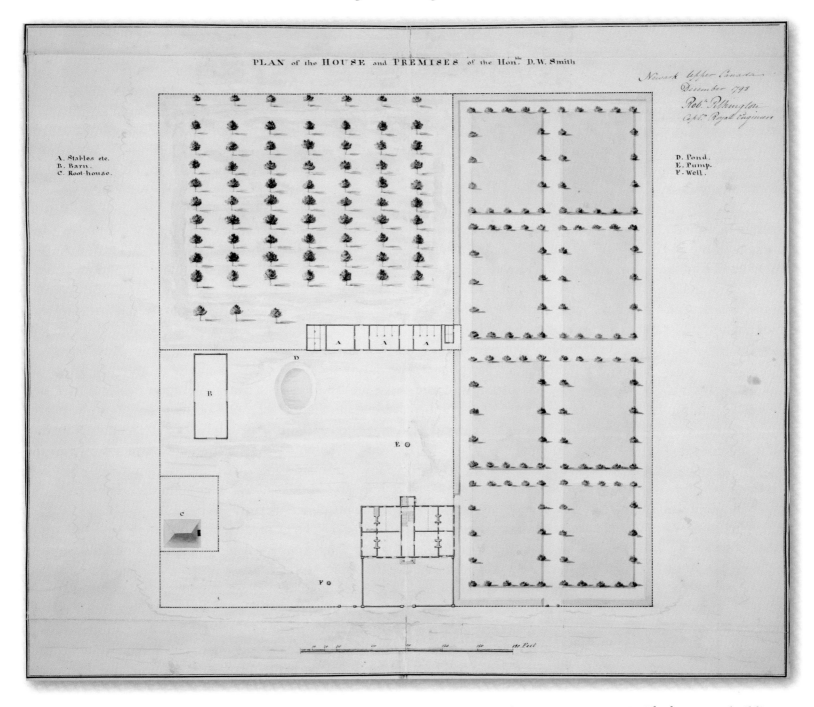

Plan of the House and Premises of the Hon.ble D.W. Smith, artist Robert Pilkington, drawing on paper, 1798. The house, outbuildings, formal gardens, and orchards occupied the entire Queen, Regent, Johnson, and King Streets block.

Courtesy of the Toronto Public Library, Toronto Reference Library, Baldwin Room, D.W. Smith Papers, B15-38.

per annum, but claimed that much damage had already been done by the occupying regular army, American prisoners, and militia. After the burning of the town only the brick walls were left standing.[10] Lot 64 was eventually severed; the eastern portion remained residential with the eventual erection of the substantial Queen Anne revival home, beautifully restored and maintained today as the Preservation Gallery. The building that occupies the Queen Street portion of the lot today, The Niagara Apothecary, is probably the most photographed building in town. Originally constructed in 1820 and initially occupied as a lawyer's office, it was renovated to its present Italianate glory in 1866 and is the oldest continuing pharmacy in the province, if not the country. Preserved by the Niagara Foundation and restored by the Ontario College of Pharmacy, today it is a pharmacy museum now maintained by the Ontario Heritage Trust.

Across Queen Street the entire block of four one-acre lots bounded by Queen, Regent, Johnson, and King Streets was granted to Acting Surveyor General of the Province David William Smith.[11] According to a plan of this property drawn up prior to his departure for England, we see a handsome symmetrical two-storey building with a widow's walk above. Frame in construction, it was described as "constructed, embellished and painted in the best style."[12] In 1803 the entire block was sold to the Crown with Smith's home designated as Government House. It is here that the bodies of Isaac Brock and John Macdonell lay in state after the Battle of Queenston Heights. Eventually the block was transferred to the Town of Niagara. In an unsuccessful attempt to maintain the county seat in Niagara, the town fathers erected the handsome court house halfway along the Queen Street portion of the block, flanked by various mercantile premises. A large market square occupied the centre of the block.

Over the years a variety of businesses occupied the King Street side of the block. In the early twentieth century a ticket station for the electric car was built; it survives today as an upscale coffee emporium. Farther along towards Johnson Street stood Greene's Livery, a somewhat ramshackle and odoriferous collection of stables and carriage barns but well patronized by locals and visitors alike. One local recalls racing down King Street to Greene's after school. After helping to clean out stables and groom some of the horses she would be allowed to ride her favourite mount down Queen Street.[13] At an hourly rental rate of $1.50 local kids could ride one of Greene's horses out onto the Commons on trails as far as Paradise Grove. However, every time the horse came to a cross-trail he would invariably try to turn back towards the stables.[14] Architectural elements of the old Livery are now incorporated into a fancy restaurant. Next door, the Town's tall stone-and-brick water tower stood sentinel for many years.

The next block between Johnson and Gage Streets was in part granted to William Crooks, one of the four Crooks brothers, all enterprising Scottish merchants. William and his brother James were the first merchants to ship wheat to Montreal and were co-owners of the schooner *Lord Nelson*, which was confiscated by the Americans and renamed the *Scourge* on the eve of the War. William married a granddaughter of Colonel John Butler and served with distinction as a captain of the militia at the battles of Queenston Heights and Lundy's Lane. He later moved to Grimsby. The other half of the block was granted to the canny Queenston merchant Robert Hamilton, who probably regarded this choice lot as a good investment. Today private residences occupy the block.

The next block of town lots was granted to members of the McDonell family. Allan McDonell of Collachie had emigrated from Scotland to the Mohawk Valley, New York, in 1773 and served in the Royal Highland Emigrants Regiment during the American Revolutionary War. His wife Helena and their two daughters were taken hostage, but eventually the family was reunited in Quebec. After Allan's death Helena and her three sons were awarded the four town lots in Niagara as partial compensation for their military service and war losses. Angus received the one-acre lot at King and Gage Streets. He dabbled in various enterprises such as potash and salt springs, but he was also a founding member of the Law Society of Upper Canada. In late 1792 he was delegated by Simcoe as first clerk of the House of

Assembly which met nearby. Later in 1804, while travelling to Newcastle to defend a Native charged with murder, he perished when the schooner *Speedy* sank in Lake Ontario during a sudden storm.

The youngest McDonell son, James purchased a commission in the 43rd Regiment but died while stationed in the West Indies.

The third brother Alexander McDonell (1762–1842) served as a lieutenant in Butler's Rangers. In 1792 he was appointed sheriff of the Home District that included Niagara. As Colonel in the militia he was captured at the Battle of Fort George and imprisoned. He also served as a land agent for Lord Selkirk and later as member of the House of Assembly for twenty years. The widowed mother Helena received the lot at King and Centre Streets. She died in 1797 and was probably buried in St. Mark's Cemetery.

The three acres (excluding Alexander's lot) were purchased by Judge Edward Campbell in 1846 and he built a substantial brick house facing the Commons. By 1864 the property was being leased by "J.B. Plumb, Alien," but in 1871 Josiah B. Plumb purchased the property from Widow Campbell for $3,000. Plumb, an American, had come to Niagara to see "the most beautiful Street in the world," namely his future wife Elizabeth Street.

Many additions and improvements were made to the house and gardens including a third floor billiards room reached by a secret staircase installed just before the private visit of HRH Prince George the future King George V. Plumb eventually became the Speaker of the Canadian Senate just before his death in 1888. In 1917–1919 the mansion was occupied by officers of the Polish army training in Camp Niagara. In 1920 the property was acquired by the White family. A daughter, Anne White Buyers,[15] recalled growing up in the house that boasted ten fireplaces, four staircases, and elaborately carved woodwork. In 1943 the house was torn down to make way for a new public school. Many architectural elements were saved and some were installed in local residences. The school, which still occupies the entire block, was called Parliament Oak School, hence the carved stone bas relief on

Alexander McDonell (1762–1842), artist William Berczy, watercolour, gouache over graphite on woven paper, 1803. McDonell's varied career included army and militia officer, office holder, politician, and land agent. The McDonell family was granted the entire block now occupied by Parliament Oak School.

Courtesy of the Royal Ontario Museum © ROM, 970.85.1.

its south wall facing the Commons. The school's name was based on a legend that during a spell of hot weather one of the sessions of the first parliament had been held under a huge oak tree on the property. Such a meeting has never actually been documented. Perhaps one could imagine the Clerk of the House of Assembly, Angus McDonell, suggested that rather than enduring yet another meeting inside the hot and stuffy Rangers' barracks, the members reconvene under a shady oak tree on the edge of his town lot.

Senator Plumb's house, photo, circa 1920. Viewed from across a corner of the Commons at Castlereagh and King Streets, Senator Plumb's mansion dominated the block now occupied by Parliament Oak School. Note the railway crossing sign at King and Gate Streets.

Courtesy of the Niagara Historical Society and Museum, #2011.025.007.

The corner lot at King and Centre Streets was granted to James Clark who had "fought with Wolfe" at Quebec. The old soldier later served as barracks master at Fort Niagara and later at the new Fort George. In the 1830s, lawyer and registrar of the county Mr. Lyons married a Mrs. Geale, a member of the Claus family that lived next-door. They built the handsome house still guarding the corner. Interestingly, the house with its splendid doorway and curious blind windows faces the side street but a large bank of windows overlooks the Commons.

The next two adjacent King Street lots, including the William Street road allowance and the two lots immediately behind, have been one parcel of land since the early 1800s. Long referred to as "Geale's Grove," this remarkable property in the midst of town has been known as "The Wilderness" for at least the past century. According to legend, the Six Nations Indians presented this four-acre property to Ann Claus, widow of Daniel Claus and daughter of the much-revered Superintendant of Indian Affairs Sir William Johnson. Ironically, the Natives had to buy the tract of land from one of the original white grantees, Lieutenant Robert Pilkington of the Royal Engineers. Ann died in 1801

and the property was inherited by her son William, who was appointed deputy superintendant of Indian Affairs. We do know Natives frequently visited Claus on official business, but they would often appear unannounced in the spring to collect buds from the huge Balm of Gilead trees from which they would make a salve for eye disorders.[16] In the middle of this Carolinian forest with over twenty-five varieties of trees and shrubs, including huge oak[17] and buttonwood trees, the first house was built near the edge of the One Mile Creek, which meanders through the property. After the burning of the town the family members apparently survived the winter in a root cellar which endured into modern times. After the war, Claus began construction of the present house farther up from the creek. The new home was a one-storey rambling bungalow with many subsequent additions which sits today contentedly under a huge canopy of trees out of view from the street. Claus and his wife Catherine kept meticulous notes of their horticultural endeavours, which provide a unique window on pioneer gardening practices of the day.[18] With only a short hiatus the current owners have enjoyed the property for over ninety years.

The Wilderness, artist Robert Montgomery, drawing on paper, 1970. The artist captured the quiet beauty and contentment of this regency villa, known today as The Wilderness, surrounded by over four acres of Carolinian woods in the midst of town.

Published in Peter John Stokes, *Old Niagara on the Lake* (Toronto: University of Toronto Press, 1971), no. 57. Courtesy of the artist, Robert Montgomery, the author Peter Stokes, and the publisher, © University of Toronto Press.

The corner lot at King and Mary Streets was apparently acquired by John Powell Senior from the grantee Benjamin VanEvery prior to the War of 1812. Powell, a son of Chief Justice William Dummer Powell, held local government positions and served with distinction in the Lincoln Artillery during the Battle of Fort George. His wife Isabella was a daughter of Adjutant General of Upper Canada and former Queen's Ranger officer, Major General Aeneas Shaw. Another Shaw daughter, Sophia, was said to have been a love interest of Isaac Brock. As early as 1818 Powell began construction of his new home of brick but finished in stucco, grooved to resemble cut stone blocks so fashionable in the Regency period. Again, large front windows faced onto the Commons. After Powell's death in 1826 the family continued in the home for another ten years when lawyer and businessman James Boulton acquired the property. There have been a number of changes over the years but the home, now known as Brockamour because of the possible Brock connection, is operated as a popular bed and breakfast.

The Powell-Cavers House (Brockamour), artist Robert Montgomery, drawing on paper, 1970. The solid symmetrical façade of this handsome regency house surely reflects the builder's appointed position as registrar of the county. Generous windows provide wide vistas of the Commons.

Published in Peter John Stokes, *Old Niagara on the Lake* (Toronto: University of Toronto Press, 1971), no. 56. Courtesy of the artist, Robert Montgomery, the author Peter Stokes, and the publisher, © University of Toronto Press.

The last two lots on King Street facing the Commons are occupied by a private late-Victorian brick home and sometime gallery, and by the Pillar and Post Hotel. The two original Crown grantees were loyalist John VanEvery and William Duff Miller, stationer and local government official. The latter must have flipped his grant, as he built his new home after the war at the corner of Mary and Regent Streets and it still stands, recently restored by the hotel. The main portion of the Pillar and Post facing John Street was originally a canning factory that hired at its zenith hundreds of seasonal workers. A railway spur was extended northward along John Street West to provide service to Camp Chautauqua.

The road allowance for what is now John Street East was originally known as "The Carriage Trail" or "The Carriage Road Trail" and was well within the Military Reserve by up to fifty feet. This created jurisdictional conflict between the town and the federal government as to who was responsible for road maintenance, snow removal, and so forth. Moreover, the property owners along John Street had to cross over federal property for access to the road. It was not until the 1960s that these legal difficulties were finally settled whereby the Crown produced quit-claims to the lands for nominal financial consideration from the relieved property owners.[19]

The twenty-plus-acre lot on John Street between King and Charlotte Streets was granted to Lieutenant Robert Pilkington. Besides being a good artist he was also a favourite of Mrs. Simcoe, which may account for his being the happy recipient of some choice pieces of land. However, much of this lot, which was known locally as the "23 acre fields," was in the flood plain of the One Mile Creek. In the 1860s William Dickson's third son, the Honourable Walter H.

Dickson,[20] owned this lot and he may have erected several small cottages for his help, and possibly a small racecourse on the property.[21] There has been one happy survivor from this period — the "Dickson-Potter House." This is a delightful mid-Victorian board-and-batten cottage nestled amongst drooping trees. It is approached by a small bridge over the One Mile Creek. Local historian Kaye Toye has enjoyed looking out onto the Commons for ninety years. The old railway right-of-way that cut diagonally across this lot is now preserved as the Upper Canada Recreation Trail. The rest of the property has undergone residential development.

Beyond Charlotte Street[22] the high and somewhat foreboding brick and stone walls give a taste of what lies behind — which can only be glimpsed through closed wrought-iron gates. Peter Russell, the administrator of the province after Simcoe left for England, was granted 160 acres that included the John Street frontage all the way to the end of the present picket fencing. With the move of the capital to York in 1797, Russell was forced to sell his lands, including his leased

Vine-covered wall, photo Cosmo Condina, 2011. The privately built substantial brick, stone, and cement wall along John Street East was probably encroaching on the edge of the Military Reserve.

Courtesy of Cosmo Condina.

The Dickson-Potter house, photo Cosmo Condina, 2010. The current owner has enjoyed the ever-changing views of the Commons from her front veranda for ninety years.

Courtesy of Cosmo Condina.

property, "Springfield" in the middle of the Commons, and this tract of apparently unimproved land. He sold the land to William Dickson, who had already built his brick mansion at King and Queen Streets.

Dickson had arrived in Niagara at age sixteen and may have initially worked for his cousin, the merchant Robert Hamilton. Eventually the canny Scot became a lawyer, judge, land developer, and member of the Legislative Council. Along the way he was involved in a duel in which his antagonist, fellow lawyer and member of the assembly William Weekes, was fatally shot.[23] In Dickson's war loss claims he enclosed a drawing of a brick bungalow which was completed a year before the outbreak of war and was probably situated on his John Street farm property. After the war he may have built a two-storey house on the western end of his John Street property that was eventually called Rowanwood. Although he continued his law practice most of his energies were directed to his large land holdings on the Grand River. Finally in 1827 after his wife's death, he actually moved there to directly oversee the development of Dumfries Township and its prosperous village of Galt. The Honourable William Dickson (Dickson was appointed a member of the Legislative Council and given the title of "Honourable" for life) returned to Niagara in 1836 probably taking up residence again at Rowanwood to devote the remnant of his life to "high and solemn purpose."[24]

Meanwhile, Dickson had divided up amongst his sons the rest of the huge estate. The "homestead" was given to his eldest son Robert, who proceeded to build his two-storey brick home and the extensive stables behind over the foundations of the original brick bungalow. He called his estate Woodlawn. Like his father, Robert was a lawyer and was very involved in community activities. He was also captain of the local cavalry troop of militia and frequently drilled his troopers on the Commons opposite his home. He and his wife had no surviving children so his estate was left to one of his numerous nephews. Eventually his youngest brother, the Honourable Walter H., who had inherited Rowanwood from his father, also acquired Woodlawn.

In the 1870s the Dickson properties were sold to Americans who were part of that group of wealthy bankers and industrialists who sought relief for their families from the heat of Buffalo and Cleveland in leafy Niagara-on-the-Lake. A Civil War veteran and executive with the Buffalo and Erie Railroad, Brigadier General Henry Livingston Lansing

The Honourable William Dickson, artist Hoppner Meyer, watercolour, 1842. Merchant, lawyer, land developer, office holder, duellist, yet non-combatant during the War of 1812, Dickson owned 160 acres along the southern edge of the Commons.

Courtesy of the Niagara Historical Society and Museum, #988.199.

purchased Woodlawn in 1873 and is thought to have been responsible for the third floor addition and tower. Next door, J.H. Lewis bought Rowanwood as a summer home and may have renovated the original frame building, as it is later described as a stone residence. George Rand Senior, a self-made man who eventually became chairman of Buffalo's largest bank, purchased the Woodlawn estate in 1910 which he promptly renamed Randwood and proceeded with many additions to the house, as well as extensive landscaping. Nine years later he added Rowanwood to the estate and erected barns and gatehouses along Charlotte Street. After his father's untimely death in a plane crash, George Rand II continued stewardship of the estate; Rowanwood was torn down in 1920[25] to make way for a park, but instead the present Devonian House was erected on the site for the newly-wed Evelyn Rand Sheets. Mrs. Sheets, an accomplished equestrian, was often seen riding her horse along John Street and on the Commons.

More outbuildings were added along Charlotte and further extensive landscaping of the grounds was carried out,

The Dickson-Rand House (Randwood), artist Robert Montgomery, drawing on paper, 1970. On the foundations of William Dickson's prewar country house, son Robert erected a substantial two-storey brick home. Later, summering American families added a third floor, a belvedere, and other embellishments.

Published in Peter John Stokes, *Old Niagara on the Lake* (Toronto: University of Toronto Press, 1971), no. 54. Courtesy of the artist, Robert Montgomery, the author Peter Stokes, and the publisher, © University of Toronto Press.

including the first in-ground swimming pool in town. A gazebo-like station was built on the edge of the estate for the family's private stop on the Michigan Central Railway line. George also had built the high wall around much of the estate. Eventually the property was inherited by George II's son Calvin. Most of the estate was eventually leased to the Niagara Institute but then sold to the Devonian Foundation, which in turn sold the property to the School of Philosophy. Now in private hands, there are currently plans for development of this remarkable property.

The Honorable William Dickson gave his second son and namesake, William Jr., the ten acres on John Street to the east of present Randwood. Rather than develop his Niagara properties, William Jr. decided to move to Dumfries to develop the family's holdings there, and so in 1829 he sold his lands for £200 to Robert Melville, a retired Captain of the 68th Regiment, which had been stationed at Fort George. This "public spirited, good-natured gentleman"[26] built the nucleus of the present two-storey brick house of three bay design with a very elaborate front doorway. He called his property Brunswick Place, apparently because he had met his wife in New Brunswick. Soon Melville was elected manager of the newly formed Niagara Harbour and Dock Company and a street in the new dock area was named after him. But his good fortune was not to last: he had to step down from the financially troubled Dock Company and each of his three young sons died before reaching their teens. The banks foreclosed on the property in the year of Confederation.

In the 1880s the Honourable William's grandson, Robert George Dickson, purchased the property, made extensive embellishments and additions to the house, and renamed the estate Pinehurst, acknowledging a large grove of pine trees on the property. Robert and his twin brother, J. Geale Dickson, were avid golfers and were largely responsible for laying out the Fort George links on the Commons opposite Pinehurst. In 1895 the property slipped out of the Dickson family once again. A succession of American families owned the property, renamed Brunswick Place. The longest owners were the Letchworths, famous for their sumptuous parties

still remembered fifty years later. The lady of the house, a petite, five-foot-tall woman, was a regular sight on the Commons riding sidesaddle on her horse Blue Shadows with her red setter Matey running alongside.[27] Artist Trisha Romance and her family are the current proud owners of the restored property. Architectural elements of Brunswick Place have been incorporated into several of her paintings.

The rest of the land between Dickson's purchase and the river was granted to William McClellan. During the American Revolutionary War he was captured by Natives and rings were inserted in his nose and ears before his escape to Canada. According to his petition for land he settled on this gore-shaped tract of land adjacent to the Queen's Bush in 1783. His son Martin had also been captured by another group of Natives but was liberated at Cherry Valley. During the War of 1812, Captain Martin McClellan of the First Lincoln Militia told his wife on the eve of the Battle of Fort George that he would not survive the fighting the next day. He gave her his pocket watch and purse for safe keeping. The next day he was mortally wounded by a musket ball that passed through his empty vest pocket where his watch was usually kept.[28] He was buried in St. Mark's cemetery and his gravestone has now been affixed to an interior wall. After the war the land was eventually sub-divided and passed through several families including the Chittenden, Warren, McIntyre, Watt, Longhurst, and Nelles families. Today the property is occupied by private residences, Peller Estates Winery and Riverbend Inn. The immense white oak sentinel on the southern edge of the John Street road allowance near the intersection with the Niagara Parkway, and several trees in the Reserve to the southeast of the intersection towards the river are first growth. These trees have been silent witnesses as LaSalle, Simcoe, Brant, Brock, and various Royals passed by.

The final boundary of the Military Reserve was the Niagara River. Starting northward from John Street East the area including the present parking lot was occupied at one time by several cottages. To the north of this was a popular picnic area that extended into Paradise Grove which, for a while, was kept clear of brush and fallen branches. There was

Brunswick Place, photo Cosmo Condina, 2011. Cosmo's photo of Brunswick Place on a misty morning belies the rich architectural detail of this stately home that has gazed out over the Commons for over 180 years.

Courtesy of Cosmo Condina.

a stairway down the steep cliff to a mooring for small boats which brought picnickers from the town.[29] Farther along, two deep gullies along the western edge of the Niagara Parkway are remnants of the old railway line. Just beyond this was the Half-Moon Battery built during the War of 1812 period to counteract the opposing American River batteries. This was a two-storey semi-circular rampart built into the high riverbank. Unfortunately, it was destroyed by the Niagara

Parks Commission when it extended the Niagara Parkway to the restored Navy Hall.

All the land along the Niagara River below the moderately high riverbanks from Navy Hall to the end of King Street was up to forty acres of low marshland. During some severe winters the banks were covered by heaped up river ice which could crush and sweep away substantial wharves and buildings. Moreover, the land was often flooded in the spring, leaving rotting stagnant cesspools during the warm summer months. Aside from a few plots set aside for merchants near the site of present Melville Street, this part of the shoreline was occupied by one or two ferry huts, an inn, and the guard house at the end of King Street. This was the edge of the Military Reserve/Commons on the eve of the War of 1812.

In 1831, the NHDC, consisting of a group of local influential citizens, was granted ownership of all the marshland by the Crown.[30] Within the year they began the process of draining and excavating a deep basin, reclaiming approximately forty acres.[31] Ramps for launching ships and a marine railway were installed. Shipbuilding was the prime purpose of the company and the first boat, the schooner *Princess Victoria*, was launched in 1833, the same year that it opened its dry dock. Business was booming. Niagara was now the largest shipbuilding facility in Upper Canada, with a great surge in employment; in seven years the population of Niagara more than doubled. At least twenty-seven ships were built between 1832 and 1864.[32] Other industries were attracted to the dock area, including a tannery and a brewery thanks to abundant spring water nearby on the Commons. Nevertheless, the company was deeply in debt to the Bank of Upper Canada which itself was greatly overextended.

SS **Chief Justice Robinson**, artist Francis Granger, watercolour, circa 1855. Built by the Niagara Harbour and Dock Company during Niagara's heyday as the busiest ship-building centre in Upper Canada, this steamer proudly plied the waters of Lake Ontario under Captain Duncan Milloy.

Courtesy of the Niagara Historical Society and Museum, #2006.016.008.

In 1853 local entrepreneur Samuel Zimmerman bought out the bankrupt company. With financial backing from the town, Zimmerman brought the Erie and Ontario Railroad to town with direct access to the docks, thus coordinating railway and steamship schedules. He began the manufacture of much needed railway cars in the same foundry already producing steamships. His untimely death four years later was a severe blow to the company's ambitious plans, and within ten years no steamships were being produced, and the once-booming facilities were in disrepair. However, a brisk steamship business continued well into the twentieth century and the railway was also well patronized, but the boom years were over.

Other well-known boat building companies[33] prospered along the waterfront for a while, but they too have folded. There were also several family-operated commercial fishing businesses that operated out of this reclaimed area, now long gone. Canning and basket factories and the Niagara Oak Tannery also provided employment in the dock area for a time.

It is not the purview of this book to document all the residential and commercial buildings in this reclaimed area that roughly includes all that between Ricardo Street and the Niagara River. However, a few buildings are of note. The active Niagara-on-the-Lake Sailing Club still uses NHDC's original 1834 storehouse on the dock. The NHDC's

Mouth of the River from Ramparts of Old Fort George, artist L.R.O'Brien, wood engraving, circa 1880. This fine engraving reveals the industrial development of the waterfront, originally the marshlands of the Military Reserve. Note in the foreground the cultivation of a portion of the ramparts of the old abandoned fort reclaimed as common lands.

Originally published in George Monro Grant, ed., *Picturesque Canada*, vol. 1 (Toronto: Balden Bros., 1882), 374.

manager's office, tucked into the riverbank overlooking the harbour, has been carefully restored as a guest house. Other frame buildings built by the NHDC survive as private residences. A later brick building that served as the town's water pumping station has been turned into a vibrant artists' gallery.[34] The early twentieth century Foghorn Station on River Beach Road has been renovated by the Niagara Foundation as a guest cottage. Two early lighthouses still stand as silent reminders of a bygone era. The iconic, beautifully restored Whale Inn at the foot of King Street once welcomed sailors and travellers. Built in the 1830s by the Elliot family on reclaimed NHDC land it is now a private residence. So ends the tour around the edge of the original Military Reserve/Commons.

CHAPTER 22

Nibbling at the Edges

The earliest and largest surrender of a portion of the Military Reserve/Commons was the exchange of James Crooks's 21.25 acres at Mississauga Point for five newly created four acre town blocks from Reserve land.[1]

The willingness of the government to give up some of its Military Reserve in the 1820s seems to have been part of a larger scheme to settle certain land issues in this part of town. During this period Niagara was coming out of a post-war depression: war loss claims were finally being paid (albeit at significant discount), Niagara was the district seat and still boasted a strategic military garrison, plans were afoot for development of the waterfront, and the proposed Welland canal[2] that bypassed Niagara was not yet considered a threat.

Although St. Mark's served as the garrison church it was not until the late 1820s that the Church of England was officially granted in perpetuity the large double block bounded by King, Byron, Wellington, and Ricardo Streets. Later the Church was granted the Davy Street road allowance. The original rectangular stone church was built more or less in the middle of this large grant; construction began in 1804 or earlier. The first divine service at St. Mark's may not have been held until August 1809.[3] After the Battle of Queenston Heights the British Army used the building as a hospital, but during the American occupation the church building was converted into a barracks and warehouse. After the torching of the town, the church's sandstone walls were left standing. As one of the few buildings salvageable, it was re-commandeered by the British Army for storing commissary supplies.[4] It was not until 1828 that the restored edifice was finally consecrated. During the boom years of the 1840s with a rapidly growing membership, a chancel and transepts were added; there have been many interior changes since. Nevertheless, the little stone church surrounded by magnificent mature trees and ancient tombstones is the very essence of an English parish church.[5]

To the northwest stands the town's only "Tuscan Villa," the first and only rectory for St. Mark's, constructed in 1858. Built of pressed yellow brick[6] (imported from England and rare in Niagara) in the Italianate style of two storeys but adorned with a tall square tower (from which one could see clear across the Commons) and wide bracketed eaves, it would certainly have impressed any visiting bishop or discerning traveller. The rectory still retains the large open lot at the rear extending to Ricardo Street.[7]

In between the church and villa stands the diminutive "Sunday Schoolhouse" erected in the 1880s. Recently restored and enlarged as the now multi-functional Addison Hall it is also the handsome repository of the original library of Rev. Robert Addison.

The sacred land now known as St. Mark's Cemetery must be one of the few cases in Ontario where the establishment of a community burying ground preceded the building of the church. The topography of the Church of England's

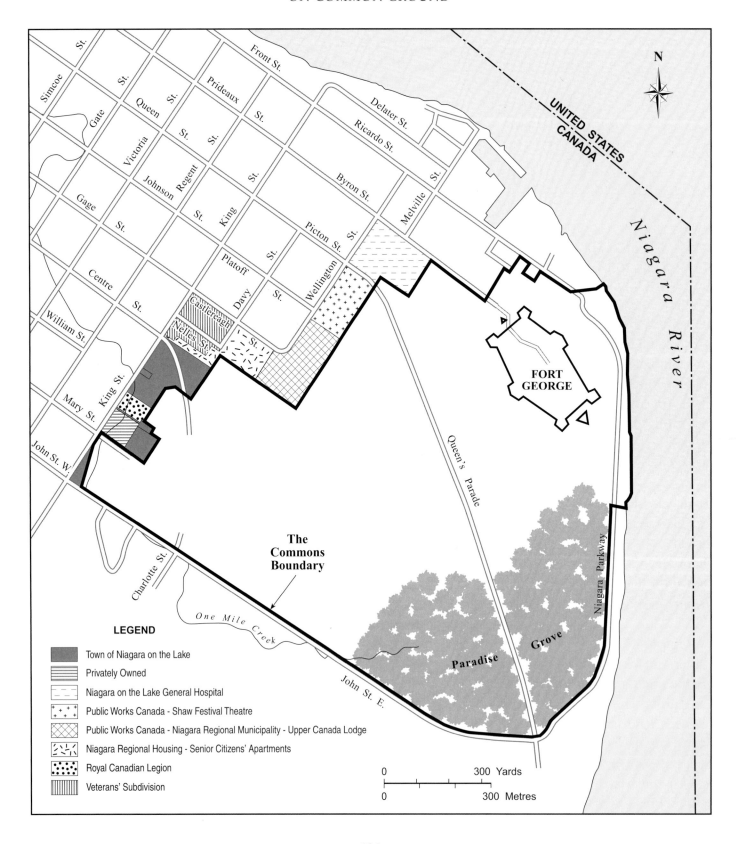

FORT GEORGE

The Commons Boundary

Niagara River

UNITED STATES
CANADA

Queen's Parade

Niagara Parkway

One Mile Creek

Paradise Grove

John St. E.

LEGEND

- Town of Niagara on the Lake
- Privately Owned
- Niagara on the Lake General Hospital
- Public Works Canada - Shaw Festival Theatre
- Public Works Canada - Niagara Regional Municipality - Upper Canada Lodge
- Niagara Regional Housing - Senior Citizens' Apartments
- Royal Canadian Legion
- Veterans' Subdivision

0 — 300 Yards
0 — 300 Metres

ABOVE: St. Mark's Church, photo Cosmo Condina, 2010. "The essence of an English parish church" after a Canadian winter storm.

Courtesy of Cosmo Condina.

FACING PAGE: Twentieth century encroachments. The areas marked according to the legend indicate twentieth century encroachments of the Commons.

grant is such that it more or less occupied a promontory of high and dry land between the river bank to the northeast and a deep ravine to the west and northwest. This ravine, the bed of an old creek that drained the Commons, would have offered some protection from the elements for early Aboriginal hunters and gatherers attracted to the mouth of the Niagara River. When the southern edge of the original church property was cut back to reduce the steep incline of Wellington Street between Byron and Ricardo Streets, early Native bones, pottery, and other artifacts were uncovered.[8] We do know that Europeans had chosen this land for burials as early as 1782. During renovations to the church in the nineteenth century, a tombstone was unearthed with the inscription "LENERD BLANCK DESEACED 5 Aug.t 1782." Blanck (originally "Planck") was a Butler's Ranger mortally wounded at the Battle of Upper Sandusky earlier in the year and was probably brought to the hospital in the Rangers' Barracks where he died.[9] It would have been a short funeral procession from the Barracks to his final resting place. For the next fifty years, until the Presbyterians and Roman Catholics established their own cemeteries, nearly all the townspeople[10] found their eternal resting place at St. Mark's. The fascinating record of burials officiated by Addison includes men, women, and children of various religious and ethnic backgrounds. Folks of colour, a Mohawk Chief, paupers, strangers, and many active military personnel are listed.[11] When the Americans occupied the town they dug extensive earthworks through the cemetery, which lends it a more picturesque contour. Brock's seat[12] rests here, and vestiges of American rifle pits can still be made out. A leisurely ramble through this ancient graveyard with its varied tombstones nestled amongst native and ornamental shrubbery and towering trees, many planted two hundred years ago is a step back into Niagara's earliest days.

The southeastern third of the original grant (between the cemetery and Wellington Street) was leased out in the 1850s for residential use, presumably to help support the parish's ongoing expenses. Eventually the properties were sold, and today are occupied by homes of quite diverse architecture.[13]

The Lenerd Blanck tombstone, 1782. Ranger Planck's marker is probably the oldest surviving tombstone in the province.

Courtesy of Donald Combe.

As an ecumenical gesture, the government also granted the Roman Catholic Church the four lots bounded by Picton, Wellington, Byron, and the Davy Street road allowance bordering the future public park. In 1834 construction began on the frame structure, fashioned in the Gothic Revival style, crowned by a tall steeple. The wooden groined interior vaulting of the ceiling, supported by Ionic pilasters, is particularly noteworthy. To meet the growing needs of the parish, a circular addition towards Picton Street, including a new fibreglass steeple, was completed in 1965.

St. Vincent-de-Paul's Church

St. Vincent de Paul Roman Catholic Church (as viewed from the open Commons), photo, circa 1930. Although the parish is not as old as neighbouring St. Mark's, its historic sanctuary and cemetery have many stories to tell.

Courtesy of the Niagara Historical Society and Museum, #984.5.22.

According to historian Joseph Masters there was an early separate school house on church property as well as an "old presbytery" for the priest.[14] The frame manse was later moved to Platoff Street and its replacement was built on the site of the school. The former gymnasium of Camp Niagara that was moved to its current site on Davy Street and renovated, still serves as the parish hall for St. Vincent de Paul.

The names on the early gravestones in St. Vincent de Paul's cemetery reflect the large Irish-Catholic immigration to the Niagara Peninsula after 1830. Perhaps the most unique characteristic of this cemetery is the plot given by the church to the Polish government in perpetuity, known as the Polish Enclosure. An iron fence surrounds the graves of twenty-four young trainees who died during the Spanish Influenza pandemic while the Polish army was training on the Commons during the Great War. The additional burial is that of a Polish chaplain who selflessly administered to his compatriots' needs.[15] Other plaques acknowledge the sacrifice of all those who died for the freedom of Poland during the First and Second World Wars. Remarkably, since 1919 this plot of sacred land has been the revered destination of an annual pilgrimage in June.

The block bounded by Byron, Wellington, and Queen's Parade remained part of the Commons until the 1940s. The town's cottage hospital situated on Dr. Hedley Anderson's property on Queen Street had long outgrown its four walls, and hence the decision was made by the town council to build a freestanding hospital on the Commons. Eventually the federal government donated the block to the town strictly for a community hospital and its support buildings.[16] Today the hospital with mostly rehabilitation and chronic care beds and an acute care clinic meets the needs of the community. The back half of the block remains undeveloped green space and may contain relics of the War of 1812.

The block bounded by Byron, Alava (Melville), Ricardo, and Wellington Streets is thought to have been the site of the

1778 Rangers' Barracks, perhaps corroborated by Butler's Rangers buttons found on the property.[17] This historic site was sold to private concerns in the nineteenth century, and most of the block is currently occupied by a nursing home.

The adjacent block bounded by Byron, Nelson, Ricardo, and Alava (Melville) was granted to the Niagara Harbour and Dock Company (NHDC) apparently in compensation for the government's granting James Crooks one of the NHDC's water lots as part of the great swap. Two small buildings, the restored harbour master's house on Ricardo, and the presently empty cottage just to the south of the hotel are remnants of the NHDC era. The massive Queen's Landing Inn currently occupies the rest of this block.

The four-acre block at the southwest corner of King and Queen Streets, now known as Simcoe Park, legally remained a part of the Military Reserve/Commons until the 1930s. The main topographical feature of this property was the wide, deep ravine, through which ran a creek that became quite turbulent during the spring run-off from the Commons. This provided a natural amphitheatre. By the mid 1800s there was great interest among urban planners to provide public parks both for the locals and tourists. In Niagara the town fathers became increasingly interested in creating a town park out of these four vacant acres, and so in 1852 they petitioned the government for these four acres for "ornamental grounds." A lease was granted with a proviso that the public have free access to the park.[18] Various initiatives were undertaken by the town to landscape the space, build a bridge across the creek, and erect a bandstand and pavilion. Henry Paffard, the much-respected town's mayor for twenty-six years, supervised the planting of trees throughout the town and in particular the "Niagara Park." A fine hedge was planted around the periphery outside of which was a wire fence to keep out roving cattle. Secure entrance gates were placed on Picton and Byron Streets.

In a controversial decision by town council, the park was leased in 1913 to Dick Taylor who operated amusements and a camp ground on the premises. Taylor gave the park its modern name, Simcoe Park.[19] He was so successful that he opened a similar but larger park at Port Dalhousie. Later the gates and fences were taken down and Simcoe Park became available to all including tourists who were allowed to camp overnight in the park. By the 1930s there was a dance pavilion and refreshment stand where the washrooms now stand. Throughout the summer season live bands would play music on Saturday nights. During the Second World War this was often the only opportunity for the trainees at Camp Niagara to meet the local girls. At five cents per dance it was a popular venue.[20] The whole community would turn out for the Sunday evening sing-songs. Dancing to a nickelodeon was available other evenings. Gradually over the next twenty years the dances became less popular. The pavilion, blown down during a severe storm, was not replaced. The once popular outdoor skating rink in the hollow met a similar fate. In the latter part of the twentieth century a modern bandshell was erected on the brow of the hollow. In 1999 an eight-foot bronze statue of John Graves Simcoe by local sculptor, Roy Asplin was unveiled in the Heritage garden within the park. On any given summer's day it is the tourists who are most likely to be found in Simcoe Park picnicking on the grassy knolls, although the local citizenry take over the park on Canada Day.

In the summer of 1962, ten unpaid actors performed two George Bernard Shaw plays on a makeshift stage in Niagara's old court house, and local lawyer Brian Doherty's dream of an annual Shaw Festival was launched. Soon it became apparent that a larger permanent theatre was needed. Several sites were suggested: expansion of the Court House Theatre onto market square, Queen's Royal Park, the Randwood estate across the Commons, and the Niagara-on-the-Lake Golf Course on the Mississauga Commons — all excluded for various reasons. There was even talk of moving buildings from the Montreal Expo '67 site to Niagara for needed theatre space. Covetous eyes were cast on the Commons at the corner of Wellington Street and Queen's Parade, a site previously occupied by the Boy Scout lodge.[21] Initially the federal government rejected the idea, but relented as it became apparent that Camp Niagara's days were numbered.

Watching Sports in Simcoe Park, Niagara-on-the-Lake*. Some of the town's youngsters are enjoying sports in Simcoe Park that had only recently been opened to the public.*

Swings in Simcoe Park, Niagara-on-the-Lake*.* Swings were always a popular attraction in public parks. Note the large picnic/dance pavilions in the background.

Both postcards courtesy of the John Burtniak Collection.

But there was another wrinkle: when the original eighteen-hole golf course on the Fort George Commons was closed by the government on the eve of the Great War it had been given the right to return should the Commons no longer be needed for military purposes. The Niagara-on-the-Lake Golf Club was already nervous the federal government would cancel its lease on the Mississauga Commons and declare it a national historic park. Anxious to retain its unique location, the Niagara-on-the-Lake Golf Club agreed to cancel its Fort George option on the condition that a long-term lease be

LEFT: Boy Scout lodge, photo, 1938. The lodge, which began its career as a barn on Regent Street ,was situated at the corner of Wellington Street and Queen's Parade — the current site of the Shaw Festival Theatre.

Courtesy of the Niagara Historical Society and Museum, #2005.027.001.

BELOW: The Donald and Elaine Triggs Production Centre, photo Cosmo Condina, 2011. This new ultra modern addition was carefully designed to fit within the Festival's leased space on the Commons.

Courtesy of Cosmo Condina.

granted for the Mississauga links. Although there were some vocal objections from local citizens, the Shaw Festival Theatre officially opened in June 1973 on 4.12 acres of the Commons leased from the federal government.

The theatre was described by the critics as "a perfect joy" and was lauded for being "carefully landscaped into its environment."[22] There have been additions since including the new Donald and Elaine Triggs Production Centre, all situated on the original plot of leased land. And during intermissions on warm summer evenings theatergoers can gaze out onto the Commons and perhaps visualize even one of the thousands of dramas big and small which have played out on the Commons over the last two-hundred-plus years.

Another ambitious proposal for the Commons was the offer of the federal lands along John Street East as the campus for the then-fledgling Brock University. Although there was local support, the mayor of St. Catharines vetoed the plan.[23]

After the Second World War the country was anxious to honour its returning veterans. A block of the Commons, originally part of the agricultural fair grounds and now bounded by King, Nelles, Davy, and Castlereagh, was set aside. Known as "The Project" or the "Carnochan Subdivision," modest houses[24] with full basements were erected on small lots along Nelles and Castlereagh Streets, financed by Central Mortgage and Housing Corporation. If the veteran had a local connection and was married with a least one child he could rent for an affordable $39 per month.[25] In 1949 Harold and Marjorie Clement were the first to move in. Later in 1962 each renter was given the option to purchase his/her home for a very reasonable $6,800 — everyone took up the offer. At the time of writing only three original renters still occupy their homes.

In the 1970s a lease was granted for 3.65 acres to erect a two-storey senior citizens' apartment on the site of the stables for the old three quarter mile racetrack. To apply one had to be over sixty-five years of age with limited financial resources.

The most recent and perhaps most controversial encroachment on the Commons was the Niagara Regional Nursing Home, Upper Canada Lodge. Other sites were offered but the Niagara region persisted. Perched on 6.04 acres at the corner of Castlereagh and Wellington Streets and extending well out onto the grassy plain, visually it certainly is the most intrusive when viewed from the Commons. Patients, staff, and volunteers surely enjoy the historic green vistas.

After the Second World War the federal government seemed anxious to divest itself of many of its properties. In the late 1940s the town was able to purchase fourteen acres of Commons along King Street opposite Central Street. This included the historic "Compound," which consisted of two early frame buildings enclosed by a high fence. The more westerly building (the barracks master's house) was quickly demolished, but the Junior Commissariat Officer's Quarters was used by the town for a "Boys and Girls Club" as well as a "Teen Town" that sponsored chaperoned weekly Friday night dances. A rear apartment was rented out to a local family. Eventually, Parks Canada decided to take back the Quarters and its tranquil 2.45 acres; they partially restored the 1816 cottage in the 1980s and are still seeking an adaptive reuse for the building.

The remaining acreage was dedicated to a recreation complex later called Veterans Memorial Park, dedicated to honour all those men and women of the town and the Niagara township, who had served the cause of freedom in the two world wars. The local baseball diamond originally was situated near the site of the old Boy Scouts' lodge, now the Shaw Theatre. In 1949 the Royal Canadian Legion sponsored the creation of a new diamond on the King Street location, eventually upgraded with night lights. Tennis courts were laid out opposite the diamond. In 1967, partly in response to the tragic drowning of the two Matthews brothers in the river, Harold Clement and a committee of fifteen raised $50,000 for the construction of a public swimming pool. Initially the pool was to be situated between the diamond and the compound, but when Noel Haines started excavating he hit a huge underground spring, so the pool was moved beside the tennis courts. A soccer pitch was added and later enlarged to two regulation-size fields after soil was brought in to raise the field preserving the archaeologically sensitive Commons.

A larger parking lot, photo, 2000. As part of the upgrading of the soccer pitches, more Commons turf was sacrificed for infrequently used parking space.

Courtesy of the author.

The Legion decided to use one of the old Camp Niagara buildings for a golden age club. A site was chosen between the Legion and the diamond. Once again when Haines tried to excavate a basement, water gushed up. The building was put on hold and eventually the group was content with the new community centre on Platoff Street.

The General Nelles Royal Canadian Legion Branch (Ontario No.124) purchased its present King Street site from the town for $500, and the new club house was officially opened in July 1967. An addition was completed in 1985 when a special cairn was unveiled to recognize those servicemen who had made the supreme sacrifice in both world wars and all those who participated in training for the military at Camp Niagara over so many generations.[26]

The entrance onto the Commons today opposite Mary Street was created during the Second World War. The Canadian Corps of Military Engineers had erected a building just off King Street. After the war the federal government sold the land and building to Canadian Canners, which in turn sold the property in 1962 to Genaire, who still retains ownership.

The Kinsmen's Lodge/day care school, formerly the Boy Scout lodge, stands next door. In the 1930s the Cubs, Boy Scouts, and Sea Cadets met in Navy Hall but after its restoration the clubs had to look elsewhere. The scouts renovated Pete Healey's old horse barn that had been moved from Regent Street in town out to the corner of Queen's Parade and Wellington Street. After the heady days of the 8th World Boy Scout Jamboree, a proposal to build an "International Boy Scouts Lodge"[27] on the site never materialized. Even before the Shaw Festival decided to build their new theatre on the site, the Scouts had been looking for another location.

One day in 1966 Noel Haines received a desperate call that the former United Mennonite Church building was stuck in the middle of the Commons.[28] The Scouts had been offered the old church building on Niagara Stone Road for removal to a new leased site adjacent to Genaire and near the Butler's Barracks complex. To avoid wires and trees the building was moved slowly on a flatbed truck across East-to-West Line, down the Parkway and onto the Queen's Parade and then was to cut across the Commons towards its destination. Half way across the grassy plain the truck sunk ignominiously to its axels.[29] Eventually it was rescued and the new lodge served its purpose for many years.

Over the years there have been many other proposals for various parts of the Commons, some of which will be covered in the chapter "Save the Commons."

CHAPTER 23

The Mississauga Commons

A climb to the roof of Fort Mississauga's tower reveals a spectacular 360-degree vista. To the east is the mouth of the majestic Niagara River and Fort Niagara beyond; to the south, over a canopy of mature trees, the old town of Niagara and the flagstaff of Fort George beyond; to the west the oldest golf course in Canada on the leafy Mississauga Commons; and to the north, a shimmering Lake Ontario with the twenty-first-century skyline of Toronto in the distance.

There is no archaeological evidence that Native peoples established any permanent villages at this juncture of the Niagara River and Lake Ontario known today as Mississauga Point.[1] By Native tradition it was a popular campsite because of the abundant fish nearby. After the disappearance of the indigenous Neutral Indians in the 1650s, the Iroquoian Seneca nation withdrew to the eastern side of the Niagara River and allowed the Mississaugas of the Chippewa nation to hunt and fish on the west side of the river. The French cultivated a "King's Garden" on the fertile mud flats of the west side of the river to supply fresh foodstuffs for their garrison across the river in Fort Niagara. However, it was not until the British established a battery on the west side of the river (at approximately Queen's Royal Park today) during the siege of Fort Niagara in 1759 that Europeans first established a military presence there. In May 1781, the Mississaugas signed a treaty whereby a strip of land extending four miles westward from the Niagara River, stretching from Lake Ontario to Lake Erie, was ceded to the

British. It certainly seems appropriate that this site should commemorate the Mississauga Nation.

Given its commanding view of the mouth of the Niagara River and being situated directly across from the well-established Fort Niagara, it is not surprising that at least one British government official recognized its strategic importance as early as 1790.[2] Nevertheless, the heights above Navy Hall were chosen for the site of the future Fort George. In 1796 Lieutenant Robert Pilkington of the Royal Engineers established a military reserve at Mississauga Point,[3] although the land set aside was only approximately one half of the 52.4 acres (21.2 hectares) of the Mississauga Commons today.

The government did recognize the maritime importance of the site. In 1804 the stonemasons of the 49th Foot built the first lighthouse on the shores of the Great Lakes.[4] The one and only lighthouse keeper was Dominick Henry, a retired officer of the Royal Artillery who lived with his wife and daughters in a log cottage nearby. Remarkably, the lighthouse, which was situated in what is now the inner edge of one of the fort's lakeside glacis (battery), survived the war[5] but was dismantled by the British in 1814 with the stone incorporated into the tower.

In February 1813, when it was apparent that Fort George's location was not ideal, Lieutenant Colonel R.H. Bruyeres of the Royal Engineers recommended that "a tower or small Redoubt to command the entrance of the

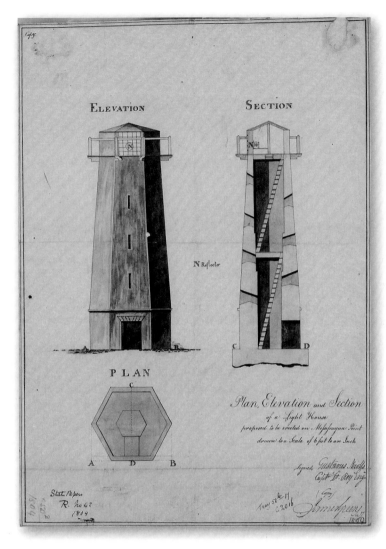

Plan, Elevation and Section of a Light House Proposed to be erected on Mississaugua Point, artist Gustavus Nicolls, drawings on paper, 1804. This is the plan of the first lighthouse built on the shores of the Great Lakes. The artificers were the masons of the 49th Regiment of Foot.

Library and Archives Canada, NMC 0006243.

Point. The fort would be "a temporary field work" in which the irregular star-shaped earthworks[7] with picketed ramparts would enclose several log barracks and a central masonry tower. Inclement weather delayed the actual start of construction past March 1814, but in a remarkable burst of war-time activity, by late July when the American army approached from the west, it was confronted by a formidable, albeit temporary, new British fortress. The fortified earthworks were nearly complete and four cannons were in place. The barracks were occupied, two bomb proof powder magazines in the ramparts were complete, as was a wooden sally port on the north side. There were also two functioning hot shot furnaces. However, the tower, being built partly from brick rubble recycled from the burned town, was still only two feet high. A few shots were exchanged and the Americans withdrew.

After the war there was much indecision as to the military importance of the Niagara installations. With Fort George in ruins emphasis was placed on consolidating the new Butler's Barracks complex at the western end of the Military Reserve and initially to upgrading Fort Mississauga. A plan which was approved by Administrator Drummond called for the construction of a huge permanent fortress on the point, ten times the size of the present fort (in fact the present fort would have fitted inside just one of the huge bastions of the proposed mammoth fort) — all at a cost of at least £90,000.[8] At one point a ploughed trace of the proposed work was outlined on the site, but that is as far as the grand scheme progressed. However, in anticipation of a future need for a larger military facility the authorities undertook to enlarge the Military Reserve. A large tract of land surrounding the Reserve that was owned by the Honourable James Crooks was swapped for a large piece of the Fort George Commons.

Meanwhile, construction of the tower proceeded slowly, not reaching completion until 1823. The finished tower measured fifty by fifty feet and was twenty-five feet high. The walls of brick and stone were eight feet thick at the base, sloping to seven feet at the parapet. In the basement were two rooms, one for storage and the other a powder

River is essentially necessary to be erected on Mississauga Point."[6] However, it would not be until after the American invasion and recapture of the site by the British that Lieutenant General Gordon Drummond, administrator of Upper Canada, ordered the fortification of Mississauga

View of Fort Niagara on Lake Ontario from the Light House on the British Side, artist unknown, engraved aquatint, *Port Folio* Magazine, 1812, 327. Naïve view of the lighthouse on Mississauga Point which was built of stone but the keeper's cottage apparently was of timber construction.

Courtesy of Lord Durham Rare Books Inc.

Plan of Fort to Be Erected at Mississaugue Pt., drawing on paper, April 8, 1816. This was the grandiose plan for a huge fortress on the point (upper right-hand corner), ten times the size of the present fort. The bastions would have extended as far as Simcoe and Front Streets. Although approved by the administrator of the province, Lieutenant General Drummond, the grand scheme was quietly abandoned by a cash-starved British government after the Napoleonic Wars.

Library and Archives Canada, NMC 17882.

magazine. The main floor consisted of two vaulted barracks rooms. In 1838 a temporary roof was finally replaced by a timber platform on the roof to support four moveable cannons. The exterior walls were originally supposed to be covered in stone, but instead were covered with a plaster or stucco parging, which has been a recurring maintenance problem ever since.

Fort Charlotte near Halifax was the only other fortification of this design — a square tower within a star-shaped earthwork — to have been built in Canada. Only Fort Mississauga has survived.

In response to the Mackenzie rebellion of 1837 some changes were made to Fort Mississauga, including adding a ravelin at the front entrance to enclose the officers' quarters, a wooden sally port reconstructed in brick, and a dry ditch around the perimeter of the fort, which necessitated construction of both a trestle bridge and drawbridge. At least one contemporary visitor to the fort was not impressed. Author Anna Jameson remarked, "The fortress itself I mistook for a dilapidated brewery. This is charming — it <u>looks</u> like peace and security at all events."[9]

Given the limited barracks space and the waning importance of Niagara in the overall military strategy in the decades after the 1822 transfer of British Army headquarters to York, Fort Mississauga was garrisoned on a limited and sporadic basis. Since the fort was heavily fortified with extensive ordnance there was always a contingent of Royal Artillery and Royal Engineers. Detachments of the various regiments that were stationed at Butler's Barracks were on occasion assigned to Fort Mississauga. Local militia served at the fort as well. As one volunteer militia man in January 1865 recalled:

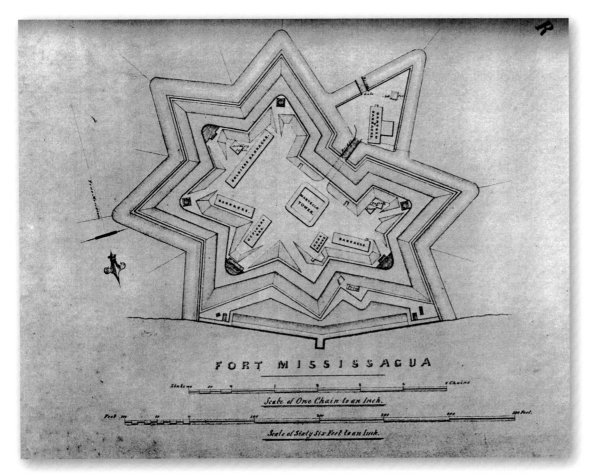

Verification Plan, drawings on paper, 1852. This insert, *Fort Mississagua*, illustrates the central brick and stone tower plus several log buildings within the earthworks as well as a new ravelin to include the officers' barracks at the front entrance to the fort.

Library and Archives Canada, NMC 11403.

… these barracks proved very cold at night, winds from the north and east swept over the bastion heavy with spray, and so raw and penetrating as to make us shudder under our blankets and overcoats.[10]

Moreover, the lake was taking its toll on the ramparts, with severe erosion being an ongoing concern. By 1858 when jurisdiction for the fort was transferred to the provincial government, the fort had been officially dismantled and the earthworks and buildings allowed to deteriorate. The garrison had been withdrawn. When historian Benson Lossing visited the site in 1860 he stated that the only "garrison" was a squatter, Patrick Burns and his family.[11] As with the other military sites along the border, when the American Civil War broke out, emergency repairs were made to the buildings as volunteer militia companies were rushed back in. Similar temporary excitement occurred in response to the Fenian Raids. In 1870 Fort Mississauga officially ceased to be a military work.

During the early Camp Niagara days the summer militia camps included occasional encampment on the Mississauga Reserve/Commons. However in 1874 the

Fort Mississauga, artist A.W. Sangster, pen and ink sketches, No. XLVIII, 1888. Cows, cows, everywhere cows. With all the interior log buildings and artillery removed the abandoned fort was taken over by the cows, both here and on the Fort George Commons as well.

Courtesy of the author.

caretaker for the Military Reserve advertised for tenders to remove in whole or in part the tower and log buildings of Fort Mississauga.[12] Thanks to protests from the mayor and historians the government backed down and the fort was saved. There was renewed interest in the site by the locals. The local militia held their annual musters at the fort. The Mississauga Commons, which included all the land bounded by Simcoe and Queen Streets and the river (the Charles Richardson House remained in private hands), became a chosen spot for picnics and various public events. However, it was never as popular as the Fort George Commons. In 1878, the first golf links were established on a portion of the Mississauga Commons. A private golf club was formed shortly thereafter, which paid an annual rent to the government. Meanwhile in the 1890s the log buildings within the fort were quietly sold and dismantled by the owner of the Queen's Royal Hotel to use in a breakwater for the hotel's riverfront.[13]

With the exception of the Camp Niagara encampment on the commons during the Great War, the Mississauga Commons (also known as the Lake Commons) has continued as a private golf course ever since. For years, the course's second green was within the fort and two tees were played from the bastions. One golfer sued the government (unsuccessfully), claiming that he was hit by a piece of falling brick from the tower.[14] The presence of this unique golf course[15] has certainly limited the public's daytime access to the Mississauga Commons and fort. Nevertheless, for generations locals have sneaked out to the fort along the river or lake paths for picnics, all-night parties, to carve their initials in the brick sally port, and as a lovers' rendezvous. (One citizen quipped that half of Niagara-on-the-Lake was conceived out there!)

In 2002, thanks to the leadership of the Friends of Fort George and financing from interested individuals, a stone dust trail was opened from the corner of Simcoe and Front Streets across a portion of the golf course to the entrance

C.E.F. at Camp Niagara. View from Fort Mississauga, postcard, circa 1916. This was the view of the military encampment on the golf course / Mississauga Common from the roof of the tower.

Courtesy of the author.

of Fort Mississauga. This has greatly improved access to this National Historic Site that continues to suffer from the ravages of nature.

The sunrises from the ramparts are magnificent. On occasion, Parks Canada opens up the old tower for tours ... a rare opportunity not to be missed.

Fort Mississauga, photo, Cosmo Condina, 2011. This view is taken from the approximate site of the 1804 lighthouse on Mississauga Point. In the foreground is the venerable tower constructed primarily from recycled bricks and stone from the burned town. Beyond is the new golf clubhouse.

Courtesy of Cosmo Condina.

CHAPTER 24

The Military Reserve Vs. The Commons: Soldiers and Citizens

Canadian literary critic and historian Northrop Frye theorized that Canadians, at least in their literature, have a "garrison mentality."[1] After all, many urban centres in Canada began as military garrisons, isolated by large distances, frequently severe weather conditions, and ferocious insects. Present Niagara-on-the-Lake is the only community in Canada to have been garrisoned by three forts.[2] Moreover, the mouth of the Niagara River was the only location along the Canadian-American international border with opposing fortresses. Occasionally there was tension between government officials trying to protect the Military Reserve as a restricted non-civilian entity and the townspeople who regarded this large open green as their common lands from the very beginning. For the most part it was an interdependent relationship. Such was Niagara's "garrison mentality."

Even today there is a strong military presence in town: restored Fort George now a living museum, Fort Mississauga on the point, the restored buildings of Butler's Barracks, and the Lincoln and Welland Regimental Museum on the Commons. The garrison's re-enactors, including the fife and drum corps, are often invited to town events, thus frequently reminding the civilians of the town's rich military heritage.

In the late 1770s and 1780s much of today's Commons was known as the King's Fields, apparently cultivated by Butler's Rangers. After they were disbanded in 1784 the Rangers and their families for the most part dispersed to their allotted lands in the township and beyond. Citizens in the tiny but growing nearby settlement of Butlersburg, or West Niagara, no doubt used the open plain already designated a Reserve to graze their livestock and cultivate small gardens as illustrated in Peachey's circa 1787 drawing, showing the edge of the future Commons. One traveller passing through in 1791 commented that land was set aside for a fort and "a large commonty for the use of the town."[3]

In 1796 construction began on Fort George on the easterly edge of the Military Reserve, whose boundaries had finally been established. Within one year, the first known written reference using the term Common was used by the local citizenry. Responding to a request by William Dickson and John McFarland to develop a portion of the southerly edge of the Reserve, the citizens' petition stated that as "the unappropriated Lands around this Town, [are] already too contracted for a sufficient common … your Petitioners humbly pray that your Honor will not permit any further Grants of the Common or Lands now used as such."[4] The request for the grant was denied. A visitor in 1800 reported Fort George "is built on the edge of a handsome green or common which is also skirted by a few tolerable looking houses."[5]

Meanwhile some locals were creating problems for the military, necessitating an announcement in the local paper that "The Digging of Holes or Pits … on the commons is forbidden."[6] Another proclamation threatened a £20 fine for cutting down trees on Crown land.[7] Only three years after completion of the fort, a frustrated commanding officer of the Royal Engineers complained, "[t]he Works are considerably injured by the quantity of Cattle that are continually grazing and treading over every part of them."[8] Officials of the British Indian Department living in the middle of the Reserve complained that locals were stealing fruit from their orchards. Several citizens living on the edge of the Military Reserve complained that fellow civilians were erecting so many enclosures on the commons for their own livestock and gardens that it was becoming far too cluttered and besides, it was interfering with their view of the Commons.[9]

Despite these minor concerns, there was considerable mercantile and social interaction with the townspeople. The garrison's commissariat officers ordered many of their supplies from local merchants and farmers and usually paid with much-appreciated cash. Lucrative contracts were signed with local carpenters, masons, teamsters, tailors, bootmakers, and other trades.

On a social level it was the officers who were most welcomed in the local shops and fine drawing rooms of town. Although some British Army officers were the younger sons of upper-class families, most were from solid middle-class backgrounds. Many were well educated and well travelled, having been posted to various far-flung British posts. Officers of the Royal Engineers received special training in drawing and drafting at Woolwich, England. Their surviving renderings of local scenes have recorded an invaluable view of British colonies. In their free time officers enjoyed many active pursuits such as riding, hunting, and fishing.[10] Polo fields, racing tracks, and cricket pitches were often established near British garrisons, including Niagara. A talented few could sing, play musical instruments, and put on theatricals.[11] The few married officers found accommodation outside the fort. Although Fort George provided a comfortable officers' quarters, many single officers also billeted with local families and close relationships often developed. Just prior to the war, Brock and some senior officers are believed to have been living in Government House but their mess was in Navy Hall. In her booklet *Remains of a Day*,[12] Plousos reconstructs a mess dinner apparently held in the officers' quarters based on the unusual findings of an archaeological excavation of the site. The varied dishes served, the broken wine and liquor glasses, and the shattered porcelain serving dishes suggest an officers' dinner party gone awry — not atypical for the day. Local gentlemen and visitors were often guests at such dinners. Too much gambling, drinking, and duelling led to the undoing of many officers and young gentlemen.

British officers generally attended divine services of the Church of England and in a few cases found eternal peace in the local burying ground. During the capital years, 1792–1796, there was much interaction among the officers, government officials, and the local upper class in assemblies (dances), card games, and special dinners. Niagara continued to be a British garrison town, albeit intermittently until 1870. The apogee of this social swirl seems to have been in the 1838–1842 period when the 1st King's Dragoon Guards were stationed at Butler's Barracks. Niagara was in the midst of a boom. The officers were purported to be all from the upper class and all the troopers were at least six feet tall and excellent horsemen. Their uniform, and in particular their regulation headgear, were especially handsome. The officers were very active in the local Turf Club and the prestigious Niagara Sleigh Club. Their recall to England was much lamented.

The non-commissioned officers (NCOs), having been promoted from the ranks, were of similar social order as the private soldiers. In a survey taken of the ranks in the British Army,[13] out of 120 men, eighty had joined in times of economic hardship and high unemployment, one was listed as a criminal, and two had joined just to grieve their parents. Only one was considered ambitious. After 1794 the majority of the ranks were raised in Ireland. Although life as a soldier may have been better than that of his civilian cousin, it was still not easy: an early rise to the sound of reveille, then six to eight hours of drilling every day to create a cohesive force and ensure automatic responses in battle, manual labour repairing the fortifications and buildings, and two meals a day. The daily pay was one shilling plus one pence for beer money.[14] However, there were many deductions (stoppages) that consumed most of the shilling.

Minuets of the Canadians, artist George Heriot, watercolour over graphite on paper, circa 1801. This rare representation of social life in the Canadas during this period records a "danse" or "assembly" attended by a wide spectrum of civilians and at least one military officer.

Courtesy of the Royal Ontario Museum © ROM, 996.124.1.

Loyal Souls: or a Peep into the Mess Room at St. James's, artist James Gilray, hand coloured engraving by Humphrey, 1797. Mess dinners, to which local gentlemen and visitors were often invited, ended badly on occasion.

Anne S.K. Brown Military Collection, Brown University Library.

Ambitious men could supplement their pay by working on public roads or odd jobs in town. Most enjoyed a few hours free time in the evening, usually spending their penny in one of the many taverns in town, but they were encouraged to wear their uniforms on such jaunts.[15] As with most garrison towns this sometimes led to fights with local toughs. After one fatal brawl between Fort George soldiers and civilian workmen in 1818, the British Army threatened to move the garrison out of Niagara. This elicited a very worried response from the town fathers.[16] Desertions, usually to the republican United States, were a constant problem.

Officer, First King's Dragoon Guards, artist Hoppner Meyer, watercolour, 1839. This young man is wearing the winter uniform of his regiment which created such a social whirl at Niagara.

Courtesy of the Niagara Historical Society and Museum, #2010.001.007.

Women and children were a common sight in the barracks of Niagara's forts. Out of every one hundred rank and file in a British regiment, up to six men were theoretically allowed to bring their wives from Great Britain. Soldiers also married local women.[17] As there were no separate quarters for married men, the husband and wife would hang up blankets around their bunk to obtain some privacy in the barracks. On the eve of the War of 1812 there were thirty-six women and fifty-four children attached to the 41st Regiment at Fort George.[18] A garrison school was provided for both the children and adult students.[19] The women served various duties as washing, ironing, mending, and cooking; wives of the non-commissioned officers were more likely to serve as midwives and as nurses in the garrison hospital. Some found extra work in town as maids to officers and townsfolk. A few enterprising women set themselves up as sutlers, selling tobacco and liquor. Generally it was felt that women made army life more bearable and reduced the desertion rate. One heartless and insensitive army regulation stipulated that in the event of a husband's death the widow would have to remarry within forty-eight hours to retain her ration rights. Otherwise she would have to move into town and fend for herself and children.

Throughout the day various drumbeats were sounded to denote regular events for the personnel in the garrison.[20] So regular were these calls that the local townspeople came to know and expect the calls as well as the soldiers. Indeed, the sounds of practice artillery and musket fire, drum calls, pipers, and military band music became a defining feature of life in the town of Niagara throughout its long military history. Even today, artillery fire at the fort is yet another daily reminder of the town's military heritage. In the early nineteenth century Fort George was the headquarters of the central division of the British Army in Upper Canada. Hence, regimental military bands were encouraged and enjoyed by both the military personnel and townspeople.[21] Similarly, Scottish regiments were stirred by their pipers. Route marches were led by bands playing patriotic music, band tattoos on the Commons were much anticipated, and public

Young Musician Practising in the Officers' Quarters of Fort George, photo Cosmos Condina, 2010. Music became an everyday aspect of life in Niagara for both the military and civilian population: the large military bands, the fife and drum corps, the Scottish pipers and fiddlers, the marches and tattoos as well as the daily rhythm of the various drum beats and bugle calls.

Courtesy of Cosmo Condina.

celebrations such as the sovereign's birthday were equally celebrated with great fanfare by the garrison and the towns-people. Such events were great morale boosters for the civilian population particularly during tough economic times. Musicians from these bands also played at town social functions including popular country dances. The lowly rank and file often amused themselves with Jew's harps.

As the nineteenth century progressed the British Army at Niagara was eventually withdrawn, which only added to the town's economic woes.

Fort George was in ruins with its eroding earthen works gradually reverting back to grassy common lands. The locals were using the Commons more than ever for grazing their cows, sheep, pigs, and horses. A common sight well into the twentieth century was a long procession of geese led by an old gander waddling its way to and from the Commons. Some townsfolk kept their animals enclosed on the Commons for the season,[22] others were concerned about safety[23] and herded their cows back and forth from their barns in town. Ted Bradley recalled that as a boy it was his job to retrieve the family cow from the Commons. While Ted was milking his cow, his fox terrier Chub would lick off the burs from the cow's hooves. When finished, the cow would turn its head and lick Chub's face in appreciation. (As late as 1921 the local town council was trying to deal with "Niagara's greatest trouble every spring … the 'Cow Question'" — cows running unattended through the streets.[24]) When the town authorized the planting of hundreds of trees in town and along Queen's Parade, each sapling had to enclosed in a small box fence to keep off the cows. One pleasant consequence of all the livestock and horses roaming the Commons was the popular pastime of gathering of mushrooms. Setting out in the predawn hours, families would vie with one another for the best spots.[25] Firewood was also being harvested from the Oak Grove, albeit clandestinely.

With the exception of the short-lived military buildups during the American Civil War and Fenian Raids, most of the buildings at Butler's Barracks were either leased out or kept boarded up, however, the military hospital in the middle of the commons was being used by local physicians as a community hospital. All the artillery ordnance was removed from Fort Mississauga and the owner of the Queen's Royal Hotel received permission to dismantle all the log buildings within the fort to use for the hotel's shore protection.[26] During this quiet period in Niagara a new social phenomenon began to emerge. Soldiers who had served in the area began to return to Niagara with their families to retire. This was especially true of the veterans of the Royal Canadian Rifle Regiment but the trend continued through the Camp Niagara years. In reality, many of Niagara's residents were former military men, either from the militia or regular regiments.

The new Canadian government passed the Militia Act in 1868 that provided for a small standing army and a large volunteer militia. The announcement that the Commons in Niagara had been chosen as the site for a summer militia camp for Military District No.2 was met with great relief. Camp Niagara, the largest of the summer camps in the country, welcomed 4,600 men that first year. The attendance was even greater the next year. Local merchants were busy selling building timber, hay, straw, candles, coal, foodstuffs, ice, and many other supplies to the camp's quartermaster. Photo galleries, souvenir shops, and penny arcades popped up along Picton and Queen Streets, catering to the soldiers and the family members who arrived on Sundays to visit them. Local citizens ventured out to the camp. In his diary entry for June 6, 1875, Town Councillor John Blake recorded visiting several militiamen and then having a good chat and smoke with the reporter from the *Globe* in his tent.[27] Summer soirees were held for the officers, and the churches were full on Sundays. With a few exceptions Camp Niagara continued annually for the next ninety-five years. During the latter part of the nineteenth century the military shared the Fort George Commons with an eighteen-hole golf course plus

Scenes on the Niagara Frontier, a military ball at Niagara, circa 1890. A well-attended local ball with both military and civilian guests.

Courtesy of the Niagara Historical Society and Museum, #2011.001.017.

Attendees of the International Golf Tournament on the Fort George Links, photo, circa 1902. The gaily decorated club house for the golf club was also the headquarters for the commandant of Camp Niagara.

Courtesy of the Niagara Historical Society and Museum, #982.384.b-9.

a few wandering cows. In fact it was reported that "cattle who venture within the limits of the camp are not infrequently commandeered by the soldiers and surreptitiously milked."[28] The commandant's headquarters and the golf club's clubhouse shared the same buildings, known as "the compound."[29] One Toronto newspaper reported that enterprising young boys were known to sneak onto the Reserve offering various home-baked goods and other delicacies.[30]

With the opening of the lakeshore firing range in 1908, there were daily marches through town, led by a rousing military band. The author's great-uncle recalled standing as a young boy in front of his grandparents' home every morning on Queen Street madly waving his flag at the passing soldiers. "One day the [lead] officer halted the column, dismounted, picked me up and placed me at the front of his saddle for a short distance — what a thrill."[31]

During the Great War, the camp was enlarged and its season lengthened with up to 18,000 men in camp at any one time. The Fort George golf course had been closed and

the Mississauga Links were soon covered with hundreds of canvas tents as well. Locals were discouraged from walking onto either campsite; in essence they had lost their commons. Nevertheless, many local families welcomed home-sick soldiers into their homes. Later, postcards and letters would arrive from Europe but on occasion the letters would ominously stopped coming.[32] The camp's impact on the town's economy was staggering. Local merchants were happy, as were the vaudeville and moving picture theatre operators on Queen Street, but others benefited too. "Bluebird Freel" had the contract for emptying all the "honey buckets" from the outhouses on the Commons, which he then transported in his horse-drawn wagon that was painted blue. Back on his farm, the buckets were then spread onto his peach orchard.[33]

In the spring of 1917, the citizens of Niagara were unexpectedly drawn into the American war effort for several months. When the United States finally entered the Great War, an officers' training camp was quickly established at Fort Niagara. However, there was insufficient accommodation for all the officers and their families in Youngstown, New York, and thus some were billeted in homes in Niagara and shuttled back and forth in small ferries[34] — an interesting vignette in Canadian-American relations.

Perhaps the townspeople's finest hour in terms of humanitarianism came with the outpouring of support for the young volunteer Poles arriving for training at Camp Niagara in late 1917. Despite some hesitation at first, the town threw open its public buildings while individual citizens offered their homes to two thousand young men over the winter while the men trained to liberate their homeland. When the Spanish Flu pandemic struck the following year, many locals selflessly nursed the stricken soldiers. A thankful Polish nation has recognized this heroic act with an annual pilgrimage ever since.

After the Great War, annual Camp Niagara resumed. The Royal Canadian Regiment and the Royal Canadian Dragoons, known as the "permanent cadre," spent their entire summer at the camp, in part to train the militia. As many came with their families they rented homes for the summer or billeted with local townsfolk.[35] The officers entertained the locals at their elegant garden parties and Christmas in July celebrations.[36] Townspeople reciprocated with receptions and special church functions. Every July 4 George Rand threw open his estate on John Street opposite the Commons to his neighbours and the Camp's officers to celebrate Independence Day.[37] Local dances in the park provided an opportunity for the young men to meet the town's daughters. However, soldiers could be intimidating; one local girl recalled driving along the edge of the Commons when a service man jumped onto her car's running board, making unwelcome advances. She rolled up the window, squeezing his fingers, and eventually dumped him off at the edge of the camp. Others had more pleasant childhood memories of playing on the commons and being treated by camp personnel to wonderful ice cream[38] or fresh bread and butter.[39] Youngsters were known to bring their sick pets to the camp's veterinarian expecting him to perform miracles.[40] It was during this period that the restoration of Fort George and Navy Hall was carried out, providing much-needed local

employment. However, the fort site was no longer available as common lands.

During the Second World War Camp Niagara operated all year round, and with it came tighter security enforced by the provost police. Again the town opened up its arms to the men and women in training. The merchants were happy and some of the town's unemployed found work in camp. One civilian, who was now able to pay her bills, was an attractive woman, "Regimental Barbara," who was often seen in the evenings riding onto the Camp astride two blankets thrown over her tawny-coloured horse.[41] The bugle calls with their characteristic notes and cadence were back. The daily parade marches through town with bands playing became once again a defining aspect of the town's daily rhythm.

To show their respect and encouragement many townsfolk turned up at the waterfront or railway spur line to bid farewell to the parting soldiers. For some of the local girls it was an unforgettable moment of emotional goodbyes to lovers and husbands.

On Sundays, drumhead services were held on the Commons as were church parades to each of the churches. On one particularly hot, humid Sunday at St. Mark's, the doors were wide open to catch any breeze and the pews were filled with sweating servicemen. The service was suddenly interrupted by the entrance of a female dog followed excitedly behind by twenty male dogs, proceeding up one aisle across in front of the altar and back out the other aisle. The incident was regaled for years.[42]

When rumours abounded that the camp was about to be closed, a press release from the army soon responded, "it is unlikely that the Canadian Government will ever again consider disposing of Camp Niagara. The camp is too fondly remembered by generations of Militiamen and wartime soldiers."[43] Camp Niagara was closed permanently within a decade. With the transfer of the property from the Department of National Defence to Parks Canada in 1969, the term Military Reserve was officially no longer relevant. Finally these hundreds of acres of rolling grassy plains and oak forest were truly common lands, Niagara's Commons.

CHAPTER 25

Flora and Fauna

The original Fort George Military Reserve encompassed at least four eco-systems: an oak savannah, partially treed creek-beds and ravines, the woods that are known today as Paradise Grove, and the Niagara River shoreline (riparian zone).

What is now known as the Commons and the adjacent town site was black oak savannah. A savannah refers to open fields or meadows of tall native prairie grasses with some shade-tolerant plants and 10 to 35 percent tree cover. According to Native tradition, maize, beans, and squash were cultivated on these grassy plains long before the arrival of the Europeans. One of the prairie grasses was the fragrant and versatile sweetgrass, much prized by the Natives. By 1790 the lands above Navy Hall were already open plains, "Land cleared by Kings Rangers commonly called the Generals Fields,"[1] or "a fine turf."[2] Given the prolonged and at times heavy occupation of the Commons throughout its documented history by both soldiers and livestock, many of the native grasses and wild flowers have been trampled and partially crowded out by imported invasive species[3] and weeds. Nevertheless, the areas adjacent to the woodlands do still contain some native grasses growing under a few tall trees, many of which are black oaks, hence the designation black oak savannah.

Also found growing in this transitional zone between the savannah and dense woodlot is perhaps the most iconic tree of the Commons, the French thorns. For generations, legend has it that French army officers from Fort Niagara planted the original thorns on this side of the Niagara River in the 1750s. As the story goes, the slips for these "contorted, twisted, writhing" hawthorns were brought from Europe but originated from the Saviour's crown of thorns in Jerusalem.[4] However, these hawthorns, with their pungent blossoms in the spring, scarlet "haws" in the fall, and

French Thorn Tree on a Wintry Commons, photo, 1997. This view across a wintry Commons towards Fort George illustrates, on the left, a typical young "French Thorn" tree with its dense irregular thorn-laden branches reaching down to the ground.

Courtesy of the author.

Paradise Grove ca. 1927

Paradise Grove, photo, 1927. This photo of the edge of Paradise Grove illustrates the oak savannah: tall prairie grasses flourishing under a partial canopy of oak trees.

Courtesy of the Niagara Parks Commission Archives.

treacherous spur-like thorns on long branches extending down to the ground, can also be found all along the Niagara River and onto the Niagara escarpment. Their only natural enemy appears to be wild grapevines which can eventually completely envelope them. Interestingly, in Britain after the Enclosure Acts hawthorn trees were often planted in hedgerows by the new owners anxious to keep the "commoners" out of their former common lands.

Generations of townspeople and outsiders have returned every year to the oak savannah for the gathering of mushrooms, usually in late summer. For over 150 years cows were almost always grazing on the Commons, thus fertilizing the already rich turf. Perhaps the remarkable diversity in colour, size, and shape of these delicacies that bursts forth

every year can be explained by so many horses from so many different locales over so many years, having cantered across the Commons, thus bringing in many diverse fungal spores. Moreover, some fungi have a symbiotic relationship with oaks. Families still rise early in the morning to excitedly stake out their favourite mushroom sites on the Commons.

Early maps of the Military Reserve reveal several creeks in shallow ravines draining the savannah. Some of these have been flattened or diverted, particularly those draining towards the Niagara River. The hollow in present Simcoe Park is a remnant of one of those natural drainage systems. The One Mile Creek[5] skirts the southern edge of the Commons before cutting across the western corner near present King and John Street. There huge willow trees[6] still thrive on the

A Group of Historic Thorn Trees, artist unknown, watercolour. This rendering depicts a grove of French thorns in the early spring. Once all the foliage is out and given the long dense branches hiding long thorns, it can be almost impossible to even crawl under a mature tree without injury.

Courtesy of the Toronto Public Library, Toronto Reference Library, John Ross Robertson Collection, T17060.

ever-present moisture.[7] The creek then meanders under King Street and through "the Wilderness." There remnants of first growth flora have survived and hence one can deduce what these original creek beds must have been like: immense oaks, sycamores, Balm of Gilead, with various other Carolinian shrubs, trees, and wildflowers.

The remarkable woodlot on the southeastern tip of the original Military Reserve has never been cultivated. It has been

Fungi on the Commons, photo, Jim Smith, 2011. There is a great variety of fungi on the Commons, many regarded as delicacies by the locals. These photos should not be regarded as an invitation to sample these particular specimens.

Courtesy of Jim Smith.

variously known as the Queen's Bush, the Oak Grove, Ontario Heights,[8] and most recently Paradise Grove. The latter name apparently originated with the Michigan Central Railway, which advertised excursions to a picnic area within the oak forest. A few romantics have claimed that soldiers gave the name to their favourite rendezvous spot for lovers' trysts.[9]

For millions of tourists approaching the old town from the Niagara Parkway, passing along Queen's Parade[10] under the canopy of Paradise Grove towards the expansive grassy Commons beyond, this is their first introduction to the town. The huge oak trees in the woods and on the savannah were a prime reason for the establishment of Navy Hall in 1765. Oak was favoured by British boat-builders. Oak bark was also used by early local tanners. Some townspeople regarded these woods as common lands for firewood and timber. We do not know how many giant oaks were harvested but a few were left standing perhaps as a wind-break as several first growth trees have survived. Mrs. Simcoe records pleasant walks in "the woods near Navy Hall"[11] in the mid 1790s. After the war, maps of the site indicate "Plantation of Young Oaks"[12] or a "bush of Scrubby Oaks."[13]

The one unfortunate incursion into this oak forest was the 1860s building of the Erie and Ontario Railway spur line from along John Street East diagonally across the grove towards Navy Hall. It passed through "the cutting," an excavated hollow twenty feet deep and eighty feet wide, cut through the woods. An 1894 map[14] indicates, in the western section near Queen's Parade, a station at which passengers could disembark.[15] Apparently they would then proceed across to the eastern section to picnic under a small octagonal pavilion. This spur line, which apparently was later used to bring in Polish volunteers to Camp Niagara during the Great War, was abandoned shortly thereafter; its course is still visible as part of a large somewhat overgrown drainage ditch. According to early photos and postcards, much of the eastern grove was eventually cleared of underbrush and thinned out to provide for a public picnic area. Townspeople and tourists would board small boats at town

A White Oak on the edge of Paradise Grove, photo Cosmo Condina, 2011. This stately white oak tree is probably a survivor of first growth forest. Although black oaks predominate, the slower growing white oaks coexist in Paradise Grove.

Courtesy of Cosmo Condina.

docks and be rowed upstream, climb a staircase up the river embankment and picnic in the grove. Later a small portion of the southeastern tip of the grove was leased for small cottages. These were taken down with improvements to the River Road and the Niagara Parks Commission (NPC) parking lot at the end of John Street East. During the 1930s there was also a shallow gravel quarry in the middle of the eastern grove.

Meanwhile, around the corner in the western grove near John Street a carousel was set up in the 1890s. Possibly on lease from the railway company, it was not a money-maker and was soon dismantled and moved to the Exhibition Grounds in Toronto. Three small gas huts were also situated deep in the western grove during the Second World War.

Today Paradise Grove consists of seventy-three acres, of which sixty-five acres are owned by Parks Canada and eight acres are owned by the NPC. Strictly speaking, the southern half of the NPC's grove is not in the original Military Reserve. NPC however supervises the maintenance of the entire grove. A recent inventory of the flora[16] confirmed the existence of at least six different varieties of oak, some first growth.[17] Carolinian trees abound including Sassafrass, sycamore, black cherry, flowering dogwood, and even a rare huge black gum. Birch, beech, black walnut, butternut, chestnut,[18] hickory, locust, and maple, as well as several conifers, are also to be found. Wildflowers such as hepaticas, violets, may-apples (which are often found under white oaks), Solomon's Seal, star-flowered Solomon's Seal, cardinal flower, bloodroot, and rue Anemones brighten the forest

Carousel in Paradise Grove, photo, circa 1890. The Lewis family is seen here enjoying a ride on the carousel set up on the edge of Paradise Grove and operated by the Wills brothers, vaudeville actors. After apparently only one year of operation it was dismantled and transported to the Exhibition Grounds in Toronto.

Courtesy of Bob Lewis.

Naturalized sunflower on the Commons, photo, Cosmo Condina, 2010. Various plants have become naturalized on the Commons and in Paradise Grove. On the right in the distance one can see the Shaw Festival Theatre, which has gradually become one with its carefully landscaped environment.

Courtesy of Cosmo Condina.

floor. Even naturalized Lily of the Valley is abundant. Ferns are also present. Undergrowths of wild sweet briar, wild raspberry, and poison ivy keep many humans away today.

As part of its management plan for the long-term protection of the grove and adjacent savannah, the NPC has undertaken to remove several invasive species including Norway maple, European buckthorn, and garlic mustard, both by selective cuts and controlled burns. Controlled burns, which must be carefully timed in the spring, burn off the buildup of debris and small invasive woody plant seedlings while increasing the production of nutrients for both flora and fauna.[19] This "friendly fire" also sets back the early growth of invasive grasses and weeds while the native warm-season prairie grasses are still dormant. The Natives recognized the value of controlled fires as well as natural fires set off by lightning strikes long before the arrival of Europeans. On the southwest edge of the woods where the Second World War military hospital was built, several naturalized species of trees, shrubs, and flowers have survived.

Much of the Niagara River shoreline has changed since the 1830s: the section from Navy Hall to the foot of King Street bears no resemblance to the forty acres of marshy floodlands. Upstream from Navy Hall a steep embankment with large oak trees near the edge, as well as white birch, locusts, maples, walnuts, poplars, hawthorns, low shrubs, and sumac[20] still characterize this portion of the river's edge. Naturalized lilacs and apple trees are found closer to Navy Hall.

The fauna of the Military Reserve/Commons reflects the flora in the various ecosystems. Out on the savannah, the mammal populations of mice, voles, groundhogs, rabbits, foxes, and the more recently arrived coyote, seem to be subject to population cycles. Bears and wolves were once a potential menace for livestock kept on the Commons. As a ready source of fresh water, the creek beds supported a greater variety of animals, including amphibians, reptiles, and fish in the streams. Salmon were apparently abundant in the One Mile Creek on the Commons. The mouth of the Niagara River has long been known for its great abundance and variety of fish, in particular sturgeon and whitefish. The government wharf at Navy Hall has been a favourite fishing spot for nearly 250 years. The woodlands provided a daytime refuge for many of the savannah predators, but was also home to raccoon, squirrel, chipmunk, skunk, and deer. The presence of beavers is occasionally evident by freshly cut birch trees on the river bank. Opossums are recent arrivals.

With two notable exceptions, the bird population today probably resembles that of the early years of the Military

White Fish, artist Elizabeth Simcoe, pen and ink sketch, Navy Hall, May 16, 1796. The mouth of the Niagara River has long been known for its abundant whitefish and sturgeon. A whitefish chowder served to French explorer LaSalle by indigenous people was the first recorded meal on the west side of the Niagara River.

Archives of Ontario, Simcoe Family fonds, F47-11-1-0-193.

Reserve. No doubt many birds were frightened away during the tumultuous years of Camp Niagara, at least during the summer months when training was most active. The open grassy plains surrounded by tall trees are ideal for raptors: eagles,[21] hawks, owls, peregrine falcons, and kestrels are still sighted, as are turkey vultures. It is not unusual during a long walk on the Commons today to see at least one red-tailed hawk watching from a tall tree. Meadowlarks, bobolinks, and red-winged black birds are often sighted over the grassy plains. Today, mechanical cutting of the tallgrass is delayed so that these ground-nesting birds can raise their young unharmed. Orioles, Blue Jays, cardinals, woodpeckers, chickadees, and sparrows are heard in the creek beds and the woods. The plaintive call of Mourning Doves counterpoints the raucous screams of crows. Wild turkeys nearly extinct, have been re-introduced to the area and are often seen feeding in the oak savannah.

Great numbers of "Musquito hawks" [*sic*] over the Commons were described by New York Governor DeWitt Clinton on a visit in 1810.[22] Research so far has failed to reveal whether these birds have any modern counterpart although Mrs. Simcoe suggested they might have been "whipper wills" [*sic*].[23]

In September 1914 a passenger pigeon named Martha dropped dead from her perch in an American zoo, thus marking the end of a species that had numbered between 3 and 6 billion when Europeans arrived in North America. The pigeons' extinction was due to a lethal combination of relentless hunting by settlers, loss of forest habitats where the birds fed voraciously on acorns and other nuts, and the fact that mating pairs produced only one offspring (squab), which after a few weeks would be pushed from the nest onto the forest floor to fend for itself. Mass migrations of these pigeons over Niagara were recorded by many: Mrs. Simcoe found the phenomenon "a surprising sight."[24] A visiting army officer gave perhaps the best description:

> I have seen a flock of pigeons undoubtedly two or three miles wide, and which was three or four hours flying past one spot ... I have seen

Ectopistes migratorius, Passenger Pigeons, artist John James Audobon, hand-coloured aquatint, engraved, printed and coloured by R. Havell (& Son), London. Although numbering 3 to 6 billion when Europeans arrived in North America, these beautiful birds were extinct by the early twentieth century.

Courtesy Natural History Museum © The Natural History Museum, London.

the Indian boys on the plains of Niagara knock down more with their sticks, than an equal number of person occupied at the same time with their guns. The flight is frequently so low as to pass within two or three feet from the ground.[25]

The Niagara River is famous for its water birds: as a flyway in spring and fall for huge flocks of migrating birds such as swans and geese, as an open water refuge for overwintering ducks and gulls from the north, and as a summer home for other species from the south.[26] Many of these birds provided a welcome food source for Natives and early townsfolk.

It is beyond the scope of this book to review all the known insects on the Military Reserve, but several species of flying insects are noteworthy.

Mankind has long been plagued by inundations of grasshoppers. Shortly after her arrival in the summer of 1792, in her diary, Mrs. Simcoe recorded with horror:

> Here are numbers of winged grasshoppers. They are hard, scaly and ugly as rhinoceros, and the colour of dead leaves. The high grounds above Navy Hall are so covered with them that the whole field appears in motion.[27]

From its earliest years of settlement Niagara was known for being unhealthy. Sir John Johnson, although pleased with his nephew's new appointment at Niagara, despaired for his health;[28] even HRH Prince Edward, Colonel of the Royal Fusiliers, was cognizant of Niagara's bad reputation.[29] Small pox was still endemic (particularly among the Natives), consumption (tuberculosis), measles, and "catarrh" (probably pneumonia), among other afflictions, struck down Niagara's population on occasion, but it was "the fever and ague" that was most widespread. It spared no one: recurrent severe episodes forced a jaundiced Lieutenant Governor Simcoe to finally request a leave of absence to England; Administrator Russell and his sister were both laid low for weeks; during one summer, out of a garrison of three- to four-hundred soldiers at

Fort George, "scarcely… fifty were fit for duty."[30] In the 1830s one visitor to Niagara called the citizens "yellow heads."[31]

The common symptoms of the ague were recurrent episodes of shaking rigors, extreme malaise, with severe headaches and muscle pains followed by high fever and then chills. Some patients developed liver failure or widespread bleeding and died. Unlike most diseases of the day, the ague could at least partially be controlled by "Peruvian Bark," or cinchona. Local home remedies included Sassafrass tea and a beverage from boiling wild strawberry leaves and roots. Severe cases were subjected to bleeding and purgatives.

Physicians and their patients had long ascribed the transmission of various diseases, but in particular remittent fevers, to the effluvia or miasma arising from swamps and lowlands. In Niagara many suspected the marshlands or swamp along the Niagara River below Navy Hall. It was also noted that mosquitoes were especially prevalent around standing water. In fact, soldiers from the Fort George garrison offered to fill in the swampy area without compensation so long as they were supplied with "the requisite tools, and be allowed a puncheon of rum, to protect them from the contagion or evil effects of the pestilential miasma."[32] Their offer was refused. Amongst the Natives only the infants were afflicted, which in part was attributed to adults covering their bodies with various "greasy substances."[33] By the 1850s reports of the ague at Niagara die out. We know today that the fever and ague was a type of malaria due to a parasite transmitted by female mosquitoes of the species *Aedes quadrimaculatus*. Some experts hypothesize that the disease made its way to Upper Canada with British regiments that had been previously stationed in the West Indies where the disease was endemic. The drainage of the wetlands by the Niagara Harbour and Dock Company as well as the clearing of swamps elsewhere in the township may explain the eventual local disappearance of the malaria. Quinine which is present in Peruvian Bark is still used today in the fight against malaria. Mosquitoes continued to be a pest, especially for the trainees at Camp Niagara. Local contractors conducted intensive spraying programs every summer during Camp Niagara and prior to the World Boy Scout Jamboree in 1955. Nearby residents enjoyed the near absence of mosquitoes during the "spray years."[34]

Other flying insects of note include monarch butterflies, which occasionally descend en masse upon the flowers of Common Milkweed on the Commons. Tremendous numbers of fire flies in Paradise Grove continue to fascinate on a warm summer's evening.

CHAPTER 26

Save the Commons

Almost from the moment the boundaries of the Fort George Military Reserve were established by the colonial government in 1796, the first formal petition to encroach upon the lands was presented.[1] Many more would follow.

In January 1797 a petition was read in the executive council from thirty prominent citizens in Niagara. This was in response to a petition by William Dickson and John McFarland[2] for a portion of the southern edge of the Reserve in what is now known as Paradise Grove. The concerned citizens' petition read in part:

> … That for the well being of all residents in town, & in particular of the industrious lower classes — a range of Common or Town Parks are of indispensable necessity for pasturing Milch [sic] Cows & draft Cattle … your Petitioners humbly pray that your Honor will not permit any further Grants of the Common or Lands now used as such….[3]

The petition for the grant was disallowed.

However, by the 1820s the colonial government was willing to give up a significant portion of the northeastern part of the Military Reserve. The change of heart was based on several factors. The threat of another war with the Republic to the south seemed remote. Moreover, the military presence at Niagara had shifted to Butler's Barracks

to the west and Fort Mississauga at the mouth of the river, and the Fort George site was being allowed to deteriorate. The military decided they required a larger defensive area around Fort Mississauga; hence the great swap occurred, whereby in exchange for his holdings at Mississauga Point, the Honourable James Crooks was granted five new blocks on the Reserve for development. There were other ongoing community issues that needed attention: the Church of England had established a community burying ground and a substantial church on Reserve land decades earlier without an actual land grant, hence the government finally proceeded with a formal grant in perpetuity. In an ecumenical gesture, the Roman Catholics were granted four acres for their parish lands. Such largesse seems to have been welcomed by all. However, when the Niagara Harbour and Dock Company petitioned for the forty acres of swampy land and water rights along the Reserve's riverfront there was considerable grumbling both by military officials as well as local merchants. When the government hesitated, the Lieutenant Governor intervened[4] and the property passed into private hands forever.

By the mid 1830s the British government, in an effort to cut expenses, withdrew regular troops from Upper Canada and instructed local military officials to lease some of their buildings and lands. The commandant's quarters in the middle of the Reserve were leased; lands on the Reserve were divided into ten-acre plots and were to be leased out.

Mackenzie's rebellion in late 1837 brought these plans to a crashing halt. Several British regiments were rushed back to Niagara and a building boom of military buildings at Butler's Barracks ensued. Fifteen years later, with the threat of war or insurrection once again diminished, the British government proposed an enrolled pensioner scheme: in an effort to maintain some military presence but also reduce pensioners' costs, veterans would be granted small two- to three-acre plots upon which they could erect a home and cultivate the land. The locals objected to this potential loss of their commons[5] and before any decision was made the military lands were transferred to the Province of Canada; the various buildings were leased out and a variety of schemes for the use of these "surplus lands" was entertained. Fortunately, all these schemes to divide up the Military Reserve/Commons fell through but it was the American Civil War and the Fenian scare that ended any further discussion to carve up the Reserve. On this occasion when the troops were rushed back to Niagara most of the leased military buildings were not available for the troops. In order to avoid a similar embarrassing experience, the new government of Canada decided to retain the lands strictly for military purposes such as summer militia camps with no thought of selling the land — at least not for half a century.

In the 1850s promoter Samuel Zimmerman extended the Erie and Ontario Railway into the town of Niagara. Initially, the plan was to run the tracks directly across the Commons to the waterfront. The government resisted and forced the railway to run along the edge of the Commons on King Street towards the river instead, as well as a spur line along the Carriage Trail (John Street East). A decade later, despite some resistance, the railway ran a spur line through the Oak Grove and forced the relocation of Navy Hall.

In the early 1880s Niagara's postmaster, Robert Warren,[6] dreamed of establishing a summer camp similar to the American Chautauqua held annually near Jamestown, New York,[7] "under Religious, Temperance and Educational auspices, for Literary, Social and Scientific purposes."[8] His original plan called for the transformation of his own farm on the River Road and the nearby Paradise Grove lands — which were under lease at that time by the Michigan Central Railway Company — into a campground to be known as the Fort George Assembly. After considerable discussion (but apparently no vocal citizens' objections) the Dominion government turned down the request.[9] Instead the assembly purchased the ninety-two-acre former Crooks' property on Lake Ontario at One Mile Creek where the Canadian Chautauqua came into being, consisting eventually of two hotels, cottages, tents, and a large four-thousand-seat amphitheatre. Although the assembly eventually failed, the Chautauqua neighbourhood still retains its unique vibrant community spirit. However, on passing through Paradise Grove today with its huge oaks and remnants of first growth Carolinian forest, one cannot help but feel very thankful for the government's groundbreaking decision.

In the latter half of the nineteenth century there was a growing interest in Ontario's heritage; local historical societies were being formed, often spearheaded by "spinster guardians." Centennial celebrations of the arrival of the Loyalists in 1884 and the opening of the first parliament of Upper Canada in 1892, both held on the Commons, received much local and provincial attention. Well-attended centennial reunions for St. Mark's and St. Andrew's soon followed. Much of the planning and documentation for these events was due to the untiring efforts of local teacher, historian, and author Janet Carnochan. Miss Janet as she was affectionately known, was the driving force behind the formation of the Niagara Historical Society in 1895. Twelve years later, this petite dynamo proudly opened Memorial Hall, the first purpose-built museum in Ontario. Without her fearless leadership the present Commons would probably not exist today. In 1898 a successful petition to the government by Miss Janet curtailed the railway's activities in Paradise Grove and "the Fort George enclosure."[10] In 1905, Miss Janet learned of a federal scheme to subdivide and sell in ten-acre residential lots the Military Reserve. In her remarkable "Letter from the President of the Historical Society, Referring to the Military Grounds," she castigates the government for

Janet Carnochan, artist E. Wyly Grier, oil, circa 1920. More than any other person, "Miss Janet" deserves credit for saving the Commons we know and appreciate today.

Courtesy of the Niagara Historical Society and Museum, #988.246.

having only recently spent great sums for upgrading the Fort George and Mississauga common for military purposes and for even suggesting the possible desecration of these lands:

> The Pass of Thermopylae, the Plains of Marathon, the field of Bannockburn and that of Waterloo, the Plains of Abraham all rouse patriotic feelings, and the Plains of Niagara should do no less.[11]

Miss Janet then repeated a request that had been presented to the government by town officials ten years earlier,[12]

in which the Military Reserve be placed in the hands of the Niagara Falls Park Commissioners and that the "ground be retained, as now, a heritage for coming generations." The federal government quietly retreated, deciding to retain the land as a Military Reserve, thus protecting it for another fifty years. A few years later, the historical society, appalled at the state of Navy Hall, convinced the government to stabilize the building.

From the eve of the Great War until the return of peace in 1945, the Military Reserve served as home turf for Camp Niagara. New barracks were added and the old buildings of Butler's Barracks were recycled for various uses. There were

Old Navy Hall, photos, circa 1908. The historic commissariat building known as Navy Hall was allowed to deteriorate. Reacting to a groundswell of public indignation from historians and local townspeople, the federal government finally initiated a partial restoration.

Courtesy of the Judith Sayers Collection.

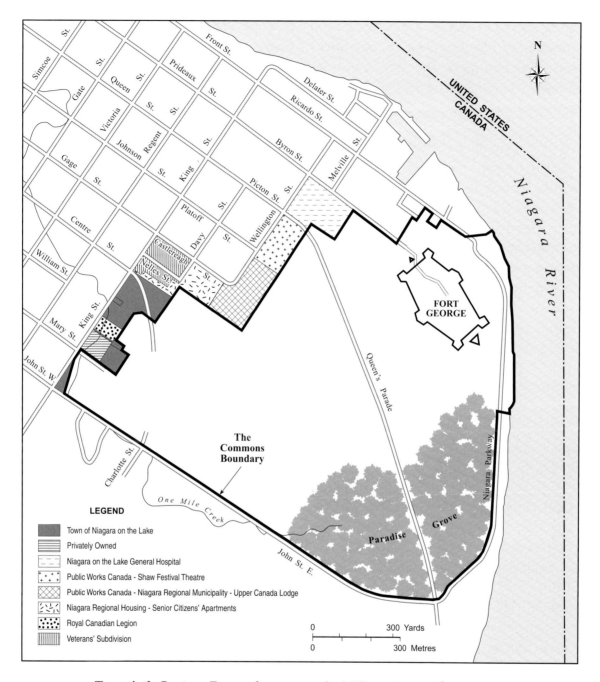

LEGEND

	Town of Niagara on the Lake
	Privately Owned
	Niagara on the Lake General Hospital
	Public Works Canada - Shaw Festival Theatre
	Public Works Canada - Niagara Regional Municipality - Upper Canada Lodge
	Niagara Regional Housing - Senior Citizens' Apartments
	Royal Canadian Legion
	Veterans' Subdivision

0   300 Yards

0   300 Metres

Twentieth Century Encroachments on the Military Reserve/Commons.

a few minor incursions on the edge of Paradise Grove, but for the most part the Military Reserve remained intact. After the Second World War the many surplus buildings were turned over to the War Assets Corporation for disposal. Some were moved offsite and found new uses.[13] The local population became very concerned as they witnessed several historic buildings being systematically demolished. Though strapped for funds, the Niagara Town and Township Recreational

Council purchased the two old buildings in the compound as a centre for a "Boys and Girls Club" and a "Teen Town." A local family leased a rear apartment. The council, in a desperate attempt to preserve surviving historic buildings, also obtained a lease on the ordnance gun shed, the commissariat storehouse, and the two-storey barracks. For a community deeply mired in a post-war slump, such heroic measures are truly remarkable. With resumption of the summer camps, the leases were summarily cancelled, but by then Ottawa realized that Niagara was indeed dedicated to preserving its built and natural heritage. Eventually in 1969 the Department of National Defence turned over the lands to what is now Parks Canada. The compound was reclaimed by the federal government, and together with the other three buildings they were designated as The Butler's Barracks National Historic Site.

The overwhelming success of the Shaw Festival in the old court house soon necessitated a search for a new dedicated permanent festival theatre. Several sites were suggested but eventually attention was directed to the edge of the Commons on the corner of Queen's Parade and Wellington. Here stood the vacated Boy Scout lodge which in turn had been the original site of the town's baseball diamond. Initially the federal government rejected the request, but with the prospect of Camp Niagara closing the feds agreed to lease 4.12 acres. An old agreement with the Niagara-on-the-Lake Golf Club had to be retired as well. There were vocal objections to the loss of this historic corner of the Commons across from the hospital; nevertheless, the theatre opened in June 1973 and was lauded for being so carefully landscaped into its environment. Today it's difficult to imagine the town and indeed the Commons without the Festival Theatre ensconced on that corner.

Also in the 1970s another piece of the Commons was designated for community use — a needed senior citizens' apartment building on the site of the old fair racetrack on Castlereagh Street. How could the government have turned down such a "motherhood" project?

The one modern encroachment on the Commons that galvanized public resentment and anger more than any other project surely was the Niagara Region's Upper Canada Lodge Nursing Home. Perched on the corner of Wellington and Castlereagh Streets on six acres of virgin commons, this 40,000 square foot complex, with an asphalt parking lot for sixty to eighty vehicles and provision for more if needed, pushed the urban space out towards the historic Indian Council House site and Otter Trail. The unique "viewplanes" across the Commons were irrevocably distorted. Although

Margherita Austin Howe, C.M. (1921–2006). For several decades Margherita, as a concerned citizen, spearheaded various activist projects including "Operation Clean (Niagara)" for which she was inducted into the Order of Canada. As a founding director of The Niagara Conservancy she was actively involved in several attempts to save the Commons.

Courtesy of the Howe family.

well-intentioned by some, it was soon revealed that the nursing home was not needed at that time. The Niagara Region had documented that there was a significant shortage of vacant long-term beds in the city of Niagara Falls and already an excess of empty beds in Niagara-on-the-Lake's existing nursing home. Nevertheless, eighteen potential sites for the home were chosen in the municipality of Niagara-on-the-Lake, several much closer to Niagara Falls.[14] The vacant space of the Commons attracted the most attention. Despite demonstrations, numerous letters from heritage groups and concerned citizens, and an OMB hearing, the land was leased to the region and irreparable damage to the Commons has resulted. In the midst of the fray, an official of the Historic Sites and Monuments Board did reassure a concerned citizen that "Parks Canada will not consider any future developments of this sort on the Commons."[15] A small comfort. The negative outcome did partially contribute to the formation of an advocacy *vox populi* group, The Niagara-on-the-Lake Conservancy, and taught the various heritage organizations the importance of working together whenever future threats should arise — and soon they did. Hopefully the staff, patients, and volunteers of Upper Canada Lodge today appreciate their unique location.

The increasing popularity of Niagara as a tourist destination resulted in tremendous seasonal traffic congestion in the old town. To this end a volunteer traffic committee[16] was formed in 1988 and consultants[17] were hired to study the traffic and parking situation. The final recommendation to council consisted of extension of Nelson Street and expansion of the Fort George parking to accommodate 118 cars and twenty buses. This would result in the loss of over 250 trees and a portion of the grassy, archaeologically sensitive Commons behind the hospital. Understandably, there was much resistance to this further encroachment on the Commons: a well-received petition was circulated in town by Jim Smith, and concerned citizens and heritage organizations made presentations at a special public meeting in January 1991. Recognizing the strong public opposition to this report the superintendent of Niagara National Historic Sites advised the lord mayor

Laura West Dodson, C.M. (1925–2007), photo taken at her beloved Willowbank, circa 2005. Laura worked tirelessly for several decades to preserve Niagara's rich natural and cultural heritage, for which she was inducted into the Order of Canada. As president of the Niagara Conservancy, she was a strong advocate for the integrity of the Commons. Arguably her greatest accomplishment was the establishment of the Willowbank School of Restoration Arts in nearby Queenston.

Courtesy of Judy MacLachlan.

that "we must consider the question to be finally and forever closed."[18] In the midst of all the discussions one citizen suggested that in order to accommodate tourists, subterranean parking under the Commons should be considered.

The strong debate over the urban boundaries for the town also focused on the Commons. If the Commons were included in the urban boundaries then any development could be approved by the town, with the agreement of Parks Canada. If outside the boundaries then any proposed development would have to be approved by Regional Council which generally is more restrictive. Today, the Commons is not within the town's urban boundaries. Parks Canada has not permitted the Commons to be included in the town's heritage district or the designated National Historic District citing that the Commons is already protected (see epilogue).

In 2002, another proposal was discussed behind closed doors to develop a new Shaw employee parking lot on the previously untouched grassy lands of the Commons between the Shaw Festival Theatre and the Upper Canada Lodge parking lot on Wellington Street.[19] In exchange for this piece of land that the town would develop, Parks Canada would receive ownership of a small triangle of land at King and John Street which had been the railbed for the Michigan Central Railway. A strong write-in campaign by the heritage[20] and ratepayers organizations in town as well as concerned citizenry resulted in Parks Canada withdrawing from the negotiations on the premise that the two pieces of property were not equal in size. Within six months the town was back offering, in addition to the triangle of land, the town-owned land on which was situated the Kinsmen Scout Lodge near Butler's Barracks. *Vox populi* was sounded once again. The town has withdrawn its proposal — at least for now.

One spring morning the town's citizens opened up their weekly newspaper to find on the front page an architect's rendering of a thirty-storey office/condo tower on the Commons that was about to be approved by town council. After gasps of horror, on turning the page they realized that they had just been taken in by an April fool's joke.[21]

As during the previous two hundred years, there will undoubtedly be more proposals for encroachments on the integrity of the Commons, many well intentioned. In fact, at the time of completion of this book in early 2012 there are two potential significant proposals[22] for the Commons itself and one overlooking virgin green common land.[23] Historians and conservationists acknowledge that there will always be a fine balance between the preservation of this special verdant place and the forces for change that are inevitable in a dynamic community. Hopefully this humble volume will inspire future generations to protect the integrity of the Commons.

Epilogue

Today, the entity "Niagara National Historic Sites" represents a complex of designated National Historic Sites in and near Niagara-on-the-Lake: Fort George, Fort Mississauga, Navy Hall, Butler's Barracks, Queenston Heights, Mississauga Point Lighthouse, Navy Island, and the Battlefield of Fort George. The estimated 285 acres that remain of the original Fort George Military Reserve and now known as the Commons are *not* designated. Requests to the Historic Sites and Monuments Board of Canada in 1986[1] and to the federal government again in 1991[2] for designation of the Commons were turned down. However, contained in the Commemorative Integrity Statement (CIS) formulated for each designated site in 1998 there is reference to the "historic place" of that site. In the case of Fort George its historic place is:

> the extensive cleared area extending to the Niagara River and across the Commons, which provided clear fields of fire; and the viewplanes to the river, Butler's Barracks and the town.[3]

Similarly, in the CIS for Butler's Barracks:

> the historic place is therefore not only the immediate area of the five buildings, but includes the entire area enclosed by the palisades, the locations of the buildings and facilities outside the palisade (commandant's quarters, etc.) and that part of the Commons occupied by Camp Niagara. Effectively, the entire area of the Commons is included.[4]

In essence, since the historic place is considered the extent of the designated site, the present Commons is included in the designations of both Fort George and Butler's Barracks. Moreover, the Management Plan for the Niagara National Historic Sites, accepted in 2007 and up for review in 2012, clearly states as a "Key Action" that "Parks Canada will not consider additional encroachments on the Commons." This would seem to indicate that the Commons today is protected from both major intrusions as well as minor encroachments along the edges. However, further encroachment requests will be decided by the Minister of the Environment, who hopefully would listen to local concerns.

Today all the Niagara National Historic Sites are administered and maintained by Parks Canada, with the exception of Paradise Grove, which is maintained by the Niagara Parks Commission.

The restored Navy Hall building is not open to the general public but is available for special meetings and private functions. The wharf is open to all and continues as a popular fishing spot and diving site. Occasionally various watercraft are allowed temporary mooring at this historic location. Fort George is open to the public throughout the year. Of the four surviving buildings of Butler's Barracks only the two-storey barracks is open to the general public. It serves

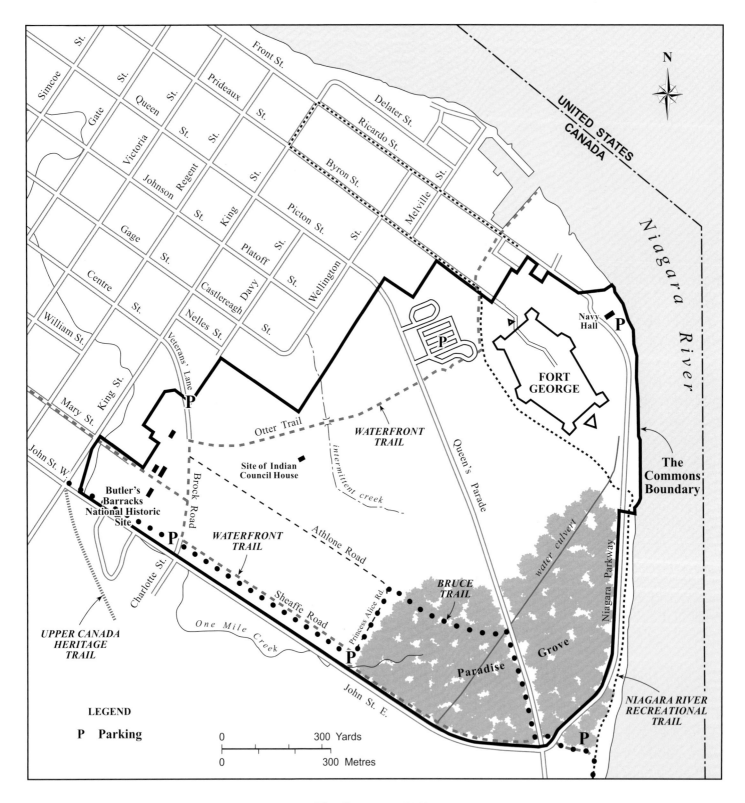

The Commons 2011.

Junior Commissariat Officer's Quarters, photo, author, 2000. What is to become of this historic 1816 building ... one of the oldest surviving military residences in Ontario?

Courtesy of the author

as the museum for the Lincoln and Welland Regiment. The ordnance gun shed and commissariat stores are currently used for storage. Hopefully an adaptive reuse for the 1816 Junior Commissariat Officer's Quarters can be implemented soon. The temporary B Company building is the sole survivor of several that were constructed on site in the late 1950s or early '60s. At least three were eventually moved offsite. The present building is currently used for storage.

Over the past two centuries there have been many trails that crisscrossed the Military Reserve/Commons. The oldest appears to be the byway from the John Street/Niagara Parkway intersection northwestward through the Oak Grove across the Commons, joining present Picton Street and ending at the intersection of present King and Queen Streets. Since Victorian times it has been known as the Queen's Parade. From this now improved and slightly elevated road one can truly appreciate the wide expanse of the green Commons on both sides.

The Otter Trail, named after Canada's first Canadian-born general in the Canadian army and long-serving commandant of Camp Niagara, General Sir William Otter, today extends from the Fort George parking lot southwest across the Commons to Butler's Barracks. Originally this important trail passed just north of the fort's gates and down to Navy Hall. Looking up from Ricardo Street one can still see the stone embankment that edged this road. Travelling towards Butler's Barracks on the Otter Trail one crosses a cement bridge that was erected in 1914 by the Royal Canadian Engineers' Corps.[5] A bit farther on the left is the site of the Indian Council House and military hospital. The Otter Trail ends perpendicular to another trail that started at the main entrance to Camp Niagara on King Street opposite Centre Street. This latter trail, known as Brock Road,[6] passed through the Butler's Barracks complex to the original officers' quarters where the John Street/Charlotte Street parking lot is now located. The other road/trail coming in off King Street opposite Mary Street was not opened up until the Second World War.

During the Second World War several trails were paved and named roads. Most of these roads were repaved in the 1990s to provide greater access.

There are two tree-lined trails that pass northeast parallel to present John Street. The trail closest to John Street, now known as the Sheaffe Road,[7] ran along a railway spur line. During the Camp Niagara days, thousands of soldiers arrived or departed by train. The other trail, known as the Athlone Road,[8] is not paved and is designated an off-leash site for dogs. Both the Athlone and Sheaffe Roads intersect with the Princess Alice[9] Road coming in off the second John Street entrance. This large rectangle of grass outlined by Brock, Sheaffe, Princess Alice, and Athlone Roads was the main campsite during the early militia days of Camp Niagara.

The new eastward extension of Sheaffe's Road skirts Paradise Grove on the left and John Street East on the right until it reaches the intersection of the Niagara Parkway and John Street. This new trail continues into the Niagara Parks

Camp Life, Back from the Ranges, photo, crossing the bridge, 1915. The cement bridge built by the Royal Canadian Engineers Corps in 1914 on the Otter Trail is still present today.

Courtesy of the author.

Commission's (NPC) portion of Paradise Grove and intersects with the NPC's Recreation Trail. Turning northward onto this trail and travelling beside the Niagara River one can continue down to Navy Hall or, halfway along, join the trail that follows around the southwestern edge of Fort George. On joining this trail one crosses between two deep ravines on either side — the remnants of the old railway cutting. The Fort George portion of the trail eventually passes the parking lot on the left and continues to Byron Street and town.

The trails of the Commons connect with three much larger trail systems. The Waterfront Trail actually begins at the Fort George parking lot (it can also be accessed at the John Street/Parkway parking lot or at the foot of Nelson Street at the river's edge), follows the Otter Trail to Brock Road, and eventually makes its way to the Mary Street exit and follows Mary Street to the Lakeshore Road. The trail can now be followed all the way to Burlington.

A side trail of the long-established Bruce Trail begins at the John Street/Charlotte parking lot. It follows the Sheaffe Road and turns left onto the Princess Alice Road until reaching the Athlone Road. Turning right, the trail passes through Paradise Grove (passing a huge pile of earth that hopefully will be moved soon) and emerges onto the Queen's Parade. Following southward to the John Street/Parkway intersection it hooks up to the Recreation Trail that can be followed to Queenston Heights, the official start of this trail. The Greater Niagara Circle Route follows the NPC's Recreation Trail and the Waterfront Trail through the Commons. The fourth connecting trail is the Upper Canada Heritage Trail which follows the old railway right-of-way from York Road northward beside Railroad Street, then cross-country eventually emerging onto Charlotte and then John Streets at the western tip of the Commons, connecting with a Sheaffe Road extension.

Recently Parks Canada unveiled its own trail on the Commons, "Spirit, Combat, and Lore: A Walk to Remember." It begins at Queen's Parade and includes several stops where a variety of interpretative displays relate various aspects of the history of the Commons.

Given the varied and important natural and cultural landscape of the Commons as well as the historic buildings thereon, it would now seem appropriate that representation be made to have the Commons designated as an UNESCO World Heritage Site.

As we make our way across the Commons and contemplate the hundreds of thousands of military and civilian men and women who have passed this way before, we are reminded of the old biblical adage that our lives are as fleeting as the grass in the field.[10]

Sunrise on the Commons.

Courtesy of Cosmo Condina.

Notes

INTRODUCTION

1. There are many uses of the term "commons" today including the House of Commons (commoners), common meeting areas in colleges, computer commons in public libraries, and commons in cyberspace.
2. Officially changed to Niagara by an Act of Parliament in 1798.
3. Kevin R. Shackleton, *Second to None: The Fighting 58 Battalion of the Canadian Expeditionary Force* (Toronto: Dundurn, 2002), 17.

CHAPTER 1

1. R. Pilkington, *Upper Canada Gazette or American Oracle*, vol. 3, no. 26, April 19, 1797.
2. *The Petition of Inhabitants of Newark* (1797), LAC, RG 1 L3, vol. 381(a) no. 1 a-e.
3. Susan Lasdum, *The English Park* (London: Andre Deutsch Limited, 1971), 75.
4. *Ibid.*, 196. Comment was attributed to author Henry James.
5. The Open Spaces Society, established in Britain in 1865 as "The Commons Preservation Society," has rescued many important "common lands." The society estimates there are still over seven thousand registered commons in England today.
6. W.A. Armstrong, *Demographic Factors and the Agricultural Labourer* (Agricultural History Review, 1981).
7. Asa Briggs, *A Social History of England* (London: Weidenfeld and Nicolson, 1983), 174.
8. Mary Beacock Fryer and Christopher Dracott, *John Graves Simcoe, 1752–1806: A Biography* (Toronto: Dundurn, 1998), 92–93, 230.
9. *Ibid.*, 237–38.
10. J. Ross Robertson, *The Diary of Mrs. John Graves Simcoe* (Toronto: William Briggs, 1911), 228. Entry for June 3, 1793.
11. In Connecticut, "the town green" is regarded as the most iconic feature of its landscape, reflecting the state's strong sense of history and civic pride.
12. Many of the New England greens became quite worn down and shabby until the patriotic 1820s when they underwent a rejuvenation, and they have been carefully preserved ever since. Litchfield, Connecticut, and Woodstock, Vermont, have retained outstanding examples of village greens.
13. In cities such as London and Edinburgh there are still private green Georgian squares that are enclosed by a fence and a locked gate. Gramercy Park in Manhattan has a similar arrangement.
14. Michael Bliss, *Harvey Cushing: A Life in Surgery* (Toronto: University of Toronto Press, 2000), 305–09.
15. *Haldimand Papers*, vol. 45, Library and Archives Canada (LAC), Add MSS 21764, 380.

16. *Stamford Township Papers*, Archives of Ontario, April 12, 1792, RG 1.

17. *Ontario Historical Society Papers and Records*, vol. 25 (Toronto: Ontario Historical Society), 274–75.

18. Established on fifty acres of the Military Reserve in 1846, the grounds today surround the Centre for Mental Health.

19. Grass, trees, and water are regarded by many as the three important elements of any landscape.

20. In his treatise on public vs. private land ownership, "The Tragedy of the Commons," Garret Hardin surmised that if too many commoners use the common lands or if some use more than their share, the resources of the common lands will eventually be exhausted to the detriment of all. Environmentalists have extended this concept to concerns over the pollution of our common atmosphere and the overharvesting of our seas.

CHAPTER 2

1. *Stage 4 Salvage Excavation of the King's Point Site*, Archaeological Services, Inc. (March 2007).

2. John Wilson, *1973 Excavations at Fort George*, Manuscript Report No. 116 (Ottawa: Department of Indian and Northern Affairs,1974), 88. See also, Peter Sattelberger, *Evaluation of the Indian Council House/Garrison Hospital & Commandant's Quarters Archaeological Collections Fort George Commons N.H.S., Niagara-on-the-Lake* (Parks Canada Agency, 2001).

3. Chert is flint-like quartz. Vast amounts of flint are found at the mouth of the Niagara River at Fort Erie.

4. Early French maps indicate the name Ongiara, but after 1650 the name Niagara appears. The former may indicate the Neutral name whereas Niagara may reflect the Iroquois pronunciation.

5. Frank H. Severence, *An Old Frontier of France*, vol. 1 (New York: Dodd, Mead and Company, 1917), 40.

6. There is some question whether "Montreal Point," which appears on the early French maps, is the same as later named Mississauga Point, or whether it refers to the bend in the river near present Queen's Royal Park.

7. Brian Leigh Dunnigan, *Siege 1759 The Campaign Against Niagara*, revised edition (Youngstown, New York: Old Fort Niagara Association Inc, 1996), 61.

8. See chapter 5.

9. Extract of the report of John Collins to Lord Dorchester, Quebec, December 6, 1788, see E.A. Cruikshank, ed., *Records of Niagara 1784–1789*, no. 40 (Niagara-on-the-Lake: Niagara Historical Society, 1929), 58.

10. For an excellent description of the importance of oak in European navies, see William B. Logan, *Oak The Frame of Civilization* (New York: W.W. Norton & Company, 2005).

11. *Haldimand Papers*, vol. 45, LAC, Add MSS 21765, 176–77.

12. Powell to Haldimand, November 18, 1780. See E.A. Cruikshank, ed., *Records of Niagara 1778–1783*, no. 38 (Niagara-on-the-Lake: Niagara Historical Society, 1927), 27. Powell complained of the poor position of the Butler's Rangers Barracks, which he felt should have been built out on Mississauga Point opposite Fort Niagara. Cruikshank surmised that the site was chosen because of the proximity of large logs for the buildings. Butler may also have realized that the Point would be much more exposed to the cold prevailing northwest winds off the lake.

13. "Captain Peter Ten Broeck's Account with Lieutenant Colonel Butler," *Haldimand Papers*, Spring 1779, Reel #46, 154.

14. Bolton to Haldimand, March 4, 1779. Cruikshank, *Records of Niagara 1778–1783*, no. 38, 9–10.

15. *Ibid.* Also, Guy Johnson to Haldimand, May 9, 1781, Cruikshank, *Records of Niagara 1778–1783*, no. 38, 9–10.

16. Haldimand to Bolton, June 7, 1779. Cruikshank, *Records of Niagara 1778–1783*, no. 38, 12. The first settlers on the Canadian side included Michael Showers (see Walter Butler, *Haldimand Papers*, vol. 46, 217); Peter Secord (see "Diary of Francis Goring," Niagara-on-the-Lake Library, Janet Carnochan Room), August 4, 1780. "Peter Secord commenced farming on the west side of the River");

James Secord (brother of Peter); Isaac Dolson; and Samuel (Samson) Lutes.

17. *Ibid.* "A Survey of the Settlement at Niagara, 25 August 1782," 42.

18. *Haldimand Papers*, vol.45, LAC, Add MSS 21764, 380.

19. The Allen McDonell who was Niagara's first surveyor was probably Allen (Allan) McDonell (McDonald), who was a sergeant in Butler's Rangers during the American Revolutionary War. He married Nancy (Ann) Johnson, widow of John Comfort, who had been granted Lot 12.

20. Butler to Matthews, March 31, 1783, and May 3, 1783. Cruickshank, *Records of Niagara 1778–1783*, no. 38, 49–52.

21. "McDonnell Map," in *Haldimand Papers*, vol. 85, 71–72, NMC 3169.

22. Haldimand to De Peyster, May 24, 1784. E.A. Cruikshank, ed., *Records of Niagara 1784–1787*, no. 39 (Niagara-on-the-Lake: Niagara Historical Society, 1928), 33–34.

23. *Ibid.* Haldimand to De Peyster, March 29, 1784, 15–17.

24. *Ibid.* Butler to Matthews, May 8, 1784, 19–20.

25. *Ibid.* Haldimand to De Peyster, May 24, 1784, 33–34.

26. Early claimants included "Col. John Butler, John Seacord [*sic*], Lt. Pilkington."

27. Jones's immediate predecessor, former Butler's Ranger officer and land surveyor Philip Rockwell Frey, had modified Tinling's maps but left the colony in disgust due to the conflicting pressures of the military officials in Quebec and the realities of the local settlement. The remarkable career of surveyor Augustus Jones is well documented in his entry in the *Dictionary of Canadian Biography*.

28. Augustus Jones to Collins, District of Nassau Letter Book, 5:65, June 15, 1792. See E.A. Cruikshank, ed., *Records of Niagara 1790–1792*, no. 41 (Niagara-on-the-Lake: Niagara Historical Society, 1929), 140–41.

29. Proceedings of the Land Board, Niagara, June 24, 1791. Cruikshank, *Records of Niagara 1790–1792*, no. 41, 118.

30. John Grier owned a tannery and dwelling house on the shoreline, southeast of the foot of King Street. The tannery was destroyed by the American bombardment on October 13, 1812. (Department of Finance, War of 1812 Losses, Record Group, 19E 5(a) claim # 60.)

31. "Petition of William Dickson," July 31, 1792. E.A. Cruikshank, ed., *Petitions for Grants of Land 1791–1796*, Ontario Historical Society Papers and Records (OHSPR), vol. 24 (Toronto: Ontario Historical Society, 1927), 54–55.

32. One would wonder how a silversmith could keep busy in the tiny community of Butlersburg in the late 1780s. Perhaps he was fashioning silver trade goods for the British Indian Department.

33. This included William Dickson, Peter Russell, David William Smith, and Robert Pilkington, as well as early settlers William McClellan and Arent Bradt.

34. Early grantees included Anthony Slingerland, David William Smith, John Butler, John Secord Senior, John Secord Junior, Jacob Ball and sons, Edward McMichael, Robert Addison, and Daniel Servos.

35. See chapter 24.

36. *The Petition of Inhabitants of Newark* (1797), LAC, RG 1 L3, vol. 381(a) no. la-e.

CHAPTER 3

1. For more information on campaign furniture see Nicholas A. Brawer, *British Campaign Furniture Elegance under Canvas, 1740–1914* (New York: Harry N. Abrams, Inc, 2001).

2. William R. Riddell, *The Life of John Graves Simcoe* (Toronto: McClelland and Stewart, 1926), 227.

3. Matavai Bay, Society Islands, April 1769. See John Ross Robertson Collection, #4610. The botanists Joseph Banks and Daniel Solander on Cook's first voyage aboard the *Endeavour* are reputed to have camped in the canvas houses in April 1770 on the edge of Botany Bay, the future site of Sydney Australia.

4. Riddell, *The Life of John Graves Simcoe*.

5. *Ibid.*

6. John Ross Robertson, *The Diary of Mrs. Simcoe* (Toronto: William Briggs, 1911), July 26, 1792, 125.

7. *Ibid.*, 141.

8. Joseph Bouchette (1774–1841) made the first survey of Toronto Harbour in 1792. He was a nephew of Surveyor-General Samuel Holland, the British officer who befriended James Cook at Louisbourg and introduced him to cartography.

9. Joseph Bouchette, *The British Dominions in North America*, vol. 1 (London: 1832) 89.

10. James Freeman Clarke, *Revolutionary Service and Civil Life of General William Hull; Prepared from his Manuscripts by his Daughter Mrs. Maria Campbell: Together with the History of the Campaign of 1812* (New York: 1848), 289–90.

11. Peter Russell to Elizabeth Russell, September 1, 1793, Russell Papers, Toronto Public Library, Toronto Reference Library, Baldwin Room.

CHAPTER 4

1. Originally this creek drained towards the Niagara River, passing through present Simcoe Park.

2. Peter Russell (1733–1808), see *Dictionary of Canadian Biography* (Toronto: University of Toronto, 1976).

3. Peter Russell to Robert Prescott, September 24, 1796. E.A. Cruikshank and A.F. Hunter, eds., *The Correspondence of the Honourable Peter Russell*, vol. 1 (Toronto: Ontario Historical Society,1932–36), 41–42.

4. Russell Papers, Toronto Public Library, Toronto Reference Library, Baldwin Room.

5. Peter Russell to Robert Prescott, September 24, 1796. Cruikshank and Hunter, *The Correspondence of the Honourable Peter Russell.*

6. The 84th Regiment of Foot (Royal Highland Emigrants) was the only provincial corps serving in Canada that was put on the British regular establishment and hence granted a regimental number. The two battalions consisted primarily of veterans of the Seven Years' War and the Highlanders who had settled in the Mohawk Valley. A few members of this regiment were stationed at Fort Niagara and their commanding officer, Allan Maclean, was commander of the "upper posts," including Fort Niagara, 1782–1783. As with the other provincial corps it was disbanded in 1784.

7. After Murray's death, this property was acquired and developed by Robert Hamilton. Professor Alun Hughes of Brock University has done much research on this area, which is now known as Power Glen.

8. *Receiver General's Record Book*, July 25, 1793.

9. Cruikshank and Hunter, *The Correspondence of the Honourable Peter Russell*, vol. 1, 41.

10. Elizabeth Russell to Mrs. Kiernon, January 18, 1793, Toronto Public Library, Toronto Reference Library, Baldwin Room, Elizabeth Russell Papers.

11. *Ibid.*, October 1, 1793.

12. Peter Russell to J. G. Simcoe, February 28, 1797. Cruikshank and Hunter, *The Correspondence of the Honourable Peter Russell*, vol. 1, 150–51.

13. Robert Pilkington, "Plan of the Premises of Mr. President Russell, 1797," *A True Copy of Original Plan in the Dominion Archives* (Ottawa, 1915). Niagara Historical Society Museum, #986.006.

14. Elizabeth Russell to Mrs. Kiernon, February 24, 1794, Toronto Public Library, Toronto Reference Library, Baldwin Room, Elizabeth Russell Papers.

15. The compromise legislation passed during the second session of the first parliament of Upper Canada held in the Butler's Rangers Barracks in 1793 was limited slavery: all slaves, upon reaching twenty-five years of age, were to be set free; no slaves could be brought into the province; adult slaves remained slaves until death unless manumitted by their rightful owners.

16. Michael Power and Nancy Butler, *Slavery and Freedom in Niagara* (Niagara-on-the-Lake: Niagara Historical Society, 1993), 18.

17. Elizabeth Russell to Mrs. Kiernon, October 1, 1793, Toronto Public Library, Toronto Reference Library, Baldwin Room, Elizabeth Russell Papers.

18. *Ibid.*

19. Peter Russell to Robert Prescott, September 24, 1796. Cruickshank and Hunter, *The Correspondence of the Honourable Peter Russell*, vol. 1, 41–42.

20. Peter Russell to J.G. Simcoe, February 28, 1797. Cruickshank and Hunter, *The Correspondence of the Honourable Peter Russell*, vol. 1, 151–52.

21. Peter Russell to Robert Prescott, February 23, 1797. Cruickshank and Hunter, *The Correspondence of the Honourable Peter Russell*, vol. 1, 145–46.

22. Peter Russell to J.G. Simcoe, February 28, 1797. Cruickshank and Hunter, *The Correspondence of the Honourable Peter Russell*, vol. 1, 151–52.

23. *Upper Canada Gazette or American Oracle*, November 9, 1796.

24. Pilkington, "Plan of the Premises of Mr. President Russell, 1797."

25. Peter Russell to Robert Prescott, November 4, 1797. Cruikshank and Hunter, *The Correspondence of the Honorable Peter Russell*, vol. 2, 11.

26. For an excellent account of the role of the First Nations in the War of 1812, see Carl Benn, *The Iroquois in the War of 1812* (Toronto: University of Toronto Press, 1998).

27. Young Mary probably had consumption (tuberculosis). She died on January 10, 1797.

28. Curiously, the British Indian Department's fiscal year always began on Christmas day.

29. "Proposed Establishment of the Indian Department For The Year One Thousand Seven Hundred and Ninety Eight To Commence The 25ᵗʰ December 1797." Cruikshank and Hunter, *The Correspondence of the Honorable Peter Russell*, vol. 2, 53.

30. Robert S. Allen, "The British Indian Department and the Frontier in North America 1755–1830," *Canadian Historic Sites*, Occasional Papers in Archaeology and History, no. 14 (Ottawa: Department of Indian and Northern Affairs, 1975), 67.

31. Public Records Office, CO 42, vol. 421, 49–53.

32. Military Secretary for Prevost to Lieutenant General Drummond, March 1, 1814. E.A. Cruikshank, ed., *The Documentary History of the Campaign upon the Niagara Frontier in 1812–1814*, vol. 9 (Welland: Tribune Press, 1898–1908), 202–03.

33. The original town lots are still intact, known today as the Wilderness. See chapter 21.

34. William Claus family papers, LAC, MG 19, F1, 1810–1816.

35. *The Upper Canada Gazette*, February 8, 1797.

36. Richard D. Merritt, Nancy Butler, and Michael Power, *The Capital Years: Niagara-on-the-Lake 1792–1796* (Toronto: Dundurn, 1991), 241.

37. Kerr's original house on Prideaux Street was burned in December 1813, but he rebuilt a substantial brick house on the original foundations. The house survives today at 69 Prideaux Street.

38. Proceedings of a Board of Claims, St. David's U.C., August 12, 1813, #19. Dr. Kerr, "Case of Instruments, at the Council House, The Doctor being on duty at York," LAC, British Military Records, Claims of Losses, vol. 82–85, 1812–1870, reel C1645.

39. Russell to the Duke of Portland, May 26, 1799. Cruikshank and Hunter, *The Correspondence of the Honorable Peter Russell*, vol. 3, 206–07.

40. E.A. Cruikshank, *The Battle of Fort George* (Niagara-on-the-Lake: Niagara Historical Society, 1990), 44.

41. *Grants to Provincial Corps, District of Nassau, A List of Reduced Officers of the Indian Department Settled in the District of Nassau*, Archives of Ontario, RG 1, Crown Lands Department Series, C-1-9, vol. 3, item no. 9.

42. Alan Holden and William Smy, *Casualties of the Militia of Lincoln County* (Colonel John Butler Br., UEL Association of Canada, 2002), 10.

43. Janet Carnochan, "Weddings at Niagara, February 11, 1798," in the article "Early Records of St. Mark's Church and St. Andrews Churches, Niagara," *Ontario Historical Society, Papers and Records*, vol. 3 (Toronto: Ontario Historical Society, 1901), 54.

44. Present site of the city of Buffalo. This was considered a neutral location to meet with the Six Nations representatives (mostly Senecas) still living in the United States.

45. Cruikshank and Hunter, *The Correspondence of the Honorable Peter Russell*, vol. 3, 77.

46. Peter Russell to D.W. Smith, February 5, 1798. Cruikshank and Hunter, *The Correspondence of the Honorable Peter Russell*, vol. 2, 78.

47. F.R. Berchem, *The Yonge Street Story 1793–1860* (Toronto: McGraw-Hill Ryerson, 1977), 17.

48. Larry L. Nelson, *A Man of Distinction Among Them* (Kent, Ohio: Kent State University Press, 2000), 155–56.

49. Alexander MacDonnell, "Diary of Lieutenant Governor Simcoe's Journey From Humber Bay to Matchedash Bay in 1793." E.A. Cruikshank, ed., *The Correspondence of Lieut. Governor John Graves Simcoe*, vol. 2 (Toronto: Ontario Historical Society, 1922-31), 74–75.

50. Joseph Brant's son John was only eighteen years of age at the onset of the war and hence was not considered old enough to be the principal chief.

51. Military Secretary for Prevost to Lieutenant General Drummond, March 1, 1814. Cruikshank, *The Documentary History of the Campaign upon the Niagara Frontier in 1812–1814*, 202–03.

52. Carl F. Klinck and James J. Talman, *The Journal of Major John Norton 1816* (Toronto: The Champlain Sociey, 1970). This publication provides a thorough biography of Norton as well as Norton's complete journal.

53. The St. Jean-Baptiste Society was formed in Toronto to recognize Rousseaux's contribution to the early settlement of York/Toronto.

54. Rousseaux St. John, John Baptist, *Dictionary of Canadian Biography* (Toronto: University of Toronto, 1976).

55. Green to John Johnson, July 8, 1799. Cruikshank and Hunter, *The Correspondence of the Honorable Peter Russell*, 261.

56. *Ibid*.

57. Butler's Barracks, Indian Council House, and Commandant's Quarters, May 2, 1817, LAC, National Map Collection.

58. James R. Henderson, *Results of 1970 Excavations in the Fort George Military Reserve*, Manuscript Report No.116 (Ottawa: Department of Indian and Northern Affairs, 1973).

59. David McConnell, *A Study of the British Military Buildings at Niagara-on-the-Lake, 1814–1837*, Manuscript Report No.191 (Ottawa: Department of Indian and Northern Affairs, 1977), 53–59.

60. Dunford Report (1823), LAC, RG 8, I, vol. 414.

61. For an exhaustive review of the archaeological studies of this property see Peter A. Sattelberger, *Evaluation of The Indian Council House/Garrison & Commandant's Quarters Archaeological Collections, Fort George Commons N.H.S., Niagara-on-the-Lake* (Parks Canada Agency, 2001). Sattelberger also noted that far more post-contact Native artifacts were found near the officers' quarters for the Indian Department than over by the Indian Council House, which would seem to indicate that far more councils were held near the former building than the latter.

62. *Sketches of the Military Reserve at Niagara*, LAC, December 14, 1835, National Map Collection.

CHAPTER 5

1. Captain Hugh Arnot to General Gage, November 29, 1765, William L. Clements Library, Thomas Gage Papers.

2. The first occupant was Captain James Andrews, commanding officer on Lake Ontario. Commodore Andrews, his crew of forty seamen, a company of the 34th Foot, and several military officers including the retiring commandant of Fort Niagara all perished when their ship the HMS *Ontario* disappeared just east of Niagara during an especially violent hurricane on October 31, 1780. His widow and three daughters were apparently allowed to continue residence at Navy Hall. All three daughters married military officers.

3. Bolton to Carleton, enclosing a memorandum from Captain Andrews, LAC, MG 21, G2, vol. 144, 75–76.

4. For an excellent summary of the history of the Navy Hall site see David Fleming, "Navy Hall, Niagara-on-the-Lake," *History and Archeology* 8, Department of Indian and Northern Affaris, 1976, 3–52.

5. Haldimand to DePeyster, May 24, 1784. E.A. Cruickshank, ed., *Records of Niagara 1784–1787*, no. 39 (Niagara-on-the-Lake:Niagara: Niagara Historical Society, 1928), 34.

6. LAC, MG 11, C0 42 vol. 70, 52.

7. E.A. Cruikshank, ed., *Correspondence of Lieutenant Governor John Graves Simcoe*, vol. 1 (Toronto: Ontario Historical Society, 1923–31), 30.

8. LAC, Simcoe Papers, microfilm A606. See also, Mary Quayle Innis, ed., *Mrs. Simcoe's Diary* (Toronto: Macmillan Press, 1965), 6.

9. Innis, *Mrs. Simcoe's Diary*, 109. Entry for October 25, 1793. Jack Sharp belonged to Sheriff Walter Butler Sheehan who lived on the river road. The Simcoes so admired his dog that Sheehan loaned his pet to the vice-regal family during their stay.

10. Prince Edward was the father of the future Queen Victoria.

11. Innis, *Mrs. Simcoe's Diary*, 79. Entry for August 17, 1792.

12. *Ibid.*, 97. Entry for July 2, 1793.

13. Benjamin Lincoln, *Journal of a Treaty Held in 1793 with Indian Tribes North-West of Ohio, by Commissioners of the United States*, Collections, 3rd series, vol. 5 (Massachusetts Historical Society, 1836), 123–24.

14. LAC, RG 8, I A. vol. 728, 195.

15. *Ibid.* vol. 120, 49.

16. LAC, MG 13, WO 55/875, 183A–184, B-2817.

17. LAC, RG 8, II, vol. 34, p. 108ff. Annual Report on Barracks in Canada 1864.

18. Janet Canochan, *History of Niagara* (Toronto: William Briggs, 1914), 10.

19. Walter Haldorson, *The Reconstruction of Fort George and Navy Hall 1937–1940* (Niagara-on-the-Lake: Paul Heron Publishing Limited, 1991), 35.

20. The original foundations could not be found. The new site is slightly south of the original location.

21. According to restoration architect Peter John Stokes, McQuesten often insisted that restored old frame/log buildings be clad in stone to afford them greater protection. Personal communication.

22. The original wharf actually extended further north. At low water, huge original supporting beams can still be seen.

CHAPTER 6

1. Butler's Rangers were expected to pay for their own arms and uniforms — the prime reason offered for their higher stipend. See LAC, Haldimand Papers, Add MSS 21756. Reel A-659.

2. Captain Walter Butler to Captain Brehm, August 8, 1779. LAC, Haldimand Papers, Add MSS 21765, 128.

3. Powell to Haldimand, November 18, 1780. E.A. Cruickshank, ed., *Records of Niagara 1778–1783*, no. 38 (Niagara-on-the-Lake: Niagara Historical Society, 1927), 27.

4. *Ibid.*

5. *Ibid.* Captain Walter Butler to Captain Brehm, August 8, 1779. For a modern transcript see Wm. A. Smy, *An Annotated Nominal Roll of Butler's Rangers 1777–1784 With Documenatry Sources* (St. Catharines, Friends of the Loyalist Collection at Brock University, 2004), 19–22.

6. Captain Walter Butler, eldest son of Lieutenant Colonel John Butler and Catherine Bradt, was a lawyer by training. After serving as an ensign in the 8th Regiment Foot, he became a Captain in the Indian Department and later Senior Captain in Butler's Rangers. He was killed in action at West Canada Creek, October 30, 1781.

7. Smy, *An Annotated Nominal Roll of Butler's Rangers*, 19–22.

8. *Ibid.*

9. Account of Captain Peter TenBroek to Lieutenant Colonel Butler, 1779, LAC, Haldimand Papers, Add MSS 21765, 154.

10. Fred Habermehl, *St. Mark's Storied Past* (Niagara-on-the-Lake: St. Mark's Anglican Church Archives Committee, 2006), 108–09.

11. *The Petition of William Dickson*, July 31, 1792. E.A. Cruikshank, ed., "Petitions for Grants of Land 1791–1796," OHSPR, vol. 24 (Toronto: Ontario Historical Society, 1927), 54–55. Guthrie's handy proximity to the burying ground

may give some credence to the old adage, "Physicians and surgeons bury their mistakes."

12. St. John de Crevecoeur, "A Visit to Niagara, July 1785," *Magazine of American History*, October 1878.

13. John Collins to Lord Dorchester, December 6, 1788. Cruikshank, *Records of Niagara*, no. 40, 58.

14. Proceedings of Land Board, Niagara, March 29, 1790. Cruikshank, *Records of Niagara*, no. 41, 20–21.

15. November 18, 1789. Unpublished transcripts of the diaries of Francis Goring. Janet Carnochan Room, Niagara-on-the-Lake Public Library.

16. Collins to Dorchester, December 6, 1788. Cruikshank, *Records of Niagara*, 58.

17. Simcoe to Clarke, June 4, 1793. Cruikshank, *Correspondence of Lieutenant Governor John Graves Simcoe*, vol. 1, 348.

18. July 2, 1800, *General Statement of Public Property in this Province Commencing with the Year 1792 and Ending in 1799*, LAC, Civil Secretary's Correspondence, Upper Canada Sundries, 1791–1800, RG 5, A1, vol.1A, 427.

19. Right Reverend Jacob Mountain to Henry Dundas, September 15, 1794. Cruikshank, *Correspondence of Lieutenant Governor John Graves Simcoe*, vol. 3, 91.

20. Simcoe to Dorchester, September 5, 1794. Cruikshank, *Correspondence of Lieutenant Governor John Graves Simcoe*, vol. 3, 40.

21. *Ibid.*, vol. 5, 74.

22. July 2, 1800, *General Statement of Public Property in this Province Commencing with the Year 1792 and Ending in 1799*, LAC, Civil Secretary's Correspondence, Upper Canada Sundries, 1791–1800, RG 5, A1, vol.1A, 427.

23. Stuart Sutherland, ed, *Two British Soldiers in the War of 1812: The Accounts of Shadrach Byfield and William Dunlop* (Toronto: Iser Publications, 2002), 37.

24. *Ibid.*

25. *Ibid.*

26. *Ibid.*

27. *Ibid.*, 38.

CHAPTER 7

1. Milton W. Hamilton, *The Papers of Sir William Johnson*, vol. 11 (Albany: The Universtiy of the State of New York, 1953), 309.

2. See LAC, Colonial Office Papers, MG 11, "Q" ser., vol. 13, 329–31, for a list of officers and rangers (foresters) in the Indian Department, June 15, 1777.

3. Mary Beacock Fryer, *King's Men The Soldier Founders of Ontario* (Toronto: Dundurn, 1980), 28–30.

4. *Instructions for the good Government of the Branch of the Indian Department within the District of Detroit* (Manuscript, 1786), author's collection.

5. St. John de Crevecoeur, "A Visit to Niagara, July 1785," *Magazine of American History*, October 1878.

6. Silas Hopkins, *Reminiscences of Niagara*, no. 2 (Niagara-on-the-Lake: Niagara Historical Society, 1904), 55.

7. John Collins to Lord Dorchester, December 6, 1788. E.A. Cruikshank, ed., *Records of Niagara 1784–1789*, no. 40 (Niagara-on-the-Lake: Niagara Historical Society, 1929), 58.

8. *The Petition of William Dickson*, July 31, 1792. E.A. Cruikshank, ed., "Petitions for Grants of Land 1791–1796" *Ontario Historical Society Papers and Records*, vol. 24 (Toronto: Ontario Historical Society, 1927), 54–55.

9. R.H. Bruyeres, *Report of the State of the Public Works and Buildings*, September 12, 1802, LAC, RG 8, I Series C, 383, 6.

10. Janet Carnochan, *History of Niagara* (Toronto: William Briggs, 1914), 141–42.

11. Peter A. Sattelberger, *Evaluation of The Indian Council House/Garrison Hospital & Commandant's Quarters Archaeological Collections Fort George Commons N.H.S., Niagara-on-the-Lake.* (Cornwall: Parks Canada Agency Ontario Service Centre, 2001). Far more post-contact Native artifacts were found in the area of the Officers' Quarters than the Indian Council House.

12. Alan Taylor, *The Divided Ground* (New York: Alfred A. Knopf, 2006), 24–25.

13. *Ibid.*, 23.

14. *Instructions for the good Government of the Branch of the*

Indian Department within the District of Detroit (Manuscript, 1786), author's collection.

15. Hopkins, *Reminiscences of Niagara*, no. 2, 55.

16. William Claus (1765–1826) see *Dictionary of Canadian Biography* (Toronto: University of Toronto Press, 1976).

17. LAC, MG 11, CO 42, vol. 321, 49–53.

18. Isabel Kelsey, *Joseph Brant 1743–1807 Man of the Two Worlds* (Syracuse: Syracuse University Press, 1984), 587.

19. Peter Russell to the Duke of Portland, July 29, 1797. E.A. Cruikshank and A.F. Hunter, eds., *The Correspondence of the Honourable Peter Russell*, vol. 1 (Toronto: Ontario Historical Society,1932–36), 227–28.

20. *Ibid.*, 228.

21. Chief Red Jacket (circa 1751–1830) was arguably the greatest orator in Native-American history.

22. Chief Farmers Brother was known for his very long speeches.

23. Peter Russell to the Duke of Portland, July 29, 1797. Cruikshank, *The Correspondence of the Honourable Peter Russell*, vol. 1, 227–28.

24. Up until the War of 1812 the Natives living in Western New York, mostly Senecas and Tuscaroras, continued to receive annual presents from the British government at the Council House on the Commons.

25. Major James Givins (circa 1759–1846), also known as the Wolf, was eventually appointed superintendent of the Indian Department of Upper Canada in 1827. See *Dictionary of Canadian Biography*.

26. Earle Thomas, *Sir John Johnson Loyalist Baronet* (Toronto: Dundurn, 1986), 148.

27. E.A. Cruikshank, ed., *Records of Niagara in the Days of Commodore Grant and Lieut.-Governor Gore* (Niagara-on-the-Lake: Niagara Historical Society, 1931), 63–64. Also, LAC MG 19 F 1 Claus Papers, vol. 9, 239–40.

28. Cruikshank, *Records of Niagara in the Days of Commodore Grant and Lieut.-Governor Gore*, 84–89. Also, LAC MG 19 F 1 Claus Papers, vol. 9, 263–79.

29. Carl Benn, *The Iroquois in the War of 1812* (Toronto: University of Toronto Press, 1998).

30. E.A. Cruikshank, ed., *The Documentary History of the Campaigns Upon the Niagara Frontier in 1812–1814*, vol. 4 (Welland: Tribune Press, 1896–1908), 123.

31. M. Edgar, *Ten Years of Upper Canada in Peace and War: 1805–1815* (Toronto: William Briggs, 1890), 167.

32. Peter Porter to John Armstrong, Secretary of War, July 27, 1813. Cruikshank, *The Documentary History of the Campaigns upon the Niagara Frontier*, vol. 6, 283–84.

33. During the short American occupation of York in April 1813, Angelica Givens, wife of Indian Department Deputy Agent Major James Givins, complained to American commander Dearborn that her home had been wantonly vandalized. He implied that he was unable to grant protection to anyone connected with the Indian Department. Statement of John Strachan D.D., LAC, RG 19 E5(a) War of 1812 War Loss Claim of Major Givins, no. 234.

34. Researchers at Fort George, "The British Indian Department," *The Niagara Advance*, 15th Annual Historical Issue, 1985, 31.

35. LAC, RG 8, vol. 258, 204–08.

36. Philpotts to Gibson, September 22, 1815, LAC, RG 8, I, vol. 555, 215–17.

37. Reid to Wright, September 26, 1819, LAC, RG8, I, vol. 293, 34.

38. *Plan, Section and Elevation of the New Hospital at Fort George*, LAC, H3/450/Niagara/1823, NMC 5223.

39. *A translation of Council Minutes with the Six Nations of Indians held at Fort George on 3rd Day August 1826*, Manuscript in the Servos Papers of the Niagara Historical Society, Access. #2002.044.001.

40. Niagara Historical Society, *Catalogue of Articles in Memorial Hall* (Toronto: Niagara Historical Society, 1911), 41, item #3935.

41. *Souvenir Historical Map of Niagara, County Lincoln, Ontario*, Compiled and Drawn by Frank Johnson, June 1, 1894.

CHAPTER 8

1. Haldimand to DePeyster, May 24, 1784. E.A. Cruikshank, ed., *Records of Niagara 1784–1787*, no. 39 (Niagara-on-the-Lake:Niagara: Niagara Historical Society, 1928), 34.

2. Patrick Campbell, William F. Ganong, *Travels in the Interior Inhabited Parts of North America in the Years 1791 and 1792* (Toronto: Champlain Society, 1937), 148.

3. See Yvon Desloges, *Structural History of Fort George*, Manuscript Report No. 189 (Ottawa: Department of Indian and Northern Affairs, 1977). See also Gouhar Shemdin and David Bouse, *A Report on Fort George* (Ottawa: Department of Indian and Northern Affairs, 1975), and Robert S. Allen, "A History of Fort George, Upper Canada," *Canadian Historic Sites* (Ottawa: Department of Indian and Northern Affairs, 1974), 61–93.

4. The Half-Moon Battery had an underground chamber possibly as a powder magazine. It was destroyed when the Niagara Parks Commission extended the Parkway northward towards Fort George in 1931.

5. For a more complete description and history of the stone powder magazine see chapter 9.

6. LAC, MG 23, H 1 (1), series 3, book 7, 197.

7. LAC, MG 23, G 11 (17), series 1, vol. 23, 156–57.

8. John Maude, *Diary of John Maude*, Niagara Historical Society, no. 11, 36–37. Also John Maude, *Visit to The Falls of Niagara in 1800* (London: Longman, Rees, Orme, Browne and Green, 1826), 171.

9. Report by Bruyeres, LAC, RG 8, I series C, 387, 15.

10. A description of the fort by an American informant, apparently before the Battle of Queenston Heights described the fort as being reduced in size. National Archives and Records Services, RG 77, Fortifications Map File, DR. 113, sh. 51/2.

11. Wesley Turner, *The Astonishing General: The Life and Legacy of Sir Isaac Brock* (Toronto: Dundurn, 2011), 165.

12. E.A. Cruikshank, ed., *The Documentary History of the Campaign Upon the Niagara Frontier 1812–1814*, vol. 5 (Welland: Tribune Press, 1898–1908), 97–98.

13. These volunteer warriors under Chiefs Farmers Brother and Red Jacket were actually paid by the American government.

14. Joseph Willcocks (1730–1814) took an active leadership role in the burning of Niagara. He was killed during the siege of Fort Erie the following year.

15. American surgeon Mann reported that one third of all the soldiers were incapacitated with "effluvia from sinks" and that there were only three surgeons available to treat seven-hundred soldiers in hospital. See Silas Hopkins, *Reminiscences of Niagara*, no. 11 (Niagara-on-the-Lake: Niagara Historical Society, 1904), 33.

16. Peter Porter to John Armstrong, Secretary of War, July 27. Cruikshank, *The Documentary History of the Campaign Upon the Niagara Frontier*, vol. 6, 283–84.

17. "Diary of Charles Askin," December 12, 1813, *Askin Papers*, vol. 32 (Michigan Pioneer Historical Society, Lansing, 1903), 513–15. During their occupation, the Americans did not erect any new barracks within the fort.

18. It is not clear whether the occupying Americans or the British built the new stone/brick powder magazine inside the fort.

19. Scott later became the American hero of the Mexican War.

20. Donald E. Graves, ed., *Soldiers of 1814: American Enlisted Men's Memoirs of the Niagara Campaign* (Youngstown: Old Fort Niagara Association, Inc., 1995), 33–34.

21. Charles Bagot to Sir John Sherbrooke, October 6, 1817. LAC, RG 8, I series C, vol. 674.

22. LAC, MG 12 B, W.O. 55, vol. 1551 (7), Appendix A, 15.

23. David McConnell, *A Study of the British Military Buildings at Niagara-on-the-Lake, 1838–71*, Manuscript Report No. 226 (Ottawa: Department of Indian and Northern Affairs, 1978), 4–5.

24. W.L. Calvert and R.P. Bolton, *History Written with Pick and Shovel* (New York: The New York Historical Society, 1950), 61.

25. Toronto *Mail and Empire*, 1897.

26. Janet Carnochan, *History of Niagara* (Toronto: William Briggs, 1914), 259–60.

27. The debate is well covered in Walter Haldorson's *The Restoration of Fort George* (Niagara-on-the-Lake: Paul Heron Publishing Limited, 1991), 14–19.

28. *Niagara-on-the-Lake Times*, May 2,1913.

29. Beryl (Taffy) Jones-Lewis who worked closely with her husband on all his projects.

30. Major archaeological digs have since been conducted on the site. See John Wilson and Linda Southwood, "Fort George on the Niagara: an Archaeological Perspective," *History and Archaeology*, vol. 9 (1976), 68. Also of interest, Suzanne Plousos, *Remains of a Day* (Niagara-on-the-Lake: Friends of Fort George, 2006).

31. Haldorson, *The Restoration of Fort George*, 46.

32. During this reshaping process a large tusk of a prehistoric mammoth was unearthed.

33. Its original 1814 location was too close to one of the reconstructed blockhouses and hence it was moved to a new location in the northeast part of the fort near the Brock bastion.

34. Carnochan, *History of Niagara*, 293–96.

35. This was reported at the time to be the largest and oldest tree removal ever attempted.

36. Haldorson, *The Restoration of Fort George*, 67–69.

37. King George VI was the great, great, great grandson of George III, after whom the fort was named.

38. Queen Elizabeth, after whom the QEW is named, returned to Fort George for an official visit as Queen Mother in 1981.

39. *The Esplanade, Fort George, Upper Canada*, artist Edward Walsh, watercolour, 1805. William L. Clements Library, University of Michigan.

CHAPTER 9

1. Yvon Desloges, *Structural History of Fort George*, Manuscript Report No. 189 (Ottawa: Department of Indian and Northern Affairs, 1977), 20–22.

2. E.A. Cruikshank, *The Battle of Fort George* (Niagara-on-the-Lake: Niagara Historical Society, 1990), 24–25.

3. Benson J. Lossing, *The Pictorial Field-Book of the War of 1812* (New York: Harper and Brothers, 1869), 418.

4. *Ibid.*, 405.

5. For an in-depth review of the reconstruction of Fort George see Walter Haldorson, *The Reconstruction of Fort George and Navy Hall 1937–1940* (Niagara-on-the-Lake: Paul Heron Publishing Limited, 1991).

6. Portions of foundations of the guardhouse and the centre blockhouse are the only other surviving remnants of the original fort.

CHAPTER 10

1. For an excellent summary of the battle see, E.A. Cruikshank, *The Battle of Fort George* (Niagara-on-the-Lake: Niagara Historical Society, 1990).

2. A recently discovered letter confirms that as early as May 21 armed American ships could be seen massing at the mouth of the Niagara River. George Adams to William Adams, May 21, 1813. Niagara Historical Society, # 2011.037.001.

3. Reminiscences of John Carrol, *Reminiscences of Niagara*, no. 11 (Niagara-on-the-Lake: Niagara Historical Sociey, 1904), 31–32.

4. Cruikshank, *The Battle of Fort George*, 42.

5. *Ibid.*, 44.

6. James Crooks owned a farm with several buildings near the mouth of the One Mile Creek that he called Crookston. The old firing range on the Department of National Defence property, now transferred to Parks Canada with part of "Chautauqua," is the approximate landing site. Designated a National Historic Site, there may be as many as 160 British soldiers buried there.

7. John P. Boyd, "Documents and Facts Relative to Events During the Late War" (1815), 4–5.

8. The American generals later attributed their cautious

advance through town to their concern for possible hidden explosives which had caused them so much grief at Fort York one month earlier.

9. John Norton, *The Journal of Major John Norton* (Toronto: The Champlain Society, 1970), 325.

10. Brigadier General John Vincent to Prevost, May 28, 1813. William Wood, ed., *Select British Documents of the Canadian War of 1812*, vol. 2 (Toronto: The Champlain Society, 1920–1928), 103–07.

11. Although he had served with distinction in the American Revolutionary War, by 1813 Dearborn was grossly overweight and quite incapacitated. His men called him Granny.

12. On April 27, while approaching the abandoned Fort York, Brigadier General Zebulon Pike and between three hundred and four hundred American troops were killed when the powder magazine exploded.

13. May 27, 1813, Major General Morgan Lewis to Dearborn, *The Weekly Register*, Baltimore, vol. 4, no. 15, 239.

14. May 28, 1813, Isaac Chauncey to William Jones, *The Weekly Register*, Baltimore, vol. 4, no. 15, 240.

15. Cruikshank, *The Battle of Fort George*, 47.

16. See British Military and Naval Records, 1812–1870, Claims of Losses, RG 8 I, vols. 82–85, Reel C-1645.

17. Cruikshank, *The Battle of Fort George*, 53.

18. May 27, 1813, Dearborn to John Armstrong, *The Weekly Register*, 239.

19. Kyle Upton, *Niagara's Ghosts at Fort George* (Niagara-on-the-Lake: Kyle Upton Publisher, 1999), 106–07.

CHAPTER 11

1. John Ross Robertson, *The Diary of Mrs. Simcoe* (Toronto: William Briggs, 1911), 125.

2. Richard Aldington, *The Duke: Being an Account of the Life and Achievements of Arthur Wellesley, 1st Duke of Wellington* (New York: Viking Press, 1943), 28.

3. Dennis Carter-Edwards, *The Commissariat Officer's Quarters at Niagara*, manuscript for Parks Canada, 1982.

4. For an exhaustive review of the uniforms, flags, and equipment of the British Forces, particularly during the War of 1812 period, see René Chartrand, *A Scarlet Coat* (Ottawa: Service Pubications, 2011).

5. LAC, MG 13, W.O. 44, vol. 590, 261–62.

6. James Davidson, *Reminiscences of Niagara*, no.11 (Niagara-on-the-Lake: Niagara Historical Society, 1904), 24.

7. Major Richard Martin, *Furlough to Sergeant John Morgan*, August 3, 1842, author's collection.

8. David McConnell, *A Study of the British Military Buildings at Niagara-on-Lake, 1838-1871*, Manuscript Report No. 226 (Ottawa: Department of Indian and Northern Affairs, 1977), 50–52.

9. T. Dube, *The Enrolled Pensioner Scheme in Canada West, 1851–1858, with Specific Reference to the Plan at Amherstburg* (M.A. Thesis, University of Windsor, 1982), chapter 1.

10. Mayor John Simpson to Governor General's Office, June 27, 1853, LAC, RG 7, G 20, vol.55.

11. Coffin to Commissioner of Crown Lands, March 9, 1858. LAC, RG 15, vol. 1685.

12. *Ibid.*

13. Coffin to Assistant Commissioner, Crown Lands, June 10, 1865. LAC, RG 15, vol. 1693.

14. *Ibid.*

15. *Report … Fitting up No.6 Cavalry Stables as a School Room for 84 Scholars at Niagara*, January 3, 1852. LAC, MG 13, WO 44, 591.

16. Born in England, Kirby moved to Niagara as a young man and married into an early Niagara family. After serving as caretaker of the Military Reserve he was appointed to the more lucrative position as Collector of Customs. Although best known as the author of *The Chien d'Or*, one of Canada's first novels, he also wrote *Annals of Niagara*. Unfortunately, much of the content is more legend than fact.

17. Kirby served as caretaker/custodian of the reserve 1867–1871. Other caretakers include Captain J.B. Geale, 1870s–1890s, Bob Reid Jr., 1912–1933, and later Will Richardson.

18. William Kirby to W. Coffin, April 20, 1869. Canadian Department of the Environment, Departmental Files, 754-0, vol. 1.

19. Coffin to Assistant Commissioner, Crown Lands, June 10, 1865. LAC, RG 15, vol. 1693.

20. David McConnell, *A Study of the British Military Buildings at Niagara-on-the-Lake, 1814–1837*, Manuscript Report No. 226 (Ottawa: Department of Indian and Northern Affairs, 1977), 71.

21. List of Sundry Repairs, August 4, 1819. LAC RG 8 I, vol. 124, 158–60.

22. Memo, December 18, 1846, LAC RG 8 I, vol. 153, 122–25.

23. Doug and Betty Hunter were early adult chaperones for this group. Alumni of Teen Town still meet occasionally. See also, Jim Smith, *NOTL Recollections*, *The Niagara Advance*, November 26, 2005.

24. The Canadian Fencible Regiment was a British regiment raised in Canada for limited service in British North America.

25. The Count de Puisaye house, circa 1794, still stands on the River Road at Line 3.

26. LAC, RG8, I, vol. 556, 88–92.

27. August 24, 1822, LAC RG 8, I, vol. 294, 98–101.

28. Reid to Wright, September 26, 1819, LAC, RG 8, I, vol. 293, 32–35.

29. *Plan, Section and Elevation of the New Hospital at Fort George*, LAC, H3/450/Niagara/1823, NMC 5223.

30. Janet Carnochan, *History of Niagara* (Toronto: William Briggs, 1914), 117.

31. Reports upon the Military Hospitals in Canada, Skey, Quebec, July 27, 1833, LAC, RG 8, I, C Series, vol. 302, 57–59. Also August 12, 1836, LAC, RG 8, I, C series, vol. 303, 35.

32. General Report on Barracks in Canada, 1864, LAC, RG 8, II, vol. 34, 109.

33. Carnochan, *History of Niagara*, 117.

34. The inscription on the stone reads "The Site of The Military Hospital and Indian Council House."

CHAPTER 12

1. LAC, National Map Division, H3/440—Niagara-1837, neg. C-42432.

2. *Plan of the 206 Acres in the TOWNSHIP of NEWARK otherwise called NIAGARA including 4 Acres in the TOWN of NIAGARA in UPPER CANADA. The property of the Hon.ble DW Smith Esqre Surveyr General*, W Chewett, Manuscript Collection, Toronto Public Library, Toronto Reference Library, Baldwin Room, D.W. Smith papers, vol. 1, 1802, 37.

3. Lord Selkirk, November 20, 1803, *Lord Selkirk's Diary 1803–1804* ed. Patrick White, vol. 35 (Toronto: The Champlain Society, 1958), 151.

4. The tower would not be completed until 1826.

5. E.W. Durnford to "Office," April 24, 1818, no. 30 (Niagara-on-the-Lake: Niagara Historical Society,1917), 42.

6. LAC, National Map Division, V3, Niagara, 1816, neg. C-42434.

7. *The Scourge* and a sister ship *The Hamilton* (originally called *Diana*) went down while flying American flags during a violent storm in Lake Ontario in August 1813 and remain well preserved in their watery grave where they have been the object of much underwater research. They are presently owned by the Hamilton-Scourge Foundation of Hamilton, Ontario.

8. This area was later developed into Chautauqua Park now known as the Mississauga Beach area.

9. With his millwright John Abbot, Crooks established a paper mill at his industrial complex of West Flamborough and hence claimed the 125 pounds sterling bounty awarded by the Legislature for the first paper to be produced in the province.

10. H. Vavasour, 1822, no. 30 (Niagara-on-the-Lake: Niagara Historical Society, 1917), 42–44.

11. This one-acre lot had been severed and eventually was sold to Charles Richardson. Lawyer, member of the House of Assembly and Clerk of the United Counties of Lincoln and Welland, Richardson built a substantial home on the

property in 1832. During the late Victorian era additions and extensive verandahs were added. It is now restored as The Charles Inn. There is some evidence of a stone-lined tunnel from the Richardson House out towards Fort Mississauga. Thus far, the existence of such a passageway has not been substantiated.

12. H. Vavasour, 1822, no. 30, 42–44.

13. *Report of a committee of the Honourable Executive Council respecting a proposed exchange of part of the Military Reservation near Fort George*, April 16, 1823, Niagara Historical Society, no. 30, 44–45.

14. Alava, Castlereagh, Collingwood, Nelson, Picton, Platoff, and Wellington. Alava Street ran between Byron and Ricardo Streets but later become incorporated into the longer Melville Street. Alava was a Spanish nobleman who claimed to have the distinction of being the only military figure present at both Trafalgar and Waterloo.

15. Lincoln County Registry Office Records, Town of Niagara, New Survey, Block 39, H 5554, 2b., 1–2.

16. *Ibid*.

17. John L. Field, *Janet Carnochan* (Markham: Fitzhenry and Whiteside Limited, 1985), 36–42.

CHAPTER 13

1. See *The Men of Nassau*, ed. William A. Smy (Colonel John Butler [Niagara] Branch, The United Empire Loyalists' Association of Canada, 1997). The original return is in the Archives of Ontario, RG 1, Crown Lands Department, series C-1-9, vol. 3, Grants to Provincial Corps, District of Nassau, Item no. 9.

2. The Niagara Historical Society's Museum has in its collection a very rare Daniel Servos Commission as Captain in the First Battalion of the Militia of the District of Nassau. Servos Collection, box 109, FA 69.3.154.

3. Pacifists such as Quakers, Mennonites, and Anabaptists were excused from service but were required to pay an annual fee.

4. For an excellent summary of the Lincoln Militia see, Alan Holden and William A Smy, *Casualties of the Militia of Lincoln County in the War of 1812* (St. Catharines: Colonel John Butler [Niagara] Branch The United Empire Loyalists Association of Canada, 2002), 4.

5. For one particularly amusing description of a militia muster see: Anna Jameson, *Winter Studies and Summer Rambles in Canada* (London: Saunders and Otley, 1838), 167–69.

6. Janet Carnochan, *History of Niagara* (Toronto: William Briggs, 1914), 141.

7. Holden and Smy, *Casualties of the Militia of Lincoln County*, 3.

8. Paul Couture, *The Farmer Soldiers of Niagara: The Lincoln County Militia in the War of 1812*, unpublished manuscript, 7.

9. Thomas Merritt (1759–1842) had served as cornet in John Graves Simcoe's Queen's Rangers in the American Revolution. (One of the captains of the troop and future builder of Willowbank, Alexander Hamilton was sidelined by boils, which can be a painful condition if you are spending any time in the saddle.)

10. William Hamilton Merritt (1793–1865) was the promoter of the first Welland Canal. His *Journal of Events Principally on the Detroit and Niagara Frontiers, During the War of 1812*, published in 1862, and a comprehensive version edited by Stuart Sutherland, *A Desire of Serving and Defending My Country: The War of 1812 Journals of William Hamilton Merritt* (Toronto: Iser Publications, 2001), gives much invaluable information on the War of 1812. Merritt strenuously petitioned the colonial government to recognize the achievements of the Lincoln militia during the War of 1812, which eventually persuaded the government to strike commemorative General Military Service medals for Fort Detroit, Chateaugay, and Crysler's Farm but Queenston and Chippawa went unrecognized.

11. Also known as Runchey's Corps after their white commander, Lieutenant Robert Runchey of the flank company of the First Lincoln Regiment.

12. George Hamilton to William Jarvis (his father-in-law), June 5, 1812. Cruikshank, ed., *Records of Niagara: A Collection of Contemporary Documents and Letters, 1812*, no. 43 (Niagara-on-the-Lake: Niagara Historical Society, 1934), 29–30.

13. Holden and Smy, *Casualties of the Militia of Lincoln County*, 5.

14. *The Report of the Loyal and Patriotic Society of Upper Canada, With An Appendix, And a List of Subscribers and Benefactors* (Montreal: William Gray, 1817).

15. William Kirby, *Memorials of the Servos Family*, no. 8 (Niagara-on-the-Lake: Niagara Historical Society, 1901), 17.

16. These two companies of fifty men each served under white officers, Thomas Runchey and James Sears. Some units were kept in service to act as a police force during construction of the second Welland canal in the 1840s.

17. Joseph Masters, Ars Niagara Historica, *http://historyniagara.niagara.com/Marshall/MHTMLFolder/index.htm*.

18. Captain John Powell (1809–1881) followed in his father's footsteps as the registrar of the County of Lincoln and as a prominent officer in the Lincoln militia. He apparently leased the commandant's quarters on the Commons during the 1830s.

19. During this period of heightened alert along the border a company of the French-speaking Quebec Militia was stationed at Niagara. One particularly dark moonless night the Quebec and Lincoln militiamen were ordered to patrol along the Niagara River. As they set off across the Commons, the commander of the French Canadians had insisted that they lead. As the soldiers proceeded, there suddenly was great commotion and cursing in French from up ahead ... in the pitch dark the unsuspecting Quebecers had marched into the twenty-foot-deep railway "cutting." Masters, Ars Historica Niagara.

20. The St. Catharines 19th is an antecedent of the present Lincoln and Welland Regiment.

21. *Militia General Orders*, General Order 12, May 5, 1871, 1.

22. Cameron Pulsifer, ed., "Narrative of the Volunteer Camp at Niagara June 1871," *Canadian Military History*, vol. 12, no. 4, 40.

23. Toronto *Daily Globe*, June 7, 1871, 1.

24. Pulsifer, "Narrative of the Volunteer Camp at Niagara June 1871," 44–45.

25. *Ibid.*, 45.

26. *Ibid.*, 41.

27. *Ibid.*, 43.

28. *Ibid.*, 45.

29. *Ibid.*, 47

30. *Ibid.*, 50 This story would gladden the hearts of the guides who lead the ghost tours at Fort George every summer and fall.

31. *Ibid.*, 51.

32. J. Trevor Hawkins, Robert G. Mayer, Lynne Richard-Onn, *Toward a History of Camp Niagara Niagara-on-the-Lake, Ontario, Canada* (London: Mayer Heritage Consultants Inc., 1990), 4.

33. Hand-written notebook, inscribed, "12th Battalion York Rangers 1888," author's collection.

34. For a summary of Otter's remarkable career, see *Dictionary of Canadian Biography*.

35. "A Marksman Killed," *The Times*, September 24, 1896, vol. 3, no. 5.

36. "12th Battalion York Rangers 1888," author's collection.

CHAPTER 14

1. For the preparation of this chapter I am very much indebted to the researchers and authors of the following two publications: J. Trevor Hawkins, Robert G. Mayer, and Lynne Richard-Onn, *Toward a History of Camp Niagara Niagara-on-the-Lake, Ontario, Canada* (London:Mayer Heritage Consultants Inc.1990); J.Trevor Hawkins, Robert G. Mayer, and Lynne Richard-Onn, *An Oral History of Camp Niagara Niagara-on-the-Lake, Ontario, Canada* (London: Mayer Heritage Consultants Inc.,1993).

2. Hawkins, Mayer, and Richard-Onn, *An Oral History of Camp Niagara*, 24.

3. The *Niagara Times*, June 12, 1914. Hughes was reported to

have said, "They are first-class for little picnic affairs, but troops get no real training whatever at Niagara."

4. There were two notable exceptions: The Royal Canadian Regiment, which was Canada's only professional infantry regiment on the eve of the Great War, and the newly formed Princess Patricia's Canadian Light Infantry battalion, named after the popular daughter of then Governor General of Canada, Prince Arthur Duke of Connaught.

5. Eventually there were five Canadian Divisions in Europe.

6. Hawkins, Mayer, and Richard-Onn, *Toward a History of Camp Niagara*, 26.

7. Straw-filled mattresses.

8. Hawkins, Mayer, and Richard-Onn, *An Oral History of Camp Niagara*, 28.

9. *Ibid.*, 29.

10. The rebuilt Oban Inn on Front Street still welcomes guests.

11. There were over forty different bugle calls. Even the cavalry horses responded to several calls.

12. Florence Wright, *The Niagara Camp*, no. 28 (Niagara Historical Society: Niagara-on-the-Lake, 1923), 56.

13. *Ibid.*

14. Hawkins, Mayer, and Richard-Onn, *An Oral History of Camp Niagara*, 33.

15. For a good discussion of shell shock see Tom Brown, "Shell Shock in the Canadian Expeditionary Force, 1914–1918: Canadian Psychiatry in the Great War," *Health, Disease and Medicine Essays in Canadian History*, ed. Charles G. Roland (Hamilton: Clarke Irwin Inc., 1984), 308–32.

16. Recollections of W.H.C., personal communication. As a young man W.H.C. was hired to fill in the trenches on the Mississauga Commons when the golf course was reinstated.

17. Hawkins, Mayer, and Richard-Onn, *An Oral History of Camp Niagara*, 38.

18. Wright, *The Niagara Camp*, 58.

19. Hawkins, Mayer, and Richard-Onn, *An Oral History of Camp Niagara*, 39.

20. The road was known as Pancake Lane as there were a number of farms along the road that grew buckwheat.

Mayor W.H. Harrison felt that the name Progressive Avenue projected a more modern image.

21. Hawkins, Mayer, and Richard-Onn, *An Oral History of Camp Niagara*, 40.

22. Reminiscences of W.H.C., personal communication. W.H.C. was given the job of transporting by wagon the bodies back to Camp Niagara.

23. Wright, *The Niagara Camp*, 60.

24. *Ibid.*

25. Hawkins, Mayer, and Richard-Onn, *An Oral History of Camp Niagara*, 41–42.

26. Wright, *The Niagara Camp*, 60.

27. Hawkins, Mayer, and Richard-Onn, *An Oral History of Camp Niagara*, 42.

28. *Ibid.*, 31.

29. *Ibid.* 37.

30. Wright, *The Niagara Camp*, 58.

31. *Ibid.*, 59.

32. Hawkins, Mayer, and Richard-Onn, *Toward a History of Camp Niagara*, 41.

33. Wright, *The Niagara Camp*, 59.

34. Mrs. Norris originally showed motion pictures in a rented hall in town, but in 1915 she built a movie house, the much-renovated Royal George Theatre of today.

35. Harry James, personal communication.

36. Lieutenant Colonel A.D. LePan, *Polish Army Camp*, no. 35 (Niagara Historical Society: Niagara-on-the-Lake, 1923), 53.

37. Lieutenant Colonel A.D. LePan, *Polish Army Camp Diary*, LAC, RG 30 E, vol. 277, entry for December 1, 1917. Joseph Masters, *Niagara Reminiscences*, Ars Historica Niagara, *http://historyniagara.niagara.com/Marshall/MHTMLFolder/index.htm*.

38. Ann Buyers, "This Old House," *Niagara Advance Historical Issue*, 1998, 6–7.

39. Lieutenant Colonel LePan, *Polish Army Camp Diary*. The Western Home at the end of King Street was built as the new court house and jail after the War of 1812. Later it became the headquarters for Miss Rye's "Western Home."

40. Lieutenant Colonel LePan, *Polish Army Camp*, 56.

41. Major Young, *The Polish Force in Niagara*, no. 35 (Niagara Historical Society; Niagara-on-the-Lake,1923), 24. Most of the uniforms had to be refitted as the Polish recruits were generally shorter and of more stocky build.

42. Also known as Haller's Army after their military leader in Poland, General Josef Haller (1873–1960).

43. Lieutenant Colonel LePan, *Polish Army Camp*, 53.

44. Captain Smith's son was actor Jay Silverheels, who played "Tonto," the Lone Ranger's Native sidekick.

45. Young, *The Polish Force in Niagara*, 24.

46. Masters, *Niagara Reminiscences*.

47. Lieutenant Colonel LePan, *Polish Army Camp*, 59.

48. *Ibid.*, 58.

49. The celebrations were actually premature by several months but this did not dampen the enthusiasm.

50. See *Niagara Advance*, April 2, 2009. Photo in the collection of the Niagara Historical Society.

51. Masters, *Niagara Reminiscences*.

52. *Ibid.*

53. Recollection of DH, personal communication.

54. Prince Arthur was the third son of Queen Victoria. He had served as Governor General of Canada (1911–1916) and was senior military officer in Canada at the time.

55. Poniowtoski served as an officer on the Polish staff for a time.

56. Lieutenant Colonel LePan, *Polish Army Camp*, 50.

57. *Ibid.*, 56.

58. John M. Barry, *Influenza* (New York: Viking Penguin, 2004), 4.

59. Lieutenant Colonel LePan, *Polish Army Camp*, 56. It is uncertain whether all forty-one deaths among the Polish soldiers were due influenza.

60. Henry Radecki, *The History of the Polish Community in St. Catharines* (St. Catharines:Project History, 2002), 202.

61. Hawkins, Mayer, and Richard-Onn, *An Oral History of Camp Niagara*, 50. Recollection of Josef Ziolkowsky, North Tonawanda, New York.

62. Elizabeth's father and grandfather had both been military men. Her brother, Joseph Masters, was very active in municipal affairs in Niagara-on-the-Lake. His *Niagara Reminiscences* and *Neighborhood Notes* (online at Ars Niagara Historica) provides a remarkable and invaluable history of the town.

63. Elizabeth C. Ascher, *Polish Relief Work at Niagara*, no. 35 (Niagara-on-the-Lake: Niagara Historical Society, 1923), 27–43.

CHAPTER 15

1. Kaye Toye recalls finding the carcass of a cow that had fallen into one of the trenches in the late 1920s.

2. An outline of a few trenches can be seen on the golf course near the sixth green.

3. The Royal Canadian Dragoons were the most senior cavalry regiment in Canada.

4. Noel Haines, oral communication.

5. Kaye Toye, oral communication.

6. In 1936 the Lincoln Regiment and the Lincoln and Welland Regiment were amalgamated into the Lincoln and Welland Regiment, with headquarters in St. Catharines. The Lincoln and Welland Regimental Museum is currently ensconced in the surviving two-storey barracks building of Butler's Barracks.

7. G. Allan Burton, *A Store of Memories* (Toronto, McClelland and Stewart, 1986), 53.

8. J. Trevor Hawkins, Robert G. Mayer, and Lynne Richard-Onn, *An Oral History of Camp Niagara Niagara-on-the-Lake, Ontario, Canada* (London: Mayer Heritage Consultants Inc., 1993), 80.

9. Burton, *A Store of Memories*, 55–56.

10. When the RCD became an armoured regiment in the Second World War, the Royal Canadian Mounted Police eventually took over the highly popular Musical Ride, which is still performed today.

11. Hawkins, Mayer, and Richard-Onn, *An Oral History of Camp Niagara*, 76.

12. *Ibid.*, 77.
13. In 1936 the Governor General's Horse Guards were formed by the amalgamation of the Mississauga Horse and the Governor General's Body Guards.
14. John Marteinson, *The Governor General's Horse Guards: Second to None* (Toronto: Robin Brass Studio, 2002), 143.
15. Noel Haines, oral communication.
16. Douglas Hunter, oral communication.
17. Allen Merritt, who attended the McMaster University COTC, oral communication.
18. Kaye Toye, who often saw the handsome brigadier on his white steed, oral communication.

CHAPTER 16

1. John L. Field, ed., *Bicentennial Stories of Niagara-on-the-Lake* (Niagara-on-the-Lake: Bicentennial Committee,1981), 74–75.
2. Many of the details contained in this chapter were obtained from the excellent publication, J. Trevor Hawkins, Robert G. Mayer, and Lynne Richard-Onn, *An Oral History of Camp Niagara Niagara-on-the-Lake* (London: Mayer Heritage Consultants Inc.,1993).
3. Hawkins, Mayer, and Richard-Onn, *An Oral History of Camp Niagara*, 91.
4. *Ibid.*
5. *Ibid.*
6. *Ibid.*, 110.
7. *Ibid.*, 117.
8. *Ibid.*, 118.
9. Margo Fyfe's mother's brick house at King and Mary Streets across from the Commons was one such temporary home for officers' wives during the war years.
10. Hawkins, Mayer, and Richard-Onn, *An Oral History of Camp Niagara*, 92.
11. Hope Elliott Bradley, personal communication.
12. Hawkins, Mayer, and Richard-Onn, *An Oral History of Camp Niagara*, 114.

13. J. Trevor Hawkins, Robert G. Mayer and Lynne Richard-Onn, *Toward a History of Camp Niagara Niagara-on-the-Lake, Ontario, Canada* (London:Mayer Heritage Consultants Inc.,1990), 50.
14. Hope Bradley, oral communication.
15. Hawkins, Mayer, and Richard-Onn, *An Oral History of Camp Niagara*, 97.
16. Hawkins, Mayer, and Richard-Onn, *Toward a History of Camp Niagara*, table 5. There were over forty bugle calls.
17. Hawkins, Mayer, and Richard-Onn, *Toward a History of Camp Niagara*, 94.
18. Suzanne Dietz, *Honor Thy Fathers and Mothers* (Youngstown: BeauDesigns, 2008), 8.
19. Hawkins, Mayer, and Richard-Onn, *An Oral History of Camp Niagara*, 95.
20. *Ibid.*, 96.
21. *Ibid.*, 115–16.
22. *Ibid.*, 116.
23. *Ibid.*, 99.
24. *Ibid.*, 97.
25. *Ibid.*, 103.
26. Field, *Bicentennial Stories of Niagara-on-the-Lake*, 129.
27. Cathy Macdonald, Ideela Serafini, and Sue Swayze, *Sixty Years of Remembrance* (Niagara-on-the-Lake: General Nelles [Ont.N0. 124] Branch, Royal Canadian Legion, 1987), 16.
28. J Hawkins, Mayer, and Richard-Onn, *An Oral History of Camp Niagara*, 104.
29. Field, *Bicentennial Stories of Niagara-on-the-Lake*, 128.
30. Hawkins, Mayer, and Richard-Onn, *An Oral History of Camp Niagara*, 100–02.
31. Kaye Toye, *Kaye' Memories*, unpublished.
32. Hawkins, Mayer, and Richard-Onn, *An Oral History of Camp Niagara*, 133–135.
33. Farmerettes were young women who came out from the cities to work on the fruit farms during the summer months.
34. Field, *Bicentennial Stories of Niagara-on-the-Lake*, 75.
35. Hawkins, Mayer, and Richard-Onn, *An Oral History of Camp Niagara*, 127.

36. *Ibid.*, 128.

37. *Ibid.*, 126.

38. *Ibid.*, 131.

39. *Ibid.*, 128–29.

40. Some of the other Units that trained at Niagara during the Second World War, in addition to summer militia camps: 1st Garrison Battalion Engineers Corps, 10th Infantry Battalion, Royal Canadian Army Service Corps, 48th Highland Regiment, Algonquin Regiment, Royal Canadian Army Ambulance Corps, Argyll and Sutherland Highland Regiment, CWAC ,Lorne Rifle Scottish and Lorne Scots Regiments, Dufferin and Haldimand Regiment and Rifles, Royal Hamilton Light Infantry Regiment, Lincoln and Welland Regiment Queen's York Rangers, Midland Regiment Royal Canadian Army Dental Corps, Peel and Dufferin Regiment, Kent Regiment, Perth Regiment, Queen's Own Rifles of Canada Regiment, Saskatchewan Horse, Sault Ste. Marie and Sudbury Regiment, Royal Canadian Army Electrical and Mechanical, Scots Fusiliers of Canada Royal Canadian Army Ordnance Corps, South Alberta Regiment, Royal Canadian Army Medical Corps, Toronto Scottish Regiment, Royal Canadian Engineers, Veteran Guards of Canada, and Royal Canadian Regiment.

CHAPTER 17

1. The council obtained a lease for the nominal sum of one dollar per year on the circa 1817 Soldiers' Barracks, the gun shed, and commissariat store house to protect them from demolition.

2. J. Trevor Hawkins, Robert G. Mayer, and Lynne Richard-Onn, *An Oral History of Camp Niagara Niagara-on-the-Lake, Ontario, Canada* (London: Mayer Heritage Consultants Inc., 1993), 141.

3. Cathy Macdonald, Idella Serafini, and Sue Swayze, *Sixty Years of Remembrance* (Niagara-on-the-Lake: General Nelles Branch, Royal Canadian Legion, 1987), 36.

4. *Ibid.*, 33.

5. Hawkins, Mayer, and Richard-Onn, *An Oral History of Camp Niagara*, 147–148.

6. *Ibid.*, 149.

7. *Ibid.*, 150.

8. *Ibid.*, 153–54.

9. *Ibid.*, 153–57.

10. *Ibid.*, 158.

11. *Ibid.*, 162.

12. Mike Dietsch later served as lord mayor of Niagara-on-the-Lake and Member of the Legislative Assembly.

13. The downstairs served as the regiment's interior parade square.

14. Hawkins, Mayer, and Richard-Onn, *An Oral History of Camp Niagara*, 167.

15. Special thanks to Bill Smy for providing information on this special event.

16. Hawkins, Mayer, and Richard-Onn, *An Oral History of Camp Niagara*, 168. The author is greatly indebted to the authors J. Trevor Hawkins, Robert G. Mayer, and Lynne Richard-Onn for their two excellent publications, *Toward a History of Camp Niagara Niagara-on-the-Lake, Ontario, Canada* (1990), and *An Oral History of Camp Niagara Niagara-on-the-Lake, Ontario, Canada* (1993). Without their in-depth interviews of so many service men and women, important individual recollections of Camp Niagara would have been lost forever.

CHAPTER 18

1. The Provincial Marine was established by the British government to supervise naval operations on the Great Lakes. Its prime function was to act as a naval transport for the army, although it transported civilian personnel and private goods as well. On the eve of the War of 1812 it was encouraged to take on a more aggressive role. In 1813 the Provincial Marine was taken over by the British navy.

2. Niagara merchants who owned their own ships included William and James Crooks as well as the Hamilton family of Queenston.

3. For excellent reviews of the naval aspects of the War of 1812, see Robert Gardner, ed., *The Naval War of 1812* (London: The Caxton Publilshing Group, 2001); and Robert Malcomson, *Warships of the Great Lakes 1754–1834* (London: The Caxton Publishing Group, 2003).

4. The Honourable John Hamilton (1802–1882) was the youngest son of the Honourable Robert Hamilton, who bequeathed a large estate to each of his children. John prospered as the owner of several increasingly larger steamships and is known as the father of navigation on Lake Ontario. He served as a member of the Legislative Council of the Province of Canada, and after Confederation as a senator until his death. His home, Glencairn, still stands on the Niagara River near Queenston.

5. For more information on Niagara's waterfront, see Isabelle Ridgway, *Sailing Out of Niagara ... Since 1833* (Niagara-on-the-Lake: Niagara-on-the-Lake Sailing Club, 1989).

6. *Ibid.*, 12.

7. R.L. Rogers, *History of the Lincoln and Welland Regiment* (St. Catharines: Lincoln and Welland Regiment, 1954), 17.

8. The much-respected businessman and sailor Captain Duncan Milloy built his residence, Oban House, at the corner of Front and Gate Streets. It was later enlarged and became known as the Oban Inn. Milloy died prematurely at age forty-six, but his family continued to control the Niagara Dock until 1899.

9. The *City of Toronto* caught fire and was destroyed while being repaired in a shipyard at Port Dalhousie in 1883.

10. *Col. Daniel McDougal and Valuable Documents*, no. 23 (Niagara-on-the-Lake: Niagara Historical Society, 1925), 58–59.

11. *Niagara Mail*, September 19, 1860.

12. A.J. Clark, "Confederate Blockade Runner 'The Chicora' Now Flying the Canadian Flag, 1911, Niagara Navigation Co," no. 23 (Niagara-on-the-Lake: Niagara Historical Society, 1925), 48–49.

13. The *Chippewa* was the first vessel in the fleet to be of all-steel construction.

14. The Niagara Navigation Company was eventually absorbed by the Canada Steamship Company in 1920.

15. J. Trevor Hawkins, Robert G. Mayer, and Lynne Richard-Onn, *An Oral History of Camp Niagara Niagara-on-the-Lake, Ontario, Canada* (London: Mayer Heritage Consultants, 1993), 78.

16. *Ibid.*, 55.

17. In the 1950s other boys would show off their diving skills from a high-diving platform erected on the edge of the town wharf. Jim Smith, personal communication.

18. Boys would often "hike a ride" as far as the pump house by hanging onto the stern chains from the side-wheelers. Donald Harrison, personal communication.

19. John Field, ed., *Bicentennial Stories of Niagara-on-the-Lake* (Niagara-on-the-Lake: Bicentennial Committee, 1981), 114.

20. Harold Clement, personal communication.

21. In late summer, the steamships provided a one-day excursion for locals to the exciting Canadian National Exhibition in Toronto.

22. For more information on the *Cayuga* and the many memories she gave, see Carole M. Lidgold, *Memories of Cayuga Ontario's Love Boat* (Scarborough: Brookridge Publishing House, 1995).

23. Samuel Zimmerman (1815–1857) was married to a local St. Davids girl, Margaret Ann Woodruff. A successful canal contractor and railway promoter, he ironically met his untimely death in a tragic railway accident while crossing the Desjardins Canal near Hamilton.

24. The site of the turntable is marked with a small plaque at Riverbeach Drive and Turntable Way.

25. The old Navy Hall building was moved from near the riverbank up closer to the Fort George ruins to make way for the spur line, although it was never extended this far north. (See chapter 5.)

26. *Niagara Mail*, as cited by John Jackson and John Burtniak in *Railways in the Niagara Peninsula* (Belleville: Mika

Publishing Company, 1978), 61. As the authors point out, for many the train's unsettling steam whistle was an unwelcome intrusion in the peaceful landscape, but would later become a nostalgic memory of the railway.

27. Francis Petrie, "Area Had First Railway in Ontario in 1835," *Niagara Falls Review*, May 13, 1968.

28. In 1875 the Erie and Niagara Railway was taken over by the Canada Southern Railway. In turn, it was absorbed by the Michigan Central Railroad. This later became part of the New York Central Railroad.

29. Burtniak, *Railways in the Niagara Peninsula*, 173.

30. Remnants of the old rail bed along Railroad Street and through to the corner of King and John Streets (now the Upper Canada Heritage Trail), plus several small stone bridges have survived. The deep ditch for the spur line in Paradise Grove and the two remaining gullies southeast of Fort George are now part of an open drainage system.

CHAPTER 19

1. For an excellent account of Brock's four funerals, see Robert Malcomson, *Burying General Brock: A History of Brock's Monument* (St. Catharines: Peninsula Press, 1996).

2. S. DeVeaux, *The Falls of Niagara or Tourist's Guide to the Wonder of Nature* (Buffalo: William D. Hayder, 1839), 149.

3. *The Daily Globe*, October 14, 1859. Cited in Malcomson, *Burying General Brock*.

4. LAC, RG 8, C Series, vol. 256, 194.

5. Interestingly throughout the seven-month American occupation of the fort in 1813, their graves remained undisturbed.

6. "Historical Sketch of the Counties of Lincoln and Welland," *Illustrated Historical Atlas of the Counties of Lincoln and Welland* (Toronto: H.R. Page, 1876).

7. In 1840 a bomb exploded inside the base of the column necessitating eventual removal of the heroes' ashes to the Hamilton Family Cemetery in Queenston. Thirteen years later, the remains were re-interred with great ceremony in crypts in the base of the present column.

8. Janet Carnochan, *History of Niagara* (Toronto: William Briggs, 1914), 268.

9. This was the popular early daguerreotype photo studio and gallery of "Graves and Prudden," established in 1853.

10. Joy Ormsby, "The Day a Tornado Hit Town," *Niagara-on-the-Lake Review Weekly*, April 19, 1995.

11. John L. Field, "The 1884 U.E.L. Celebrations," *The Niagara Advance Historical Issue*, 1984, 24–25.

12. *Ibid.*, 25.

13. John L. Field, *Janet Carnochan* (Markham:Fitzhenry and Whiteside Limited,1985) 24.

14. For the complete report of the celebrations, see *Centennial of the Province of Upper Canada 1792–1892* (Toronto: Arbuthnot and Adamson, 1893).

15. Oliver Mowat's brother, J.B Mowat, had been the Presbyterian minister in town in the 1850s.

16. William Kirby, *Annals of Niagara* (Niagara Falls: Lundy's Lane Historical Society, 1896), 246.

17. Carnochan, *History of Niagara*, 145.

18. I am greatly indebted to Tony Roberts, curator of the Niagara Scouting Museum in Niagara Falls, Ontario, for supplying me with much of the information on the Jamboree. Especially helpful was the *Jamboree Journal*, which was published daily during the Jamboree for the attendees and then republished as a souvenir edition afterwards by Charters Publishing Company Ltd., Brampton, Ontario.

19. Children were admitted for free.

20. There were no scouts in attendance from behind the Iron Curtain.

21. Several campers arrived by bicycle from as far away as Calgary in Canada and Colombia, South America. The latter, a twenty-eight-year-old Scoutmaster from Colombia, Isrel Alfonso Acevedo Valderamma, went through three bicycles and wrote a book about his 6,000 mile trip. He recently donated his last bicycle to the Niagara Historical Society Museum.

22. As related to the author by Steven's mother, Margo Fyfe.

23. *The Niagara Advance*, July 14, 1955, 6.

24. Ian Murray was tragically killed when he fell off one of the media towers.

25. Cardinal McGuigan, archbishop of Toronto, and Cardinal Leger, Archbishop of Montreal.

26. There were 5,500 scouts in attendance from Canada. The next largest group was the Americans.

27. The plaque read:

> EIGHTH WORLD BOY SCOUT JAMBOREE: The Eighth World Scout Jamboree, the first World Jamboree outside of Europe, was held on this site August 18-28, 1955 attended by some 11,000 Scouts from 71 countries and colonies. The Jamboree was officially opened by His Excellency the Right Honourable Vincent Massey Governor-General of Canada, in his capacity of Chief Scout of Canada on Saturday August 20, 1955. This plaque commemorating the 50th Anniversary of the Jamboree was unveiled Sept. 17, 2005.

28. In 2011 a plaque was erected on the Commons by the Historic Sites and Monuments Board of Canada and Parks Canada in recognition of the Scouting Movement in Canada. "Brought to Canada in 1908, the Scout Movement, originally known as the Boy Scouts, became one of the largest and most influential organizations in the country, its membership reaching more than 280,000 in 1965. Through games and outdoor activities it promotes character-building, good citizenship, and self-reliance, reflecting the educational ideals and methods of Scouting. The 8th World Scout Jamboree held in Niagara-on-the-Lake, Ontario in 1955, was the first of its kind to be held outside Europe. The event allowed Canadian Scouts to showcase their country, generating a favourable image of Canada on the international stage."

CHAPTER 20

1. *Upper Canada Gazette or American Oracle*, June 27, 1797. The race course was apparently one mile in length.

2. Janet Carnochan, *History of Niagara* (Toronto: William Briggs, 1914), 256.

3. "Caution," *Niagara Herald*, May 9, 1801.

4. Niagara Historical Society Collection, 972.701.

5. *Burials, Niagara*, Ontario Historical Society Papers and Records, vol. 3 (Toronto: Ontario Historical Society, 1901), August 8, 1850, 73.

6. "Obituary for Mr. Adam Crysler," *St. Catharines Journal*, October 28, 1858.

7. The Moogk family video at the Niagara Historical Society Museum included a large sports event known as a "Gymkhana" in 1939, which took place on the race grounds on the edge of The Commons where the Carnochan subdivision was later built (see chapter 22). The video shows both horse racing and cart racing.

8. Donald Harrison, personal communication.

9. Kaye Toye, "Fight for the Commons," *The Niagara Advance*, Letters to the Editor, April 11, 1998.

10. J. Trevor Hawkins, Robert G. Mayer, and Lynne Richard-Onn, *An Oral History of Camp Niagara Niagara-on-the-Lake, Ontario, Canada* (London: Mayer Heritage Consultants Inc., 1993), 76.

11. Carnochan, *History of Niagara*, 258.

12. LAC, NMC #43151.

13. Harold Clement, personal communication.

14. I am very indebted to long-time golfer Al Derbyshire, who provided much information on the history of the Niagara-on-the-Lake Golf Club. His manuscript, *Niagara-on-the-Lake Golf Club* was presented at a meeting of the Niagara Historical Society, January 15, 1998. Also very informative is *Niagara-on-the-Lake Golf Club* by James A. Barclay, a published golf historian and Curator of the Golf Museum at Glen Abbey Golf Club, Mississauga.

15. Major William Ingersoll Merritt (1846–1931) was born in Canada but spent much of his life in England in the

British Army. However, he was living in Niagara during the 1870s. His grandson, Colonel Charles Cecil Ingersoll Merritt (1908–2000) was awarded the Victoria Cross.

16. James Barclay, *Golf in Canada: A History* (Toronto: McClelland and Stewart Inc., 1992), 36.

17. *Ibid.*, 37.

18. The term "links" originated in Scotland and referred to the early golf courses situated on sandy coastal dunes with few trees.

19. *The Globe*, April 8, 1882.

20. Carnochan, *History of Niagara*, 259–60.

21. *Ibid.*, 260.

22. In the nineteenth century the gutta percha ball was used, which did not fly as far as today's rubber cored balls.

23. Carnochan, *History of Niagara*, 260.

24. Derbyshire, *Niagara-on-the-Lake Golf Club*.

25. Lancelot Cressy Servos, *Practical Instruction in Golf* (Rodale Press, 1905).

26. *Ibid.*, 1.

27. Later the balls were made of rubber.

28. George Catlin, *Letters and Notes On the Manners, Customs, and Condition of the North American Indians*, vol. 2 (New York, Dover Publications, 1973), 125–26.

29. Contrary to popular belief, lacrosse was not designated Canada's national game by an Act of Parliament.

30. Today there are more women players worldwide than male players.

31. Thomas Moore, *The Poetical Works of Thomas Moore, A New Edition Collected and Arranged by Himself* (Paris: V.V. Galignani, 1842), 114. In July 2004 a commemorative plaque was unveiled on the Niagara River Parkway just south of McFarland house, which apparently is where Moore often rested under a tall oak tree, later known as Moore's Oak.

32. Carnochan, *History of Niagara*, 145.

33. *Memoirs of Col. John Clark*, Ontario Historical Society Papers and Records, vol. 7 (Toronto, Ontario Historical Society), 177–98.

34. Joseph Masters, "Games Johnny Played and When Johnny Went Marching, Games," *Niagara Reminiscences.*

35. *Memoirs of Col. John Clark.*

36. John McEwan, *Reminiscences of Niagara*, no. 11 (Niagara-on-the-Lake: Niagara Historical Society, 1904), 14.

37. *St. Catharines Journal*, March 9, 1837. The boy was the son of Jared Stocking, hatter and merchant in Niagara.

38. Masters, "Games Johnny Played and When Johnny Went Marching, Games."

39. *Ibid.*

CHAPTER 21

1. King and Queen Streets were so named on documents from the 1790s.

2. Present King, Queen, William, Mary, Butler, and Mississauga Streets all have ninety-nine-foot-wide street allowances, possibly for military considerations.

3. According to tradition, a small plot at the southeast corner of this reserve was set aside for a printing office where the government-sponsored *The Upper Canada Gazette or American Oracle* was published during the capital years.

4. The quarters for the Royal Engineers' commanding officer were deemed "the best quarters in the two provinces," and hence appropriated for the commandant's quarters. *Hillier to Darling, Queenston*, September 27, 1823, LAC RG 8, I, vol. 1328, 63; *Bolton to Durnford, Fort George*, October 9, 1823, LAC RG 8, vol. 417, 92; and *Durnford to Darling, Quebec*, October 28, 1823, LAC RG 8, vol. 417, 93–95.

5. This prestigious destination hotel was a four-storey white building with green shutters situated on the high ground overlooking the mouth of the Niagara River. It had been built by the town in 1869 with funds received from the county in compensation for having lost the county seat to St. Catharines. It soon passed into private hands. By the 1920s it was suffering from the popularity of the family automobile and was eventually demolished during the Great Depression.

6. Filming of the movie, *Dead Zone.*

7. W. Kaye Lamb, ed., *The Journals and Letters of Sir Alexander*

Mackenzie (Cambridge: University Press, 1970), 455. The editor incorrectly states that the Hend's (Hind's) Tavern was at York in 1794.

8. James J. Talman, *Historical Sketch to Commemorate the Sesqui-Centenary of Freemasonry in the Niagara District, 1792–1942* (Grand Lodge A.F. & A.M. of Canada, 1942), 5.

9. Archives of Ontario, RG 1, Executive Council Office Record Groups, Niagara Town Papers, 000970. David Secord was the founder of St. Davids hence its name. He was a brother-in-law of Laura Secord.

10. *War of 1812 War Loss Claims*, LAC, RG 8, series C, vol. 88, reel C-2636; and LAC RG 19E 5(a) vols. 3740–3758, claim # 5.

11. David William Smith (1764–1837) was the son of Lieutenant Colonel John Smith, sometime commandant of Fort Niagara. In addition to his considerable responsibilities as acting surveyor general of Upper Canada, he was also a member of the assembly and a land developer. In 1802 suffering from the ague, he returned to England, gave up his prestigious position as lieutenant of the County of York, and was appointed manager of all the estates of the Duke of Northumberland. He was knighted for his efforts in raising a militia regiment during the Napoleonic Wars.

12. François La Rouchefoucault-Liancourt, "Travels in Canada 1795," *Report of the Bureau of Archives for the Province of Ontario 13* (1916), 49.

13. M.W., personal communications.

14. J. S., personal communications.

15. Anne Buyers, "This Old House," *Niagara Advance Historical Issue, Niagara Advance*, 1998, 6–7.

16. The author has been unable to find any other reference or pharmacological explanation for the Natives' use of this natural ophthalmic remedy.

17. The last great red oak that was said to be six hundred years old came to a crashing end on July 23, 1982. Another huge but hollow sentinel was struck by lightning and burned like a Roman candle for days.

18. Diana Graves, *In the Midst of Alarms: The Untold Story of Women and the War of 1812* (Toronto: Robin Brass Studio Inc., 2007), 418–22. For the original reference, see "Garden Book of Catharine Claus," LAC MG 19, F1, Claus Papers, vol. 4.

19. For a series of letters and plans pertaining to this subject, see the collection of the Niagara Historical Society, 2011.025.009-023.

20. Like his father and older brother Robert, Walter H. Dickson served on the Legislative Council, and hence held the title "Honourable." He was later appointed to the Senate.

21. Kaye Toye, personal communication.

22. Charlotte Street may have been named after Queen Charlotte, consort of George III or Charlotte, wife of William Dickson, who owned so much land in the area.

23. Dickson had taken offence to disparaging remarks made by reformer Weekes concerning the former Lieutenant Governor of the province, Peter Hunter. Unlike many of his peers, Dickson was a non-combatant during the War of 1812 but was taken prisoner by the Americans in June 1813.

24. James E. Kerr, *Sketch of the Life of Honourable William Dickson* (Niagara-on-the-Lake: Niagara Historical Society, 1917), 31.

25. According to Kay Toye, the stone taken from the demolished Rowanwood was used as a firm foundation for Charlotte Street nearby.

26. Anna Jameson, *Winter Studies and Summer Rambles in Canada* (London: Saunders and Otley, 1838), 55.

27. Kaye Toye, personal communication.

28. History of Captain Martin McClellan given at a meeting of the Beaverdams Historical Society, September 15, 1897.

29. Masters, *Niagara Reminiscences*.

30. Lot 9 on the river just north of Navy Hall was set aside for James Crooks as part of the great land swap.

31. Isabelle Ridgway, *Sailing out of Niagara … Since 1833* (Niagara-on-the-Lake: Niagara-on-the-Lake Sailing Club, 1989), 8.

32. *Ibid*, 21.

33. C. and C. Yachts and Shepherd Boat Works.

34. The Niagara Pumphouse Visual Arts Centre.

CHAPTER 22

1. Crooks also received water lot 9 near Navy Hall.
2. The first Welland canal was opened in 1829 and was derisively called "Mr. Merritt's ditch" after its promoter, William Hamilton Merritt.
3. There is considerable debate as to the actual date of completion of the church building. Edward Walsh's 1804 watercolour of Niagara from across the river portrays a completed exterior to the church and yet Robert Addison's reports to the Society for the Propagation of the Gospel in Foreign Parts suggest later dates.
4. For an excellent history of St. Mark's Church, see Fred Habermehl and Donald Coombe, *St. Marks, Persons of Hopeful Piety* (Niagara-on-the-Lake: Archives Committee St. Mark's Anglican Church, 2000).
5. Dean Stanley, quoted by Janet Carnochan, *History of Niagara* (Toronto: William Briggs, 1914), 319.
6. These bricks, which were rarely used in Niagara, are purported to have been brought to Canada as ballast.
7. Some early maps show several small buildings enclosed within a fence on this portion of the land, perhaps part of the Rangers' Barracks complex.
8. Reverend John McEwan, *Reminiscences of Niagara*, no. 11 (Niagara-on-the-Lake: Niagara Historical Society, 1904), 19–20.
9. Fred Habermehl, *St. Mark's Storied Past* (Niagara-on-the-Lake: Archives Committee St. Mark's Anglican Church, 2006), 108–09.
10. A few early family members were buried in Butler's Burying Ground on the edge of town, which is now a protected site.
11. *Burials Niagara*, Ontario Historical Society Papers and Records, vol. 3 (Toronto: Ontario Historical Society, 1901), 66–73. The earliest tombstone still standing in the church yard is that of Elizabeth Kerr, who died in 1794, aged thirty-four years. She was the daughter of Molly Brant and Sir William Johnson and wife of Doctor Robert Kerr.
12. This large boulder originally sat near the beach. Isaac Brock is purported to have often sat here gazing across the river towards Fort Niagara. It was moved inside the churchyard for protection on the insistence of historian William Kirby.
13. The ultra-modern home designed and occupied by artist Campbell Scott, which blends into the corner of Byron and Wellington Streets, is a case-in-point. On the corner of Wellington and Ricardo Streets, the charming brick Victorian Baggs-McGaw House sits nestled on the brow overlooking the Niagara River basin. Former president of the Confederate States of America, Jefferson Davis, was entertained there in 1867.
14. Joseph E. Masters, *Niagara Reminiscences*, Ars Historica Niagara, *http://historyniagara.niagara.com/Marshall/MHTML Folder/index.htm*.
15. Father Jan Jozef Dekowski (1882–1949).
16. Should the property no longer be needed for a hospital, the entire block would revert back to the Crown.
17. Donald Harrison, whose family owned the property, personal communication.
18. Mayor John Simpson to the Governor General's Secretary, November 2, 1852, LAC, RG 7, vol. 54, no. 5727.
19. Joseph Masters, "Families – The Taylor Family," *Niagara Reminiscences*, Ars Niagara Historica.
20. Jim Smith, oral communication.
21. An old barn from Regent Street had been moved to the site and turned into a rustic Lodge for the Scouts twenty-five years earlier. The Scouts had already made plans for a new location when the Shaw Festival made its overture.
22. Clive Barnes, *New York Times*, June 1973.
23. Harold Clement, personal communication.
24. These houses were typical "war time houses" built during and after the war in many Ontario communities.
25. There were several small houses that were slightly cheaper.
26. See Cathy Macdonald, Idella Serafini, and Sue Swayze, *Sixty Years of Rembrance* (Niagara-on-the-Lake: Standard Fine Printing and Graphic Design, 1987), 43.
27. "Niagara Boy Scouts Open Building Fund Campaign on Anniversary of Jamboree," *Niagara Advance*, August 16, 1956.

28. Noel Haines, personal communication.

29. Noel has noted that there is quite a variation in the sub-soil as one crosses the Commons. Geologically, the plain of the Commons is part of the compacted bottom of Lake Iroquois (ancient Lake Ontario) with soil remnants from the last receding "Wisconsin Glacier."

CHAPTER 23

1. Some early French maps denote this point of land as Montreal Point, although other maps refer to a bend in the river near Queen's Royal Park as Montreal Point.

2. Robert Mathews to Evan Nepean, July 9, 1790, LAC, MG 11, CO 42, vol. 72, 209.

3. LAC, Map Division, H3/440 –Niagara-1837, neg. C-42432. This later map shows the original boundaries of the military reserve as outlined by Robert Pilkington.

4. LAC, RG 8, I, A1, vol. 923, 42–43.

5. Some argue that the Americans did not destroy the lighthouse because they reasoned that there should continue to be a guiding light for mariners at the mouth of the river.

6. Bruyeres to Prevost, February 13, 1813, LAC, RG 8, I, A1, vol. 378, 17.

7. Generally, star-shaped traces were not popular amongst military strategists since they were difficult to defend and took up so much interior space.

8. LAC, Map Division, V3, Niagara, 1816, neg. C-42434.

9. Anna Brownell Jameson, *Winter Studies and Summer Rambles in Canada* (Toronto: McClelland and Stewart, 1965), 41.

10. Charles Hunter, *Reminiscences of the Fenian Raid*, no. 20 (Niagara-on-the-Lake: Niagara Historical Society, 1911), 6.

11. Benson J. Lossing, *The Pictorial Field-Book of the War of 1812, the Last War of Independence* (New York: Harper and Brothers, 1868), 419.

12. *Notice to Tender, Niagara*, Archives of Ontario, Kirby Papers, November 9, 1874.

13. Joseph Masters, "Fort Mississauga," *Niagara Reminiscences*, Ars Niagara Historica.

14. Gray to Minister of National Defence, February 18, 1946, LAC, RG 24, vol. 6351, HQ71-7-8, vol. 2.

15. The golf course occupies approximately twenty hectares of the Mississauga Commons today.

CHAPTER 24

1. Carl Klinck, *Literary History of Canada* (Toronto: University of Toronto Press, 1965), 342.

2. Fort George, Fort Mississauga, and the palisaded Butler's Barracks in the 1840s and '50s.

3. Patrick Campbell, *Travels in the Interior Inhabited Parts of North America in the Years of 1791 and 1792* (Toronto: Champlain Society, 1937), 148.

4. LAC, RG 1 L3 vol. 381(a) no. 12a-e , 1797.

5. John Maude, *Visit to Niagara* (London: Longmans, Rees, Orme, Brown and Green, 1826), 171.

6. R. Pilkington, *Upper Canada Gazette*, vol. 3, no. 26, April 19, 1797.

7. Thomas Merritt to Wm. Holton, December 29, 1809, and subsequent proclamation. E.A. Cruikshank, ed., *Records of Niagara 1805–1811*, no. 42 (Niagara-on-the-Lake: Niagara Historical Society 1930), 95.

8. Report of Lieutenant Colonel R.H. Bruyeres, LAC, RG 8, I, vol. 383, 6a.

9. Joseph Edwards to Major William Halton, April 17, 1810, LAC RG 5 A 1, vol. 11 4795–4798.

10. There was a spring-fed fishing pond stocked with fish just outside the northeastern bastions of Fort George that was strictly for the officers.

11. Thin, young ensigns, attired appropriately, usually portrayed the female roles in these plays that were often open to the general public.

12. Suzanne Plousos, *Remains of a Day* (Niagara-on-the-Lake: The Friends of Fort George, 2006).

13. J. MacMullen, *Camp and Barrack Room: or the British Army as it is* (London: 1846).

14. This explains why breweries and brew pubs usually

15. Ferdinand Brock Tupper, *The Life and Correspondence of Major-General Sir Isaac Brock K.B.*, 2nd edition (London: Simpkin, Marshall & Co., 1847), 32.

16. Bob Welch, "Niagara has Strong Military Ties," *Niagara Advance Historical Issue*, vol. 10 (1980), 25.

17. Soldiers wishing to marry were required to ask permission of their commanding officer.

18. Women and children were reportedly found cowering in a powder magazine when Fort George was "liberated" by the Americans in May 1813.

19. Historian Joseph Masters' father and uncle were both attendees of the Regimental School at Fort Mississauga where their father was stationed. (See Masters, Ars Historica Niagara, *http://historyniagara.niagara.com/Marshall/MHTMLFolder/index.htm*).

20. It seems that after the American Civil War bugle calls became more popular at infantry camps. The cavalry had a long tradition of bugle calls.

21. The list of baggage left behind by the retreating British troops after the Battle of Fort George included fourteen clarinets, two bassoons, ten flutes, two French drums, one trumpet, one "serpent," and one kettle drum. LAC, RG 8 I, C 1227.

22. Common lands, on occasion, were leased at half a dollar per acre. Only fences could be erected with no permanent buildings. The lease could be annulled at any time. See LAC RG 1 L3, vol. 381 (A) reel C–2236.

23. In the early years there was always the fear of wild animals; occasionally animals strayed or were stolen from the commons as noted in *The Spectator*, vol. 1, no. 8, 22 March 1816.

24. "Niagara Has a New Cow By-law," *Niagara Advance*, vol. 3, no. 12, May 5, 1921.

25. This annual competition is still held today.

26. Masters, *Niagara Reminiscences*.

27. Diaries of John A. Blake, Niagara Historical Society Museum.

28. "At the Niagara Camp," *Toronto Star*, June 20, 1903.

29. The old Junior Commissariat Officer's Quarters and barrack master's house.

30. C.W. Jefferys, *Toronto Star*, June 20, 1903.

31. A. Bruce Davidson, personal communication.

32. R.H., personal communication.

33. Jim Smith, personal communication.

34. Joseph Masters, "U.S. Enters World War I," *Niagara Reminiscences*. Masters operated one of the ferries.

35. Some friendships nurtured during this period seventy years ago are still retained today. Personal communication.

36. Kaye Toye, personal communication.

37. *Ibid.*

38. *Ibid.*

39. Noel Haines, personal communication.

40. *Ibid.*

41. Anonymous, personal communication.

42. J. Trevor Hawkins, Robert G. Mayer, and Lynne Richard-Onn, *Towards a History of Camp Niagara Niagara-on-the-Lake, Ontario, Canada* (London: Mayer Heritage Consultants Inc., 1990), 41.

43. *Ibid.*, 28.

CHAPTER 25

1. Plan of the Military Reserve, 1790. The original in the National Map Collection was copied by J. Simpson in 1909 and is in the collection of the Niagara Historical Society, 986.004.

2. J. Ross Robertson, *The Diary of Mrs. John Graves Simcoe* (Toronto: William Briggs, 1911), 125.

3. The large grassy field along present John Street has been recently over seeded for a polo and equestrian field. The soccer pitches in Veterans Memorial Park have received similar attention.

4. Janet Carnochan, *History of Niagara* (Toronto: William Briggs, 1914), 291–92.

5. The One Mile Creek eventually drains into Lake Ontario.

The Friends of One Mile Creek group is dedicated to protecting the creek throughout its drainage area.

6. Early descriptions of this portion of the Commons include huge willow trees and an "unhealthy" swampy area.

7. The yellow irises (flags) so prevalent there in the spring were originally planted on the edge of the creek near the Dickson-Potter house in the 1940s and have "escaped" down the creek.

8. LAC, RG 24, vol. 6337, HQ 71-1-2. As this name appears nowhere else, there is conjecture that it was a bureaucratic error.

9. An early twentieth-century trade brochure listed the "lover's lane" between the Fort George Ruins and Paradise Grove as an appealing feature of the town.

10. Queen's Parade was an unimproved trail/road from John Street to Picton Street until it was much improved in the 1950s. However, in the 1890s the town authorized the planting of five hundred trees to line the roadway.

11. Robertson, *The Diary of Mrs. John Graves Simcoe*, September 8, 1795, and 312, May 25, 1796.

12. Plantation does not necessarily indicate that it was planted, but merely consisted of mostly young oak trees.

13. *Plan of Niagara*, Archives of Ontario, 1845, D 6.

14. *Souvenir Historical Map of the Town of Niagara, County Lincoln, Ontario*, compiled and drawn by Frank Johnson, June 1894.

15. The site of this station is still evident as a grassy area surrounded by woods.

16. An extensive inventory of the flora of Paradise Grove was undertaken in 2003, but the data was unfortunately lost. The NPC is currently conducting an ongoing study of the property.

17. Another study involving the taking of core samples from oaks in the Grove confirmed that some of the giant trees are first growth.

18. Although early accounts refer to chestnuts in the woods, American chestnuts were wiped out by a blight due to a fungus. The unrelated horse chestnuts now found in part of the woods, were probably plantings around the Second World War hospital site.

19. The Natives recognized the value of controlled burns long before the arrival of the Europeans.

20. Robertson, *The Diary of Mrs. John Graves Simcoe*, 290. Mrs. Simcoe refers to many Sumach by the river. She made a lemonade-like drink from the flowers.

21. A large number of eagles were noted in the area in 1788–1790. Silas Hopkins, *Reminiscences of Niagara*, no. 11 (Niagara-on-the-Lake: Niagara Historical Society, 1904), 55.

22. William W. Campbell, *The Life and Writings of De Witt Clinton* (New York: Baker and Scribner, 1849), August 1, 1810

23. Robertson, *The Diary of Mrs. John Graves Simcoe*, 335.

24. Robertson, *The Diary of Mrs. John Graves Simcoe*, 209.

25. Colonel Landmann, *Adventures and Recollections of Colonel Landmann, late of the Corps of Royal Engineers*, vol. 1 (London: Colburn and Co., 1852), 277.

26. For more detailed information, see R.W. Sheppard, "Water Birds of the Niagara," *The Canadian Field-Naturalist*, vol. 59, no. 5 (Sutton West, Canada, 1945), 151–69.

27. Robertson, *The Diary of Mrs. John Graves Simcoe*, 131.

28. Earle Thomas, *Sir John Johnson Loyalist Baronet* (Toronto: Dundurn, 1986), 148.

29. Edward Augustus, Duke of Kent and Strathearn to Major General Alured Clarke, RE family of Lieutenant Wulff, October 6, 1792, author's collection.

30. Landmann, *Adventures and Recollections of Colonel Landmann*, vol, 2, 20–22.

31. Hopkins, *Reminiscences of Niagara*, 51.

32. Landmann, *Adventures and Recollections of Colonel Landmann*.

33. John Douglas, *Medical Topography of Upper Canada* (Canton: Watson Publishing International, 1981), 40. Originally published in 1819.

34. Marie Webb, personal communication.

CHAPTER 26

1. The original petition of William Dickson and John McFarland has been lost but is inferred in the petition written in response. LAC, RG 1, L3, vol. 381. (a-e).
2. Both merchant/lawyer Dickson and shipbuilder/farmer McFarland already owned land nearby. For more information on John McFarland, see David F. Hemmings, *The House of McFarland, A Master Shipwright's Legacy* (Niagara-on-the-Lake: Bygone Publishing, 2011).
3. LAC, RG 1, L3, vol. 381. (a-e)
4. Lieutenant Governor Colbourne.
5. Mayor John Simpson to the Respective Officers of the H. M. Ordnance, June 27, 1853, LAC, RG 7, G 20, vol. 55, reel H 1363.
6. Warren served as postmaster for over forty years.
7. The New York Chautauqua continues to educate and entertain thousands every summer.
8. Margaret Peake Benton, "Chatauqua's Heyday," *Niagara Advance Historical Issue* (1981), 34–35.
9. Joseph Masters, "The Warren Family," *Niagara Reminiscences.*
10. The Honourable R.W. Scott, Secretary of State to Janet Carnochan, October 1, 1898.
11. Janet Carnochan, *Letter from The President of the Historical Society, Niagara-on-the-Lake Ontario, Referring to the Military Grounds*, Niagara, June 28, 1905.
12. *The Times*, September 24, 1896.
13. See chapter 17.
14. Experts agree that every effort should be made to place patients in facilities close to their family and friends.
15. Henri Tetu, secretary, Historic Sites and Monuments Board of Canada to Dorothy Middleditch, October 4, 1985
16. This volunteer committee under the capable leadership of Dr. Ed Lemon was much complemented for their conscientious efforts.
17. Proctor & Redfern, St. Catharines.
18. Walter Haldorson, superintendent to Stan Ignatczyk, lord mayor, May 23, 1991.
19. This property is part of the original portion leased to the Niagara Region for its future parking needs.
20. Niagara Historical Society, founded in 1895, which owns the Niagara Historical Museum with its outstanding collection of Niagara artifacts; Niagara Foundation, founded in 1962, dedicated to the preservation of the built and cultural heritage of Niagara; Friends of Fort George, formed in 1982 to support Parks Canada's properties and programs in Niagara; and the Niagara Conservancy, formed in 1987 to serve as strong advocates in the community. The local chapter of PENS (Preserve Established Neighbourhoods Society) has also been a vocal advocate for the Commons.
21. John McPhee, *The Town Guardian*, April 1, 1992.
22. Parks Canada is considering the construction of a bermed two-storey observation deck near the southern edge of the woods edging the Fort George parking lot. Tentatively called the "Agora," or meeting place, it would provide interpretive displays of the Commons that could then be viewed from the elevated deck. At the western edge of the Commons there is a proposal to build a new much-needed museum for the Lincoln and Welland Regiment near the site of the old parade ground. It would represent the first new permanent building on the site in 170 years and could alter the viewscapes of Butler's Barracks. More open land would probably be paved over for parking.
23. Tentative plans were announced by the Shaw Festival in the spring of 2011 for a new theatre on private lands just to the southeast of present Queen's Landing Hotel on Byron Street. Although not on the present Commons there would be great pressure to use some of the virgin common lands across the street for overflow parking; moreover, there would probably be a request for a walkway across the Commons to the Shaw Festival Theatre.

EPILOGUE

1. Minutes of the Historic Sites and Monuments Board of Canada, Charlottetown, June 16–21, 1986.
2. Richard D. Merritt on behalf of the Niagara Historical Society to Walter Haldorson, superintendant, Niagara Historic Sites, March 7, 1991.
3. Niagara National Historic Sites: Commemorative Integrity Statement, Parks Canada, Ontario Region, June 1998.
4. *Ibid*.
5. The Royal Canadian Engineers were formed in 1908 as a professional military branch of the Canadian Army.
6. The portion of this road close to Centre Street is now known as Veterans Lane.
7. Major General Roger Hale Sheaffe succeeded Brock as commander of forces at Queenston Heights. He was later knighted for his efforts.
8. The Earl of Athlone (born Prince Alexander of Teck) was the Governor General of Canada during the Second World War.
9. Princess Alice, Countess of Athlone, was a granddaughter of Queen Victoria and wife of the Governor General. The vice regal couple visited Camp Niagara in 1940.
10. Bible, 1 Peter, chapter 1, verse 24.

Bibliography

ARCHIVAL SOURCES

Library and Archives Canada (LAC)
Record Groups (RG)
    RG 1. Upper Canada, Executive Council, L3 Upper Canada Land Petitions.
    RG 5 A 1. Upper Canada Sundries.
    RG 7. Governor General's Correspondence, 1850s.
    RG 8 I. "Series C", British Military and Naval Records; RG 8 I A; RG 8 II.
    RG 19. E5(a). Finance. War of 1812 War Loss Claims, 3728–3759.
    RG 15.
    RG 24.
    RG 30. E. LePan Papers.

Manuscript Groups (MG)
    MG 11. Colonial Office Papers (CO) 42 (Canada). The original papers are located in Public Record Office, Great Britain.
    MG 13. War Office Papers (WO) 1,17, 44, 55. The original papers are located in the Public Record Office, Great Britain.
    MG 19. F 1 Claus Family Papers and Records of British Indian Department.
    MG 21.
    MG 23.
    MG 24. Crooks Family Papers; Merritt Family papers.

Haldimand Papers. Additional Manuscripts (Add MSS. 21661–21892). The original papers are located in the British Library. Also available on microfilm reels.

National Map Collection (NMC).

Archives of Ontario
RG 1. Crown Lands Department Papers and Executive Council Papers: Stamford and Niagara Township Papers; Niagara Town Papers.

Kirby, Merritt, Norton and Street Papers.

Toronto Public Library, Toronto Reference Library (TRL), Baldwin Room
Elisabeth Russell Papers.
Peter Russell Papers.
David W. Smith Papers.

Lincoln County Registry Office Records: Town of Niagara

Niagara Historical Society Museum
Servos Family Papers.

National Archives and Records Service, U.S.
RG 77.

William L. Clements Library, University of Michigan, U.S.
Thomas Gage Papers.

PRIMARY SOURCES

Askin, Charles. *Askin Papers*. Vol. 32. Michigan Pioneer Historical Society, 1903.

Boyd, John P. "Documents and Facts Relative to Events During the Late War." 1815.

Campbell, Patrick and William Ganong. *Travels in the Interior Inhabited Parts of North America in the Years 1791 and 1792*. Toronto: Champlain Society, 1937.

Catlin, George. *Letters and Notes on the Manners, Customs, and Condition of the North American Indians*. 2 vols. London: Tosswill and Myers, 1841. (Reproduced by Dover Publications, 1973).

Cruikshank, Ernest A., ed. *The Documentary History of the Campaign upon the Niagara River Frontier, in 1812–1814*. Vol. 9. Welland: Tribune Press, 1896–1908.

_____. *Correspondence of Lieut. Governor John Graves Simcoe*. 5 vols. Toronto: Ontario Historical Society, 1923–31.

Cruikshank, Ernest A. and A.F. Hunter, eds. *Correspondence of the Honourable Peter Russell*. 3 vols. Toronto: Ontario Historical Society, 1932–36.

De Crèvecoeur, St. John. *Voyage dans la haute Pensylvanie et dans l'état de New-York*. Paris: Maradan, 1801.

Edgar, Matilda. *Ten Years of Upper Canada in Peace and War 1805–1815: Being the Ridout Letters with Annotations*. Toronto: William Briggs, 1890.

Firth, Edith G., ed. *The Town of York: 1793–1815*. Toronto: The Champlain Society, 1962.

Graves, Donald E., ed. *Merry Hearts Make Light Days: The War of 1812 Journal of Lieutenant John Le Couteur, 104th Foot*. Ottawa: Carleton University Press, 1994.

Hamilton, Milton W. *The Papers of Sir William Johnson*. 14 vols. Albany: The University of the State of New York, 1953.

Holden, Alan and William Smy. *Casualties of the Militia of Lincoln County in the War of 1812*. St. Catharines: The United Empire Loyalists Association of Canada, Colonel John Butler (Niagara) Branch, 2002.

Klinck, Carl F. and James Thalman, eds. *The Journal of Major John Norton, 1816*. Toronto: Champlain Society, 1970 (reprinted in 2011).

Lamb, W. Kaye, ed. *The Journals and Letters of Sir Alexander Mackenzie*. Cambridge: University Press, 1970.

Landmann, Colonel. *Adventures and Recollections of Colonel Landmann, late of the Corps of Royal Engineers*. London: Colborn and Co., 1852.

Masters, Joseph Edward. Niagara Reminiscences and Neighbourhood News. *http://historyniagara.niagara.com/Marshall/MHTML Folder/homepg.htm*.

Maude, John. *Visit to the Falls of Niagara in 1800*. London: Longman, Rees, Orme, and Green, 1826.

Smy, William A., ed. *Men of Nassau*. St. Catharines: Colonel John Butler (Niagara) Branch, 1997.

_____. *An Annotated Nominal Roll of Butler's Rangers 1777–1784*. Welland: Friends of the Loyalist Collection at Brock University, 2004.

Sutherland, Stuart, ed. *A Desire of Serving and Defending My Country: The War of 1812 Journals of William Hamilton Merritt*. Toronto: Iser Publications, 2001.

_____. *Two British Soldiers in the War of 1812: The Accounts of Shadrach Byfield and William Dunlop*. Toronto: Iser Publications, 2002.

Tupper, Ferdinand B. *The Life and Correspondence of Major-General Sir Isaac Brock, K.B.* 2nd edition. London: Simpkin, Marshall & Co., 1847.

White, Patrick, ed. *Lord Selkirk's Diary 1803–1804*. Toronto: Champlain Society, 1958.

Wood, William C.H., ed. *Select British Documents of the Canadian War of 1812*. 3 vols. Toronto: Champlain Society, 1920–28.

SECONDARY SOURCES

Adlington, Richard. *The Duke: Being an Account of the Life and Achievements of Arthur Wellesley, 1ˢᵗ Duke of Wellington.* New York: Viking Press, 1943.

Allen, Robert S. "A History of Fort George, Upper Canada." *Canadian Historic Sites: Occasional Papers in Archaeology and History No. 11.* Ottawa: Department of Indian and Northern Affairs Canada, 1974.

_____. "The British Indian Department and the Frontier in North America 1755–1830", *Canadian Historic Sites: Occasional Papers in Archaeology and History No. 14.* Ottawa: Department of Indian and Northern Affairs Canada, 1975.

_____. *His Majesty's Indian Allies: British Indian Policy in the Defence of Canada, 1774–1815.* Toronto: Dundurn, 1992.

Allodi, Mary, Peter Moogk, and Beate Stock. *Berczy.* Ottawa: National Gallery of Canada, 1991.

Andre, John. *William Berczy Co-Founder of Toronto.* Toronto: Borough of York, 1967.

Armstrong, W.A. "Demographic Factors and the Agricultural Labourer." *Agricultural History Review,* 1981.

Barclay, James. *Golf in Canada: A History.* Toronto: McClelland and Stewart Inc., 1992.

Barry, John. *Influenza.* New York: Viking Penguin, 2004.

Benn, Carl. *Historic Fort York 1793–1993.* Toronto: Natural Heritage/Natural History Inc., 1993.

_____. *The Iroquois in the War of 1812.* Toronto: University of Toronto Press, 1998.

Berchem, F. R. *The Yonge Street Story 1793–1860.* Toronto: McGraw-Hill Ryerson, 1977.

Bernat, Clark and Joy Ormsby. *Looking Back Niagara-on-the-Lake Ontario.* St. Catharines: Vanwell Publishing, circa 2005.

Bernier, Serge. *Canadian Military Heritage, Vol. III, 1872–2000.* Montreal: Art Global, 2000.

Bernier, Serge, et al. *Military History of Quebec City 1608–2008.* Montreal: Art Global, 2008.

Bliss, Michael, *Harvey Cushing: A Life in Surgery.* Toronto: University of Toronto Press, 2000.

Bouchette, Joseph. *The British Dominions in North America.* 2 vol. London: 1832. Brawer, Nicholas. *British Campaign Furniture Elegance Under Canvas 1740–1914.* New York: Harry N. Abrams Inc., 2001.

Briggs, Asa. *A Social History of England.* London: Weidenfeld and Nicholson, 1983.

Brumwell, Stephen and W.A. Speck. *Cassell's Companion to Eighteenth-Century Britain.* London: Cassell & Co., 2001.

Burton, G. Allan. *A Store of Memories.* Toronto: McClelland and Stewart, 1986.

Calver, William and Reginald Bolton. *History Written with Pick and Shovel.* New York: New York Historical Society, 1950.

Campbell, William W. *The Life and Writings of De Witt Clinton.* New York: Baker and Scriber, 1849.

Carnochan, Janet. *Centennial St. Mark's Church Niagara 1792–1892.* Toronto: James Blain & Son, 1892.

_____. *History of Niagara.* Toronto: William Briggs, 1914.

Carter, W.H. *North American Trade Silver.* Revised and edited by Lar Hothem. Lancaster. Ohio: Hothem House, 1996.

Carter-Edwards, Dennis. *The Commissariat Officer's Quarters at Niagara.* Manuscript for Parks Canada, 1982.

_____. *Military Reserve Niagara-on-the-Lake.* Agenda paper. Ottawa: Historic Sites and Monuments Board of Canada, circa 1984.

Centennial of the Province of Upper Canada 1792–1892. Toronto: Arbuthnot and Adamson, supposedly sponsored by the Province of Ontario, 1893.

Chartrand, René. *Canadian Military Heritage, Volume II, 1755–1871.* Montreal: Art Global, 1995.

_____. *A Scarlet Coat: Uniforms, Flags and Equipment of the British Forces in the War of 1812.* Ottawa: Service Publications, 2011.

Clarke, James Freeman. *Revolutionary Service and Civil Life of General William Hull: Prepared from his Manuscripts by his Daughter Mrs. Maria Campbell: Together with the History of the Campaign of 1812.* New York: 1848.

Condina, Cosmo. *Niagara-on-the-Lake.* North Vancouver: Whitecap Books, 1984.

Cruikshank, Ernest. *Camp Niagara*. Niagara Falls: Frank H. Leslie, 1906.

_____. *The Battle of Fort George*. Niagara-on-the-Lake: Niagara Historical Society, 1990.

Dale, Ron. *The Invasion of Canada*. Toronto: James Lorimer, 2001.

De Crèvecoeur, St. John. "A Visit to Niagara July 1785." *Magazine of American History,* October, 1878.

Desloges, Yvon. *Structural History of Fort George*. Manuscript Report No.189. Department of Indian and Northern Affairs, 1977.

DeVeaux, S. *The Falls of Niagara or Tourist's Guide to the Wonder of Nature*. Buffalo: William B. Hayden, 1839.

Dictionary of Canadian Biography (DCB). eds. William Claus, James Givins, Augustus Jones, Robert Kerr, John Norton, William Otter, St. John Rousseaux, and Peter Russell. Toronto: University of Toronto.

Dietz, Suzanne. *Honor Thy Fathers and Mothers*. Youngstown: Beau Designs, 2008.

Douglas, John. *Medical Topography of Upper Canada*. London: Burgess and Hill, 1819.

Dunnigan, Brian Leigh. *Siege — 1759 The Campaign Against Niagara*. Revised edition. Youngstown: Old Fort Niagara Association, Inc., 1996.

Field, John L., ed. *Bicentennial Stories of Niagara-on-the-Lake*. Niagara-on-the-Lake, Bicentennial Committee, 1981.

_____. *Janet Carnochan*, Markham: Fitzhenry & Whiteside, 1985.

Fleming, David. "Navy Hall, Niagara-on-the-Lake." *History and Archaeology* 8. Department of Indian and Northern Affairs, 1976.

Fryer, Mary Beacock. *King's Men: the Soldier Founders of Ontario*. Toronto: Dundurn, 1980.

Fryer, Mary Beacock and Christopher Dracott. *John Graves Simcoe, 1752–1806: A Biography*. Toronto: Dundurn, 1998.

Gardiner, Robert, ed. *The Naval War of 1812*. London: The Caxton Publishing Group, 2001.

Gayler, Hugh J., ed. *Niagara's Changing Landscapes*. Ottawa: Carleton University Press, 1994.

Graves, Dianne. *In the Midst of Alarms: The Untold Story of Women and the War of 1812*. Toronto: Robin Brass Studio Inc., 2007.

Graves, Donald E., ed. *Soldiers of 1814: American Enlisted Men's Memoirs of the Niagara Campaign*. Youngstown: Old Fort Niagara Association, 1995.

Habermehl, Fred and Donald L. Combe. *St. Mark's Persons of Hopeful Piety*. Niagara-on-the-Lake: Archives Committee of St. Mark's, 2000.

_____. *St. Mark's Storied Past*. Niagara-on-the-Lake: Archives Committee of St. Mark's, 2006.

Haldorson, Walter. *The Reconstruction of Fort George and Navy Hall 1937–1940*. Niagara-on-the-Lake: Paul Heron Publishing, 1991.

Hardin, Gerrit. "The Tragedy of the Commons," *Science*, No. 3859 (December, 1968): 1243–48.

Hart-Davis, Duff. *Audobon's Elephant*. London: Weidenfeld & Nicholson, 2003.

Hawkins, J. Trevor, Robert G. Mayer, and Lynne Richard-Onn. *Toward a History of Camp Niagara Niagara-on-the-Lake, Ontario, Canada*. London, Ontario: Mayer Heritage Consultants, 1990.

_____. *An Oral History of Camp Niagara Niagara-on-the-Lake, Ontario, Canada*. London, Ontario: Mayer Heritage Consultants, 1993.

Hemmings, David F. *The House of McFarland: A Master Shipwright's Legacy*. Niagara-on-the-Lake: Bygones Publishing, 2011.

Henderson, James R. *Results of 1970 Excavation in the Fort George Military Reserve*. Manuscript Report No.116. Ottawa: Department of Indian and Northern Affairs, 1973.

Holmer, Richard. *Redcoat: The British Soldier in the Age of Horse and Musket*. London: HarperCollins, 2001.

Hunter, A.T. *History of the 12th Regiment, York Rangers*. Toronto: Murray Printing Company, 1912.

Innis, Mary Quayle, ed. *Mrs. Simcoe's Diary*. Toronto: Macmillan of Canada, 1965.

Jackson, John N. and John Burtniak. *Railways in the Niagara Peninsula*. Belleville: Mika Publishing Company, 1978.

Jamboree Journal: Souvenir Edition. Brampton: Charters Publishing Company, 1955.

Jameson, Anna B. *Winter Studies and Summer Rambles in Canada.* London: Saunders & Otley, 1838. "New Canadian Library Edition." Toronto: McClelland and Stewart, 1990.

Jenkins, Phil. *An Acre of Time: The Enduring Value of Place.* Toronto: Macfarlane Walter and Ross, 1996.

Kelsey, Isabel Thompson. *Joseph Brant 1743–1807: Man of Two Worlds.* Syracuse: Syracuse University Press, 1984.

Kirby, William. *Annals of Niagara.* Niagara Falls: Lundy's Lane Historical Society, 1896.

Klinck, Carl. *Literary History of Canada.* Toronto: University of Toronto Press, 1965.

Lasdun, Susan. *The English Park: Royal, Private & Public.* London: Andre Deutsch, 1991.

Lidgold, Carole M. *Memories of Cayuga Ontario's Love Boat.* Scarborough: Brookridge Publishing House, 1995.

Lincoln, Benjamin. *Journal of a Treaty Held in 1793 with the Indian Tribes North-West of Ohio, by Commissioners of the United States.* Massachusetts Historical Society, 1836.

Logan, William Bryant. *Oak: The Frame of Civilization.* New York: W.W. Norton & Co., 2005.

Lossing, Benson J. *The Pictorial Field-Book of the War of 1812: The Last War for Independence.* New York: Harper & Brothers, 1868.

Loyal and Patriotic Society of Upper Canada. *A Report of the Loyal and Patriotic Society of Upper Canada: With an Appendix and a List of Subscribers and Benefactors.* Montreal: William Gray, 1817.

Macdonald, Cathy, Idella Serafini, and Sue Swayze. Niagara-on-the-Lake: General Nelles (Ont. No. 124) Branch, Royal Canadian Legion, 1987.

Maclean, Hugh D. *To Many People … Many Things.* Niagara-on-the-Lake: T&C Associates, 1981.

MacMullen, J. *Camp and Barrack Room: or the British Army as it is.* London: 1846.

Malcomson, Robert. *A Very Brilliant Affair.* Toronto: Robin Brass Studio, 2003.

_____. *Warships of the Great Lakes 1754–1834.* London: the Caxton Publishing Group, 2003.

Mathieu, Jacques and Eugen Kedl. *The Plains of Abraham: The Search for the Ideal.* Sillery, Quebec: Septentrion, 1993.

Marteinson, John. *The Governor General's Horse Guards Second to None.* Toronto: Robin Brass Studio, 2002.

McConnell, David. *The Indian Council House.* A Report Prepared for the Niagara Complex team, circa 1975.

_____. *Paradise Grove.* A Report Prepared for the Niagara Complex team, circa 1975.

_____. *A Study of the Military Buildings at Niagara-on-the-Lake, 1814–37.* Manuscript Report No.191. Ottawa: Department of Indian and Northern Affairs, 1977.

_____. *A Study of the Military Buildings at Niagara-on-the-Lake, 1838–71.* Manuscript Report No. 226. Ottawa: Department of Indian and Northern Affairs, 1977.

_____. *A Study of the Military Buildings at Niagara-on-the-Lake, 1871–1978.* Manuscript Report No. 244. Ottawa: Department of Indian and Northern Affairs, 1978.

Merritt, Richard, Nancy Butler, and Michael Power, eds. *The Capital Years Niagara-on-the-Lake 1792-1796.* Toronto: Dundurn, 1991.

Moore, Thomas. *The Poetical Works of Thomas Moore: A New Edition Collected and Arranged by Himself.* Paris: V.V.Galignani, 1842.

Morton, Desmond. *The Canadian General Sir William Otter.* Toronto: A.M. Hakkert, 1974.

Nelson, Larry. *A Man of Distinction Among Them: Alexander McKee and the Ohio Country Frontier, 1754–1799.* Kent, Ohio: Kent State University Press, 2000.

Niagara Historical Museum. *Looking Back 100 Years — 100 Artefacts.* St. Catharines: Vanwell Publishing, 2007.

Niagara Historical Society Publications. Nos: 5, 11, 12, 19, 20, 23, 26, 28, 30, 34, 35, 38–44.

Ontario Historical Society Papers and Records: Vol. III, VII, XXIV, XXV, LV, LXXXIII.

Page, H.R. *Illustrated Historical Atlas of the Counties of Lincoln and Welland.* Toronto: H.R. Page, 1876.

Parks Canada. *Niagara National Historic Sites Commemorative*

Integrity Statement, 1998.

_____. *National Hstorical Sites of Canada Mangement Plan*, 2007.

Phair, Graham. *Snapshots of the Home Front 1939–1941*. St. Catharines: Vanwell Publishing, 2009.

Plousos, Suzanne. *Remains of a Day*. Niagara-on-the-Lake: The Friends of Fort George, 2006.

Power, Michael and Nancy Butler. *Slavery and Freedom in Niagara*. Niagara-on-the-Lake: Niagara Historical Society, 1993.

Publications Committee. *Old Town Niagara: A History*. Niagara-on-the-Lake: The Friends of Fort George, 2005.

Pulsifer, Cameron, ed. "Narrative of the Volunteer Camp at Niagara June 1871" *Canadian Military History*, Vol. 12, No. 4.

Radecki, Henry. *The History of the Polish Community in St. Catharines*. St. Catharines: Project History, 2002.

Rennie, A. James. *Niagara Township: Centennial History*. Niagara-on-the-Lake: A. James Rennie, 1967.

Riddell, William R. *The Life of John Graves Simcoe*. Toronto: McClelland & Stewart, 1926.

Ridgway, Isabelle. *Sailing out of Niagara ... Since 1833*. Niagara-on-the-Lake: Niagara-on-the-Lake Sailing Club, 1989.

Robertson, John Ross. *The Diary of Mrs. Simcoe*. Toronto: William Briggs, 1911.

Rogers, R.L. *History of the Lincoln and Welland Regiment*. St. Catharines: Lincoln and Welland Regiment, 1954.

Roland, Charles, ed. *Health Disease and Medicine*. Hamilton: Clarke Irwin 1983 Inc., 1984.

Sattelberger, Peter A. *Evaluation of the Indian Council House/ Garrison Hospital & Commandant's Quarters Archaeological Collections Fort George Commons N.H.S., Niagara-on-the-Lake*. Cornwall: Parks Canada Agency Ontario Service Centre, 2001.

Secrest, Meryle. *Frank Lloyd Wright*. New York: Harper Perennial Publisher, 1993.

Sendzikas, Aldona. *Stanley Barracks*. Toronto: Dundurn, 2011.

Servos, Lancelot. *Practical Instruction in Golf*. Pennsylvania: Rodale Press, 1905.

Severence, Frank H. *An Old Frontier of France*. 2 vols. New York: Dodd, Mead and Company, 1917.

Shackleton, Kevin R. *Second to None: The Fighting 58 Battalion of the Canadian Expeditionary Force*. Toronto: Dundurn, 2002.

Shemdin, Gouhar and David Bouse. *A Report on Fort George*. Ottawa: Department of Indian and Northern Affairs, 1975.

_____. *A Report on Butler's Barracks*. Ottawa: Department of Indian and Northern Affairs, 1975.

Sheppard, R.W. "Water Birds of the Niagara." *Canadian Field-Naturalist*. Vol. 59, No. 5, 1945.

Smy, William A., ed. *The Butler Bicentenary*. St. Catharines: Colonel John Butler (Niagara) Branch, 1997.

Stacey, C.P. *Six Years of War: The Army in Canada, Britain and the Pacific*. Ottawa: Minister of National Defence, 1955.

Steel, R. James. *The Battery: The History of the 10th (St. Catharines) Field Battery Royal Canadian Artillery*. St. Catharines: the 10th Field Battery Association, 1996.

Stokes, Peter John. *Old Niagara On The Lake*, Toronto: University of Toronto Press, 1971.

Taylor, Alan. *The Divided Ground: Indians, Settlers and the Northern Borderland of the American Revolution*. New York: Alfred A. Knopf, 2006.

Thalman, James J. *Historical Sketches to Commemorate the Sesquicentenary of Freemasonry in the Niagara District, 1792–1942*. Grand Lodge AF & AM, 1942.

_____. *The Civil War of 1812*. New York: Alfred A. Knopf, 2010.

Thomas, Earle. *Sir John Johnson Loyalist Baronet*. Toronto: Dundurn, 1986.

Thomson, Don W. *Men and Meridians, Vol.1*. Ottawa: Department of Mines and Technical Surveys, 1966.

Truettner, William H. *The Natural Man Observed: A Study of Catlin's Indian Gallery*. Washington: Smithsonian Institution Press, 1979.

Turner, Wesley B., ed., *The Military in the Niagara Peninsula*. St. Catharines: Vanwell Publishing, 1990.

_____. *The Astonishing General: The Life and Legacy of Sir Isaac Brock*. Toronto: Dundurn, 2011.

Upton, Kyle. *Niagara's Ghosts at Fort George.* Niagara-on-the-Lake: Kyle Upton, 1999.

Venning, Annabel. *Following the Drum: The Lives of Army Wives and Daughters, Past and Present.* London: Headline Book Publishing, 2005.

Warner, Malcolm and Julia Marciari Alexander. *This Other Eden: British Paintings from the Paul Mellon Collection at Yale.* New Haven: Yale University, 1998.

Webster, Donald B. *Georgian Canada Conflict and Culture 1745–1820.* Toronto: Royal Ontario Museum, 1984.

Wellig, Timothy. *Restoring the Chain of Friendship.* Lincoln: University of Nebraska Press, 2008.

Whitfield, Carol. "Tommy Atkins: The British Soldier in Canada, 1759–1870." *History and Archaeology 56.* Parks Canada, 1981.

Whitfield, Faye. "The Initial Settling of Niagara-on-the-Lake, 1778–1784." *Ontario Historical Society Records and Papers.* Vol. LXXXIII, No. 1. 1991.

Williamson, Ron. *The Stage 4 Salvage Excavation of the King's Point Site (AhG5-24), 225 Ricardo Street, Town of Niagara-on-the-Lake, Ontario.* Toronto: Archaeolgical Services Inc., 2007.

Wilson, Bruce. *As She Began: An Illustrated introduction to Loyalist Ontario.* Toronto: Dundurn, 1981.

Wilson, John. *Excavations at Fort George.* Manuscript Report No.l16. Ottawa: Department of Indian and Northern Affairs, 1974.

Wilson, John and Linda Southwood. "Fort George on the Niagara: An Archaeological Perspective". *History and Archaeology 9.* 1976.

Winchester, Simon. *The Map that Changed the World.* New York: HarperCollins Publishers, 2001.

THESIS

Doyle, J. Anthony. *Loyalism, Patronage, and Enterprise: The Servos Family in British North America, 1726–1942.* Ph.D., McMaster University, 2006.

NEWSPAPERS

Canadian Illustrated News (Montreal and Hamilton). 1872, 1875.

The Daily Globe. 1859, 1871.

Hamilton Spectator. 1899.

Mail and Empire. 1897

Niagara Advance. 1921.

Niagara Herald. 1801.

Niagara Mail. 1860.

Niagara-on-the-Lake Times. 1913, 1914.

The Spectator. 1816.

St. Catharines Journal. 1837.

The Times. 1896.

Toronto Globe. 1882, 1899.

Toronto Star. 1903.

Upper Canada Gazette or American Oracle. 1796, 1797.

The Weekly Register (Baltimore). 1813

Modern Newspapers:

Masters, Joseph. "Niagara Reminiscences and Neighbourhood News." *The Niagara Advance.* 1949–1955.

"Annual Historical Issue." *The Niagara Advance.* 1971–1988.

Smith, Jim. "Niagara Reminiscences," *The Niagara Advance.*

Niagara-on-the-Lake Review Weekly.

The Niagara Guardian.

The Town Crier.

Niagara Falls Review.

St. Catharines Standard.

New York Times

Index

School of Philosophy, 218
Schooners:
    Diana (*The Hamilton*), 285
    Lord Nelson (*The Scourge*), 107, 210
Scott, Campbell, 297
Scott, Colonel Winfield, 69, 83
Sebastopol, Crimea, 183
Second World War, 11, 12, 13, 39, 73, 102, 147 150, 151, 153, 154, 157,
    163–64, 184, 227, 228, 231, 232, 248, 254, 255, 263, 270, 289,
    291, 300, 302
Secord, David, 207, 296
Secord, James, 274
Secord, John Jr., 123, 275
Secord, John Sr., 275
Secord, Peter, 274
Senior Citizens' Apartments, 184
Seven Years' War, 22, 34, 55, 169, 276
Servos, Lancelot Cressy, 199
Sharp, Jack, 44, 279
Shaw, Adjuvant General Aeneas, 41, 213
Shaw, George Bernard, 228
Shaw, Isabella, 213
Shaw, Sophia, 213
Shaw Festival, 194, 226, 264, 297, 301
Shaw Festival Theatre, 148, 194, *230*, 231, 232, *255*, 266
Sheaffe, Major General Roger Hale, 180, 186, 192, 302
Sheaffe Road, 186, 192, 270
Sheehan, Walter Butler, 51, 279
Sheets, Evelyn Rand, 217
Sherlock, Steve, 160
Shinty (Shinny), 201
Showers, Michael, 274
Simcoe, Charlotte, *30, 188*
Simcoe, Elizabeth, 17, 29, 30, 32, 45, *46*, 91, *188*, 215, 253, *256*, 257
Simcoe, John Graves, 12, 17, 25, 29, *30*, 31, 32, 37, 40, 43–45, *46*, 51,
    188, 206, 210, 215, 218, 257, 286
Simcoe Park, Niagara Park, 77, 109, 132, 140, 159–60, 161, 177, 182–
    83, 188, 228–29, 250
Six Nations, *see* Natives
Six Nations Reserve (Grand River Valley), 148, 149, 150
Sixteen Creek, Oakville, 17
Slavery (Upper Canada), 32, 34, 276
Slingerland, Anthony, 275
Small Pox, 36, 257
Smith, Captain (Chief) Alexander G., 239
Smith, David William, 107, 207, 210, 275, 296

Smith, Nathan, 29
Soccer Pitches, 102, 203, 204, 231, *232*, 299
Solander, Daniel, 275
Spanish Influenza, 133, 227
Springfield, 27, *31*, 32, 40, 216
St. Andrew's Brotherhood of the Anglican Church, 132–33
St. Andrew's Church, 181
St. Davids, 84, *89*, 154, 175, 176, 292
St. Johns, Quebec, 137
St. Mark's (The English Garrison Church), 40, 70, 187, 223, *225, 227*,
    248
St. Vincent de Paul Roman Catholic Church, 142, *227*
St. Vincent de Paul Cemetery, *142*, 227
Stamford, 17
Stanard, Asa, 107
Stanley Barracks, Toronto, 17, 145
Stationary Hospital (Fort George), 130
Steamships:
    Britannica, 169
    Cayuga, *153*, 154, 160, 161, 165, 172, 174, 187
    Chicora, 171–72
    Chippewa, *172*, 292
    Cibola, 172
    City of Toronto, 170, 292
    Corona, 172
    Frontenac, 169
    Princess Victoria, 220
    Transit, 169
Stokes, Peter John, 279
Stone Barracks, 207
Stone Powder Magazine, 65–68, 70, 73, 79–82, 205
Stratford Festival, *194*
Sullivan, Major General John, 22

Teen Town, 102, 231, 264
Tench, Frederick, 191
Tennis Club, 202
Tent Pegging, 193–94
Thorold, Ontario, 116
Thirteen Colonies, 17, 25
Tinling, Lieutenant, 23, 275
Toronto (York), 17, 27, 30, 32, 39, 40, 42, 46, 51–52, 60, 63, 66, 69, 76,
    114, 116, 128, 130, 145–46, 149, 154, 169, 171, 172, 174, 181, 187,
    215, 236, 254, 276, 278, 296
Toronto (York) General Hospital, 114
Toye, Kaye, 160, 174, 192, 215, 289, 290, 296